Star Crossed Serpent III: 'The Taper That Lights The Way'

Star Crossed Serpent III: 'The Taper That Lights The Way'

Being

The Letters of Robert Cochrane Revealed

Published by

Mandrake of Oxford

PO Box 250

OXFORD

OX1 1AP (UK)

Printed on acid free paper certification from three leading environmental organizations: the Forest Stewardship Council™ (FSC®), the Sustainable Forestry Initiative® (SFI®) and the Programme for the Endorsement of Forestry Certification (PEFC™)

Other books by Shani Oates and available from Mandrake:

Tubelo's Green Fire: Mythos, Ethos, Female, Male and Priestly Mysteries of The Clan of Tubal Cain, isbn 978-1-906958-07-7

The Arcane Veil: Witchcraft and Occult Science from the People of the Dark-ages to the People of Goda, of the Clan of Tubal Cain.
978-1-906958-35-0 (£25/$40 hbk)

Without prejudice

Please note, in compiling the information contained in this book to explain a rationale for the often confused and conflicting accounts of the history and legacy of the Robert Cochrane tradition, none of the names or events shared here break any confidences oaths or individual rights as all of it is already in the public domain, albeit in diverse places. My own position and knowledge of these matters has merely enabled me to organize them to a sensible account. This is no less than the charge to which I am obliged to serve in duty to the truth. This body of work reveals for the first time the full and unedited content of all letters in our current possession, and written by Robert Cochrane, aka Roy Bowers. Some of these have appeared before only partially, some not at all. Many of them have been adulterated; all of them have been represented. None of them have ever appeared chronologically, having appeared in different books, under different authors, obscure compilations, and almost always separated into categories of recipient. This bold and innovative construct presents a framework around which a cross referenced and lateral history totally supports, reinforces fact, or breaks down outmoded conjecture. Truly, no other history can boast such a rounded, expanded and balanced and open window into the lives and times of the Craft's most esteemed personages.

fff

12th Night 2016, on this day of the 9th Knot completed.

Dedicated to all seekers of Truth, of the Word and of the Real.

Live well, Love tenderly, Die well.

Take all you are given

Between those two fires that declare us for Her own;

In life and in our departure from it, nurture others, always.

Give all of yourself.

Accrue your green leaves and scatter them to the wind

Contents

This is the Taper that lights the way.
This is the Cloak that covers the Stone,
That sharpens the Knife
That cuts the Cord
That Binds the Staff
That's owned by the Maid
Who tends the fire
That boils the Pot
That scalds the Sword
That fashions the Bridge
That crosses the ditch
That Compasses the Hand
That knocks the Door,
That fetches the Watch
That releases the Man
That turns the Mill,
That Grinds the Corn
That makes the Cake
That feeds the Hound
That Guards the Gate
That hides the Maze
That's worth a light
And into the Castle that Jack built.

Foreword

"In fossilised superstitious traditions, there are profound secrets folded within the most mediocre beliefs and action. These great secrets, secrets of the souls and destiny, are only apparent in the open light, not in the illusionary world of Ye Old English Wiccen. If the witches are to survive then the religion must undergo some violent and radical changes. Changes that will open up the ritual for examination, so that the spiritual content may be clearly seen. Changes that must kick over many sacred cows to see whether these old cows still give milk." [1]

This volume completes and concludes the trilogy of *The Star Crossed Serpent*. Written to define and clarify 'The Robert Cochrane Tradition,' that is to say, *our Tradition*, according to its *own tenets*, and by its *own people*, it expressly uses its *own historical archive of letters and articles* to distinguish it from any account written by others, which by that default, must remain conjectural, and massively inhibited by presumption. Since the death of Roy Bowers aka Robert Cochrane, the founder of our Clan—The Clan of Tubal Cain, many such accounts have accumulated throughout the passing decades. The need to address their troubling inaccuracies has necessitated the publication of a separate but supplementary volume. Adjunct to this trilogy, yet of complimentary accord, it is entitled: Tubal's Mill,[2] an auto-biographical critique constructed to tackle directly all areas of confusion and error accrued over the past five decades. In that volume all discrepancies find explanations of considerable depth to highlight by contra-distinction, what we are not, especially via the measure and assumption of others beyond the bounds of our vital tradition. And though the very nature of the beast inclines to a certain amount of duplication within this volume, *Star Crossed Serpent III*, rest assured it is scant enough to ensure ease of reading and contextual flow, yet thorough enough to maintain integrity of purpose. Both tomes honour all source materials used in their construction. Moreover, SCS III expresses a very natural history, one that is conveyed through its unique chronology. Revealed cumulatively via inclusive letters and documents, they lead the reader on, page by page, guided and supplemented by 'in-house' information. Finally, a first hand account of our history is established here in this seminal work. Of and by the people involved, Truth is at last served. The Saga of our Clan, of our Tradition is synthesised using the words and experiences of the people involved, forming a lyrical composition of all voices in unison. By contra-distinction, *'Tubal's Mill'* takes an analytical stance. It scrutinises and probes, taking apart all previous and extant error and propaganda. Paying particular attention to deliberate falsifications, it holds them all to account. The disservice to the Craft generated by repetition of those errors is unprecedented. Public acceptance of that illusory edifice has suppressed a creative and intuitive evolution borne of true understanding for all seekers of its mysteries. And so, by sharing our knowledge of the facts, spoken of intimately and candidly, our first-hand experience exposes those rotten foundations. So, two very different yet vitally complimentary tomes.

In Part One of SCSIII, we explore the tenets of our Mythos by textual example, to set the stage for all that is revealed in Part Two: The Chronology itself. Much of the valuable resource material explored in this volume is readily accessible to the public for study and inspiration. But it must be respectfully asserted that interpretations thereof, will vary immensely with proximal accord *to the source of that material and to the experience and tutelage within its aegis as an extant and hereditary Tradition.* Part

Three of SCSIII, and its completion is served through a companion guide, entitled *Cochrane's Clan: The Devil's Crown,* which is to be published separately. This concludes the Star Crossed Serpent Trilogy. It brings closure of detail through analysis within the Mysteries 'proper.' All texts are dutifully explored in full context of a Clan lived through its cumulative history as a mystery tradition; this tenet is key to this and all other tomes in this trilogy. Known to many as *The Robert Cochrane Tradition,* our insights shared here serve to bring new life and light to many of the tenets Bowers introduces within the body of his letters that precede it. We have cast out all malignant shadows of confusion and obscurity, promulgated as they were through a previous and regrettable dearth of facts.

To address that history constructively, we are required to include certain other material that has only recently reached public attention as a published cache of documents[3] and which have attempted an explanation of the early years of Bowers' Craft history prior to 1963. A marginal achievement occurs in a considerable anomaly, manifest in a letter which relates to persons whose collective presence is plausible in one solution only. In this, our conclusions differ immensely from those suggested by the the author of that aforementioned tome. The opportunity to present an historical account of the many remarkable people involved, has been an honour as exacting as it was privileged. To that end, it is observed how several documents from that cache are so deeply questionable, they remain entirely without validity or conclusion, though not without explanation. Any such disputed document is flagged where appropriate to alert the reader of the relevant anomaly for deeper analysis or study.

The imperative here then, was to generate a valid chronology for all extant documents to properly illustrate and demonstrate *The Robert Cochrane Tradition.* To date, no other such structure exists; and so, this foundational commentary enables insights regarding the more elusive aspects that challenge the reader both singularly, within each separate document, and collectively, as a continuity throughout Bowers' greater body of works. As a concise record, it provides an instantly accessible account in real time, of events as they occurred and affected the persons concerned. All works are cross-referenced and events validated where possible by solid anchor points. It has been a monumental undertaking, especially so, given the paucity of material available for cross-referencing. What these works reveal in their unfurling pattern, is a diversity of style and distinctions of influence that change and develop the way Bowers expressed his own vision; one that is never lost or hidden throughout. Once fully formulated, he ruthlessly discarded all areas of conflict, asserting finally that very personal view without compromise or concession, an act that led to a break up of the people within his Clan.

Several documents are certainly dated after Bowers' death, and are either not included here as they obviously contribute nothing to his legacy, failing to add any measure of understanding; or, they are included to expose duplicity, error, confusion, and where necessary, deliberate fabrication. Other documents, more recently acquired, have yet to be validated by the passage of time and other reference material. At this time they remain conjectural and have therefore been placed tentatively within the Chronology and may be subject to removal or re-evaluation in the future. Those placed with surety serve to stabilise and link others around them. These are stated clearly. Of the documents that allege to be prior to 1963, but few of the handwriting samples upon them are verifiable. Just to compound matters further, the scant examples available for comparison are in marked contra-distinction to the questionable pieces that flag concern. Nothing supports these anomalies to be contemporary with the typed text they accompany. And it absolutely goes without saying, that handwritten comments and signatures upon typed documents do not prove authorship of them, nor do they 'fix' a time when either text was created, hand-written or typed. These can be added at any time, and by anyone. Again, where pertinent, these are studied in greater depth within the tome constructed for such examination—'*Tubal's Mill.*'

No previous work has even attempted to categorise a referenced context for this occulted tradition, and so we hope it will be viewed as a pivotal and inspiring study. It does not claim however to be written in stone, as it gestures only the most probable ordering possible at this time. Further knowledge and/or further documentation may radically change this current understanding. Their eventual placements will challenge and strain extant perceptions, too long held erroneously as fact. Conjecture now finds clarification, refuting almost all that precedes it. We strongly encourage all students of the arte and seekers of truth to engross themselves in the often difficult task of reading *all* documents thoroughly. They deserve and demand rigorous, disciplined scrutiny; a stimulus, truly interested parties will find most fruitful. Our commentary is absolutely candid. Our references solid. Laid bare for all students, the work is free of all constraint, bias, and agenda, serving only Truth: what is 'held' here is primary. Adjunct to the two other volumes of this trilogy, we underscore remaining concepts central to the maxims and idioms of what others have named '*The Cochrane Tradition.*'

Whilst this may appear a complementary descriptive, serving as it does to distinguish it from others branches of 'Traditional Craft', we are and remain, quite simply—the *People of Goda, the Clan of Tubal Cain.*' We were so named by our ancestors themselves, and we honour them best in that retention. These pages explore subjects that have again laboured under decades of tautological diminishment. Most importantly, they beset a framework, a context upon which the message spins out, threading, weaving and darting, hither and thither a charm in the making: of revelation, an epiphany of intent, a register of all souls bound to its aegis that clamour for bald representation. Be it here granted. Be it here witnessed. Be it here known.

Any history of the Clan should be recorded and written only by those who People it still. Through this approach, all influences to the greater history of the Craft finds consideration by default. We are proud of that legacy, and share its wisdoms both mindfully and with cherished awe. Experience and valued first-hand mentorship engenders the gift of continuity throughout Bowers' works that have puzzled followers of the arte for five decades since his death. Too long have those works circulated, expounded by others unqualified to do so. Expansion across various media publications will hopefully also shift the tide of generalisations assigned by others, to our Tradition, known and named as— *The Robert Cochrane Tradition.*' [4]

From living and working those beguiling Mysteries, their means of conveyance through sacred poetry and metaphor touched our souls, traversing the arcane road of the fool and the devil he serves. Truths illustrated here, disseminate still, a view exoteric to those it harboured within the confines of the esoteric. Any suggestion to the contrary is otherwise false. Impersonal sources provide only the most fundamental of templates, leaving in their wake, a huge lacuna, into which all manner of rumour and speculation have rattled and blustered. Negligible tangent has since drifted into media free-fall. Illumination of the *'Cochrane Tradition,'* dispelling all extant errata, is therefore a worthy testament to the valour of mentors past and those yet to be. From this non-existent moment in the now, those rivers flow free of prior obstruction. Integrity is the core principle upon which CTC is predicated. The reader may finally witness the 'True' history of this Clan prescribed through an inherent mysticism, intrinsic to its Craft. It is properly:

"…the transmission of 'gnosis revealing praxis,' for the individual and the collective, in a manner that evolves the seeker via Antinomian cognition. Promethean sacrifice, Cainite exile and Titanic endurance. This arcane stream immerses the seeker in its dark light, where 'wisdom' is sought and won by the fire of the soul, straining after the light of truth, itself revealed as divine." [5]

Part I
Cochrane's Clan
Chapter One:
Origins and Definitions

"The path we have chosen, was thrust upon us, 'thereby,'" he said, filling his pipe, "hangs a Strange Story." [6]

As we walk our chosen path, wisdoms impart subtle keys to its many levels. These are keys earned in situ, via experience, they unlock increasingly new levels of seeing, and always in accordance to inbuilt parameters of relevant symbology, applied to intrinsic virtue. To that end, Roy Bowers was deliberately obtuse. For those beyond the bounds of his personal tradition, the message locked into his letters, is generally accepted as one— 'open' to considerable interpretation. Given their original purpose, that view holds reasonable grounds for such assumptions. In reaching all who read them now, their yield suffers, and is variable at best. Periodic re- reading/re-assessment instigates insightful re-visioning. Subjective and collateral awareness of his 'method, induces automatic, periodic self- assessment.'

Exposed to public scrutiny, the Bowers/Cochrane letters have accrued compound views not consequent to their original purpose, their vital and express determinatives slowly deviated from all arteful context. Their original and once intimate state, as a shared dynamic between mentor and student, devolved into the spectre of public opinion. In that blatant arena, their message is irrevocably misappropriated. The media observes an absence of subtle inference lost upon the casual voyeur reading them, disadvantaged in time and proximity, to discreet nuances that stubbornly remain beyond the remit of all who would seek to know, just what, hides there.

Naturally, there can be no definitive, single perception of them, less still, a rigid or singular way to interpret these Letters. For those encouraged to forget, as missives, and this must be stressed, they spoke their intent to *one* person only—the recipient with whom a rapport underpinned continued dialogue, mindful of the subtle yet implicit context. That dialogue has become a monologue serving new agendas. With respect therefore to all those drawn to read the enigmatic comments within them, please hold them dearly, for they were never written for the scrutiny of, nor to be subject to opinion of, any other than their original recipients. Privileged treasure indeed. Perhaps it is also fair to add, and even more important to underscore, how the very Muse and Virtue that had inspired Roy Bowers to express his thoughts and understanding, especially within those few letters and articles written during the final years of his life, drawn from the very 'Source' that founded and nurtured his Clan and Tradition. Known in the outer as CTC, we were (and remain), vitalised from its all-encompassing Egregore. In lieu of this, those works retain an iconic animism, born of that core.

As a *grammerie (Anglo-Saxon for book of evil/ sorcerous/ crafted/ magickal words)*, they offer manna to the discerning mind, receptive to the Muse. Repeated reading and study therein, inculcates substantial yields comparable to any other Arcanum. That is to say, you take from them what you experience, which may differ considerably from those of the writer, in terms of intent and purpose, of understanding and application, of latitude and aptitude and finally; of depth and draft. *They remain an invaluable and vital repository for those beyond the conclave of the Clan itself.*

Who we are: Nomenclature

Of the many terms used in Initiatory Craft—speaking as advocates for the abandonment of all abhorrent labels, which is not to deny the very necessary distinction between all groups using Craft or Witchcraft either, in an Initiatory, or non-Initiatory capacity; none, are mutually inclusive. Everyone needs to know the base line. A clear understanding from the onset may avoid contention after the event. If we seek communication and discourse with others, then an awareness of the base line is imperative; this avoids getting mired within semantics. We are defined by terms used, either by outright celebration of who we are, or in the mask of ambiguity that conceals through circumspection or discretion. We all make a choice, witting or otherwise.

Exact terms are requisite for reference, naturally, serving, as they must, a recognisable application to any given thing. Surely though, when applied to extant, living traditions, people or organisations, it should be a rule of thumb to ask those concerned, how they view and name *themselves*? Might we not reasonably hope for such courtesy? Beyond that, any label offered is by default in error; at best imprecise and at worst, offensive. And yet, so very much has gone awry. It is noted, how, even possessed of this vast media outlet, many things remain misunderstood and misrepresented. This highlights the need for constant and unrelenting updates to check the steady flow of information, ensuring it remains firmly on track and secure in its dissemination.

To that end, we introduce for examination, a term applied somewhat indiscriminately to others as much as to ourselves, when in reality, it properly describes neither. If there remains an insistence upon its usage, then it should fall towards those of Bowers' tradition only. The term in question is *Cochranite*, composed we suspect as an adjective (to describe his particular belief and approach to the mysteries) rather than the noun that would properly refer to his tradition, alone and none other. This we have come to realise, *is* the very nux of many problematic terms and applications. Bowers' works and visions evolved solely under the aegis of the Clan he formed and headed as its crucial source and catalyst. But just as Jesus may not be considered a Christian, Bowers may not himself be Cochranite. Moreover, unlike Jesus, whose followers adopted that eponym to define themselves, they are under no predilection to become initiates within a conclave of similarly bound cohorts; at least not as laymen since the first century. Since then, priests, monks and other smaller denominations involve oath-bound Inductions before one is admitted to their mysteries, and these are always defined by the rule under which they practise their particular branch of 'Christianity,' again, an adjective.

So for those who choose to be considered 'followers,' at best the term is a misnomer, and at worst an oxymoron. Cults tend to define themselves by adopting the name they follow as a descriptive and a noun, which highlights the unhealthy tendency towards fundamentalism. Often, if a group of people are considered a threat, by fanatical behaviour; or as questionable, by suspicious behaviour, they acquire this eponymous distinction. The suffix: "...*ettes*" or "...*ites*" are socially adopted forms of jocularity, applied pejoratively by some. Hence 'we' the People of Goda, are not followers of Roy Bowers/Robert Cochrane; but we may be better understood as being 'of ' his family. We serve the gods of our 'father's father,' so to speak. Our father is a beloved ancestor, one of several revered 'others,' but he is not a god and is not worshipped per se.

Another earnest distinction therefore arises with the terms 'Cochrane inspired' and 'Cochrane derived,' the former disseminates a broad and very public legacy and the latter, a suggestion of connectivity, an imperative borne as fruit, from his singular, initiatory and closed tradition, that which withholds its direct and very discreet, private legacy to its own *People of*

Goda, of the Clan of Tubal Cain. In that regard, so much misunderstanding exists across the broad spectrum of Traditional Craft. We often lament for what *should* be known as common knowledge. Of course, this is not the fault of any seeker or pilgrim along this Wayfaring Craft, but the fault of those who in knowing better, would yet obfuscate the truth for their own self-serving causes. Sadly, much dis-information continues to be widely circulated concerning this very matter, asserting a perspective totally at odds with Bowers' views.

There appears to be a fundamental lack of comprehension with regard to the operative system of Clanships, formed from one or more groups of peoples or families of people who hold and preserve the traditions of culture and memories of the 'folk,' as sheltered within an overarching body named for its leading exponent's *tutelary* ancestor, or deity (sometimes one and the same of course). These peoples offer allegiance to a Head-Kinsman, whose sworn duty is to serve them, to protect them, to provide for them and to be responsible for their bodily and spiritual well-being. A deeper and more involved explanation of this may be found in the aforementioned *Tubal's Mill: The Round of Life (A critique of the historicity of the Robert Cochrane Tradition)* again penned by this author.

Therefore, we are also obliged to disabuse the concept of many 'Clans' of Tubal Cain, as impossible as it is absurd. Bowers instigated *one Clan only*, named for 'Tubal Cain;' that singular construct has continued since that inception; that Tradition thrives still. For posterity, let history record that within its aegis however, one 'Cuveen of the Ram' exists in California, fully aligned in troth to the Clan. Beyond that, various kith and brethren reside in allegiance to it. Clans are historically composed of various groups or collectives; though always in allegiance to the *one Head-Kinsman*. It can be no other way.[7] We are not being exclusive so much as we are refuting inclusivity by desire; acceptance and recognition comes through due election and admittance only.

It was thus in 1966 and remains so now in 2016.

The one to come. Though earlier founders and holders of our tradition remain unnamed to the public, it is their works that we, *'The People of Goda, the Clan of Tubal Cain'* hold as the *'Robert Cochrane Tradition'* and its Legacy as Covenanted Heirs, in succession through three Magisters; continuing directly that unabated aegis of the Clan from Roy Bowers, through *Evan John Jones*, appointed by Bowers to be his Tanist (spiritual heir), vouchsafed by his wife who was the Lady and Maid of the Clan, to be its physical heir and leader. Evan John Jones, past Magister and Head-Kinsman of the Clan of Tubal Cain, publicly bequeathed that authority to ourselves, naming *Robin-the-dart* as *his* Tanist successor in turn. He appointed *Shani Oates* as Lady of the Clan, serving as its virtue holder through her acknowledgement as Clan Maid. The future of the Clan resides in the promise and troth of another yet to be—*Ulric 'Gestumblindi' Goding*, stands as appointed Tanist in endurance of this remarkable and arcane tradition. His own transition to Magister when the time comes, will witness a smooth transition between himself and the Clan's current Magister, *Robin-the-dart*. Given the mechanics of the Clanship system, as stated previously, it could not again be otherwise. Our appointments are unequivocal, and as a vital tenet of The Law, were confirmed in person, several times by our mentor and predecessor in the Clan, Evan John Jones. As holders of Cochrane's legacy, declared privately and in public via a document that was finally published just three weeks before E. J. Jones died in August 2003, we continue to serve and lead the Clan, in sacred troth, through the aegis of its ancestry.

A Conspiracy to Fraud. History marks for posterity the gravid significance of all appointments under The Law. History reveals and records a specious deed instigated to undermine our leadership a decade after our inception. Media inflammation regrettably brought to light a private matter involving the expulsion of a former clan member, cast out primarily for gross misconduct. Failing to grasp the mechanics and purpose of that expulsion, that person continued to act outside and beyond the 'rightness of things,' choosing to add fraud and hubris to a catalogue of troth-breaking events to present herself and her new partner as 'additional' titular heads, thus exhibiting the irony of supreme ignorance for the system they sought to usurp. Totally lacking in conviction or bravado, she naturally waited until E. J. Jones was no longer around to refute her extraordinary fantasies, before she emerged to expound them.

That anyone gave credence to their claims or consideration for its plausibility, reveals more about their own ignorance of operative Traditional Craft, than it does a lack of discernment and knowledge of the peoples involved, not to mention a lack of respect for the Sworn Word of a Craft Elder who'd legitimised his legacy under the Law, appointed through and of his own Tradition in ourselves. Quite frankly, as shameless pretenders, they should both have been shunned and spurned by everyone who encountered them, and especially by those who claim to be key exponents and esteemed 'Elders of Traditional Craft' per se. Those who fained neutrality merely abetted their gross deceit, inhibiting a swift and just dismissal of a ridiculous and farcical footnote that has since cast a blight upon our Clan. And yet the facts of the matter were never hidden and the truth was ever common knowledge. Not everyone cares. Not everyone is intrigued by this event or its regrettable politics. But, anyone even remotely intrigued by this political embroilment might perhaps consider how those involved acquired the backing and support to escalate and promote them so devastatingly *some ten years after* we had worked in silence as a discreet presence, evolving our tradition. Whose agenda for example, would that have served to do so? Be at least aware that there are those who can manipulate media to this extent, to falsify and support an entirely insidious and fraudulent claim, *entirely without evidence,* and furthermore, use blatant lies to undermine a legitimate position. Be vigilant!

We extend our unreserved gratitude towards those whose better actions supported us throughout, aiding a complete resolve. Addressing these pragmatic issues here, so concisely, all lingering misunderstandings disintegrate the matter, returning it to the nothing is always was. As in all things, Truth will out. Under The Law, we remain connected and contacted to the vital ancestry of our tradition that inspires all works still. Time and Tide corrected that brief interruption to the work as we battled to 'hold' all we'd been 'given.' Generating an even stronger Clan, it is now one less willing to suffer fools gladly. We are indeed *Od's* men and we stand with greater pride than ever, of our legacy. We are grateful for the annealing process this experience has afforded us. How wise our mentor was, when he said how nothing is ever of no value and no time is ever wasted.

A sacred name. Of course, the titular element of the Clan name, like any other, if desired, is subject to another's choice of adoption. It is not owned and therefore may never be copy-righted, not by any of us. Common sense and due caution should prevail in all instances of 'naming,' especially those invoking a sense of the 'other.' Adopting a self-appointed name for one's clan is vastly different from the bestowal by authorized adoption into an original 'Clan' of its given name! What is gifted in spirit, remains so. Neither its authority and legitimacy, nor its unique and official status is challenged by those foolish enough to believe that same authority accompanies the 'appropriation' and use of an assumed name. Indeed, such persons would do well to study the arcane notions of naming and the burden of Wyrd that such engages.

Wyrd, is bound forever within the Oath of its making; a most holy undertaking. As John (E. J. Jones) remarked—it is a gravid matter, and not to be taken lightly, nor falsely. We are after all, a Suzerainty, not a Sovereignty; and that makes all the difference. That is a very different relationship and undertaking. It behoves a very different world-view, requiring an arcane yet living tradition to actuate its uniquely liberating universal camaraderie, not to mention a profound brotherhood.

The activities of the Clan as a collective centralised around its founder Roy Bowers (aka Robert Cochrane) and his (own) core group, which is believed to have been briefly known as the *'Thames Valley Coven.'* Very quickly he made a dramatic leap forward, inspired by traditions that had become known to him, all of which fuelled his own experiences gained thus far along his search for his heritage. In seeking out the 'blood and bone' of his fore-fathers, his resulting corpus of works remains uniquely unambiguous, and self-evident. Examples are emphasised where relevant throughout this book to the contexts in which they are quoted. Needless to say, he used any and all means to express those tenets by way of analogy and allegory. His genius recognised the kernel of truth in many things that most people overlooked. In creating a Clan-ship, Bowers extended his own aegis. The formulation of a group mythos evolved into his *Clan Tradition* to encompass those other groups and peoples whose own traditions, adjunct to his own, formed a 'collective,' an occult 'tour de force.'

Vital inclusions, not to be understated, were sourced through Evan John Jones, whose presence within Bowers' coven and Clan, shaped and inspired Bowers' trajectory, exponentially. Bowers was keen to share his knowledge and experiences, and eagerly wrote of quite specific directives brought to bear upon his development of his tradition. Another major influence, of course, was the 'Old Man' he speaks of in numerous letters and documents.[8] His identity has thus far remained elusive, but we have discerned a viable candidate; again, not explored here, but in *Tubal's Mill*, where it refutes candidates proposed in other publications.

Others associated historically with Roy Bowers and his Clan require further clarification in order to properly place them in their rightful understanding. This is deemed necessary to dispel rising misconceptions in their regard. Neither 1734, nor The Regency form any part of the actual legacy of the Robert Cochrane Tradition. They were created by its influence only. All may indeed feed the *public* legacy Cochrane fuelled by his active engagement, directly and indirectly through his works.

The 'order of 1734'

'1734' is the name Joe Wilson chose to describe all he had created from sources and teachings available to him, including all that Bowers had shared with him through letters of correspondence. The information within those communiqué's were sourced from within, yet beyond the bounds of CTC's closed initiatory teachings and tradition, naturally distinct from them, hence Wilson's own insistence on other additional sources as fundamental to the primacy of his tradition, an important emphasis that should counter poorly presented explanations from those less familiar with these facts. Too many misunderstandings abound across all media concerning the traditions of others, particularly with regard to anything tracing influences from Roy Bowers, aka Robert Cochrane. Error arises in the hollow between fact and truth.

In order to dispel those vague and often woolly misconceptions and repeated half-truths, based no doubt on poor information, or incorrect sources, we here set out an explanation relative to the facts concerning the establishment of '1734.' Devised in consultation with

Stuart Inman, a Doyen of Toteg Tribe and one of the current guardians of '1734,' his views and knowledge on this matter should adequately clarify their status. Wilson independently formed '1734' as a unique 'method' that enables its students to 'see' and 'understand' a more intuitive approach to the Craft and it Mysteries. This influential approach would eventually change the generic systems of American Craft he and many others had previously subscribed too. Inman briefly summarises his experience of this as a method that can draw someone into a working system, through into what becomes a tradition. It can be said therefore to combine all elements into the uniquely envisioned '1734.' Though of course, all further discussion on that matter is better engaged directly through the guardians of 1734.[9] And so, at no time had Joe Wilson ever been, nor claimed to be a part of the Clan or indeed, Cochrane's Tradition.

Based on Wilson's idiosyncratic understanding of Bowers' six letters, received in private correspondence through the first six months of 1966, Wilson sought further understanding of his Craft from others who had known and worked with Bowers.[10] During the early 1970s, an opportunity arose for Wilson to travel to England, where he met and worked primarily with certain members of *The Regency.*' These were Norman Gills and Ruth Wynn Owen. Ruth in particular served to further en-flesh Wilson's own teachings founded in the tradition of a person we know only as 'Sean,' in America. Joe Wilson was therefore moved to create '1734' core/ nucleus as an organic process he evolved along unknown trajectories.

Although Bowers' letters do touch upon certain aspects of his Clan's lore, he did not impart CTC lore as a mentor to one inducted into its mysteries. Rather, he shared certain aspects, drawn from his larger corpus of experience to embellish and deepen Wilson's understanding of another tradition he *was* already a student of, via his mentor—'Sean.'[11] Thus Bowers was drawing from his own diverse store of Craft knowledge. The 'method,' termed by Wilson as '1734,'continues to thrive within those exponents gifted with its guardianship and dissemination.[11] Interested parties are encouraged to discover these teachings directly from that source. Whatever needs to be learned, should rightfully come from the lips of those who speak the mysteries of a tradition and never the tongue of others. Our own mentor, in like manner adopted Bowers' impetus to reach out to those beyond the media circus, to those real seekers, the genuine followers of the arte, especially when and where they have taken sincere steps towards acquiring an understanding of their Craft's intrinsic Mysteries.

CTC *IS* Robert Cochrane's Tradition. Founded by him, just as the '1734' method was founded by Joe Wilson. Rather, '1734' is a way of viewing the notion of tradition. Formulated from the three separate spheres of influence, noted above, Sean, Roy Bowers and Ruth Wynn Owen, Wilson birthed the '1734' Egregore as a distinct Virtue, entirely separate from that of CTC, as it should and must be. The current holder/s of those separate Virtues serve and are each served by their own distinct Egregore. '1734' is therefore not CTC and CTC, equally, cannot be '1734.' Neither exists within the other, and neither formed from the other.

When discovering Bowers' words anew, their reading and working will undoubtedly strike a chord of dissonance or harmony. They will influence by default. Of those with whom personal correspondence was shared, certain wisdoms pass through their kenning. Truth be-told, much remains hidden still, unshared, hoarded for some future event, or feature of revelation. Not by ourselves, for all we have, we share here. To those persons, we beseech of them to share also their treasure, for his legacy to the world, abides in those gems he offered freely, given to those who would listen, when all around him danced another's tune. Out of step, he put his 'Faith' into the 'Word,' in the vain hope it would reach the many, deafened by the cacophony that suffocated him. Nonetheless, those works may not be deemed as, nor confused with, its distinct teachings experienced in actuality, *within and through that tradition*, amongst its members alone, whose individual initiations through the spirit of the Clan's own Egregore, concatenate mutual gnosis. Rather, it may at best serve only to articulate a basis upon which they may build their own praxis.

The Mysteries present a complex mechanism for all pilgrims and seekers of spirit, nurtured and guided by attendant hosts of beings and entities. Witnessed and experienced as societal groups, primarily through our 'cultural' lens, we may refine that further as individuals within and without those groups. The great depths of Marah, as 'Her' unending and ineffable wellspring of accrued thought and memory, is channelled into numerous streams to form the Web of Wyrd across this amazing planet, peopled as it is, by so many traditions, beliefs, faiths and religions. Historically, these Mysteries have retained a strong initiatory presence in various but, limited conclaves, dedicated and committed to furtherance and exploration. These achieve the greatest success where engaged as full-time 'priests' for want of a more apt term,' as mendicants of those works. Gnosis is absorbed and disseminated more efficiently through communities nurtured by the presence of its priests, who exist, live and find thrift therein. Yet, typically, communities falter where disquieting currents rise as superstitions, fuelling parallel traditions or cultic practice, and less frequently as actual religions. Thus the 'One' source finds a 'Way,' via the few, to influence the many. We may build upon the groundwork others have facilitated for us, not as elitists, for very few of us are able to perform that task ourselves; each will serve, one way or another, and all may share whatever bounty, we as human beings collectively generate in our daily lives.

The camaraderie of all such groups of 'workers,' no matter the field of labour, gather and create ways of expressing attendant lore to reflect that work, in turn formulating attendant rites and rituals in their execution. These underpin the myriad traditions that encompass all aspects of our lives. Remember, there is no separation betwixt what is deemed the sacred and the mundane, all too often (and in error), these find further division and classification. There is nothing new under the sun, and it is for each of us to explore and discover our place within the above schema. Many 'yearn' for alternative modes of access to those Mysteries, though in reality, these may only ever be achieved by gruelling work. Individuals may act upon a combination of instinct and personal contact with the spiritual currents of their own locale, or by acquiring admission to others (essentially a group of people), who have also honed their individual contact and instinct formed around and guided by a tutelary spirit.

This quite specific entity is the inherent guiding force behind such groups, better known as its Egregore. It is abundantly clear, that even within a community stream, there exists an Egregore that is not accessed by all, yet its influence is felt and will eventually reach all who are, or choose to be receptive to that force. Importantly, both the individual and the group may achieve some form of external generic, spiritual initiation. That does not depend on belonging to a group, nor being 'admitted' to their practises. Our modern society is now so deeply multi-culturalised, where centuries of cross pollination has embedded deep seeds within the soul, to the extent where many find their own spiritual locale incongruous to their soul's deep yearning. This tendency has extended the distance plausible between direct 'physical' mentorship. Thus, influences felt across the web of Wyrd, pull ever harder and tighter to sate a visceral longing within. We reach out to those whom we feel could share those journeys with us. So may we long continue as the few that must retain the core, nurtured by it sufficiently to generate a dissemination of teachings that will guide others toward the achievement of their own epiphanies, ultimately of personal significance.

This is what Roy Bowers referred to as 'The Faith,' a beacon of light in a dark world. To bring this to meet the question of influence and access, we would add that all that becomes 'known,' may be shared in ways that do not encroach upon the individual's realisation and experience, continuing via the 'Mystery Schools' existing in our time, as forums and various media, including books, literature and lecture modalities. These facilitate enquiry and may accelerate the individual further along a particular pathway they feel especially drawn to. We believe this may be how the Mysteries set the loom, that threaded the fabric of a greater community together, establishing the pattern of their lives, asserting how they act and recognise the 'other' within them; and how they are served, highlighting the lack of ego required for such works. We are grateful to those whose kindnesses acknowledge our own works. Many have responded deeply and sympathetically to them, whether shared in books, articles or even personal correspondence. They offer support for its vibrant core, expressing desires that may continue to vitalise future connections to ever-greater force. Through application of these external current, their works bring all of us closer to a synergistic focus.

Bowers once used the analogy of the 'Tree' to great effect. In time honoured fashion then we use the image of the 'Tree' by way of his analogy: the root forms by force of spirit, seeding the 'mind-fields,' with inspiration. Once that seed formulates its roots within that nurturing virtue, it grows a sturdy trunk. Its branches arch upwards to collect nourishment required for growth, from both the Source and from the winds that shape and form it. Those same winds blow its leaves across the landscape, harvested by those with ears to listen to the subtle whisperings they carry. Likewise, its fruits are gathered by those who stand close to the tree (its community), who may choose to keep or share such abundance with other communities. In turn, they may also enjoy that bounty in its consumption (immediate gratification), or by wise action, planting deeply those seeds to nurture and partake fully of the source that inspired the parent tree. That fruit will hybridise and evolve its own strain, incrementally of genera.

Our Clan, 'Cochrane's Clan,' is such a tree. Our branches are our own limbs, our lifeblood draws through the sap all it needs to remain self-sustaining. A tree remains a tree, supported by its own roots, even when amongst a forest of others. It is entirely different from a network of interconnecting railway lines or road networks and grids that can in contradistinction, 'branch' off from the central trunk. We emerge amidst a sea of confusion, of epithets and associations, so that we may lay bare all we are, and all we are not.

The 'Cochrane Tradition' *is* Cochrane's actual Clan, being that singular tree where: One is one, and all alone, and ever more shall be so! This Clan of Tubal Cain, founded by him to express the tenets of his own tradition, continues; it thrives still. It cannot be separate from it, yet its names resides not in that external form.

'In Nomine Rex'

At the end of her year's note-pad for 1966, Valiente records an attendance in that year for what Ronald White termed the 'largest public Halloween Rite to date' at the Rollright Stones. Over 50 people attended. This was probably the event that inspired Ronald White to adopt an open approach to public rituals as a seasonal continuum. Hence this event almost certainly set the birth in mind for *'The Regency.'* Valiente notes another strange anomaly, one of many more to come, that Bill Gray did not know Ronald White when he attended a very early ritual (again as described by Valiente as one of the first) held by *'The Regency'* in 1967. But that is another matter which I shall return to. For now and with regard to the role and status of *'The Regency,'* fair clarification must be given to distinguish it as an independent tradition in its own right. To that end, forbearance must be upheld for those inclined to veer to either pole, for the giddy roll betwixt the two, doth not harmonise. To that end, *'The Regency,'* let it be known, <u>never was, 'of '</u> the Cochrane Tradition. Nor was it ever foolish enough to claim such for itself. Neither did it place itself into the category of 'follower.' Its own founders were too independent for that. And those who would cast it so, do those founders of *'The Regency'* a great disservice. There is no reason and no cause to do so. Media trends in fashionable buzzwords spread misnomers that present little bearing on their worth or value. And so, by association they and others inspired by Cochrane, have therefore fallen in some way to the inappropriate terminology of *'Cochranite.'* Another ill placed descriptor is *'Cochrane derived.'*

The rise and fall of *'The Regency'* has been explored fully in *'Tubal's Mill,'* and so brief mention only is awarded here to elucidate only this terminology of nomenclature where relevant to their role within this archive of letters served by SCSIII. Quite incorrectly, due to the initial reference by one author to *'The Regency'* as formed from either 'several, 'or 'remaining' members of the 'Clan,' others less witting, or concerned to check for themselves the veracity of that suggestion, have accepted it as fact and repeated it. Sadly repetition of error never establishes fact, only specious rumour or opinion. It remains in error. Two of the founding members of *'The Regency'* had certainly been leaders of a separate 'second' kin-ship group[12] formed *within the aegis of the Clan* of Tubal Cain in Bowers' lifetime. Those two men were Ronald White/Chalky and George Stannard/Winter. Others from among their own group that shifted into *'The Regency'* with them, were likewise considered 'kindred.' That distinction is of extreme significance. Moreover, their own works and lore only set the mythos and praxis of *'The Regency,'* not the Clan's. Whence they departed the Clan to co-found 'The Regency,' they took only what 'they held.' No more, and no less.

Others, namely Anne S., who also contributed to the instigation of 'The Regency,' were mainly Inductees (probationary or temporary guests) of The Clan and not Members of Full Admission. Some were also casual guests of Ronald Chalky White's group, including (again) Anne S., George Desmond Bourke, Gerard Noel (aka John Math), Geoff and Louise Hampton-Cole and Norman Gills. Distinct from these are Bill & Bobbie Gray, and A.M. who were Inductees of the Clan only and not part of Chalky's group. Doreen Valiente and Evan John Jones were among the select few Members of Full Admission in the Clan besides Roy and Jane Bowers. E. J. Jones was singularly qualified (having invaluable input to the understanding and praxis of 'Tradition') to continue 'Cochrane's Tradition,' that is 'Cochrane's Clan.' **Jones was therefore appointed by Bowers as Tanist to succeed him.**

By contra-distinction, Chalky and George largely influenced only their own group, led by them, briefly aligned to the Clan. In fact, this was the basis of the many disagreements and altercations Bowers had with them. They saw things very differently, as several of the enclosed letters within the chronology highlights. Their histories reveal how Bowers was at constant pains to have them understand his wishes, to act upon his teachings and to have them align their praxes in accordance with his own, to build a cohesive Clan, operating from the same fundamental principles. But, as the letters readily assert, Ronald Chalky White and George Winter often disagreed with Roy Bowers on even the most basic of those principles. Their works are separated from those of Jones and Bowers by a clear demarcation of content and intent. One needs only read *The Pagan's Handbook*, or indeed anything produced by 'The Regency' to note the significant differences from the core tenets outwards. They exhibit their own love of a more 'Celtic' (sic) and romanticised craft that nestled into the Neo-Paganism of the 1970s and 1980s. They are in no way aligned to the grittier, less sensual, earthier graft that Bowers had formulated from the historical magicks and beliefs of his ancestral tradition. Comparison of anything written by Bowers (and Jones for that matter, who differed only in style) with anything written by Chalky and George will highlight this immediately. There is no need here to impress upon them, again, the works speak for themselves.

Even before Bowers' tragic death, Ronald White and George Winter's group had already begun to flex their independence, a matter which escalated the friction between them. As kindred, after his death, they simply had no choice but to go their own way, leaving behind a tradition they had worked within, but had not formed.[13] They had loose associations with that tradition through the Clan, but they were by no means major players. As our mentor pointed out, they were kindred, not Clan. Quite bluntly, they did not have Bowers' permission, nor that of his widow and Maid, to continue his specific teachings and works, nor those of his Clan.[14] That singular authority and Virtue did not fall to them, nor to any other beyond the bounds and aegis of the Clan that beheld it. *The Virtue remained within the Clan*, and has remained so, ever since.

In her note-pads, Valiente marks the attendance of the inaugural meeting of *'The Regency'* in 1967 (note, not 1966 as claimed by some others). Evidently, when Bill Gray (as a former member of the Clan) did attend a meeting, he did not like what he saw, for he never attended another.[15] Meetings were initially hosted at the flat of a mutual friend, Ruth Wynn Owen, another co-founder, until considerable differences of opinion led her away from *'The Regency'* to form Y Plant Bran. Her input to both was however, instrumental to Joe Wilson in formulating his '1734' [16] modality.

Anyone reading for themselves *The Regency*'s own works (exemplified quite definitively within their source work, the '*Pagan Handbook*'), will find no difficulty in noting their manifestly un-Cochrane- like works. These works and teachings, authored solely by Chalky and George, diverge, quite significantly (as they should), from those of Roy Bowers, concentrating on those issues that fuelled *their own* traditions and lore, quite independent of his. More latterly, their works remain principally defined through those rightfully attributed to *The Regency,*' a self-defined 'group' (not a coven, a distinction they were most insistent upon). It was co-founded to preserve their own, quite individual works, now accessible on a website dedicated to them, available to all interested parties for study. Their corpus has a unique trademark, as does that of Bowers and Jones, (E.J.J.). Illustrated without ambiguity, the explorations of the Pagan lore they'd retained, albeit adjusted slightly by unavoidable natural influences from within.

The Clan may rightfully determine an appreciation of its own works. With respect, *The Regency*' were no more, and no less than *kindred*. In their life-time, its exponents never claimed to be anything else. Decades have passed without explanation of these matters; regrettable in hindsight. But then, there was never a need to; nor should there have been. It was no-one else's business beyond those few people concerned. Time has shifted the course of action, and so, were it even desired, to be properly recognised today as kindred within the Clan, a declaration of that intent would be correct procedure, a re-acknowledgement of the Clan, under its Head-Kinsmen. As independents, this is something they no longer feel is appropriate for them, and something they no longer feel serves their own aegis. There is no enmity in this. It is simply the way it is. Their former kindred status was not preserved nor was it renewed through the Clan's successive Magisters. They led their own group and founded their own tradition, from their own works. And those works do not in any way inform those of the Clan, and vice versa. For a while, Bowers explored everything put before him. Then he began discriminating what he felt was 'right' for its trajectory and refined it:

> "Since we have decided to follow strictly traditional patterns, we have had to scrap nearly everything that was valid previously. During the formation of traditional practise, it must be remembered that nothing has come to us as a bulk commodity, but as a series of small; but increasingly interesting information."

In his own words, he says to Chalky:

> "This is the way Jane and I have been working, and will work in future."[17]

Every missive, every document written *from Bowers,* initially to members of his coven, very probably the *The Thames Valley Coven,* and his Clan; *The Clan of Tubal Cain.* He advises *them all.* **He** gives instruction. No-one else. Four other documents that remain unaccounted for in terms of authorship and context provide information only – no instruction. Even then, that information is entirely incongruous and at utterly at odds with everything else Bowers has ever written. This strongly suggests another author. These few precious documents were once held by two people who'd used them as an aid to form an initial basis to later re-structure their own group upon. In saving these documents, Chalky and George have enabled us to further en-flesh other surviving documents and letters Bowers shared with a selected few, within and without his Clan. Together, they establish a composite structure hitherto unfamiliar to many outside real Old Craft Traditions. Because of that, much nonsense has been accrued in ill formed attempts to grasp the complexity of those old modalities; to the modern mind, they abound with alien concepts.

Therefore, a lack of reference or context, has facilitated all kinds of conjecture, none of which stands up to scrutiny or study. All we ask, is that using what we share here, that people who do care about the truth, do exactly that. Through such insight and first-hand knowledge, we strongly refute any suggestion that promotes *The Regency'* as an enterprise, *Cochrane derived*, and so would Chalky and George, despite however much others may choose to promote this nonsense as their own wish fulfilment. As for being *Cochrane inspired*, possibly, but only initially. The works that sourced *'The Regency'* are their own, and those works did not inform Bowers' *Coven or Clan*. Saying otherwise, and repeating it, will never make it fact. Without documentary evidence that irrefutably reconciles such wish - fulfilment, there is only an extant dearth of contrary documentation, and so conjecture it must remain. Comments given thus far by others on this subject simply do not hold up to any scrutiny and fail utterly to confirm or support any such claim.[18]

Those who value the unique works of Chalky and George, should not wish it otherwise, for their mentors, or for themselves. Their gift to the Pagan Community, especially throughout America, is highly valued. It stands on its own feet. It needs no other. From Ethos to Mythos, they neither contain nor continue any of the Clan 'Traditions or Rites' (despite certain superficial similarities alluded to by nomenclature), instigated by Bowers as its founder, and leader of his Clan, until his death in 1966. As E. J. Jones informed us on more than one occasion that:

> "Jane had not deeded them Roy's material,[19] so they simply couldn't use it even if they'd wanted to." He later added how "they [Chalky and George], had no desire to do so, and no right to do so either."

Differences in theology and practice remain divergent between The Clan and *'The Regency.'* Essentially 'Pagan' by their own definition, their Craft conflicts imposingly from Bowers own, as Bowers was frequently strained to note and remedy. Evan John Jones (E. J. J.) explained this without equivocation, very simply, that:

> "The snag with The Regency will always be—'What are they working'? Chalky and George had their own system [very loosely] based on some of Roy's material and teachings, so if one wanted to be pedantic about it, they could claim to be kindred to Clan. Chalky and George never claimed Clan status for The Regency and neither do the new Regency people as far as I know." [20]

We may confirm, as E.J.J. states above, those old boys certainly did not. They'd honoured 'what they were given.' Not until after Evan John Jones' death in 2003, in recent time, has that idea been aired by newer members of the current incarnation of The 'New' Regency, and then, retrospectively *for* (not by) their former mentors. Speculation is ever the fuel for escalation of any new controversy, and few people ever study the material presented before adding to the fire. In such haste, several important factors have been overlooked. Cherry-picking selected comments out of context do both the writer and the reader a disservice, and a thorough examination of the entire corpus is required in order to gain a true perspective of the events these documents record. Early works by Regency members naturally reveal negligible traces of Bowers unique style. How could they not? Still, they show swift signs of releasing those influences by the time they were advertising themselves as a Pagan group in 1968 in an interview for *'Man, Myth and Magic,'* entitled: 'The Messiah of Highgate Hill.' Ronald White resigned as 'Leader' from *'The Regency,'* just a few years later in 1974.

Of primary significance in the aforementioned statement, is the status of The 'New' Regency relative to the Clan. And that, E.J.J. explains with absolute precision, was *kindred.* A status they have shown no desire to uphold, neither desired nor requested. As members only of the Clan, being neither leader nor founder, their respective and distinct heritage remained within their separate groups after Bowers' tragic death. From that group, they simply continued as a more open and public face, named The Regency, free entirely of the Clan's aegis. Being independent and autonomous of it, means of course, they have no call upon its name or works, including those of its founder, Roy Bowers. Ironically, in claiming the identity of The Regency as an element distinct from the Clan, the underlying premise of it becomes abundantly clear. John of Monmouth says:

> "Contrary to current opinion, the Royal Windsor Coven did not become The Regency. It continued as the RWC. The Regency arose *out of the seeds of the Clan*, and the vision of Ron White."

This bold and retrospective statement begins to makes sense of these anomalous claims. The agenda is here flagged at last, raising an alert traceable through the entire commentary that accompanies the recent publication of several letters we have named: 'the Monmouth Cache,' to distinguish them from others held longer, and as widely available works penned by Roy Bowers. In reality, the bulk of these letters illustrate a very different bearing upon the 'Cochrane Tradition' than had been previously assumed, especially recently. Bowers, his works, his Traditions and his legacy through The Clan, remain explicit throughout them. Some of those letters almost exclusively pertain to members of the (separate) 'group' headed by Chalky and George who enjoyed what Marian Green recalls as *a loose company of folk who gathered ad hoc to celebrate in pagan fashion, the seasonal round*. This absolutely must be understood as a group entirely independent of the Clan of Tubal Cain. The Clan was of course led by Bowers overall under his Clan leadership alone.

But always, as we cannot stress enough, the documents really do speak for themselves. Whatever Chalky may or may not have named his own informal gathering is unrecorded. But if it was the 'Royal Windsor Coven,' then it was a name so secret they never used it, not even amongst themselves. In fact it finds no mention in any document until several years after Bowers' death. Stranger than even this, and appreciated only when one realises that several of those missives headed as 'dangerous,' 'secret' and to be destroyed immediately after being read, never to be rerecorded or uttered - not even there is that name recorded!

With the exception of one alleged ambiguous abbreviation noted as a later diary entry,[21] (unfortunately not provided by that claimant), it remains without explanation or validation. Beyond anything awarded other than retrospectively,' no factual documentary evidence therefore exists that confirms even a hint towards the alleged existence for any group by the name *Royal Windsor Coven*. No name is ever so secret that even its members fail to refer to it, especially in their private and official correspondences to one another. Certainly, the *Thames Valley Coven* is mentioned several times, especially where it counts, that is, on the document designated for its members to sign under oath (see *Writ and Constitution*' document (d). Conversely, the RWC as an allegedly secret name, finds mention but briefly and retrospectively, and then, only after 1974 whence Ronald White resigned as leader, effectively winding down *The Regency*, ceasing its public activities around 1976/7.

Bowers' widow, the Maid and Lady of both Bowers' Coven & Clan, held the heritage and lineage of both in her husband's life-time as its Magister, and after his death. Historically, this has always been the way Clans and their traditions are continued. No matter what factions splinter from an established Clan, the Clan itself as an office and a family, as a heritage and a duty, remain always and entirely with the Head-Kinsmen, (jointly or severally, depending upon whether the Clan is Matriarchal or Patriarchal) holding absolute authority, but duty bound to serve all his

People within it, as kith or kin, be that one person or twenty-one. How a Clan operates within the Craft is touched upon in this volume, but is covered extensively by the author in the afore-mentioned separate publication (*Tubal's Mill*), a little of which may be quoted here.

> "Initially derived from the Gaelic form 'Clann,' meaning 'children,' it later embraced the term in a less metaphorical sense and began to encompass a broader sense of those children as a 'family'—effectively a 'People,' being the larger unit of a kinship, a description that very much conforms to the social structure of the Scottish Clan/n system. As a collective, based within a specific culture, they shared common customs, most importantly of beliefs, superstitions, folklore and magicks."

Bowers explores those duties, the charge to the ancestors, the work itself, mentorship and tradition. Above all, Bowers' notion of the mechanics of Clanship, of fealty within the hierarchy as it flows from the Egregore through the principals of titular heads, and then the gyfu of 'return,' back towards the Egregore—a perfect symbiosis. Underpinning his exemplary facet of magickal enterprise, is the grist for the Mill, that is, the true context for the winding of its cogs. Clans became organised into trades and guilds, each possessed of apprentices, customs, rites and lore; each possessed of strict 'family' codes of adoption and rejection. Blood and Bone—the source of virtue within every Egregore

> "I in turn recognise the authority of others who are higher than myself, and that authority, once stated, is absolute, do what we may…
> My job, is to train and organise, fulfil the letter of the law, and to function, to discipline and to curse, as well as to elevate and expound. . We have to train any new members to a certain level, develop any hidden power they may have, and finally to teach them how to

manipulate virtue. We may be the last of the old school, but we still uphold the old attitudes and expect the same. Above we two rises another authority whose writ is older than ours, to that authority, we give absolute allegiance, and whose function it is to train us and work with us ... I was in the fortunate position of having been blooded, therefore I have some hold on their ears." —Bowers.

Monmouth[22] offers a most curious and contrary explanation of 'Clan,' one that has no historical basis in any reality or fact. Designed to support propositions declared throughout his book, it casts a glamour over the true meaning. His explanation creates a cloud of obfuscation and confusion where none existed. Quite simply, the *term 'Clan' has never been a descriptor for a group of people that include guests attending Sabbats not initiated into their 'coven.* Therefore the question why this is even raised, begs address, since the view held by Bowers of what exactly constitutes a Clan 'is' neither ambiguous nor sparse in application. More than that, it was his alone to define, to defend and to pass on; none other! There is not a single letter, or document that fails to clarify Bowers' purpose in full, correct and historical understanding, as (named) families and bonded units of a People. From that first early founding of his Clan, everything ranging from his intimate missives to his discussions with Justine Glass regarding the Mysteries of the Breton Menhir, underscore how for him, everything revolved around 'his Clan.' We offer here but a small selection as examples for readers to consider when-cross referencing.

With regard to the Knots, as the more frequent Esbats, or the larger gatherings of mixed groups, covens and Clans, held less often, known as Sabbats, and whether either or none engage guests, has always been a matter individual preference, according to the Tradition of the people involved. In most Traditions, *both Sabbats and Esbats remain closed to outsiders,* admitting members only, to attend either or both, as desired. Therefore, any depth of intimacy, as here noted by Valiente, existing between regular members of an Esbat group, may naturally be expected to 'dampen' somewhat whence compared to the grander formality of the Sabbats, and where other less regular members or kin-ship groups within their bonded Clan, may join them, (although the opposite extreme is also just as common). Even so, neither a lack of, nor an escalation of intimacy would signify either party as 'guests;' conversely, mere attendance at any rite would not qualify any guest inclusive within the term 'Clan.

To distinguish one from the other by this criterion, Monmouth attempts to support his usage of the term Clan. He cites Bowers' application of it with regard to the gathering of people in question in receipt of the Round Robin letter, see doc (zi). However, Bowers specifically addressed: *his Clan which included other **members** from kindred groups alongside his own personal group— which may have been The Thames Valley Coven.* This is entirely distinct from the view expressed by Monmouth, of a Clan consisting of: '*his coven and its **guests**.*' This is a considerable error, a fundamental under sight which reveals how little is really known of True Craft and how they operate. Far too many things are assumed, repeated and taken as read. It should never be so. If a thing holds truth, then it can be shown to do so.

To put it succinctly, one is either:

- a *'guest,'* that is: a non-member of the People, generically, a 'non-initiate'/cowan/outsider),

Or, one is:

- a *member* of the People, therefore a fully Inducted person, apprenticed by Admission to The Clan.

Bowers, of course, had guests and Inducted members of *his* Clan and *his* own group *in attendance*, but those guests were never referred to as

Clan members! Their presence at a Rite did not confer that status upon them! Moreover, Bowers *did* maintain his Esbats for *Clan and Coven* only—*no* guests! His Sabbats however included members from *groups (including kindred groups) from within* his Clan, and occasionally guests who belonged to neither group within the Clan; he even 'guested' other Clans. In fact, Bowers refers jovially to a meeting of the Clans, in a letter to Norman Gills, confirming both Clans as distinct from each other.[23] Clearly, 'Clan,' is not the term used to distinguish the inclusion of a guest attending a Sabbat; the deference of the Sabbat, does however. That is to say, the Sabbat includes guests alongside Clan and Coven, the Esbat excludes them. Being 'Clan' has no bearing on the matter as they attend both with impunity!

Confusion resides entirely in strange opinion presented throughout Monmouth's book, for which we struggle to find reason or cause. He is completely mistaken in his usage and application of the term 'Clan.' Rather troublingly, he cites (those errors as based on) Valiente's understanding and use of the difference between an *Esbat* and a *Sabbat*. We must therefore defend Valiente from Monmouth's attempts to persuade us *her* opinion upholds *his* premise in this regard. Hers naturally remains contra to any misappropriation and misunderstanding of her knowledge, and her own intent by him, particularly when using the term 'Clan.'

In sharing her experiences, Valiente makes no comment anywhere, throughout all her works that even remotely suggest the usage of Clan infers the distinction of 'guest.' [24]Valiente merely confirms the unease Inducted Members of his *Coven* felt, where subjected to the presence of guests at the Sabbats. Esbats were occasions not open to guests. She fantastically confirms these to be the preserve of members only. Though she uses her more familiar term *Coven*, she nonetheless makes the distinction of an Esbat as a meeting where 'guests' are not permitted to attend. Valiente had worked with Bowers' group less than a year, attending several meetings, yet she later qualifies her astute understanding regarding Bowers' use of the word, Clan and what is meant by 'Clan.' In addition to its natural and historical usage to denote several groups within a family, in allegiance to its Head-Kinsmen, she explains Bowers' natural reticence for the term 'coven,' feeling that it was too closely associated with Gardnerian Wica. Hence his departure from it. His preference for the term 'group' distinguished the different assemblies forming around him at that time. Being quite comfortable with the term coven herself, she had no issue explaining any matter relative to Roy Bowers and his People, so continued to use it generically. Her familiar and inter-changeable usage of the term 'coven' describes people attending both Esbats and Sabbats who were not guests, but who were in fact Inducted members.[25] It really is that simple. Valiente uses the distinctive term 'Clan,' several times when making specific comment about Bowers' 'People', an inclusive term twice of note: firstly when she states the name of his group as the 'Clan of Tubal Cain'[26] and again when describing the final break-up of his 'Clan,' of all the people concerned, in lieu of the problems between Bowers and his wife.

Monmouth presses yet further into Bowers personal usage of the following terms, coven, group and clan. He states quite baldly that Bowers never refers to the *Clan of Tubal Cain* at all. Bowers does in fact use that full title as least twice, and each time, to refer to its members as exactly that: as the *'People of Goda.'*[27] He also refers repeatedly to *The Clan*, referring always to his 'People' as Members of it. Of considerable importance, all should remember, Bowers wrote but few letters, and to even fewer people, all of whom knew who he was, what his position was etc. There was no need to present constant reference to imperious credentials! Once introductions were made, there was absolutely no need to make repeated pronouncements to those same few people involved!

We look now to the one particular document[28] Monmouth draws his opinion of 'Clan' from, so that we may better explore his misunderstanding of what is a credo for life, setting the pattern of our being. Looking at its contents, this letter is obviously the follow-up 'Round - Robin' to the attendees of *The Ritual of the Covenant of Hallows,'* in 1964. Bowers does indeed head up that document to: 'The Clan.' What is interesting, and has been ignored in both those documents, is how Bowers makes references throughout them to his own, personal 'group' within The 'Clan."

This immediately refutes the idea it defers to guests. It commits expressly to another situation that in speaking for itself, truth is revealed. Those documents were sent to members of the People of the Clan only, as the heading alone declares, and *not* to any guest. Within the body of those texts, Bowers' comments do however draw significant attention to the fact that not all its people were in the same group. Again, by specifically referring to his own group (though it is not certain, it was probably *The Thames Valley Coven*), the core within the Clan he established around it. He reiterates the correct and historical usage of what a Clanship is and how it functions. Where Bowers refers to guests at all in that document (but does not address, as they are of course absent from inclusion in this missive), he names them as such, and as attendees, additional to the People of his Clan. He does not include them in his use of 'Clan,' not ever.' Further claiming that, *"Bowers makes 'little further use of the term, five times only, two of which, reference Tubal Cain"* (generically), and *"none at all regarding the actual Clan of Tubal Cain,"* Monmouth is in serious error. His research is readily established as utterly without truth. It is incorrect on all points. Bowers refers to *The People, to Tubal Cain,* and to *The Clan of Tubal Cain,* jointly and severally. In each instance, the context relates directly to his Faith, wherein each and every person is described in total by him, as: 'a 'member' of '*The People of the Clan of Tubal Cain*.'

The following list is not exhaustive, but provides a general overview of the majority of the references that may quite easily and randomly cited by even the most casual observer.

1. As referenced earlier, Bowers uses the term *"my clan and your clan,"* in his first letter to Norman Gills when discussing how they must all meet-up to 'work.'

2. With Bill Gray #X they jest about the probable *Clan* Shakespeare belonged to.

3. #to 'ickle deric.' Again Bowers refers to *"my clan"* with regard to its beliefs assigned to them as a particular group of crafters.

4. #V to Bill Gray, he refers to another Craft family known to him in Dorset as a *'Clan.'*

5. #VIII to Bill Gray, he mentions The Clan at least three times in this letter alone. He refers to himself as: *"master of a small clan,"* its *"devil in fact."* He then remarks about a person associated with someone Bill is enquiring about. Bowers says of him that he is: *"a living friend (one of the Clan) of ours"* And, he adds how *"the Clan is badly out of balance, we number five men and one woman."*

6. #1 to Joe Wilson: Bowers writes: *"I am a member of the People, of two admissions, ..."* and quite specifically: *"I am a member of the People of Goda, of the Clan of Tubal Cain.* As such, he informs Wilson about the migration of the *Clan* system in the US, from the Craft traditions of England.

7. #2 to Joe Wilson: Bowers mentions Clan in this letter alone more

than five times! He challenges Wilson on his knowledge of the mysteries, explaining them in terms of discreet male and female mysteries, of how their *'clans'* were divided into matriarchal and patriarchal *clans*; how the Plantagenets were the devil's own *Clan*, and how his Faith concerned itself as the *'Order of the Sun—the Clan of Tubal Cain.'*

8. #9 to Norman Gills, established previously in parlance, one *Clan* to another, he relates trouble brewing among everyone known to them at that time in the Craft; Bowers laments the forthcoming retribution and grim outcome for someone close to him at the behest of the 'Families,' he says: *"As such, when the Clans' people get to hear of it…"* In this momentous letter, the topic concerns a network of Clans across the Craft known to Bowers and to some extent, to Norman Gills also, and of its ability to act as one unit when and if expedience demands it. Again, the troubled matter spoken of is a private one, concerning only those Family Headed Clans, whose existence as closed alliances, comprised of Inducted Members only, highlights not just the severity of the problem facing the person mentioned, but just how removed from the facts Monmouth's propositions are.

9. In the document (ii) entitled: 'To All Elders,' Bowers declares: *"We are an Eight Clan"*

    In this document, all *Inducted Members,'* (not guests of any nature) are those whom he attempts to persuade how, variety and *'choice,'* enjoyed within a *'simple cuveen,'* are quite inimical to the Mythos as a *Clanship,* whose working Egregore requires everyone to share the same beliefs, to hold to the same gods, and to desire the same grail, pursuing the same Mysteries, as a collective. These are essential directives in order to be effective as a unit. Without those things, higher levels of work, he warns, are simply not achievable.

At long last, there is a gift here, an opportunity to lay to rest another absurd and ill-considered suggestion that for over a decade, alleged how Bowers reneged his duty under the law to his people of the Clan. Ironically, the document used to assert that premise, reveals its own falsehood. Entitled thereafter as: *'The Basic Structure of the Craft,'* there exists the suggestion that it was something Bowers was developing as a *private* grimoire for himself and Jane to work alone.[29] And worse, that it was worked and kept secret from the other members, ignorant of its existence. Thankfully, erudition and research are able to unequivocally lay that nonsense to rest. Any reader may clearly see to their own satisfaction within the manifest document (ii) [30] that it was written for and shared amongst those whom Bowers addresses as Elders: (ergo 'members' Inducted by that definition), quite *freely with all of them as the people of his Clan.* Bowers writes:

"As such, what is written here, is not absolute, but open to suggestion and comment, so that it can really become a group opinion, and not an opinion forced upon the group.. Therefore, we ask your honest comments upon these matters. These opinions will be considered and accepted providing they form a coherent pattern, and are related to the living truth of the mysteries. . ."

It is worth a small digression here, to affirm the import these few sentences hold in relation to his Clan. Bowers' opening gesture alone, denounces many of the claims that assert a detrimental analysis regarding Roy Bowers, as a person, as a leader, and of the material he presents. To that end, attempts to shift what has been known previously of these matters by these new documents, again only serve to prove those claims as nonsense. How bold then to cite them as evidence for re-viewing who exactly formed *The Clan*, who was in it, and most importantly, 'who' exactly should be credited with its works. On all points relative to these matters, Monmouth's claims escalate Bowers' alleged dictatorial and overbearing manner, to flagrant 'power-mongering,' leading him to propose that Bowers' assumed an authority he believes was not rightfully his, but the rightful preserve of another. Finally, he even challenges *Bowers' genius, his unique insight* through similar unsubstantiated erosions that fall like dominoes, one after the other in the face of all we are now able to share as pre- existent Truth.

It is an easy matter to give opinion, and all opinion is a welcome trial, it should never, ever, be considered otherwise. Suggesting an interpretation is just the same as laying claim to being in the 'know.' Both remain nothing more than speculation. Only an informed opinion, backed up by clear and unambiguous evidence may claim those facts as truth. Check everything claimed, against everything that 'is said' to support or confirm those allegations, word for word, line by line. Never take it 'as read.' It is far too easy to suggest the interpretation of material; so, as to assist, in its understanding, when one wishes to manipulate the opinion of the reader, especially where others may not have access to it. Equally, it is not helpful, and generates only doubt and confusion, when material that is available, quite blatantly goes overlooked, in order to present a view contrary to what is clearly, evident within it. It is unworthy to make opinion that wrestles the original intent into another suited to the bias of the writer, or their purpose in the writing. It is suspicious when nonsense casts a veil over clarity and obfuscation over surety. And so, digression aside; we may now continue our précis:

10. #5 Bowers explains quite excitedly to Norman Gills his hindsight regarding The 1965 Halloween Rite (afore-mentioned) *attended by The Clan, in addition to outsiders...*

Despite the fact that Bowers admits to Gills he needed to hide the major keys from those outsiders (Norman had not attended this particular rite), Bowers, was thrilled things had gone very well. Continuing to chatter at length, before closing his letter, he adds that he'd been very busy recently with *The Clan* who were responding to his re-organization and experimental ways of shifting 'virtue' around the body...these were methods *he'd devised regarding the Broom and the Witch's Cradle.*

11. Addendum to 'The Covenant for Hallows'—'Round-Robin' (zi) addressed to all, recipients as *"The Clan"...*

Most telling of all things discussed in this one document, cited by Monmouth (which alone is truly worthy of much study), is the fact that at the bottom of the page, Bowers opens his message to *Clan*, which includes an invitation to attend a more prosaic general meeting, comprised in anyone's understanding of the term, an enclave of 'Inducted Members.' Obviously, Bowers is not referring to, nor eliciting the opinion of, or presence of, outsiders—the alleged 'guests.' By inviting all *'Clan' members* to attend and discuss its business at the next meeting, which he names, somewhat ironically in this context, an ESBAT!!! Here without doubt, and straight from the horse's mouth! Clan is not a body that includes outsiders barred entry to those Esbat meetings. Furthermore, in referring to *them as members,* they are evidently not outsiders or guests! Even in the absence of all other points listed previously, this quoted comment alone impugns yet further, the fragmented logic, that 'Clan' must therefore refer to the 'coven + guests, 'who would, if his premise held any measure of truth, pronounce strict attendance upon such persons for the Sabbats only, and no Esbats. Bowers provides unmitigated proof of his own use of both terms, casting away totally, the false assumption that Esbats excluded Clan members and that Clan was a term used by Bowers when referring to the inclusion of guests (to his 'coven') when attending the Sabbats. We are what we are, and over and over, the very claims alleged otherwise, merely add to the increasing pile of evidence to prove the contrary. The shame is that these matters are even necessary to explain here at all, when all should have been either common knowledge, or matters remaining without deliberate confusions cast by the mischief of others, for whatever cause or agenda that served. We do wonder why? Whom does it serve?

Everyone on that 'Round-Robin,' including Bill Gray, was an actual member of his own group, within the Clan! This is why, both his own group, and other persons assigned to his Clan from the other group, are invited to attend his particular group's private, Esbat!

12. Importantly, we come to what must be the most famous and well-known of all his works—'*The Witch's Esbat,*' *written late1963, albeit not actually* published until Nov. 1964, New Dimensions magazine. Bowers relays his impressions experienced during an entranced stupor; "*I become aware of everyone else IN THE CLAN, as if they were in me. I can feel them all.*" Rather poignantly, Bowers reiterates the emotional intimacy of his 'people.' Elders from each of his two groups within his *Clan* who were present for this rite. They are clearly listed, though their names were changed for the sake of anonymity in the magazine: *Six men, one woman, all devoted to each other, and above everything else, to our gods.*"—Arthur, Roy, Jane, Peter, John and Dick.

Arthur was very probably the very same 'Arthur E.' referred to earlier, but Peter and 'Blackie' remain allusive as yet. [31]

Despite it being very much based in real and actual events, Bowers freely admits massaging the facts quite dramatically to create a more meaningful article. Certainly, there is <u>no</u> mention in any documents extant at the time of its writing, of Ronald, George, Laurence, Avril, or any of the others who do not feature until some time later, materialising in the second group, established by his two apprentices at that time: Dick and John. When Doreen Valiente joined Bowers' Clan in 1964, she noted only (the same) four others beside Roy and Jane Bowers: (Jane, Roy, John, Dick, Arthur and Peter or Blackie)

13. Bowers continues his directive in a later missive that stresses again the importance of them being a shared collective if their works are to achieve success in a shared Egregore. Coercive compatibility. In the document headed; 'Dear Brothers and Sisters,' Bowers discusses the desired culmination of his work as an adept. In this Rite, he finally acquires the means to fulfil the Mythos of his Tradition. Virtue is transmuted via the seven+one spiral, in the ring of making therein discussed. Of its promise he clearly warns them:

"It is also a basic matter, unless this can be done successfully, we may as well work individually and forget all about a Clan, since we do not deserve one, or for that matter have the interest of the gods."

This was possibly the very last instruction he actually gave them as Clan, and certainly, the last time they worked together as such. After this, everything began to fall apart. All eight people working together in this Rite, are named and listed, on document [s].

To summarise then: Bowers refers to those attendees, as 'Clan.' Elders are of the 'People,' that is, from within his Clan. All Elders are seasoned members of the people. All are Inducted. NB: *No Guests*. If read objectively and understood fully, the context of this one letter alone contravenes almost all the nonsense propagated and the fantasies generated that has marred the true beauty of these mysteries—as ever, they are hidden in plain sight. We would wish that such knowledge may allow everyone to move forward in their understanding of these treasures. And the final point to address is:

- The way *The Regency* used and understood various terms, particularly where their guests *did* attend Sabbats, which 'must' therefore, automatically transfer and impose upon Bowers, their idiosyncratic use of them.

Attempts to draw non-existent parallels between Bowers' Clan system and the system later employed by *The Regency,* do so, in order to assume parity between the Clan and the phantom RWC. But their distinctive usage serves only to defeat that purpose by accentuating their fundamental disparity. In attempting to create a margin for what is hitherto a fantasy, Monmouth, again, is sorely at pains to assert a working pattern for them. Surely, if they had one at all, this would be unnecessary?

Neither Bowers' own group, nor his Clan were ever named the Royal Windsor Coven, and no amount of juggling with semantics or their activities will change that fact. By striving to describe the alleged workings of that phantom coven in the marking of the lunar Esbats, *"to form the distinction between"* an alleged Royal Windsor Coven ..and the Solar Sabbats of *The Regency"* that celebrated rites for that 'coven plus any guests,' their incompatibilities and inconsistencies with the Clan are highlighted to the detriment of that intent. Neither within nor without the Clan's own histories, both oral and written, does knowledge exist regarding even the name, Royal Windsor Coven prior to 1974, whence that name began to assert itself upon the drifting tides of rumour and comment. It remains to this day without 'existence' except through 'rumour' alone. We know with certainty the name given to Bowers' *Clan* was never that.

Drifting in and out of the 'Society of Keridwen' [sic], and of *The Clan*, Ronald White and George Winter, though always '*members of the people*,' were sometimes leaders of their own alliances and associates that were often outside *The Clan*, and but few of those were committed to them long term, as they quickly discovered. But when Ronald White and George Winter did attend, it was as members of *The Clan*. After Bowers' death of course, all White ever referred to was *The Regency*. A point noted by E. J. Jones, whose astute observation comes from the direct knowledge that '*they had no right*' to do otherwise. Jane Bowers had not sanctioned neither usage of nor familiarity with Clan Works.

Simply put, it means that those two men, worked with and alongside Bowers as '*members of the people*' of his Clan, but also as independent persons, as members of other alliances and leaders of their own. Moreover, whatever name Chalky and George eventually may have chosen for their loosely allied group/coven, both before and after Bowers' death in 1966, that subjective choice has *no bearing whatsoever upon The Clan itself, ergo, it is of no relevance to it in any capacity!* Bowers' Clan remains a distinct source and trajectory, a legacy continued through his own tradition that formed and fuelled his People and his Clan. His legacy and continued inspiration to the world, naturally continues through all his works, and by all those who cherish them, and work them. We have always supported and encouraged this unique and magical source of gnosis for all who engage in the Mysteries. For as the man said: "*there are no secrets,*" sacred, certainly, retained as inner mysteries explored through the cultural tenets of that tradition, bound in troth—absolutely. So it was in ancient times; so it remains today.

Preferring now to concentrate on the actual Clan of Roy Bowers, and its traditions as meted through its known works, very little more time will be given to the why's and where-fore's of the alleged name of the second, separate group, throughout this book. All that was needed here for the purposes of this volume was a context to establish the meaning and significance of 'Clan.' The matter of an alleged group calling themselves the 'Royal Windsor Coven' has been properly explored elsewhere.[32] Suffice to say, all the evidence best supports a spurious 'phantom.'

Bowers' tradition, that is: *The 'Cochrane Tradition' and its legacy, continue within The Clan alone*, that is, *his Clan* and through no-one else, in any way, whatsoever. His Clan was a closed tradition then, and it remains one, still; it cannot be otherwise. The spheres of influence from all three distinct traditions, CTC, The Regency and '1734' have sometimes abutted where they have been absorbed by practitioners down the line; but this should not confuse their separate and distinct origins, nor their yet current separate states of Tradition and Praxis.

The Law Applied

The context of '*take all you are given*' and the charge to '*give all of yourself,*' must and should remain within the whole instruction, which maintains that 'what I hold' remains even after we have '*given,*' this implicitly refers to the bounds of a '*Closed Tradition,*' and hints at the troth by which that law is applied. Herein elucidated, and with a degree of finality: '*what I have* [in my possession], *I hold*' [to myself alone]. The vow to uphold that Law, is taken as part of Admission to *The Clan*.

The significance of that, cannot fail to clarify all other propagated nonsenses. Obviously, *The Clan of Tubal Cain* established by Roy Bowers (aka Robert Cochrane) is predicated on his traditions and experiences, authenticated by *his unique works*, and easily distinguishable from others,' whose own discrete traditions, evident throughout *their works*, afford them and no other, as singular authorities in their individual regard. Of course, in time, other individuals have since established their own Traditions, citing Bowers works as foundational to them; but these again, serve most efficiently to flag influences perceived directly or indirectly, from his teachings. These may be categorised fairly and accurately as precisely that:(directly) influenced by ie. *The Regency.'*

- Influenced and inspired by ie. '1734.'

One crafter in the US, Russell Erwin said:

"Seems like all other streams of the Craft besides the CTC merely assert some degree of influence or inspiration, some founding principles, which have been creatively received from Cochrane's few surviving and now widely disseminated letters or articles. From what I gathered from John of Monmouth's book, the Regency made no effort to incorporate any of what seem to have been Cochrane's specific ideas into their separate work as the Regency. I think that Joe Wilson got to participate in some Regency workings. Maybe I read that in Joe's auto-biography which floats around online in various states of unfinished." [33]

Noted here, proper distinction may easily be given clarification as having:

- 'Indirect' influence: Every other group or tradition *inspired* to *follow* his teachings.

That being totally contra to the principle of:

- A *private, closed* Tradition, cannot by definition 'be(come)' nor be 'of' nor *'belong within,'* the public domain.

It is Beyond The Remit of Anyone Not Admitted as A Member of Its People. Moreover, reading its works, or even working its rites, will not change this. Only by rites of Induction or Admission may anyone consider themselves to be *of that tradition.* In ALL other circumstances, at best, any outsider may only ever qualify themselves as 'influenced by.' Belonging is never an assumed status. In like manner of surnames, the gift remains a family protocol. Were the latter a status so easy to achieve, then anyone could claim to belong as an initiate of many other 'entry specific' groups. .Any other term used, adopted, or applied to one-self, or to another, is fictitious and void of any significance.

The following are but few examples. Again, they are by no means exhaustive: OTO; SOL; Thelema; Ked; Cultus; etc; *all* of whom express their Traditions as defined by their Induction/Initiatory status.' All these traditions are known to the public, their existence may not be private or secret, but their traditions are, and remain so, subject to their unique modes of Admission. Their names confer initiatory status, and may not be appropriated. For example, despite the enormous breadth of Wica/Wicca as a tradition, only those *physically initiated* into the lineage defined as the 'Gardnerian Tradition,' may refer to themselves as such. Others, who may follow Gardner's works, and by indirect influence, work those rites as faithfully as possible, may never consider themselves to be 'Gardnerians.' But they can name themselves as Wiccan, ie, a movement influenced by the tenets of his system. Again, only where initiated (subject to all requisite proofs of course) into any named tradition, does one become named 'for' it.. Beyond this, all that can be added, is that they are merely subject to its abiding influences. Ergo, a 'Gardnerian' is not a *follower of* Gerald B. Gardner, but properly, *an initiate of* his tradition.

Likewise, despite indiscriminate use in describing a follower of, and to infer status within, the title—so-called 'Cochranite' cannot exist in any reality, and does not relate to anything in truth. The term means nothing, has no standing, and no validity whatsoever. If one is 'Inducted' into *his* tradition, then one has become a member of the '*People of Goda*,' a member in fact, of *The Clan of Tubal Cain*.' Nothing more; and nothing less. These and only these, are valid terms of description.

Our preferred descriptive must therefore reflect the fact that '*The Clan of Tubal Cain*' alone, continues *as The 'Robert Cochrane Tradition*.' That is to say again, for total and absolute clarity. We are *not* Cochranite, *not* Cochranian, *nor* Cochrane influenced. These are misnomers. They do not apply to us, and should not apply to any who follow his works by inspiration or enquiry. Neither is *The Clan based* upon his works (as it *is* his works) nor is it '*inspired*,' by him for the same reasons (nor he alone, to date, for that matter). Derived from, could serve well enough, but is not entirely accurate, as subsisting ambiguities within its semantic interpretation leave it open to misunderstanding, particularly regarding its singular authenticity as a continued tradition sourced and founded by Bowers.

As *The* 'Robert Cochrane Tradition,' CTC, continues its works, maintained now for over half a century, by *The People of Goda* alone. Facts are always simple. Truth is always inviolate. With regard to our status as a Craft Tradition, our position has been woefully misunderstood and far too frequently misrepresented. This is largely due to a plethora of nonsense written by non- members riding on its coat-tails, and by those seeking mischief. Even so, it is vital to remember, we have only ever stressed the right to claim only what is ours—what we have we hold; and from that point of virtue and truth we give all of ourselves. In this we offer but one way, one pathway only, within the whole corpus of the Mysteries and of the Craft. We are merely one river flowing towards the Ocean. And we are one Tree rooted in the earth, thriving within a forest. We are no more; and no less.

"CTC is a tree, our branches are our own limbs, our lifeblood that draws through the sap all it needs to remain self-sustaining. For a tree remains a tree even when in a forest."

2
The
Mythos
of a People

The Mythos of a People, *is* its People, aligned symbiotically to its Egregore. Both evolve through awareness, alongside the mediating perceptions of an ever-increasing spiritual alignment. Change must develop naturally, unconsciously. Conscious change is rooted in subjectivity, human frailty, desire etc and therefore manipulated against the Truth to which the Egregore must remain bound. Individuals forge links with others through a shared cumulative experience, conjoined through traditional rites whose ancestry continues to inspire, and be inspired by that diverse heritage. Served once, and still, by all souls who hold dear its vital legacy, it remains one that daily never ceases to induce awe. This is the very nub of the following comment to Bill Gray that his Clan is very probably the last to follow the path of the Mysteries within Traditional Craft at least.

> "We have our own disciplines and our own symbology, and as much as we can believe it, we think we might be the last to possess the real mysteries of the past.......you see, basically a second tradition of thought has been lost, a dual tradition in which nothing was as it appeared. This was the real secret behind the mysteries, and dancing peasants have very little in common with that philosophy."

Bowers here refers again to his favourite distinction of the male and female mysteries, that for most of his life, he'd believed were lost to him. That is, until another brought them as their gift. Together, those disparate traditions were engaged to re-discover the third—that of the priestly mysteries. Unfortunately, that knowledge made him appear rather elitist when his frustrations marred his consideration of others and their works. Enabled through integral fusion, his completed Tradition thus engaged sympathetic magick at its most profound potency—whence spirit becomes en-fleshed and earthed once more. Bowers oft expounded magick as an occult science, very much the 'Natural Science' favoured by Agrippa. As a modality, subject to regular research by the great minds of academia, past and present, Frazer especially, in branding its tenets as a misunderstanding of the natural laws of nature, sets fine example of how a horrible under-sight, eventually overwhelms public opinion. Frazer denounced Agrippa's 'acts of sympathy' as pseudo-science, describing them as mere deviances of pseudo magic, finding expression as art. This induced Bowers to respond quite critically. Stressing a rather distinct application of it to the theology of (religious) science, he asserts a view contra to more generic practical demonstrations of it as superstition, found in both positive magics (sorcery), and negative magics (taboo).

Nonetheless, sympathetic magic with a 'k' is the foundational principle of a purer magick, found in all forms based in theurgy and thaumaturgy. This rather obviously suggests that sympathetic magick is a far deeper praxis than it first appears: *'leaping in the fields to make the crops grow,'* or *'burning fires to raise the Sun.'* Rather, it is beholden to an older, more instinctive synergy. Gross misunderstandings of these simple, but arcane principles, have repeatedly exposed them to attack. Viewed and commented upon rather scathingly by many historians and theologians alike—Frazer et al, for example, whose unanimous lack of vision, presumes falsely the importance of the fundamental structure of these rites.

Certainly, these suggest primitive attempts to coerce or regulate natural occurrences, and certainly they fail to address the principles of Fate, and our alignment within it. At least, superficially, they do. This is where true magick crosses all boundaries of theory, science, sorcery, taboo, religion and art, to be acts of desire, fuelled by the human instinct to 'overcome' Fate. In the field of animism, we pitch 'Will,' in accordance with Wyrd—the grand conjunction where human force merges with the cosmic force of The 'Natural' World. There is no point of separation, and no part of us that is not, 'of ' it.

Bowers' philosophy on this matter, of being in alignment with one's Fate to the extent we may anticipate it, judge, dodge, assess, pre-empt, prepare and advance our own causality. Precognitive attunement and unsubtle sentience together, form the twin-edged blades of the sword we carry as spirit, honed in focus, to battle against apathy and despair. Balance, wrought only within the field of Nature, is where 'Will' staves all too briefly, the onslaught of an unrelenting Fate. So yes, when *The Clan* make grand gestures to the starry canopy, invoking the moon, placing offerings upon the earth, lighting fires to the sun and making love in their names; we do so as needful acts of evocation. Given up to the self 's own desire to retain connective awareness of itself as 'divine,' these become acts, as Bowers rightfully declares, undertaken with arcane kenning, and not, as peasants dancing to ensure the sun will rise.

Our lineage heralds the laudable gifts of Roy Bowers, a uniquely tuned-in, focussed and intuitive person of singular vision. Born 'knowing,' the fire burned brightly within him, dazzling all who worked with him and who follow his works. He set his era ablaze with challenge, innovation and contention. He set and broke precedents. His innovations and claims resound still, remaining a facet of topical debate on all matters related to the 'Craft.' Bowers, deeply inspired by the whole history of his Craft, was able to incorporate its relevancies into the subtler methodologies of his teachings and Mythos. He said:

"What do witches call themselves? They call themselves by the names of their Gods."

Adding that 'Truth', was also the absolute name for the Godhead, utterly beyond any religious affiliations, systems and illusion, he also believed that each person's vision represented individual subjective Truth. Roy Bowers emphatically rejected any association between his perception of the nature of witch and pagan; yet he keenly asserted that the Old Craft retains even now, discernible vestiges of the ancient pagan mystery cults. Traditional Craft as a practising arte, is frequently described as neither pagan nor religious. This single aspect is a vital principle of spirituality that defies definition. So how do we reconcile such views? Abstraction of belief is too rigorously subjective.

Religion is one of humanity's essential traits; we are self-aware and aware of the divine. Paganism as a reference to our apprehension of the divine, reflects the human condition, it is our natural state. It is our belief, and magickal practice evolves from this fundamental premise. Atheism is not a natural state. Cults are by their nature sectarian; religion is not. Therefore, it is perception, and not belief, that divides us. Perception separates us, not only from the rest of humanity as individuals, but from the All. Mysticism is the driving force within diverse religions that recognises this impedance and which seeks to elevate its adherents beyond these self-inflicted boundaries. Truth is above all doctrine, and the Word is received by everyone with ears to hear it. Belief, whether rooted in spirituality or religion, becomes hide-bound by magickal praxis and indulged by the individual practitioner. Mysticism remains the driving force towards Truth, after all, the maxim 'There is no Religion higher than Truth,' stands today. Magick is practised within and without the

Craft. In fact, the essence of all true religion is magick. In magickal terms, the Priest and the Magus are one.

For Roy Bowers, the Craft was a:

"Mystical religion, a revealed philosophy, with strong affinities to many Christian beliefs. The Faith is concerned only with truth; that brings man into closer contact with the Gods and himself—the realization of truth as opposed to illusion—fulfilled only by service. This grail quest correlates with the fulfilment of gnosis under the 'Order of the Sun,' the life's work of a true mystic."[34]

Roy Bowers wrote extensively on the subject of 'Truth,' affirming its quality as eternal, where it forms an intrinsic link between that premise and the concept of the 'People,' of whom he pronounced as follows:

"So we come to the heart of the People, a belief that is based upon eternity, and not upon social needs or pressures—the 'witch' belief then is concerned with wisdom, our true name then is the Wise People, and wisdom is our aim." [35]

It is worth clarifying too the prominence of demarcation, extant within the 'nameless arte,' of traditions within folk magicks and of their recorded histories, where a dearth of female voices exist, unheard. Slowly, some breach that gulf, whereby through them, the Wisdom of the Muse is known. Eloquent female writers are stepping out to share their own Craft Traditions, providing a much needed counter weight to balance those of the toad men. Sadly, especially other men, particularly with regard to cunning crafts, do not award them the same kudos.

"... the modern artist...is a poet without a theme...[having] a delightful little love affair with himself. I was listening to one explain a painting of a woman, and I realised that he wasn't talking about *woman as she is*, but the pitiful creation *of himself, he called woman.*"[36]

Within the Mystery Traditions apropos its Crafting, the ideal of 'woman' remains highly regarded. The issue resides within the middle ground, where the active 'priestly' role of the divine feminine, mourns and laments her missing element within the triadic mysteries. Deep within the psyche of these ancient Isles of Britain, a feint voice, drowned by the more active magickal roles of the kitchen witch and the toad man alike, is constant, though fading fast. Bowers firmly asserted a view that women possessed a natural affinity with the moods and tides of the Creatrix:

> "All females, irrespective of species is a lesser moon, reflecting the greater. She is made of three elements, the poor male possessing the fourth. Through these elements, she creates a chain, unbroken, that ranges from primitive childbearing and nest-making, to the goddess woman, flying in strange climates. Man is individualised and solitary—lead only by reason or passion. Woman by her physical structure, is part of the cycle of evolution, and therefore part of the group soul."[37]

In her notepads, Doreen Valiente makes a fascinating comment on the matter of an Egregore. Rather than comporting to its generic description as a 'group soul,' she proffers instead, the concept of a 'soul - group.' She explains that being of 'one mind,' accessed by all souls bonded together through their singular host (that being the 'Old Woman' and Maid of the Clan), it configures a more apt premise of the intimacy they share with her, between her and the Egregore, and through her to the Egregore.[38] Because we may all yearn so deeply for progress within that divine embrace, it is highly possible, that individual perception, in regarding the nature of 'Truth,' and of an 'Egregore,' may generate a space, where actual experience of it, may run contra to those pre-conceptions. Despite what we feel we already know concerning our observations of Transcendent Godhead as an ambivalent force, surely, in generating an imminent aspect of itself, it is able to be and become a reciprocal force as love, lover and beloved? Probably, this may be so; though in our dreams, most certainly this is true. Truth may require us to 'be' in that state of gnosis best described as 'ecstatic,' a state wherein it may be equally possible that the act of giving one's 'self' to the Self, is no less than 'perfect love'—'unconditional love.' This is not romantic love, neither is it erotic love, but a purity that is all virtue, all justice, all-calm. This foil is the reality of chaos in the mundane mirror of life.

In true 'Khaos,' comprehension occurs devoid of all pre-dispositions and all bias, affording the full subtleties of genuine experience. Having sought to affirm a pre-existent state, induced in memory; its truth expels doubt. Conviction alone enables experience in that instant of pre-conception, shattering unerringly the falsity of any superficial analysis. Simultaneously, this shared insight from within the Egregore, generates the vital catalyst for *anamnesis*. In a Platonic sense (Theory of Recollection), all preconceptions of the mind are fragmented threads that weave us tighter upon our pathways towards eventual anamnesis. The soul intuitively recalls its origins and destination; yet the paradox of intermittent existence throws our rationale towards critical mass, and ultimately the sacrifice of reason, for something more palpable. All things borne of the field of experience, induce a paradox borne of the reason of memory. With regard to the nature of chaos, Plato struggled with these aspects; no law, unless pertaining strictly to divine virtue, good and pure, could be, 'divine.'

Certainly the 'devil and all his works' instigate and inject life's experience with all manner of 'Khaos,' a function primarily of challenge, of cajolement to greater deeds. Tradition generates cohesive systems of unification, whereby people may be drawn together to serve distinct modes of expression, dependent upon a liturgy for the mediation of their faith and beliefs. These exist to inform the evolution of all, even itself; the nature of inspiration is generative and complementary of intuition, serving as catalyst and guide to all within and without its bonds. Fruitful discussion may assist us to explore further, the numerous misconceptions that surround the enigma of 'Virtue,' a thing that is probably the least understood of all occultisms. There are many types of 'Virtue' spanning the gulf from the personal to the trans-personal, elevating 'self ' within to 'Self ' without through the transmission of Divine Grace. Centralised Virtue, or the core essence, nurtures the sentience of any given collective.

At its simplest, it is the group-mind, at its most complex, it is the group-soul; they are not the same thing at all. Alone, one may be created and fed by the collective. The other feeds that collective. One, is the unity created within a group. The other, is the Unity of Creation. So it becomes obvious that one of these may be acquired through the industry of the 'self,' the 'other' is bestowed though Transmission, an act of Grace mediated by Fate and manifest in Time. Virtue at its simplest, being the mind (rational) is, at its most complex, the soul (intuition). The rationalising mind forms preconceptions that are verified or dismissed through experience while through intuition the soul 'knows,' having (Platonic) a prior knowledge. Where Virtue is embraced or when we become touched by its influences there are always restrictions on the depth of it.

Virtue is certainly a major facet of *The Clan*, and one Roy Bowers referred to intensely and with considerable frequency throughout his works and letters. Reading through them, the term Virtue appears in certain contexts that require further clarification regarding their distinctive application of it.

• From *The Witches Esbat:'* New Dimensions 1964 (see doc. u)

"Round and round in absolute silence, fingers following the pattern that the seven knots make in the cord. Willing, thinking, concentrating upon our work, the hoods of our cloaks down over our eyes, thinking, willing, visualizing the '*image of virtue*' shifting from one part of our bodies to the other, the sensations of changing like colours upon our minds eye. In the brief glimpses we get when our concentration lowers in its intensity the cave seems to be spinning around us, then back to the darkness of our hoods and our compressed wills."

Here, Bowers accents the 'image' of virtue, referring to the acquisition of the mask as the personal assumption of Trance. That raw *odic* force, or 'power,' induces the personal 'other,' the totemic self. Its image is specific, but different for, and to each person. Awareness of it, is here described as a transformation from the self to the Self, as that *odic* force draws one into the 'other.'

• Bill Gray # I

"To work witch magic properly, one must work out of doors; buildings, unless ectoplasmic displays are required, destroy '*virtue*.'"

This refers to the sweeping ancestral and elemental forces carried by the wind as literal elements, the essence of the Valkyrie as raw energy, rolling across tree-tops, hilltops and moorlands. All organic matter, being of the animistic *odic* breath also, does not impede or corrupt this flow; man-made structures of plastics, compounds steel and concrete do however.

• Bill Gray #II

"Work in silence, treading the Mill, will does it all, is the way we work, and we get results. I have crossed the moat and into the spiral castle, and seen and heard some strange things. Last Samhain, all of us had that sense of terror that denotes 'virtue,' and strangely enough, I could not hear anything except the crying of a baby."

In this sense, virtue *is* the other. It is the total sensory recognition of the sheer (power) force of the 'other,' that so overwhelms our human corporeality, our 'awe' renders us in held its grasp. We utter the words, *'in girt terror and fearful dread'* to express this mystery of our sacred troth.

- Bill Gray #III

"We work upon an anthropomorphic pattern to shift virtue from one transcending state to another."

Again, this refers to the acquisition of the Mask noted earlier. And:

"Where the 'image of virtue,' really comes into its own, is when a group has formulated an old symbol, then developed it into a 'new' symbol."

Iconic: this refers to the focussing of a literal representation of the divine, embodied with it, that with new understanding, acquires another layer of force and meaning, a new significance. The Icon has conveyed its latitude via its virtue, narrowed in perception previously by the time and tide of its creation.

- Bill Gray #V

"We have to train any *new members* up to certain standards, develop any hidden power that they may have, and finally teach them the manipulation of various images of virtue."

In this context, Roy Bowers informs Bill Gray there is the personal mask (transpersonal 'other') and the external 'Other.' There is even an Egregore to embrace and a group mind to share.

- Bill Gray #VI

"The rituals in which the male and female generative organs were used, were rituals of (a) Magick, (b) Death, (c) Resurrection, in the sense that virtue, our word for power, can be passed from one person to another (now you know why witches must pass from male to female). This virtue originally was given to 'Hecate' by union with Saturn. They between them produced a Son—'Hermes.' Now by combining his function with that of the Guide, generates in the female witch virtue by the same process, she in turn passes it to the male witch."

This refers to the active/receptive unity, where two create a third, *ad finitum*. NOT a passing of power in the modern Wican sense by any means, but an involuntary shift of an indwelling, gifted once only, completely and permanently in death, whether relative to personal virtue of the virtue held as head kinsman of a Clan. In life, by way of analogy, it sits spider-like almost upon its host, and spins a web about the people, binding and holding them together, protecting and shielding them, one to another. And:

- Bill Gray #VI

  "I for instance, cannot die until I have passed my virtue on, I carry within my physical body the totality of all the witches that have been in my family and their virtue for many centuries. If I call upon my ancestors, I call upon forces that are within myself and exterior, now you know what I mean when I speak of the burden of time."

Obviously, the fact that he did indeed die, indicates that he had satisfactorily fulfilled this criterion. Here, Bowers refers to his personal power, a battery almost, fuelled by the memories of all he holds within, as a totality. That burden finds release, once transposed to another who becomes their spiritual heir. This is a magickal act, and its gift is final, one-way and complete. It binds the memory and knowledge effectively to another, it is literally 'willed' to them.

Roy Bowers adopted Evan John Jones as his spiritual heir.

The 'Virtue'[39] of a group, the 'mind-force,' named the 'Robin' is a synchronising mechanism between its members, a psychic attachment that bonds them together within. In like manner, the *Hamingja*, is an ancestral female spirit guardian who alights upon the next Head-Kinsmen of a Clan, a grandmother figure affording protection and guidance from the realm of the 'Other.' Upon death, She departs for another in continual succession. This brief foray into the basic forms Virtue may operate through, may finally help in shaking off many misconceptions that surround the enigma of Virtue, ranging from personal to Ultimate or Divine Virtue. Central to all, Virtue is the core essence, the sentience of a collective. Quite quickly it becomes obvious that one of these can be acquired through industry, whilst another is bestowed though Transmission, an act of Grace, mediated by Fate, manifest in Time.

With regard to that nebulous 'other,' that alights upon its host, its presence is unmistakable. Where declared by others, that such a 'Virtue' is easily lost, then it becomes apparent that it may never really have existed at the onset. Sometimes, not everything exposed to hope, finds realization in actuality. Where Virtue is embraced or encountered in a person, its clarity and depth remove all misapprehension; here it is acknowledged as a sentient reality within another, and is duly honoured and lauded through the 'Rite of Transmission' (The Old Covenant).

There is no other way that authority may be ceded to another in lieu of their realization of the indwelling virtue. One is the effect where the other affects. The two are not *one and the same thing*. The first is not even a pale facsimile of the second. Being embraced within, and being encompassed by, are two very different poles relating to the whereabouts of Virtue. Truth reveals all. At best, a forlorn hope may exhibit a certain 'bloom,' a flush within the psyche. As a vital impetus for growth and change, its recipient would be well-advised to use it wisely and according to the rightness of things. Typically, this reveals that sense of fickle possession; and one that quickly dissipates:

1. Roy Bowers' *personal virtue* and *Magisterial Virtue* was gifted to Evan John Jones. As Head-Kinsman, his virtue feeds and sustains the **Group-Mind.** (the Robin) Hence, he leads - 'What I have I hold.'

2. The **Group-Soul**, (The Egregore) previously hosted by Jane Bowers, the Clan's former 'Maid' who 'gave' herself to it. This is actuated and manipulated by the Group Mind. 'Give all of yourself.' Once released from this sacred bond of duty, as 'Host' it alights upon another.

3. Once combined together, both *Clan Virtue*, and the *Egregore* form a deep symbiosis and catalyst that attracts the *'Hamingja'* ('group luck' or 'A People's Fate') through whom the Group Soul and Mind are secured and anchored firmly within an ancestral chain aligned to Fate through Kairos. This means an overarching Fate is filtered through ancestral deities, emanating a very specific 'virtue' as a recognisable signature trait. This shifts from one Head-Kinsmen to another when Time or Necessity wills it. Normative succession occurs upon 'death of the Old King' and instigation of the 'New King.' But because there was no Maid to bind it within, it settled elsewhere, and it was many years before E. J. J. discovered its whereabouts, recognised it and officially appointed that person with the authority to host the Clan officially from that point in time. That person is this author recording that deed.

With regard to the Hamingja, there is an archaic origin for this fated symbiance, one that fascinated our Mentor significantly. Over the few (too) short years we knew him, his letters are peppered with one particular point concerning the two words that should *not* be placed into the

Cauldron and why this should be so. He also highlighted when and how the opposite would be true. Making the bold shift into Thule culture, his mentoring directed us to research the cosmological myth of Creation. Speaking of all things 'outside time' in fact, are by default, also 'beyond Fate.' Here are his words expressing that concept.

> "Roy had found inspiration in a rather obscure Thulist book that had a highly original and rather ludicrous explanation for the start of fate, time, life etc. which involved spheres of ice, fire and so on with the universe existing but presented as being a symbolic cauldron, the place of stillness, immobility and with a total lack of motion or energy, where time slept in the bosom or womb of duration until the 'Godhead' pronounced the Primal Movement. With this, Time and Movement began, and Fate and the human spirit and Fate embarked upon its long climb out of the mud to the stars. Fate also shaped the old gods and goddesses who in turn shaped us while holding out the helping hand needed to raise us from the primal slime in which we were rooted, and so when we eventually triumph, fate another name for the old gods will cease to be and the cauldron will once again become still, and so on all over again. There is even a scientific term for this."[40]

From the perspective of Clan work, this realisation was quite overwhelming; the idea was quite 'instinctively' correct. Of course, the runes, *Isa, Hagal* and *Nyd* describe just such a principle. John (E. J. J.) later developed this view and published it within *The Cauldron, Feb 2002 103#* It is a remarkable exposition on the Creation of the world and of humanity placed in the greater schema, as he quotes his own mentor's assertion of that principle within his letters. This suggests and affirms the synergistic communion excelled through shamanistic rites, yet following carefully orchestrated Apollonian and Hermetic principles that bind together all mystical modes of working. At this singular apex, the 'still point' is a paradox, essentially the pinnacle of union and communion, irrespective of the methods used to achieve that state. Cutting across distinctions between the many highly physical and very pleasurable activities, these evolving sophistications eventually alienated Roy Bowers. His more critical peers preferred not to embrace those innovative and visionary shifts that many of us, decades later, are better able to appreciate for their bald honesty. John (E. J. Jones) confirms in that same article, his agreement with Bowers, that we clothe the gods with their presentation, being pure virtue in themselves. This is a view still held; we colour our lens, they have no need to.

A 'Mythos' centralizes a particular series of cultural myths that aligned to a given topography (physical or metaphysical, dependent upon the myths and/or the philosophies of those peoples engaging in their current usage). En-fleshed further, all praxis is the vehicle for their meaningful exploration as a living, extant co-existence—in other words: a way of being, a way of thinking as the wayfarers' exploration of sympathetic concepts inherent to and intrinsic of both soul and body. This medium is the province of guide, mentor, guardian and Companie in the accomplishment of that 'Work.' It is a way within the Way.

Our statement here is a pertinent marker for all seekers. It highlights the duties of all, and the concerns of the wayfarer in having guidance and support along the weary road of wael and woe. Delusion and illusion face all of us along the way, and all of us do need the honest contact of another to maintain stability and reason. Systems, groups and traditions are sadly often prone to back-patting, suffering most regrettably from an attendant ego-gratification. There is no easy way to Truth, but certainly, in Companie at least we hold to one another, through any truth exuded by reality within the work, and this reflects into the shared pool where all may bathe. This remains true even beyond its bonds. In this way, we all add to the course, the stream from which all drink.

Faith affords us impetus to the cause that burns within, need forces the hand as it were, to continue even in the face of adversity. In holding to that grim determination, we gravitate towards the circles others trace, in the land, in the air and on paper. Only through Spirit do all works exists, there for each of us to express and find expression through the voice of another. There is nothing more profound or deeply mystical than the acceptance of spirit, the lifting of the veil that shrouds the conscious homeostasis—the sentience that simply is. The eye of the beholder is illuminated into a baptism of light; the beloved becomes the lover, a guide to the ultimate reality of true existence.

Mindfully, we must remember how a true 'Initiation' comprises of at least two active parts and a third of repose:

- The first of earth and water (female qualities, ie birthing and baptism) relates to the psychic descent of the soul—the transformation—*kenoma*;

- The second of air and fire (male qualities of spirit and vigour) relates to the pneumatic ascent of spirit—the transcendence—*pleroma*.

Pneumatic initiation inculcates the understanding of our true self as surviving the process of disintegration of the illusory physical body. The third and final part, of repose, is the passive acceptance of this truth, and the acquisition of all gnosis. The purpose of initiation is to propel the psyche into the experiential and numinous world of pneuma to achieve a realisation of divinity. Maturation engenders comprehension of universal archetypes, of cultural images in their true context and an awareness of the synchronicities of Kairos (perfect or divine time) in their interpretation. Initiation is a catalyst for the comprehension of True Will, which is in fact, divine will. Through the process of initiation, we understand our true (divine) nature, negating all conflict between ego and superego. Thereafter, all acts of magick become an act of will, specifically of true will. Complete surrender evokes complete absorption of the lesser will, allowing us to act freely and spontaneously without fear of conflict. Gnosis is not a rejection of the world, but an awareness of the dual gifts of our humanity and divinity, their harmony and symbiosis. Successful symbiance is reliant upon this premise. Complete detachment defeats the purpose of life.

Gnosis, epiphany: comprehensions birthed in Kairos. Resolved riddles occur as 'moments' of lucid clarity and are drawn from within the fugue of obfuscation we ascribe to 'life.' Mythopoesis is the process of extraction from all media regarding the *'heart-of-the-matter,'* to be absorbed and 'realised' over 'time.' As expressions of inspiration, they possess the virtue of Kairos as form, presented by their mediator, and by force, as apprehended by observer/recipient. Such connections do indeed formulate all initiatory mechanics as an experiential procedure. Through layers of incredible simplicity, words and images cease their importance, reduced by degrees to symbology where science speaks to all, in ever-deeper complexity. Equilibrium falls upon the point, the vital nuance and nexus where virtue suffused with reason, verily abandons it.

Afore-mentioned was the nod to our own predilections and foibles, where the gods we form from need and desire, are in like manner, created of, and from, the Divine essence. They resonate that which is true and untrue, known and unknown. Commanding ambivalence, their amorality repeatedly challenges human morality and mortality until we too, are sifted. We are enabled to accede to the incomprehensible Mysteries of the Divine thereto find the solace of 'Self.' Only within that small mystery, may we travail to know the Greater Mysteries still. Therefore, if we treat them as archetypes, we have lost their mystery; and if we treat them as personages, then we will never achieve self-gnosis.

Here we highlight the important distinction between the 'self ' and the ego. In any 'selfless' journey, we may all sacrifice both self and ego, and in so doing, lose the purpose of being—the true self-awareness of enlightenment—gnosis is not acquired through the immolation of self, but by integration of the ego, in its cessation as 'opposer.' It is frequently the latter that challenges and restrains us, quite fiercely so; sometimes for vanity, sometimes out of fear of change. Always, the unknown creates the greatest fear. Just rarely, it fights to preserve the virtue for and of others, thus repudiating its own 'perfection.' No finer sacrifice is possible in that final scenario. None of these choices encountered along the way, are easy to overcome; they all serve the whole, each its part to play.

"A piece of advice, if I may be allowed to give it, is that, no philosophy, no creed, no god, is worth more than the love, one human being may give and receive in their life-time. This is what I meant by being 'involved.' It matters not how wise or knowledgeable one is—providing one can love, and be loved by another."

Concerns regard always the proper execution of one's duties as wayfarer, to guide and support others, to reveal delusion and illusion are all second nature to those of a priestly cast. For those of us not in receipt of such gifts, but still wish to undertake such a role, the challenges are indeed onerous, but never, insurmountable. Along the way, we all need the honest contact of another to maintain stability and reason. Between a readiness to embrace the 'Beloved' (as in surrender to) and knowing the 'Beloved' (as in a totality of awareness, consciously and subconsciously) lies a considerable distinction. The Beauty, Love and Truth 'known' by this awareness, is the lure by which we are all, inevitably 'caught.' For is not the heart already given? Is not life, the very meter of the soul's sojourn in that happy reunion, whence admittance to that cause gives rise to 'seeking', in earnest, the steps to 'Her' Golden Halls, be they formed via a myriad denominations? Each pilgrim traverses along the thread that vibrates in tune to the 'heartbeat's drum. Robin-the-dart might say:[41]

"The ferry, the ferryman and the destination are one and the same."

The stream flows through all pilgrims open to its musings along their journey, where tradition fords and forges their basic needs. Found essentially in the hearth, through succour and by shelter—the three FFFs stand for vitality of health in mind, body and soul. Beyond all kenning is the mysterious innate ability we each possess to understand and resonate with the 'primordial tradition.' What remains important to every individual, is a purposeful harmony; one that allows complete surrender to the impulse to fall—as in a lover's embrace. As early as 1909, we find Guénon writing about the 'Primordial Tradition,' which finds cognate forms, unilaterally. Guénon felt that the mysteries of our humanity could only be partially revealed; he asserted the need to study everything, in every era, before we could make true sense of our own. Only then, may we evolve in spirit, in Truth. When reading the works of such genius, we must strive to garner their insights and resist the imposition of our own. Too easy lies the temptation to 'see' highlighted all that we wish to see. Most particularly, we must distinguish between the implicit and explicit tenets of wisdom therein. All mystics believe that all things reflect the truth, even those religions deemed false by others; even so, the light within, is given to discern those truths of equal value, and strive to remain an advocate of that, where so ever it may arise. Tradition therefore exists to aid the individual upon their lonely journey. Hence, we are alone with the Alone, though guided always by the lore and law of others, whose lights guide our own, in turn. For in their truth, we find our own.

Sometimes we may reject one thing for another, almost in like manner to our choosing a life partner—it twists knots in the stomach, clutches the heart, snatches the breath, and steals the soul: yet always, it leaves us insatiate! Crossing cultures is problematic but not impossible, rare is the person who achieves this with success, as tradition is normally rooted in a culture. This will depend whether that tradition is based in 'Magick,' or 'Faith.' Again, so many conundrums and lapwings abound. It is fair to say we combine the virtue of faith and magick at their most animistic... and yet, there is always more.

Standing on the rising cusp, we poise, ready to ride the next storm, not as flotsam, but preened, strong and resolute. To date, we may add only, that as seekers of those precious, sacred mysteries, we share tribute to another, far wiser than any on the matter of the Rose, of true discretion among like Companie. Guénon understood that no-thing and no-one is of consequence, yet truth or wisdom gained, is always of consequence. That all may act according to their nature, is to be accepted, and all responses should be our own, and not another's. Finally, 'under the rose' signifies that whatever is shared under 'Her' aegis must be of mutual trust, mutual understanding and mutual worth. That is to say, were those matters to be taken beyond that Companie, those tenets would not be enforced by the Rose, but by Her thorns. Beauty masks the hidden barb, yet those guarded by that obligation and by treaty of invocation, are assured of greater delights. Not so much a vow of silence then, but more of discretion, caution and the need for honour paid to all witnesses to that act. There is very often a good reason for keeping things to oneself, but just occasionally, there is a better one for not doing so.

Truffles are indeed too rich for a babe, but hogs take all, given, or *not*.

3

Grist
to the
Mill

So much for heart and soul, but what defines the blood and bones of 'Tradition'? Some might say tradition itself abides through repetition of an established pattern, either of belief, or of action. Others might refine this further to highlight the tradition is the vital element that drives those beliefs and actions. All views on this will naturally be subjective; consideration as to where the principles of those traditions truly exist, be that in the tools of the arte, or the Craft itself, sustained in that process; or within the actions undertaken by whatever means become available. Again, fire, typically a 'traditional' element, is so imperative to any magickal rite, absence of it, would be unthinkable, perhaps? Maybe, we cannot separate fire's inherent virtue as a symbol of that element represented, from its ritualistic use as fire. Is this simply because fire is present, or is it the ceremony that attends and describes how that fire is lit? Tradition would determine one in favour of the other, or even both, inclusively. Bowers certainly held strong convictions regarding the element of fire. Many things determine 'Tradition,' including survival and repetition. In the end, all that really matters is that a 'tradition' is anything around which a particular principle may be shared and continued, be that an idea or the actuation of it. Fire, its invocation and mastery of it was a matter of discussion between Bowers and Gray, and though we do not have Gray's comments, Bowers' views are extrapolated with considerable ease:

"Experts tend to believe that the god of fire was one of the witch gods, this is not strictly true. Like yourself, we have the four elements that we invoke, and fire and your Michael are one and the same thing. We use him for purification at the simple level, and for higher symbolic work at the others. I have been in the presence of fire at an elemental level, and have seen things burst into flame, he is not a faithful servant at that level."

Numerous principles and actions of single or compound activity clearly then, constitute a 'Tradition;' some by their methodologies, others by the mechanics exerted in their actuation. For some, a determinative factor of tradition is the ritual of 'repetition.' All is 'grist to the Mill' as Evan John Jones would say; all necessary for our winnowing: oddly (or not) a process that engages the kernel, cast up to the winds. Connection with and through an Egregore is essential; intrinsic to any Clan/family, its traditions are invigorated through its virtue. This vital stream flows from the family' tutelary deity, as mediated by its totem, and totemic presence. Therefore, the Egregore of '1734,' or *The Regency*, for example, function differently to that of '*CTC*.' And yet, we also believe that the 'source of all' actually allows for a common spiritual ancestry from which we all descend, just as a common blood ancestor will be present if we look back far enough.

For those not yet Inducted to a specific Tradition, through no lack of genuine seeking, take heart, as this does not preclude any seeker, emboldened by valour, and enflamed through personal virtue and ancestry, to find fulfilment, as countless pilgrims and hermits have confirmed to us. This signifies how Traditions, drawing upon similar pools of inspiration, may be kin—'related,' without being the same. Through experience, we all begin to appreciate the Hermit's path; the undertaking of one's self as 'lamp' evokes an unhindered progress. There is much of value in the solitary path, not least thereof, is the singular mentorship in spirit, the peace available for contemplation and the sanctity of being alone. These things offer an incredibly profound pathway to successful gnosis. Whence drawn into a familial heritage or even an awareness of their existence; inexplicable, yet tangible forces will gradually propel that recipient towards a very different mentation. In that bald arena, attunement to the vibrancy of others, both incarnate and discarnate becomes possible. This effects challenges far more aggressively than the Hermit's path, stimulating evolution through quite different and unique patterns of interaction where appreciations for another's perspective attunes us to their insights, shared in blessed Companie. From the same Well, we draw our buckets, and the sweet nectar filters through the differing woods, imparting uniquely individual flavours, bringing succour to the thirsty traveller.

Unwittingly, we each attach to our carnal, spiritual and group soul, and though that thread, bind one to the other—to its core, the heart and hearth of that tradition. Our individual strands are composed of the very fibres of our own individual experiences, such that cumulatively, the weaving together of them present a more exciting, vibrant and expansive tapestry than the one borne of the hermit's single thread. Freely, the grander narrative leaps out from the linen cloth, resplendent in all its tones and subtle knots and intricate patterns, a mantle of sublime profundity and exquisite harmony, unequalled in solitude, exile or isolation. We are a social animal and fall naturally into groups and packs; drawn, to 'like' we hold to the blood. Guided by spiritual virtue that speaks collectively to all, we each share its grace as one among us. Such moments are beyond expression. Roy Bowers declared how no Fate could be worse than the exile of this beneficent heritage, a lineage that is a lifeline in an otherwise alien world. Paradox is ever the handmaiden to truth; so in that apotheosis only, do we overcome 'Fate.'

Part II
Chronology of The Events And The Works of Roy Bowers Aka Robert Cochrane Circa 1960-66

Legend: Key Explanations to all Letters

Collated from various direct sources, including personal correspondences with Doreen Valiente, E. J. Jones, V. Jones; my debt to those known and unknown is eternal and bound in Troth. To all I offer my most heartfelt thanks, your input is priceless.

Information regarding Bowers' life and beliefs prior to the appearance of several public letters is scant and subject to a good deal of 'grey magic.' Previous histories have been largely compiled from material that remains at best speculative, and at worst, specious. There is so much that remains unconfirmed. But, with the few clues we have, we may attempt to construct an educated guess, which may or may not require considerable revision, if, in the future, further information is discovered that may increase our appreciation of this man and his remarkable works. Bowers and his wife Jane were married in London in 1951, afterwards, embarking on the most fascinating journeys few of us ever get to glimpse. Theirs was a very different world. Laws regarding the occulted world were being revised and updated and the social revolution after the strictures of the war were slowly being relaxed. They matured into an era of unprecedented freedoms, sexually and intellectually. Theirs truly was a 'permissive and liberated society.' And one we are never likely to match again.

Spiritualism, theosophy and metaphysics were certainly major fascinations of his, matters oft discussed with Bill Gray in their extended correspondence. Bowers avidly read the occult literature of his time, including magazines and periodicals, eager for a glimpse into a world more familiar to him than that which surrounded his waking days. Bowers and his wife were even at one time, members of the Centre for Psychic Study/Research. He attended lectures on the paranormal, witchcraft, magick, even physics, and he began to make contact with people writing the articles and speaking at events. Much like we all do. In particular, he sought out those who defined themselves by an 'otherness.' He had immense insight and a canny grasp of the 'other,' a gift of the kenning that eludes so many.

Struggling to work and live in his mundane environment, he tried to explore the hidden aspects of the arte from amongst those folk clinging still to its vital roots. Travelling around from job to job, he shifted through foundries, jostled with artists and printmakers, meandered with canal 'bargees,' and grafted alongside other craftsmen working on the London Underground. Eventually, nurturing a new family, the Bowers' moved from inner London to the outer regions, settling in Slough around 1960/ 1. Having left a magical group behind him in London, consisting of people he'd worked with during those hedonistic early days, he began looking around in earnest for genuine seekers to engage the Mysteries that so beguiled him. In particular, he sought those who desired to follow a traditional pattern, one based in the blood and bones of his ancestors, not the eastern gods of those around him; but those of the Hearth and the Heath. Disappointment rankled him deeply; his bitterness towards the facile antics of occult themed sex parties, laced with empty rites, led by cliques beleaguered by flailing egos, shadowed him always. Referring to them as something he wished to leave behind, he asserted an air of cynical superiority.

"...they wanted to play silly beggers, so I let them..."

An initiated Gardnerian Priest named Reginald Hinchcliffe[42] offers his own views on the people involved, describing a commercial artist named Everley, as the 'prime mover' and catalyst for those he gathered around him in his attempts to establish a working group along more traditional lines. Valiente confirms this from notes she also made that it was here, in that group that Roy Bowers met Ronald White, circa 1958-60. Many of those around London throughout the early sixties were quite familiar with Charles Cardell, whose later feuds with many involved in the occult scene, were to sensationalise it for decades to come, and which sadly, brought him only ruin and despair. Initially, he'd rented rooms in the city to counsel the well-heeled, and to lecture upon the magickal world of the occult as he saw it. His views were very unorthodox, a matter of considerable friction to many he encountered. He defined sharply between the common magic of the illusionist, the theatre of tricks and trade, and the true magick of the metaphysical, occulted world; the spirit world unseen by profane eyes. These concepts have regrettably become lost in the controversy that remains unresolved still, regarding which, of Cardell and Gardner, was the mentor, and which the pupil. Cardell's devotional fervour and regard for the highest 'truth' undoubtedly impressed Bowers, who moved within those circles, rubbing shoulders with several names listed in Valiente's diaries associated with him. Other names are known already, and include Lois Bourne (then Lois Pearson.), Eleanor Ray Bone, Raymond Howard, Charles Pace, Jacqueline Murray and Olive Greene (also known as Olywn Armstong-Maddox) the source or go-between who so beguiled and befuddled both Gardner and Cardell. There are others too. Of those known to Bowers, if they were not already Wican, many were turning to its sweeping tide. Led by G.B. Gardner, a man for whom Bowers had only contempt, he believed him to be: *"an out and out fake."* Of Wica however, he said: *"I believe it could be something greater."* And yet, Bowers' own practises reveal more than a passing similarity to those led by Charles Cardell (as will be made clear). They show no similarity whatsoever, to those of Gerald Gardner.

Early beginings – 1962?

In order to fully draw out the imperative of this emphasis, we need to return once more to the invaluable and consistent resource Valiente's note-pads have proved to be. Essential in fact for cross-referencing much that transpires, and much that allegedly transpired, we must note her vast catalogue of names of all the people she and all those concerned here, revolved around. Again and again these names recur throughout the following letters. It is important to remember and to be aware how a good proportion of them are merely pseudonyms, therefore do not concern as many people as one might initially suppose. Also, as the letters show, there is more than one George (hence George W, written atop the page to distinguish him from the other George known to them); and more than one Jane, Joan, Jean, Roy, Ray, John, Dick, Diane, Diana, Ann, Anne, William, Bill and Chalkie known to Bowers and each other in the very small, and closely-knit occult community of those early days, four to five decades ago. We simply cannot imagine how few of them peopled the occult world of their time, nor how well they knew each other. They did, after all, attend the same few events, and read the same few journals, Wic/can and non-Wic/can alike.

Nomenclature notwithstanding, events and context alone serve best to separate fact from previous fictions, and are here explored and recorded for others to follow to their satisfaction. Monmouth offers a very confusing situation that involves an alleged letter from 'Laurence' to Ronald White dated I/9/1963,[43] the thrust of which contains a discussion about time spent over Christmas, with his good friends, Norman and Jean. The letter stresses his concerns that it had been a while since their last meeting/working. A fair enough comment of course. What is odd however, is that someone would choose to discuss events that occurred during Christmas nine months *later* in September! Monmouth uses this letter to generate a continuity of relationships between the persons named within the letter, ie, Norman and Jean, its recipient, Ronald White and the last meeting it discusses. And it may do, as far as that goes. But Monmouth seeks to stretch those associations further to include Roy and Jane Bowers by asserting the rite Laurence refers to is the one noted in doc (a) dated 9th March 1962, which would make it a very, very long time indeed since they last worked together – over 18 months in fact! We suggest this is highly improbable! The next odd thing of note is the dating of the letter itself. Unless Laurence is American, the date is clearly the first of September. But, if he is not, for the letter to make any sense at all, the date is either a typo or a forgery. Unfortunately a scan of this letter is not included in the extensive appendices of scans in Monmouth's book for us to properly assess its content, context and its veracity. Therefore this letter does absolutely nothing to validate any of the relationships he asserts are evident within the doc (ooo) for all these people beyond express an opinion based on unprovable possibilities within conjectural and hypothetical scenarios. Moreover, those scenarios are in *direct conflict with all material evidence* that cross-references the events which occurred at that time. It is important to recall here that Bowers had _not_ met Norman Gills. Their paths eventually crossed a couple of years later at the end of 1964, a secure date affirmed quite irrefutably via their ongoing correspondence which only began when Bowers was introduced to Norman Gills through Gerard Noel, and not via Chalky or George. Highlighting again how certain people had different/deeper affiliations with either Ronald White or Roy Bowers at that time, establishing the course of events to come. (see also (nn) Norman Gills Intro letter #1)

(ooo) Letter to Chalky, allegedly from Jane Bowers ?
Re: Confused Rite.

Notes: Anomaly: A handwritten letter below that mentions a date of March 27th within the body of the text. No year date given (ooo). It is claimed by Monmouth to have been penned by Jane Bowers and in 1962, despite the signing off as 'Joan.' But he fails to offer either proof or even a valid reason for this, asserting a date presumed only upon the letter heading of 'March.' To suggest that Gills' and Bowers' meeting is pushed back to 1962 is therefore clearly impossible and remains utterly without any validation whatsoever.

Let us study then the anomaly at heart in this hand written letter presents, most obviously due to the signature afoot the letter itself. Signed very clearly Joan, we are to presume this to be Jane? Why? She is certainly not shy when signing other documents as Jane, nor is 'Jane' substituted anywhere where Bowers' types her in to Clan documents. Using rationale, we may determine if this letter is bone fide on that account. To be legitimate, however, it could relate to one only of three separate scenarios: (1) It was written by Jane in 1962; (2) It was written by someone else in 1962 (or even earlier); or (3),it was written by Jane, sometime later in 1965 once all the people mentioned in it had all met. If neither of these are viable, then we have to consider the letter a forgery. We shall consider the possibility of each separately.

The later time-frame of 1965 stretches credulity for Jane to write about an event that involved Norman, as Roy Bowers had only just begun to write to him, so any meeting this early in their correspondence was doubtful, let alone a working. Any time later of course, puts Jean out of the picture, as Bowers' letter of 1965 to Gills remarks, lamenting that physical loss. Moreover, if Jane *had* written this letter in March 1965 once Roy and herself had met Norman Gills, even prior to Jean's death, then nothing that follows it makes any sense. Nothing Bowers had written to Bill Gray, Robert Graves, etc, his published articles, - none of it has a place in their known and validated time-frames preceding Jane's writing of this letter as late as 1965, and obviously none of those events and publications could not occur after 1965, as their dates are rock solid. The inclusion of others such as Laurence and Diane/a in the list, further diminishes the possibility Jane writing that letter in March 1965. Laurence, better known as Arthur Oakwood (see (a)) was accompanied by 'Diane/a' only prior to that date, after which time Valiente's record cites her as deceased).

Using data borne facts we may consult the calendrical records to determine in which years a weekday dated the 27th March falling straight after a weekend, noted by 'Joan' for their 'working. Figures confirm the possibilities for when that particular weekend could have occurred as 1961, making the 27th a Monday; a perfect date for 'Joan's' comments and the events which followed. This date also correlates with Bowers' arrival in Slough. Monmouth puts the date for that rite a year later in 1962 just two weeks after the events noted in (a) which by content alone makes a nonsense of both letters. As for the dates, on paper it may seem sensible to presume the 27th of March must follow *in the same year* as a letter dated 9th of March 1962, at least initially. However, the devil is always in the detail, and this scenario is no exception.

First, we should consider carefully the matter of George's Initiation, an event planned in the letter of the 9th March 1962. But, in the letter of the 27th March (no year given), George is already noted as a member of that group, which suggests that (a) refers to an induction into a different group formed some time after the ritual discussed in (ooo), rather than before it. Then, in (a) Bowers speaks of his wish to bring George in under the Virgin, that being the Saturday, just catching vestiges of the

New Moon of the 6th. Naturally this would mean that for the Initiation planned in (a) to have been the Rite discussed in (ooo) as Monmouth suggests, the Full Moon that fell on the 21st March, would be ripe still for any rite occurring between 23-25th over the weekend preceding the date of the 27th. So not a Virgin Moon by any reckoning. Once again, the facts and logistics determine a better probability in my proposal that the failed rite noted in (ooo) occurs in 1961, and precedes those noted in (a) the following year. Thankfully, we now have a better date, and one that totally supports careful consideration of the facts noted within these letters and documents. Quite obviously, however, the anchor points validated by actual calendrical data, somewhat conflicts with Monmouth's proposition which asserts this document (**ooo**) likewise dates from March 1962.

Agendas, being self-serving frequently ignore anomalies, gloss over facts and select information at the expense of truth. But if we are hungry for answers, and avidly seek the truth, then we must follow the rule of Occam's razor, accepting that whatever is left after sifting out all known or obvious error, will be the most probable. So, taking that as read, if this letter truly relates to the people mentioned as the personages we suppose them to be, then it absolutely cannot relate to the events listed in another letter dated letter 9th March 62, unless that date is also dismissed as error (as demonstrated earlier).

One other possibility remains. Valiente refers to 'Arthur's' wife who died around the same time as 'Dian_e_/_a_ ', given as the partner of Laurence. It is just possible that Arthur Oakwood (referred to by 'Robert' as Laurence – (a)) is one and the same noted here as a member of this group. 'R_a_y,' (Raymond? Everley?) is husband to 'Joan,' (named clearly in the text as distinct from 'R_o_y'). Laurence and Diana could feasibly be Arthur and Dian_e_ Oakwoood, whose signatures as 'Elders' are recorded alongside those of Robert and Jane Bentback in the 'Oath of Loyalty' to the *Thames*

Valley Coven' a document that sensibly reveals the first group Bowers led, referred to by himself: " I was once in charge of a full and balanced coven."

Analysing the note for content now, we see that 'Joan ' reprimands Chalky/Robin for waving his knife about during a shamanistic dance (discussed later), and excuses her husband Ray for his nervous laughter during the failed rite. Bowers was many things, but nervous was not one of them. The scan of this letter requires scrutiny to determine the distinction, both in written style and intent between Joan's reference to Ray, her partner and Roy, whom Chalky is meeting on Tuesday. They are *not at all* the same person. In this letter Joan reminds Chalky with whom she is addressing as Robin, that he is meeting 'Roy' on the following Tuesday. We may tentatively suggest that when Roy became introduced to Everley's group, he would indeed be seen as the 'Young Roy' noted by Monmouth in an early document (see fii).

This early meeting between Roy and Chalky provides at last confirmation to comments made by Valiente regarding an early group of people Roy very briefly joined, a coven where he'd met Ronald and George. It also makes sense of why, a year later, 'George' as a former member of Everley's group, would need to be brought in (initiated) to Bowers' 'newly' formed group under the 'Virgin.' These events are mentioned in letter (a) dated 9th March 1962, which allows for the brief time Bowers' would spend with Everley's group, before leaving to settle down and sort himself out with his own. During that year following the afore-mentioned embarrassing incident referred to by 'Joan,' involving George and Ronald Chalky White as existent members, Norman and Jean must have left before Bowers was introduced to that group. Remember, it has already been verified that Bowers and Gills did not actually meet until 1965. The alleged letter from Laurence in 1963 bemoaning time passed since he last worked with Ronald White would indicate that Laurence was no longer part of Roy Bowers' group. This ties in perfectly with comments made by Bowers to Bill Gray during a period of grief and aggravation regarding people he was working with and that he and Jane would soon be working alone. Thankfully, Dick and John appeared in 1963 and his new Clan took off from there and he left forever the 'coven' behind him. Given that Hinchcliffe recorded events that correlate with authentic and validated comments made by Bowers, this offers the only solution to an otherwise unsolvable anomaly that exists outside the possibility of outright fraud.

All clues are listed separately by Hinchcliffe regarding the 'traditional' group established by 'Everley, a commercial artist' who recruited Bowers and others in response to a newspaper ad; by Valiente, who records the information concerning the deaths of 'Jean' and Diane/a', and how Bowers knew Chalky and George back in the late 1950s, and the group that split up when Bowers argued with a commercial artist; and finally by Bowers throughout his own letters regarding a former group of people he regarded as *'silly beggers,'* and of another group he'd <u>led</u> (as distinct from a group he'd joined as a member), which had been 'a full and balanced coven,' but who *'went over to Aradia.'* Several documents in this cache presented by Monmouth, which he believes was the former property of George Stannard/Winter, provide further corroborative and fundamental clues regarding the *'Thames Valley Coven,'* via the Oath of Loyalty, three hand-written letters, and early documents concerning very 'Wican' material that Bowers later refers to as needing to be cast aside, as it does not serve their needs. He goes on to provide new innovative material he is best known for inspired by John, Bill and the 'old man of Westmoreland.'

Bowers' letters to Bill Gray and to Gills confirm their meeting as a solid anchor point for cross referencing other less certain dates. And so these riddles are not nearly so complex as they may first appear. When taken on their own, freed of all previous propositions that have befuddled and swamped the few basic and very simple factors here, the obvious is very quickly transparent. Perhaps Monmouth, in his desire to obligate a specific agenda overlooked these vital clues that point to a very different conclusion to the one he presents in 'Genuine Witchcraft is Explained.' Perhaps.

We simply cannot ignore what is written there to present suggestions based on personal desire or inclination. When approached with caution, they do speak volumes. In 1963 Gills' wife, cited by Monmouth as 'Jean,' was still very much alive. Valiente records that her death occurred sometime in 64/65 just prior to the initial correspondence between Gills and Bowers. As already noted, other reference material from Bowers however, makes it clear he does not see Gills until 1965. Therefore, it can be demonstrated that this particular letter (ooo) relates to people whose names indicated in the text, properly refer to. They are not at all the people others have presumed them to be.

To conclude then, this collection of people could not have lined up together before the end of 1964,* if at they ever could at all. There can be no proper attribution of any context for these people, until further evidence proves this signature as Jane's, or until dates can be secured for them by other means. Even though we tentatively suggest this letter's interpretation, it remains a conjectural proposition.

This letter can therefore only be:

- A forgery. Almost impossible to prove. The signature 'Joan' is wholly unlike Jane's - which again can be clearly noted in the scans (these may be published separately due to technical difficulties, but copies will be sent to both the 'Centre for Pagan Studies' in Brighton, and the 'Witchcraft Museum' in Cornwall for independent study.

- One that applies to other people with similar names. [Possible, as noted earlier]

- Of relevance to Everley's group, circa 1959-1961. [Very highly probable]

*Aside from the first option, the remaining options are not mutually exclusive. We may offer valid year dates of 1961 for the week-ending March 27th through the calendrical data. Other factors would still have to confirm any of the dates noted (including the one mentioned on the other letter of 9th March 1962 for George's Initiation) as an actual meeting of certain members of the *Thames Valley Coven.'*

(1)   Chalky (sp) Bowers uses Chalkie.

(2)   Ronald White's description in document (g)

(3)   This comment clearly defines the distinction between Ray, her husband who is   not free all week until Thursday evening at which time Joan and Ray are meeting up with Laurence and Diana....but Roy, however is free both Monday and Tuesday, Tuesday being the day Ronald White is to meet up with him.

(4)   'Blessed Be' is NOT a phrase Jane would use, consider the numerous derisory comments Bowers makes concerning such sign offs. And Jane always referred to herself as 'Jane.'

(000) Transcript of Handwritten Letter
(Allegedly from Jane Bowers)

Dear Chalky, (1)

Thank you for your letter and suggestions. I agree with you wholeheartedly that we should have the element of worship more prominent. This is a definite need felt by all of us. This after all is the whole purpose behind it. I have felt absolutely awful since our last meeting and I know everyone else felt the same. In fact I was picking up Diana and Laurence so strongly all day Sunday I had to rush and phone them. What Laurence said confirmed my own feelings. I don't think we can lay recriminations at any one person's door, although I myself do feel largely responsible and apologise to everyone for not taking a firmer stand. I don't know what Jean and Norman and George must have thought. I am awaiting their letter which I know must come, and hope it will not confirm my worst fears, that they will not feel too hurt or disappointed. It must have been a terrible let down for them. I think we should always start with everyone knowing exactly what they are going to do, and no last minute alterations. Before L&D arrived we had agreed that we were not going to have the full ceremony. Then at the last minute everything was changed. But no-one had a clue what to do. There seemed to be more people outside than in. George was not in at all. I think that he should be inside for the opening prayer. One which should give thanks and express our dedication, and then a pleas for guidance etc. We have to think up something really beautiful, and one which can be used each time to open the proceedings. You're very welcome to lead the prayers according to the occasion, and perhaps others will take a turn. After this George can go outside the circle again until the agape when he can place a small table with the only the ritual glass of wine for each and cake. This will only take a few minutes to eat, and then the circle will be broken and members can smoke or anything. We should never have personal conversation in the circle, or smoke etc. But you know all this of course. I am just letting off steam. We all know what was wrong and must vow that it will never happen again. I feel as if I am physically whipped over this. I think the gods are angry with us.

Another thing, while I am letting off steam. I am very sorry Robin, (2) but you must not use shamanistic magic like you did on Saturday with the knife. You will end by doing either yourself or someone else an injury. It is either dangerous, and really the knife/athame should only be used for meditation. I know that you wanted to try out this particular experiment, but it means that others are tensed up, and if everyone within the circle is brandishing a dangerous weapon things could get quite out of control. The ultimate use to which the knife is put is cutting or stabbing, and in the moment of frenzy might easily happen. So I do feel that this practise must be strictly banned either singly or within the group.

Ray and I would certainly like to meet and discuss these procedures, but I am afraid it will be impossible for us this week. I thought you were meeting Roy next Tuesday? (3) He has Monday and Tuesday off next week. Laurence and Diana are coming here this Thursday evening so will discuss everything with them. Ray has written out the basic forms for each festival, and I am typing and adding to them. I will send each person a copy then they can be subject to their opinions and alterations as long as we have a copy to send to Jean, Norman and George before next meeting, and everyone can learn their parts. No last minute alterations to throw everyone into confusion. Robin would you like to hold the official prayer book. You don't have to make them all up, if you like you can glean them from poems or ballads, from any source. I see from your letter you're already doing this.

Blessed be Joan (4)

PS Ray feels awful about losing control and laughing it is a sign of extreme nervousness and tension. He is very sorry. I hope Norman will be able to do something about this by hypnosis.

X...................................X

(a) Letter to Chalky dated 9th March 1962

Notes: By March 1962, Bowers was clearly intent on forming another group. He'd previously met Ronald Chalky White in a Coven in London, now left behind him in his move to Slough. Ronald 'Chalky' White, to whom the second letter listed in this Chronology was allegedly written, is relayed certain details about an initiatory rite planned later that month involving a person named simply as 'George.' This document also refers to the sponsorship by Arthur Oakwood (Laurence) of an unnamed lady, later presumed to be Diane. Avril is mentioned in another letter (c), but this lady may have been someone else altogether, and a fleeting member only. This ambiguous document generates more problems than it solves and certainly better suggests another grouping of souls than Monmouth assumes for them. Bowers is at pains to inform Chalky that all the relevant material and literature Chalky will need for the occasion will be forthcoming.

He is literally writing and typing it during and just after that exchange. Allegedly by Bowers, the signature - 'Robert' is impossible to authenticate. It is signed in the same manner as the signature on the *'Writ & Const.'* doc but at this time Bowers was still using his own surname and was very informal. Roy, or Roy Bowers. Or R. L. Bowers. It is written to Chalky, believed to be [Ronald White/Chalky- RWC] 1962. It is the only document that is dated. An absence of topical information makes cross-referencing difficult. But if legitimate, it certainly sets everything else up that follows it, and all in due order of known and externally verifiable events.

However, certain facts taken for granted, taken 'as read' quite literally, are found to have gross anomalies regarding the details they supposedly relate to in the texts. The letter is dated as written on the 9th March with a view to meeting up on the Saturday, under the auspices of the 'Virgin'. If Bowers refers to the 'Virgin' Moon, then in 1962, the date on the letter given as the 9th March fell on a Friday. Even if posted first class, this would arrive the next day, on Saturday 10th leaving very little time for Chalky to contact George and prepare him as requested. Not impossible, but a little hurried. Though it obviously does not refer to the following Saturday as the Dark Moon had already begun on the Tuesday of the 6th prior even to the writing of this letter. Bowers must be referring to the 'Virgin' as the Spring Maid, heralding in the Starry Tide of Light in the Round of Life. If Bowers did mean the Moon, however, and a literal New Moon at that, then the calendrical data again determines that for a Saturday in March, a New Moon event occurred in 1960, in 1964 and in 1966. But not in 1962. Which means he was either happy with the proximity of the dark moon on the 6th; he actually meant the Spring tide; or the letter is a forgery.

And what of the enclosures that allegedly accompany the letter comment upon meeting up for the Wild Hunt on the 13th, which in 1962 fell on the Tuesday, unusually not a Saturday. So unless they were able to meet up and work late midweek, (very doubtful), those could be notes sent another year, perhaps the year after, in 1963 or even later. In fact the next time a Saturday fell upon the 13th of March was in 1965 only (and no other date between 1957 and 1966). Other dates given in the text for cross-referencing allow us to accurately fix those events in time.

Surprisingly, amongst the many letters Bowers wrote to various and diverse peoples in those last six years of his life, he dates none of them. So this one is rather an oddity. He does however, mention within other letters, three more dates, the 13th March - the *Wild Hunt and* the 27th March, both previously discussed. One other, March 26th, is a date circa 1965 Bowers offers Norman Gills as suitable for a visit. (see (nn) Gills). The letter from Bowers to Gills discusses his need for a medium. Bowers suggests visiting Gills on the (Saturday) week-ending 26th March, bringing along John, V******, Ron and George to help prevent a tragedy befalling a member of the Clan Bowers was involved with. We need to study these dates very carefully for calendrical clues that allow us to view those documents for a full and true accord. The findings are quite astonishing.Doc: (ee) In this note, a date is given for when they are to meet up. That date is given as Saturday the 26th of March. No year is provided. This vital date has been speculated by another author as 1962. However, a Saturday that occurs on the 26th of March, occurs only in 1960 and 1966, certainly not in 1962. The week-ending is also noted in this letter But, even if Bowers had meant Sunday as the 26th, despite writing Saturday very clearly—this only falls in 1967, which is a year after his death. So the date is clearly <u>Saturday 26th March 1966,</u> again, not 1962. With regard to the people he wishes to accompany him, Bowers again, having not met John until 1963, and Audrey until very late in 1964, then the only date that correlates those people together on a Saturday in March, falls in 1966.

A general consensus of these bald facts therefore cannot fail but to present 1965 through to 1966 as the strongest time frame to correlate all events that involve Chalky, George, Bowers and Gills, rejecting unequivocally any earlier date as a non-existent fantasy. This fact become more pertinent as these pages continue. As noted here, there is one fully dated document only amongst the entire collection. Handwriting is difficult to completely validate, anomalies do exist as the Calendrical Archives confirm. Other documents are more certain, despite any lack of dates, necessitating the contents to speak for themselves. Some of these allow a much deeper insight into all contextual events, reducing previous conundrums, even as others add new ones. Some documents remain stubbornly impossible to crack at this time. Such is the way with all Historical data, they must be rigorously scrutinised and cross-referenced where possible to achieve the best and most probable sequence and veracity.

A strict date can centralise and anchor all otherwise, and uncertain events, providing a more accurate chronology overall. Some events merely alluded to, nonetheless remain questionable, requiring further letters and verifications before any useful conclusion may be formed from them. Many of those events presented by John of Monmouth, fail repeatedly to address those glaring anomalies. Without solid, supportive evidence, their placement in any factual chronology must be firmly rejected; their inclusion serves only to confuse and distort a 'natural, sequential flow.' All documents in this publication are arranged tentatively, but with greater certainty and according to chronological or verifiable cross-referenced events found within them. These are drawn from numerous accounts of that period.

As a major resource, Doreen Valiente's diaries have proved invaluable in this. She notes that between 1957 and 1962, the keeper of Anglo-Saxon antiquities in Cambridge—T.C. Lethbridge, began to take an active interest in parapsychology, making a series of documentaries on that subject. This aids us enormously to understand exactly how heavily influenced Roy Bowers was by T.C. Lethbridge's publication in 1962 on Witchcraft (*Witches: Investigating an Ancient Religion*); more so in fact than any other tome, including Robert Graves' *White Goddess*. Throughout the winter of 62/63, there was a spate of desecrations and rituals held within certain graveyards and churches across Sussex, and Bedfordshire. These briefly recurred a year later, inducing a certain reporter and close friend of Valiente's, named Leslie Roberts, to renew with vigour, his investigations into those scandalous activities, by interviewing every celebrity occultist he knew of. Bowers, having no wish to speak to him, jovially mentions in one of his letters to Bill Gray that he should caution Doreen to ensure Roberts stays away from him!

Finally, a highly irregular signature raises one final anomaly that for now, remains in question. Without reasonable proof of signatory authorship, this letter signed *Robert,* and in the same hand as the signature in 'Writ*Const.' doc: see **(d)** does present an unresolvable issue without the aid of a hand-writing specialist. For an alleged early document, this is very unusual as his normal sign off was Roy. At that time, Bowers held very closely to his own name or a very informal 'Roy Bowers.' Later documents were signed Robert or Robert Cochrane. Three Hand-Written notes exist, of which this is the first re: *GEORGE'S INITIATION.* The letter also mentions the introduction of a new person, sponsored by Arthur Oakwood. Though unnamed, she is probably the lady 'signed' on the *Thames Valley Coven* document **(d)**, which follows shortly.

(1). Bowers here refers to 'Chalky' which is probably Ronald White. Eleswhere he spells it 'Chalkie' by hand and by typewriter in at least two other authenticated documents. Robin Gynt is also a troubling affirmation, why would Bowers need to use both Robin and Chalky names in an informal letter, when common practise would be to use either a nick-name or a magical name or one's real name – to use both is a superfluous anomaly. In addition to this, <u>Robin</u> Gynt morphs into <u>Robert</u> Gynt on the 'Writ and Constitution' document! Someone appears uncertain of names and spellings in this document.

(2). Arthur Oakwood is already part of the (Thames Valley) coven. As one of the original signatories in fact, which Gynt is not. Keeping it simple, Bowers exclaims, he was not a lover of excess cant or liturgy, which again confirms the unlikelihood of his authorship of the very long and protracted document which displays extremely Wican traits, phrases, and formulae. Sadly, much of it is now vastly exposed to graffiti, displaying a marked disrespect for its original commentary. Early works are here dramatically abridged, and are obviously developed by others into a more refined and less complex rite at a later date; only to be further refined and pared down by others once more at an even later point in time.

(3) Two Kings noted are the Young and Old Horn-ed Kings referred to throughout Bowers' developing theology.

(4) Works proffered by another, very probably Ronald White, as he is the one Bowers addresses here with his comments regarding the May Festival and other dances. Bowers' responds at length to Chalky's piece of work on the festival dances (doc f). Bowers is correcting what he sees as glaring errors.

ii Wild Hunt addenda

iii Drawing of a glyph of the Stang & Crossed arrows as the 'Mask of God' diagram of a masked Stang, likened by others to a person resembling a 'Vitruvian' being. [There is a deeper significance for this image, which is discussed in *Tubal's Mill*.]

[These addenda could be from a later date, and may not necessarily be enclosures here]

Transcript of: Letter to Chalky, Robert Gynt dated 9ᵗʰ March 1962

Dear Chalky, Robin Gynt,(1)

Can you bring George, drums and prepare him for initiation on Saturday? We are going to bring him in under the virgin which is the proper time to begin anything new.

Laurence (Arthur Oakwood) (2) is going to sponsor a very old friend of his on Saturday also. She is a woman (sculptress, psychic) about

George's age. From what we have been told, she is an excellent proposition and since Arthur Oakwood has known her since she was 18, she has evidently covered the initiatory probation. Jane and I are plumping for her.

I have enclosed a copy of the full rite of initiation for entry into your Red Book, destroy the typescript when finished with it, and let me know your reactions on Saturday. I have kept it as simple as possible, I would have liked to develop upon it but our coven being what it is, would be sure to mess the ritual up, and as you know, magic depends upon continuity.

I have broken down the symbolism of the two Kings(3) and worked out the past theology of this subject. You are well out on the May Festival. The Full rite and marriage of Spring falls in the last ¼ moon of April, the May feast is a wedding breakfast and the renewal of virginity takes place on 12th Night. G. in the real Arthurian legends was always cuckolding the Old King and running off with Jack o' the Green, or the spirit of Vegetation. The Wild Hunt in Sep-Oct is the Old King chasing down the Queen's Lover, and either killing or banishing him. The modern witches are not genuine since they do not know of this. Gardner actually asks in his book if anyone knows the meaning of the Wild Hunt. You will also note that it was never called Thor's Hunt, but always Wodin. I am coming to the conclusion that we are real orthodox Kosher, and apart from one or two really closed covens, who have nothing to do with anyone at all, we are the direct heirs to the real tradition. Obviously in the Arthurian L. Launcelot was Jack o' Green, but the Grail was Christian opposition.

There are three books. Red (Rites and Law), White (Philosophy, morality). Black (magic)—you enter the relevant writings in each, always by hand.

Make sure George brings his drums (?)

Have you contacted Michael BAMPTON at Croyden as yet? He sounds a good proposition. Robert.

X......................................X

(b)Induction/Initiation Rite

Notes: As a typed document, it forms part of the full '*Writ and Constitution*' document, which Bowers sends on to the Chalkie in the next letter (e). This Rite is mentioned in letter (a) above, allegedly by Bowers—as something he is sending Chalky as preparatory instructions for George's Induction. Inserted here for clarification is a transcript that includes both the 'Induction Rite,' and the 'Writ and Constitution.' These are exceedingly important and should be read in their original form, devoid of the obscurities evident within the scans. This contrasts considerably with how we see them today, covered as they are in numerous pencil scribbling, biro notations, diagrams, ciphers and crossings out. All other documents in this chronology, though faded, can be read with some degree of patience within the scans (published separately). They do present a challenge, but the results are worthwhile, and do evoke a sense of the person not apparent in the cold transcripts. It is quite a phenomenal experience to properly witness and evolution of ideas from these early documents even though their authorship remains a mystery. That author could be Everley, Oakwood, White, or someone else entirely, but it is very, very doubtful Bowers composed it, as study will determine.

All transcripts produced here are left unedited, displaying all original typos, errors and spelling mistakes. As for this 'Writ,' as a document, it appears authentic (in as much as that may refer to its age), though again, we may not be so certain of the signatures upon this copy, for we have to remember that it is a copy only of the original, despite the map of surface pencil and biro edits added afterwards. The comment at the very bottom states quite clearly that the original was left with the HP. This 'copy' has clearly provided the working template for others to amend at a date later than its original presentation and use, distinct again from that original intent, whence it served as a sacred 'Writ,' with clearly avowed instruction not to alter or defile it.

Another consideration, of some significance is that a member of his coven, that is to say his group of people that constituted his Clan, has stated how they are totally unfamiliar with Bowers as Robert Bentback. This suggests two options, one is that he may have used it, albeit briefly before developing the Clan at which time that person came to know him; if not this, then it can only refer to someone else entirely. If the first option is true, then it reveals how much of this he quickly left behind him around 1963 when Evan John Jones joined. As for the second option, it is no secret that Ronald Chalky White coveted the aegis of his hero Richard III, of whom he believed himself in 'carnate' form. Richard the III's nickname was of course 'Crouchback.'

X...................................X

Transcript of Full Rite of Initiation (Induction)
Rite of Initiation

This is copy and must be destroyed, (1) after the full ceremony is entered into the Red Book. On no account must this copy be left around so that outsiders may read it. It will be entered into the Red Book in the woman's handwriting only, and should precede everything but the Coven Writ in the issue of the Red Book.

The Full Rite of Initiation. The Coven will assemble and the presence of at least five Elders, The High Priestess and The Maiden is required, it may be held at any time of the month, excepting the dark of the moon, although it is best if the moon is new at the time of initiation. The Maiden will wear the crescent upturned of the Virgin, or if the Coven lacks The Maiden, The High Priestess will deputise in place as the Virgin.

The Sponsor will introduce the Neophyte to t the Coven and will begin the direction of the Neophyte's entrance by a detailed description of the Neophyte's virtue and faults. The Neophyte should be present during the discussion, but not allowed to speak at any time. The Neophyte will always be referred to as it, denoting that as yet, he/she has not been born (it can be said that of the Coven describe the Neophyte, he, she, or by name that it will be a reliable guide that the Neophyte has failed entrance). When and if the Neophyte has been accepted for Initiation, it will be taken out of the room or area and the following ceremony will be held.

The Star of Morning still up at play… something in the book/ the Coven will sit and meditate for not less than ten minutes/upon the virgin and her meaning the High Priestess and The Maid hold the Cup and charge it. The Coven will then begin the quick dance to work up power then the Neophyte will be brought in the Initiator will be laid out with the following proper symbols. Staff, Coven Staff, Athame, Cord (Green) will be used, candles and water, salt and red wine, on the floor, about the altar… will be drawn the Star of Morning. Then the Neophyte is brought in, it is still unbound. By the door, it will be approached by an Elder, who will look into a scrying ball and say I see thy past, I see thy present, but I see not your future, for you are to die! upon this the altar, sponsor will seize it and bind the Neophyte then two men will carry the Neophyte to the altar of the circle. The High Priest will then raise the sword say to the Neophyte, upon the neck, and throw red wine upon its chest saying, "behold, he/she has sacrificed even life in search of the Goddess." The Neophyte will then walk alone and unaided to the Alter and kneel. The Coven will gather round in a circle and the High Priestess will begin the following prayer.

"Star of the morning, woman of the dawn, virgin we salute thee, our love we give yet never match what ye have given us. Virgin we ask thee to descend, for in this time, this place and upon this day a friend of ours is drawn towards thee and they seek thy Truth, Wisdom, Love and Joy. Virgin we ask for thy grace upon us and them and thy admittance to thy Companie." Coven: "Virgin descend and fill our hearts with joy!"

High Priest. "Glory to the She. All Life shall know her. All life shall seek her Truth. We shall raise our hearts to thee giving all." Coven begins to circle Moonwise! "In all climates and seasons we praise thee. In times of pain, we praise thee, In times of stress we call to thee. From life to death and back again we remember thee. Praise the She, blessed is the She, Thrice Blessed be. Come to us Virgin (rapid dance now) Virgin, Mother, Temptress One, come to us, come! Invo Her! Invo Her! Mother, Virgin, G——ver. Come!"

Upon the ninth perambulation, The Maiden or High Priestess will step forward and the Coven will now gather around the Neophyte and each place a hand upon his/her shoulder. The Maiden will hold the Star position then begin the charge of Initiation. During this reading, the Coven will press hard upon the Neophyte until rebirth is spoken of, then lift up the Neophyte rapidly symbolising re-birth, and the cords will be undone. The full charge is as follows...

"Behold I am She, I am the Immortal who knowest not Death, who is named G......... ye have called upon Me and I have come I who in the past was named many names, walk amongst ye again. In mutual love, I left My Mark upon thy soul's to be guarded and remembered for all time, through the joy of life and the sorrow of death and ye have not forgotten Me....... So it be... So it be....

I say to ye now in this time and in this place that ye shall arise again to worship me.... As ye were then and as ye are now, until all things that are human do come to thier and and we find peace together.

I come to you not empty handed but bring blessings and joy with

Me, and I give My convenant and word to ye now. These things do I tell thee, and trust thee to observe.

First I bring love without fear or hatred... Joy without sorrow... Compassion for those who are weak or for those who are persecuted, and most precious, a wisdom for all things that live and the things beyond life.

Secondly, I promise you fertility in body, mind and spirit, fruitfulness......so that ye might give and fertilize the world and its nations with my will.

Thirdly, I tell thee of three great magics. Life, Death, and Rebirth.

Life, so that ye may love, learn and grow, wise in joy.

Death, that ye may now of my will and know my mansions.

Rebirth, so that though will love again those you have loved before, and carry my words before ye in the affairs of thy people."

These are my teachings and my words, mark ye well that they are the holiest things of all. If in your way then seek and find these truths. Then my blessings shall always be with thee. But if thou disgraces them, then no shelter shall thou find, either in this world, nor what lies beyond, for thy own curse shall seek thee out and destroy thee, so it is, so it be, so shall it be eternal.

Ye see that I have given thee all yet asked for nothing in return, but this do I ask. I ask only for thy love and that which is most feminine in woman and most masculine in men. This shalt though offer me at the festival of the Year as ye may. I charge thee to observe thy duty to me, as I observe mine to thee.

I have spoken and so it has begun and ended. My spirits shall guide thee through all that life has to offer. My blessings upon thee.

Wise and Blessed Be...."

(When the Neophyte is brought to her feet upon rebirth, two women should have thier arms around her symbolising actual birth).

The Priest will know take up the Coven Staff and approach and begin the swearing-in with these words.....

"do you (...) swear in the name of 'A' the God to uphold the traditions of this coven, which are, love for all men and all things, joy for all life, wisdom to be still and to know when and courage to break with fear."

R. "I do"

"Do you swear to have mercy charity, humility, virtue, and to reject all that which is evil thought and evil deed?"

R. "I do"

"Do you swear that you will never peak or write of what you will see here, touch or sense amongst thy people" –

R: "I swear that my tongue shall be still upon these things upon the woods no longer are and the seas have run dry."

Priest "So it be. So it be. If thou betray us no rest shalt though find in this life or the second. For the She shall turn from thee, and ye shall join with the wolves and the end deed in the darkness." He kisses the new witch and then says "Thou art my brother/sister now. Now and I name thee... So shalt be known among us."

[over page]

The Mentor of the new witch steps forward and says:

"I am thy teacher. Come hold my hand, we will walk together until ye can walk alone."

The mentor must be of the opposite sex. Before speaking, they must kiss the new witch upon the lips with a long sweet kiss.

The Priestess now closes the ceremony with a prayer of thanks "O goddess we thank thee for thy presence. We have tried to work good on thy behalf. Bless our work before departing. O mistress mine, Coven all say "wise and blessed is the Goddess. Wise and blessed be those who follow the ways of the goddess."

And Feast.

X...............................X

(c) Hand-written letter to Chalky
from Robert Bentback?

Notes: Following on from events noted in both aforementioned letters, albeit some time later, another hand-written note is sent to Chalky discussing the imminence of the now (over) due event pertaining to AVRIL'S 'INDUCTION' possibly referred to in the 'dated' letter (a). Bowers remarks upon her difficult behaviour within the loosely forming 'second' group, and so offers Chalky advice and confers to him, the authority for himself (as overall leader and head of the Clan) to act and do what is needed to resolve the situation. He also refers to the three books in which to record the tenets of the '*Writ and Constitution of a Coven to Diana.*' If 'Avril' is the sculptress and psychic lady, stated as a good friend of 'Arthur' noted in (a) then this lady's possible identity has been explored in 'Tubal's Mill.' It is of course very difficult to speculate who this lady might be without further information. It is further compounded because a lady named Diane/a, named as partner to Laurence, may be the same person whose signature appears in the '*Oath of Loyalty*' to the '*Thames Valley Coven*,' as Arthur and Diana Oakwood. Diane/a may or may not be Avril, and Avril may or may not be the lady explored in 'Tubal's Mill.'

Additional Points:

(1) The directive to 'destroy' this material, again, ignored, despite the imperative.

(2) In large letters, a handwritten word is scrawled lengthways across the bottom of this page. It says: GWENYTH. This is a name that features amongst others in a list compiled by Valiente in 1959, of persons she believed knew and worked with Cardell. We do not know if this is a real name or a pseudonym, nor why it features in this way upon this document. But, it is definitely not written with

119

any degree of deference or reverence, nor does its odd context suggest it as others presume, that if refers to the name of the Goddess Bowers used or believed in at that time. It is not his handwriting, it is Chalky's; and he certainly did ascribe deific status to this name.

(3) After 'Basil Thomas, the message takes a tangent in content and subject matter. The hand-writing is different, which gets progressively smaller, even crossing over a previous sign-off in its attempt to squeeze in the remaining space on the note- paper

Transcript: Hand-written letter to Chalky from Robert Bentback ?

Dear Chalky,

Here is the Laws and Constitution as required. Anything left out of this can be supplied on the High Priestesses authority. I think it would a good idea to have every new initiate to the coven sign it and read it a condition of acceptance. L+A seem to like it, although I do not think that they quite realise the extent of power given to the HP. I hope you can handle Avril alright, if not boot her out on our authority, but first explain to her about the sacrifice. Do not explain about Robin Artison until she has signed, but do not explain to her about any methods in which she can use Robin. I want to keep her at boiling pitch until this mob is fully settled. (3) Sign yourself Robert Gynt when writing to Basil Thomas. Never use your real name when making contact ~~Love~~ with outsiders, they can use telepathy against you.

Robert Bentback (Roy Bowers) Priest

x..................................x

(d) Typed 'Laws + Constitution'

for *'Thames Valley Coven,'* copies given to Chalky for his own group. List of hierarchy and seniority [signatories are the Priest and Priestess: Robert & Jane Bentback (sic) + two others, pp - Arthur & 'Diana' Oakwood] Details of Sabbats, Kindred festivals, Conditions of entry, Summary of the Writ and its ritual format. Document completes with the *'Oath of Loyalty and Acceptance'* that Bowers advises Chalky everyone should declare upon entry (noted in the hand-written letter to him, as above (?). This document formed the basis for the workings of White's own group, later refined as a working document for themselves after Bowers' death.

Transcript of Typed 'Laws + Constitution

The Writ and Constitution of a Coven to Diana

The members in thier authority and seniority are as follows:

The Maiden (G-n)

The High Priestess (The Queen)

The Priest (The Server)

Summoner (The Caller)

Elders and Musician

Red Cords (Those who have passed certain unspecified tests)

Green Cords (Those who have received Initiation, but who are unskilled as yet)

Neophytes (Those who are serving a term of probation)

Meeting Places The coven will meet indoors in a properly consecrated, censed and purified room, or large hall. The Circle(s) will be drawn in such circumstances. Outdoors, the coven will meet in a sacred grove of trees given to the Goddess (such as apple, oak, alder, hazel, holly, birch and willow). Or they will meet upon or in one of the ancient and sacred sites of power. At no time will members divulge of such meeting places to anyone who is not inside the coven. At all times coven members will be expected to treat such groves, or similar places of worship with absolute respect.

<u>Ritual and Form of Service</u> The Priestess and the Elders of this coven shall each have in thier possession a Red Book, in which all functions, ritual, prayer and magical forms shall be entered down therein. At NO time does such a book leave the possession of such Priestess or Elder to be read or handled by anyone below the rank of Red Cord. The Red Book will be kept under lock and key at all times, and it will not be taken out of a place of safe-keeping, except under stringent precautions and conditions. At no time may alterations be made within the Red Book or additions therein, until such alterations and additions have been passed by the Priesthood and Elders of the Coven with unanimous assent. Upon such possessors of Red Books leaving the Coven, it is requested that all tools and writings must be handed to the coven, unless special permission has been given otherwise.

<u>Ritual and Form of Service Cont: Ritual</u>
All members will be naked excepting such times when ordered otherwise by The Priestess. All members will abide by the decision and orders of The High Priestess in respect of fasting, contemplative thinking, study of symbology and upon theology and craft. The Priest will introduce all ritual, craft and magical practise, and explain in full the meaning and purpose of such ritual, craft and magical practise, improvise that the pupil is of sufficient high standard to understand such work. The Priest

will make it his duty to rehearse and explain the meanings of all prayer and ritual and he will ascertain that each member is fully conversant with such procedure beginning the rite or magical practise proper. To enforce such powers as written above, The Priestess or Priest has the power to discipline such members who fail in thier duty towards the coven, he or she will the authority to order fasting, contemplative work, research, or banishment to such offenders.

Ritual and Form of Service Cont:

Purification and anointing will be ordered by The Priestess, and she will call all members into the circle, in pairs, greeting each male with a kiss. Her authority in all matters pertaining to The Craft is absolute, until she has invoked the summoning ritual. Upon uch occasion, she will hand the Staff to the Maiden, who is then worshipped as The Goddess Incarnate. Where there is no Maiden, the adoration should be limited to the Priestess in her capacity as the Initiator. At no other time is The Priestess adored as The Goddess. The Priestess will have the training and purification of The Maiden in her care, and should be her mentor in all points of Ritual, Craft and Magical Practise. The Maiden will be under the care and instruction of The Priestess for a time not exceeding three years, and not under thirteen months. Upon such candidate for The Maiden being found unsuitable, she will revert to her original rank and authority. The Maiden, The High Priestess and the oldest Female Elder form a Moon Triad, and all work done within the phase of the Moon will use one of these three as a focal point. The Maiden is the Virgin, The High Priestess the Mother, and the oldest Female Elder, The Destroyer. A fully—trained Maiden will hold, absolute authority within the circle., but be subjected to the advice of The Priestess outside the circle. In no case has The Maiden or The Priestess the power to alter coven writ, nor to add to such writings until the above provisos are completed. This is an absolute law, because such alterations and additions will affect the communal spirit and disrupt the continuity of consciousness. In no case may any male alter such writ or magical practise without the authority of the coven as stated. Upon such alterations or improvements being found to be necessary, the male member will first approach The Priestess who will then decide the case upon advice of the Elders.

<u>Ritual and Form of Service Cont</u>: The Rites will be held upon the following occasions and events:

1.   Esbat
2.   Sabbath
3.   Solstice
4.   Equinox
5.   Twelfth Night
6.   Initiations

The details and procedures of such events and occasions and rites will be written down and kept in the Red Book under the previous conditions. The details of the structure of such rites and craft are as follows:

1.<u>The Esbat </u>The meeting will be called by the Summoner acting upon instructions from The Priestess. He will make known it's time, place and purpose to all members. Attendance at an Esbat is not compulsory unless the procedure known as 'Calling the Cord' is ordered. Upon such an event it is imperative that all members attend without fail, unless illness, domestic trouble of a grave order, or similar events prevent such attendance. In the case of someone failing to attend to a 'calling of the Cord' they will be subject to strict disciplinary measure. The Esbat is normally held to discuss business matters and to hold a ritual and prayer meeting. Business reports giving of duties and punishments are dealt with first. Each member will report accordingly to seniority. Each member will report on magical work alone and be instructed on methods of work to be done by The Priestess or Priest. A member will also report any requests for magical work made to her/him by another member of the coven or an outsider. A certain period of time is set aside for instruction of such techniques or ritual as may be necessary. This will be done by The Priest or another member capable of such information and teaching. The mentor will also have the power to order such as those needing instruction to read certain works and perform certain duties. Each Elder must act as mentor to neophytes and instruct them according to the law and tradition of the Craft a meeting of Elders, a meeting of Initiates at which The Elders are present, and work arising there from.

Ritual

The circle will be completed, and The Priest or Summoner will call upon members to worship within the circle. The five-fold kiss and dance forms are directed by The Priestess. No member will change thier partner within the circle without previous permission or direction from The Priestess, or Maiden. Such a request can only be made through two Elders who will not be affected by this change. (This stricture [.........] as it relates to the magical continuity of the dance. After the dancing is finished The Maiden or Priestess will hand each member ginger or spice cake and a glass of white wine, mead or cider that must be drunk. She will also kiss each member on the lips and the partners will embrace each other. Coitus is not normally practised within the structure of an Esbat, but if and when such couples find it necessary, they will copulate within sight and hearing of all the other members. The Priest should precede such action and circle be broken. On no account or at any time excepting certain occasions of the year will any couple copulate, make love or do similar actions within the circle while it is charged.

Sabbaths and Kindred festivals

1. There is a different ritual for each Sabbath.

2. Dancing is prolonged and mystical in its characteristics.

3. Tools will be used and forms of symbolism to create a necessary effect.

4. Discipline is absolute within two days of any such meeting.

5. No other thought or action will be allowed within the circle once the dance has begun.

6. A defined and definite chant and dance form is always used. There can be no appeal or criticisms of such forms until the circle be broken (one hour after finishing) and at no time will members attempt to spontaneous dancing unless ordered by The Priestess.

7. All profanity, humour and satirical comment must be severely repressed.

8. At certain times within the 'build-up' of power tension is extreme. On no account do members attempt to hold conversation, or pass remarks to each other to relieve this. Instead they will direct such tensions and forces either into dance or enter into some form of physical action, such as horse paly to relieve such tension. On no account will members say anything at all except the words of the chant.

9. Apart from the chanting and ritual, no speaking is allowed at all.

10. A maximum period of twenty minutes is required before the ritual for meditation.

11. All members will make themselves conversant with the symbol of the rite and fully   capable of such.

12. Previous to such meetings it is absolutely essential that the members will fast for a period of not less than eight hours, and that they abstain from all intoxicating liquids during this period.

13. That members will not have sexual intercourse with partners for at least four days before such meetings and ritual.

14. That previous to a meeting all thoughts that are negative in concept must be severely repressed, and that action taken for an entirely selfish motive, must be subject to the strongest self-criticism.

15. That the previous night must be spent in prayer towards the aspect to be invoked.

16. At no time will members use the craft symbolism for any other purpose than what it has been designed for.

17. That no detail or information as to the place of meeting or nature of the rites be expressed to outsiders.

Any infringement of these rulings will be subject to the severest discipline.

Sabbaths and Kindred Festival. Cont:

The Festivals, Ritual and other ceremonies fall under this order.

May Eve Midsummer Walpurgis

Twelfth Night (Elonian Belateneeolia) Initiations

Marriages Funerals Kindred festivals

Election of Priestess and Maid Return of the King in October

Magical practises and ritual will be carried out under the same condition but held at the appropriate time of the month and day.

The Strictures and Laws that Initiates are under

To obey directions of The Priesthood or Elders of The Coven at all times. That they will at no time abuse their powers or boast of such.

That they will respect, maintain and preserve all tools of the Craft with due reverence to thier magical properties.

That they will be chaste to a reasonable degree in all outside liaisons, and highly selective in friendships.

That at no time will they Initiate or introduce an outsider to The Coven without first obtaining full permission of The Coven.

That they will never offer Instruction to Robin Artison without due care to The Coven and it's traditions and principles.

That they will at no time attempt to alter, corrupt abuse to enter into agreements of an evil or selfish nature with Robin Artison.

That at all times when working with Robin Artison they will exercise due care and caution to behave in a goodly and kindly manner and that thier motives are of the highest honesty and that thier desires are based on truth.

Any infringement of the above rulings will be subject to discipline. Any infringement of the rulings connected with Robin Artison will be dealt with by banishment, and the full Rite of the Bull.

The Condition of Entrance upon new Candidates

That the candidate should be drawn towards the Craft because of a vocational and mystical drive. That the cadidate should show some intuitional knowledge, and be prepared to accept the laws and conditions, traditions and craft of the Cult to develop such knowledge.

That the candidate should express his/her absolute belief in G & A and teste to find if such belief is sincere.

It may also be that the Candidate will shew inherent memery of the Craft. In such cases this may be accepted as "good intention."

That the Candidate should be neither neurotic, psychotic, or suffer from sexual lesions, abberations, perversions, or malfunctionings, no should he/she be attracted towards any anomaly of function.

That the Candidate should be coarse or insensitive.

That the Candidate be intelligent, yet not intellectual, and that he/ she will understand the function of intuition and kindred factors.

That the Candidate shall not see sensationalism in physical or psychic matters.

That the Candidate will recognise the need for discipline and instructions and pay due attention to his or her mentors and due reverence towards the ritual.

That the Candidate will not speak write or utter anything of the Craft without due reference to the Coven.

That the Candidate will serve a probationary period not less than three months and not exceeding a year and a day.

That the Candidate will swear before being accepted for probation that he/she will never disclose anything of the Coven measure, ritual or purpose to outsiders.

That the Candidate will shew unswerving loyalty to the Coven, and protect the Coven to the best of his/her personal ability.

That the Candidate will not suffer from any form of nervous or physical disorder.

Summary upon the Writ and Constitution.

That this summary has been drawn up from what is known as the Witch Cult of Europe and Britain, and of the Cults, ancestry in Thessaly and Crete. Comparison of records from various sources show considerable regional differences in detail, and in some cases the addition of regional feasts have appeared. The document above has been based on the historical and general structure of all Covens to Diana, and is authentic to such records and knowledge of such Covens. Such writ once accepted is unalterable within its basic structure. And that every initiate and Candidate must accept this writ within its fullness and without reservation. This writ is the Basic Law and as such is subject to improvement only upon superficial matter. This Law and Writ is The Law and Writ of this Coven. Repeated disregard for any part or complete structure of this Writ, will lead to banishment from such a Constituted Coven, and the automatic penalty of a self-initiated curse that may or may not be increased to the Rite of the Bull according to the severity of such punishment or banishment. The only person who can initiate discussions concerned with the Writ is the High Priestess and her say and decision is final to such discussion.

The Oath of Loyalty and Acceptance   *Windsor*

That I as an Initiate of this Coven, being a full member of ~~The Thames Valley Coven~~ do swear upon my personal honour and the name of A' to keep this Writ and never to deny, defy, alter., or use such Writ to my personal advantage or to anyone else who seeks a selfish advantage. That I will be silent upon such Writ, Articles and Ritual, Magical and Religious intent or practise to outsiders unto the death and beyond if it so be.

This do I pray to the Gods to hear me, and make not of my words, ~~and~~

~~this to Bull I cry.~~

That if I break my word as written here, then may the Bull destroy me and cast me out alone, to wander throughout all time. And that I pray to The Coven to hear me, that if I betray them I shall be under thier curse as well as mine own.

So it be!

Each candidate shall kneel before the Initiator and express his/her intention of service.

Each Initiate shall kneel before The High Priestess and express his/ her intention of service as written above.

SIGNATURES OF ALL ELDERS TO THE THAMES VALLEY COVEN

Robert Bentback Jane Bentback pp   *Robert Gynt*

Arthur Oakwood pp Diane Oakwood pp   *Will Maidenson*

(G Stannard)

(The original signatures are in the possession of the H.P.)

The Oath of Loyalty and Acceptance

WINDSOR

That I as an Initiate of this Coven, being a full member of The Thames Valley Coven do swear upon my personal honour and the name of A' to keep this writ and never to deny, defy, alter., or use such writ to my personal advantage or to anyone else who seeks a selfish advantage. That I will be silent upon such Writ, Articles and Ritual, Magical and Religious intent or practise to outsiders unto the death and beond if it so be.

This do I pray to the gods to hear me, and to make note of my words, and this to Dull I cry. That if I break my word as written here, then may the Bull destroy me and cast me out alone, to wander throughout all time. And that I pray to the Coven to hear me, that if I betray them I shall be under thier curse as well as mine own. So it Be!

Each candidate shall kneel before the Initiator and express his/her intention of service.

Each Initiate shall kneel before the High Priestess and express his/her intention of service as written above.

SIGNATURES OF ALL ELDERS TO THE THAMES VALLEY COVEN.

Robert Bentback   *Jane Bentback* pp.   *Robert Gynt*

Arthur Oakwood pp   *Diana Oakwood* pp.   *Will Maidensen (G. Slaiman)*

(*The original signatures are in the possession of the H.P.*).

~1~ 'Oath of Loyalty to the Thames Valley Coven'

*   ("The same blue pen that scribbles out Thames Valley Coven and writes Windsor above it. John of Monmouth validates this 'hand' as Ronald White's." - *Genuine Witchcraft is Explained* by John of Monmouth)

Comments regarding the signatures to the above document

The final paragraph of the last page citing the **Oath to the Thames Valley Coven** as above, is copied below to authentically reproduce the document as we now see it in (d) above.

One title pertaining to the *'Thames Valley Coven'* only has been scribbled out, and in blue biro over the black inked copy of the original (believed after Bowers' Death.) A similar blue biro signs Robert Gynt. This nonetheless conveys how the four original signatures, directly beneath the name of the coven, are directed in their oath to the **Thames Valley Coven**. What the copy shows is how there has been a lot of fuss and hype over what is clearly a classic case of text/document recycling, by another group some time after this coven/group no longer practised, or by people no longer involved or connected to this Coven; certainly it is possible The Regency or even possibly Chalky's own Coven wishing to re-use and adapt this document are the authors of the graffiti the document now sports. We know, by their own admission *'The Regency'* certainly used the pared down version A4 doc. Bowers is attributed authorship of this writ, but reading it, that seems highly unlikely, though not impossible. It was allegedly composed for his own group, allegedly named the *'Thames Valley Coven'*, people, a group he later developed and expanded as: *"the People of Goda, of the Clan of Tubal Cain."* Some things do suggest this document could relate to Bowers' group, but equally, some things diminish that possibility.

What is absolutely certain is that despite the directive to destroy this highly secretive document, regarding the immense sensitivity of the oath-bound material involved, it was ignored, as the document exists still for us now to analyse and discuss it.

Bizarrely, Monmouth cites that what is clearly an ***Oath to the***

Thames Valley Coven is an Oath the *'Royal Windsor Coven' ???!!!* despite the blatant title that says otherwise and the signatures beneath that title! No desire, no feat of will, and no sleight of hand can shift that contrary proof!

In itself, this single document utterly refutes Monmouth's entire tome, ironically predicated upon this single claim to which he repeatedly refers back, stressing all other opinion and comment as fact, based on the validation he claims this document provides. And yet, without equivocation, we can see clearly that it does not! Moreover, he extends credulity yet further by claiming the *'Royal Windsor Coven'* was a secret title!!! So secret it cannot even head an oath-bound document that is directly requested to be destroyed??? That is surely beyond all sense! How could anyone be foolish enough to believe or support such folly? And yet....we have learned to our cost that not everyone reads or works anything out for themselves but are quite happy to be led, to be told what something means, what to think or do. And those people would still say they use Craft!!!

The signatories are allegedly: Roy and Jane Bowers as Robert and Jane Bentback, plus their two coveners, Arthur and 'Diane' Oakwood. NOTE: the name is *not* Diana, the distinctive 'e' that ends Jane is the same that completes Diane. This is important because it shows a clear and distinct hand. It also shows that many have overlooked this lady's given name here. That aside, two very major things are wrong here. It is without dispute the signatures noted here are assigned to the <u>Thames Valley Coven</u> and *not* the Royal Windsor Coven. Likewise, it cannot be disputed that four are of one hand and in the same black pen. This contrasts markedly with the signatures of both Robert Gynt written in blue* and Will Maidenson, in another, very different black pen. Written onto what is essentially a copy document in which the original had only

134

those same four original signatures in black, Robert Gynt and Will Maidenson's separate signatures are obviously later additions in their own hand, and are not contemporary with the original document.

Above the oath, within the main text of the 'Writ' is a list which defines a distinct Hierarchy, asserting the positions of Maid/High Priestess (allegedly Jane Bowers) and the Priest (allegedly ROY BOWERS) above that of the Elders—which of course as Head-Kinsmen of the Clan, they should be. But why has no-one asked how Jane and Roy would therefore need to sign the document as Elders alongside their initiates? So many unanswered questions and further anomalies. Nothing should be taken as read, and certainly nothing as is given by others without validation and in clear line of sight of contrary evidence! Ever deeper controversy leads to the observation that a completely new set of identities are possible for those we have been led to believe these pseudonyms are associated with and there is better evidence to suggest this possibility.

These remarkable documents show that prior to E. J. Jones' entry to the Clan, any coven Bowers had briefly run (be that the 'Thames Valley Coven, or not)' its basic structure for ritual was reasonably ceremonial and quite generic. Through their distinctive use of a Seer, known as the Maid, they deviate from the Wican model contemporary with them. Traditional tools are utilised, and centred primarily around the Stang and the Cauldron. There is a strong emphasis upon the Law and upon the Egregore, named Robin Artison. These early explorations developed into the slower, methodical, less complex rites Bowers is better known for, whence the Gardnerian influences from Chalky and George (who were initiates via Lois Bourne) and from former associates in the London based coven to which Bowers had briefly dallied with, became much diminished.(1) Bowers and Jones together sparked a revolutionary methodology of Traditional Craft workings that combined the structure of ceremony, the art of the sorcerer, the oracular force of the Seer, and the folklore of rural craft within a devotional praxis. Collectively, these symbiotic tenets evoked the historical rituals of our cultural ancestors, many centuries past. Their primary Mythos evoked the sleeping dragon.

(1) This is not in any way to express a superior perception of work, but merely to make a clear and noted demarcation in the face of detractors who insist Bowers had a Gardnerian initiation and/or that his work * is* Wiccan.

The Writ and Constitution of a Coven to Diana

Notes: The former document is cited by Monmouth as draft for this document, which he cites as a final version. There are several reasons why this is nonsense, and those are addressed here briefly and in *'Tubal's Mill'*[45] in greater depth. First of all, we must address the composition of this document. In Monmouth's book, *'Genuine Witchcraft is Explained'* p394 he has added an extra paragraph to this named document (see his scan on page 287 of his book) which is an amended version extracted from the older document of *The **Oath of Loyalty and Acceptance to The Thames Valley Coven,'*** (see his scan on p281 of his book) in which he has substituted **'Thames Valley Coven'** name for *'Windsor Coven'* giving the impression the document exists as he presents it. However, the version he shows on page 394 **is a falsified construct.** As stated above, that name does not appear in the earlier document and the extra oath signing section he includes does not appear in the later document, as clearly shown below in this accurate facsimile. This later document some years after Bowers' death. It may even have been authored by Ronald White – it was certainly the preserve of the later Regency. Monmouth however, may have provided the new title which relates it to a Royal Windsor Coven, which does not appear anywhere on that document, thus presenting it as a 'final version' of the former *'Writ and Constitution'*. He also adds two inclusions to his transcript in his book that likewise do not appear on the actual document. The Transcript below is an absolute facsimile, which is verifiable by the scans, which by default reveals the specious addenda to the transcript provided by Monmouth in his book – *'Genuine Witchcraft is Explained.'* The two addenda are the inclusion of *'Royal Windsor Coven'* as a title, and the inclusion of the *'Oath of Loyalty'* section copied from the earlier **non-draft** copy document (d) albeit one that replaces *'Thames Valley Coven'* with *'Windsor Coven.' (see 'Tubal's Mill.')*

One final oddity worthy of attention is a diary quotation directly from Ronald White's appointments, which rather suggests a time and circumstance for the creation of this document. In fact, there is no reason to suppose it may not even refer to the previous 'full version (b) of anonymous authorship. Certainly it indicates a specific point in time when Ronald White records his scripting of an Initiatory document. Again, though assumed by Monmouth to defer to another document entirely (The Reading of the Festivals), he gives the date for this entry as the 2nd September 1966, where White states: "Begin to Write 'Initiation' Roughs & Rough out Theology." [46]

The scans he provides for the A4 Writ& Constitution (Final version) clearly show that the 'Final Version' does not appear on any of the previous early scans. This examples another attempt by Monmouth to falsify documentary evidence in order to persuade the reader what he wishes them to believe it says rather than what the reader is clearly able to see states something else entirely.

Transcript for Document: 'A4 Writ and Constitution (Final Version)'[47]

The Writ and Constitution of a Coven to Diana

The members in their order of seniority are as follows:

The Maiden

The High Priestess

The Priest

The Summoner

Elders and Musicians (Those who have shown evidence of instinctive or acquired ability beyond the ordinary)

Red Cords (Those who have passed certain unspecified tests)

White Cords (Those who have received Initiation, but those who are as yet unskilled)

Neophytes (Those who are serving a term of probation)

Meeting Places

The Coven will meet where and when specified by the Summoner.

At no time will members disclose of such meeting places to anyone who is not a coven member or under the coven's protection.

Ritual

The Priestess and the Elders of this Coven may keep a Red Book in which all germane matters can be entered. Upon such possessors of Red Books leaving the Coven, it is requested that they shall leave all such writings within the Coven.

Ritual Observances

All members will be naked excepting such times when decreed otherwise by The Priestess. In such cases a black cloak and hood must be worn. Purification and anointing will be ordered by The Priestess, and she will call all members into the circle, when possible, in pairs, greeting each male with a kiss. Her authority in all matters pertaining to the Craft is absolute, until she has invoked the summoning ritual. Upon such occasion, she will hand the staff to the Maiden, who is then worshipped as The Goddess Incarnate. Where there is no Maiden, the adoration should be limited to The Priestess in her capacity as the Initiator. At no time is The Priestess adored as The Goddess. The Priestess will have the training of the Maiden in her care, and should be her mentor in all points of Ritual, Craft and Magical practise. A fully trained Maiden will hold, however absolute authority within the working circle. In no case has The Maiden or The Priestess the power to alter Coven Writ without the unanimous approval of The Elders.

Ritual

The Rites will be held on the following occasions:

1. Esbat (The nearest convenient date to the full moon)

2. Sabbath

3. Solstice

4. Equinox

5. Twelfth Night

6. Initiations

Meetings

All meetings will be called by the Summoner. He will make known its time, place and purpose to all members. Attendance at an Esbat is not compulsory unless 'The Cord is Called.' Habitual inattendance may be the subject of enquiry.

The Esbat

The Esbat is normally held to discuss business matters and hold a working meeting. It is in three parts: a meeting of Elders; a meeting of Initiates at which The Elders are present; and work arising therefrom.

Work Ritual Observances

The circle will be completed, and The Priest or Summoner will call upon all members to worship the circle. The Five-Fold Kiss and dance-forms are directed by The Priestess. As far as possible the order of procession in work should be maintained. After the work is finished, The Maiden or Priestess will hand each member ginger or spiced cake and a glass of wine. She will also kiss each member on the lips.

Sabbaths and Kindred Festivals

There is a different Ritual for each Sabbath. A minimum of twenty minutes is required before the ritual for meditation. All members will be made conversant with the projected rite. Previous to such meetings it is essential that members will fast for a period of less than eight hours, and that they will abstain from all intoxicating liquids during this period. That no detail or information as to the place of the meeting or nature of the rites be expressed to 'outsider.'

The Festivals, Ritual, and other ceremonies come under this order.

Candlesmas

Equinox

May Eve

Midsummer

Lammas

Equinox

Halloween

Midwinter (Yule)

Twelfth Night

Initiations

Election of Priestess and Maiden

Esbat

The Condition of Entrance upon New Candidates

That the Candidate should be drawn towards the Craft because of a vocational and mystical drive.

That the Candidate will be severely tested with regard to her or his beliefs in order to find if such belief is sincere.

It may also be that the Candidate will show inherent memory of the

Craft. In such cases this may accepted as 'good intention.'

That the Candidate will recognise the need for discipline and instructions and pay due attention to his or her mentors and due reverence towards the ritual.

That the Candidate will keep silent on his or her candidacy to all outsiders.

That the Candidate will serve a probationary period, its length to be at the discretion of The Elders.

That the Candidate will be prepared to promise before probation that she or he will never disclose any item of ritual or knowledge to outsiders; and will be unswervingly loyal and honest to all Coven members.

<u>The Laws that Initiates are under.</u>

To obey the directions of The Priesthood or Elders of the Coven at all times who will at no time abuse their powers or boast of such.

That they will respect, maintain and preserve all tools of the Craft with due reverence to their magical properties.

THIS IS THE LAW AND WRIT OF THIS COVEN

X.................................X

(e) i Dance Forms, Their Meaning and Purpose
ii: The Dances: How to Draw a Magical or Religious Circle
iii: Magical Purposes and Dances.

Notes: Almost certainly not composed entirely by Bowers, it was probably written by others close to him in the late 1950s—early 60s. It contains theories rejected by Bowers (see letter (c), and some embraced by him. Best candidate is Everley, under advice from Bowers. Nonetheless, this author, White? clearly preserved its tenets for later use in The Regency after section i, the tone picks up exponentially as Bowers'—most marked in section iii..

(1). The practicalities of this is highly questionable and leads one to wonder if this was ever performed or written down as a fantasy construct only. The movements and mechanics of this rite are wholly impracticable, how can the Mistress lead the dance if she is prostrate as the Altar?

(2). Very startling and curious directive that could easily lead to rapid dehydration and kidney failure, hospitalisation and possible death!

(3). 'Young Roy' here may be a term used condescendingly by Ronald White (as there was only a couple of years between them), or another author to refer to Bower's knowledge on this subject, possibly Everley within the Thames Valley/London coven? Clearly, Bowers did not compose this document.?

(4). A sign off not even remotely characteristic of Bowers! Again, may be Everley.

143

ii. Transcript of Dance Forms: Their Meaning and Purpose

<u>May Day</u>

1. <u>Fertility Dances</u>: This is done with a centre pole that should be shaped like a phallus and crowned with flowers at the top. It is tied with cords and the dances wind in and out, representing coitus. At times of the dance, the Mistress or Master takes the centre. They are dressed as Flora or Jack o' the Green.

2. <u>The Lover's Dance</u>: This is done in the form of a waltz, and the man should have a small fir-wood phallus and the woman a chaplet or necklace of flowers. The man should give her the five-fold kiss, which follows the pattern of the dance as an active worship of the female pattern of life, love, wisdom and peace, (G) at the top. They symbolically couple the chaplet and phallus and waltz together.

3. <u>The Pole Dance</u>: This is done with the staffs to make the crops grow and avert drought. The ash staff is also called Ygrisdaal, Wodin's horse of wisdom for good or evil. The dance is fast, with a rocking motion of the legs which never cross each other. A spell for rain and warmth is chanted over a cord staff. The dancers leap high with the staffs as levers to make the crops grow. The women can also dance with a besom, made of birch, ash and bound with withy to sweep the evil out of the land. Much reference to this is in the Wild Hunt of March the sixth.

4. <u>The Goddess Dance</u>: This is done by the Mistress standing in the centre, heaped with flowers and young greenery. The Coven circle her, with women in the centre, with one arm about their partner, and the other about the Mistress. The women are dressed as Flora, the men as Jacks. The cords link everybody and it is a graceful dance. This and the Lovers dance are used for Midsummer also.

5. <u>The Rite of Spring</u>: The wild dance of growth and love. The battle for

survival. The Mistress is the Altar, as per ritual. The couple begin dancing, facing inwards and linked with their arms. They are dressed in greenery, and represent the growing Spring. The dance is fast, sunwise and can be imagined from Stravinsky's music. The partners turn individually, yet as a group. They all follow each other around the circle, with a fast shuffling step, then alter to a stamping wild head-shaking step when facing inwards or outwards. It is fast and furious, noisy and violent. It is the struggle for life. Five times round and the Mistress will lead the dancers towards the centre and dance out again, forming the apple pattern with the last couple passing the first couple in and out.(1) Shrieks, wild chanting are used. It is the last dance and will last an hour. Salt water is recommended (2) and a two hour rest afterwards before attempting consummation of the rite.

Midsummer

This dance is to recognise the opposite polarities of male and female and the waxing and waning of the year. The men take the outside of the circle facing inwards; the women, the inside of the circle facing outwards. The women dance one way the men the other. The women use a sliding gliding step sliding step, the men a stamping fast step. Sometimes the music will alter the rhythm and the members will dance (waltz) with the opposite number. It has much the same principle as the Paul Jones.
[Hand-written line in between typed lines of text: *There is a figure of eight dance around the two bonfires.*]
Dances four and two are also used from the May festival.
Midsummer Green Queen and Green King. He or she stand in the centre and couples dances in two circles. One for the women, one for the men. They symbolically couple with the centre men or woman, who holds a symbol of their sex. The outside dancers have chaplets or staffs.

Lammas

The dance of the Corn Queen. The centre is heaped with vegetables, wine, berries, and wheat. The dancers circle sunwise after the rite and each take an article from the centre and dance with it, before finally putting it [......] the circle. The Mistress is the last to put it outside the circle and when she [......] this, the dance is over. Variations are used some of the fertility dances, that is there are in some dances a centre woman and corner men. Details of more dances are found within the full ritual. No matter whatsoever is used in this dance, since it is to wish a good harvest and ripening to the land. The dance is slow and graceful representing rest and wisdom. The previous dances can be wild and [...] dances afterward but this is always slow and graceful.

September Esbat

This is thanksgiving and it is a simple rite of prayer and thanksgiving over the reaped corn and fruits. It is followed by a feast.

Halloween

The return of winter as King. The descent of **G** to the underworld. And the opening up of the Gate of Death to purify the land and kill the remaining vegetation in readyness for the next years growth. It is a dance of knives, and tied to a long cord at the centre. Two circles are drawn and a feast of red foods is laid in the centre of one, for the dead to feast upon. The other dance is wild and special, precautions are taken for this, it is magical in extreme and good nerves are needed. The Priest takes over as leader of the Coven and he centres. The ash staffs are also ridden to represent the wild horsemen, but no leaping. It is a wild dance in conclusion and very long, although it begins as simple pacing. The full rite is entered and it is one of the most closely guarded secrets of all.

There is no lights except fire and the wild dance should be reasonably frightening, although to witches death hold no terror since it is the beginning to paradise. [???]

Solstice December 21-23rd

The cauldron is brought out and leaves and brandy are burned. The 21st is the day of mourning since the Sun (son) has gone to the Underworld seeking his mother. The dancers circle the cauldron on the 23rd, chanting to G to bring the Sun back and when he reappears, it is a dance of joy, since he brings news that the Goddess will return to the Upperworld.

Twelfth Night

The dance is with candles representing the waxing of the returning Sun. He went to the Underworld as an old man and returned a baby. See Rite for details.

February 13th Brighid

The return of the Goddess. It is a dance of love and thanksgiving. Love has returned to the earth again. See rites for details. The first aspect of the Moon is invoked. The dancers are the Lovers and jubilation. There is also a dance of birth, in which the cords are loosened after Drawing Down the Moon, and the women dance by themselves and each one centres the circle by stepping out of a necklace and rejoining the dance.

Wild Hunt

The chasing of the winters forces back to the underworld Match 6th.

These are a brief summary of the main dances and festivals of the year. They are based on the witch triad of life: Life, death, and Rebirth. They also follow the five points of the star: Birth, Initiation (youth), Love,

Wisdom (rest), Peace (Death). The Goddess is the principle of Love in the theology.

The son is born on December 23rd whilst G. rules the Underworld as Queen of the Dead and A. rules the Upperworld as Winter. The Son is Robin, son of A. He shows his young strength on Twelfth Night, inception. The Goddess emerges on February 2nd to join her consort, and takes her place as Queen of the Upperworld.

In March, A. chases his forces back to the Underworld in the Wild Hunt. By this, he will regain his youth. In May, he as the Young King consummates the marriage and G. conceives the next year's son. They go through the seasons like this, until the time comes for G. to return to the Underworld as Queen of the Dead and the son languishes and dies for the love of his mother. The new one is reborn December 21st. This is a modern interpretation. In the past, there were two kings, but it makes theology confusing like that and opens the gate to primitive practise.

ii Transcript of: 'The Dances. How to draw a Magical or Religious Circle.' The religious circle. Imagine a pool with a fountain of light rising form the centre nine feet high. At the top of the fountain there is a star or similar symbol, at the top of the symbol a grail from which light flows making a magical circle nine foot in diameter. The colours are gold and white for the fountain (like wood sparks). The colour of the grail is pure sparkling white, and the flowing light the colours of the Rite. For example, the colours of a Rite to do with water would be the sea and a centre pillar of white gold and green to represent the other aspect which is complementary to the sea. Obviously to visualise these properly is a matter of time, in which hypnosis can play a very large part. Magical work is simple. Lay a ring and cord in centre of column, then pace about it after combining the necessary elements into your magical process, then when power has reached a peak, draw the cord through the ring and chant a spell over it. Then bind the cords to the object required with some other simulacular of the tools to obtain your meaning. I will explain this in more detail if anyone asks me. You should also assume the body of light necessary to the operation, but that is better taught by example rather than writing. The wand is used as a contact between the pure energy and the centre column to the physical energy to the thing magicked. I know this sound complicated but it is really very simple, if you are puzzled ask young Roy (3) for the answers.

> The Chant for Drawing Down the Moon is:
> 'Queen G. Thy Blessings we pray thy presence we crave.
> Fill our souls with thy being.
> This our home we offer, tis our land we have prepared for thee.
> Our love mind and spirit is thine to do with what ye will.
> O Mother G., divine star hear our simple prayer,
> and descend, for we are betwixt heaven and earth for thee.
> The Cattle in the byre low for thee.
> Man and women feel thy loss.
> O come our Queen, oh come to us.
> Or else the land be desolate and the crops undone.
> And love will not spring again from the young.
> Oh Mother G., woman and star hear our simple prayer.
> We guilty children grieve our loss.
> We mourn for thy being.
> We are but children by thy breast.
> Cherish us with your presence.
> Bless us with your word.
> Thy name we call as children in the dark.

Oh Mother G., woman and star.

Divinity bright hear our prayer.'

Then after this has been effected turn inwards towards the centre and begin the chant of invocation. Since I am tired I will send it on later. Any way this very brief outline and the copies of the tree and star positions of magical and religious work should keep you all contented for the next week as you begin to try them out, one word though, do not try anything for real until you have seen me otherwise you might go and do something awful. My love to you all, and may we soon prosper for ever.(4)

iii 'Magical Purposes and Dances'

Notes: This document does exhibit Bowers' notable style, which curiously concerns is the dance and ritual style referred to by 'Joan' in her chiding comment to 'Robin/Chalky', as shamanistic and dangerous in its wielding of knives during wild dancing ritual form. Bowers refers back to this very early group in a letter to Bill Gray, that conveys his dismay at their sexual antics and bemoans their lack of spiritual sincerity.

Transcript of Magical Purposes and Dances

The Shamens danced vigorously to reach a state of frenzy in which they worked magic. The ceremonial magician, whether he works with tantric, cant ... Or Cabalosic magic, also incorporates the dance form into his ritual. The witch dances to achieve a state of auto or group hypnosis, in which the conscious mind is shifted and the centre of consciousness is allowed to break through untrammelled by the stimuli of outside environment ... If you read the Rite of Drawing Down the Moon, correctly, you will realise that it shows four purposes of work. One a short prayer meeting at the beginning, two a long period of meditation to begin a mental 'circuit'. Three, the rites. The rites are divided into three major parts, and these three parts must be followed in all magical practise, irrespective for what purpose. It begins with a **fertility** ritual, from there graduates into a ritual of **vitality**, in which the opposite poles of manifestation are brought into being, and then it takes the form of **inspiration**, which is formless, being interpreted only by the person involved into her particular form.

All magical work must follow this pattern you invoke the highest presence, examine its meaning to yourself, begin work at the level of earth or Malkuth, then work your own way up to divinity or Ainsoph. One creates a temple physically, then mentally, then spiritually. These temples remain with the mind and soul afterwards to be worshipped in and drawn up for inspiration. You may create the temple in mind and matter but the spiritual temple can only be created by your own life, and it is here that the need for love, charity and all those other virtues , that everybody has talked about for thousands of years, but never discovered the meaning thereof, come in. You can create the temple by your own life but the inhabitant will only come of her own accord when she thinks you are ready. This is one of the basic reasons why magical practise cannot be mixed with other forms of spiritual manifestation, and also the purpose behind the exceedingly strict mind training in spiritual morality that all White Lodges work upon.

It is very complicated and I would be very willing to answer any questions that you might like to put about it, since I can write forever about it and never answer you, yet I can show you in ten minutes….. For instance a magical ceremony and group depending entirely upon its contacts upon the inner plains, yet those planes exist only as a group manifestation of humanity. I could direct you in how to find the Godhead, yet the results would depend entirely upon yourself. All magic depends upon the contact and the purity of that contact of the inner planes. One cannot work on the spiritualist basis of having a guide or teacher and also expect to work any form of high magic, since the two paths are totally different. Yet one can work with the recently dead, in so much as they are of the same order, and the same practise as yourself. One can however invoke the Mighty Dead, who are beings that have passed beyond incarnation and who now work directly under the control of a master, that we call A. A. is the aid de camp to the Goddess and all work is done by invoking the Mighty Dead first, then A. then G.

This is not a religious practise but it is a magical practise and very simple if you always remember the basic procedure. Never try to mix these contacts. Invoke to the highest level first as prayer, then return to the lowest form and work to the Mighty Dead next, up to down then up again to the level that you desire shown in the chart of the trees. Each position of the tree is to be meditated upon and its meaning for at least ten minutes. The corresponding emotions must also be evoked, and as you progress up the tree, swing to the complimentaries or opposites do not go directly from charity to love go to severity also and power also. When you have reached the point of contact necessary then stop there and meditate upon it for at least twenty minutes until you are infused with the totality of that contact. It is also essential that you do not cross your ideas or powers at this point and that your emotional 'background' is the same as the power you are evoking or invoking. It is then that the actual magical ceremony is entered into. Upon completion shut down your centres in the same way. Do not just walk out the circle or else you will be suffering from hallucinations for the next week. To shut down, travel back down to the lowest point, then go up to the highest and end with a prayer and physical action of opening the circle. Your contacts during the ceremony will themselves known through various means and various signs that you will learn though experience.

Light should begin at bright yellow, turn to dark blue, grey, mauve, purple then change again to the corresponding colour of the contact (earth would be russet, green, gold, ventitian red, brown, blue of the hills and so forth). You will find that a soft green would do physically and these colours will appear in 'minds eye' as the rite continues. You meditate in a comfortable position, but so comfortable you will go to sleep on it. The symbols are made of white or yellow metals and should be highly polished. The outside symbols are corresponding to the positions of the four elements, the inside symbols should be made so that it will fit into the staff above a drawn diagram that should be in the centre. You'll find that by various manipulations the symbols will all move clockwise. Now if you make a large star with five points and place this in your staff, then superimpose this upon a spiral ending with an arrowhead that the points of the star can be used as focal points of thought to be invoked by and that the arrow will fertilise or engage each position as the star turns. Now for religious purposes the star would be upon its normal order of thought and you would use this as a chant as it turns, invoking the aspects as they came to the arrow, then when a point has been reached, the Mistress gives a full Invocation and draws the power down and shapes it to the form that is desired. It is hard to explain, yet once seen it is as simple as possible. Remember though to start off with symbols on the outside of the circle to work by then turn inwards to the star, three legged man, spiral, cross of elements, a symbol and so forth. These are all directives of consciousness and they are very useful as a basic beginning to magic, and ritual. You'll find that all parts of the human organism come into play. Tough in the handling of tools and the use of them is one, a sense of smell so that certain perfumes may be associated with certain factors. Words should be whispered to achieve a state of group or self-hypnosis the words also have great relative meaning at certain parts of the ceremony. And then by being whispered, act as a depressant to oxygen supply to the head. The dance steps and movements with the tools are also important. The totality of all these movements is to produce a great 'whoosh' of directed will and power to the object desired.

Names of power these are the most potent of all symbols and should never be told to anyone outside the coven. It is possible that the other mobs use the name Gilda but we have chosen a more ancient name deliberately, because it lessens the chances of getting involved with their particular planes of manifestation.

The name we use is ended with

Ea (Virgin)	Evah (Mother)	Ge (Wise woman)
East	South	West
Life	Love	Rest

(see drawings of cross of elements and star)[See Diagrams - (vv)i]
The same principles apply with different symbolism for A. and Robin. Each have a three-fold aspect that can be multiplied to a considerable number.

X.................................X

(f) Theory of Modern Witch Practise

Notes: More information allegedly typed by Bowers best refers to Everley's group which may or may not be the Thames Valley Coven, and is sent to **Chalkie**, Laurie/Arthur, Avril/Diana and to 'Self.' The typewriter is consistent with Roy Bowers'. Some of the language and phrasing is however distinct and quite unlike Bowers'.

Attention should be drawn here to the spelling of *'Chalkie.'* Why does this spelling shift between documents? Are they to different people? Are they authored by different people? Rather uniquely, the author speaks in an entirely different tone to the person named *Chalkie, to the person addressed as Chalky.* In the few times this spelling is used, the author defers to this person rather affectionately, using fond terms such as 'dear,' *'dear old,'* and even signs off with *'love.'* it is not impossible then for this to relate to another person entirely, still assuming Bowers wrote it of course. Several people known to Bowers et al at this time would serve as candidates for this term of endearment, whose names contain White and even Black as a surname. One other known as 'Blackie,' may even had had connections to a certain Blackie Barlow, a 'Gypsy Seer,' of some past fame in the South East. One thing is obvious, they are all terms not shared on any communiqué's between Bowers and Ronald Chalky White, whose omission from the list along the top of that instructional information, very strongly supports the unreliability of these few pages to present anything except further conflict in their subject matter.

This introduces yet another anomaly, for as this missive reveals the line-up and status of people working together as an unknown group at this time, then the suggestions regarding letters (ooo) and (a) flagged previously, begin to accrue more ground. Few of these documents can be authentically attributed to Bowers and the few persons confirmed elsewhere as actually belonging in his group at that time. This information is another example of instruction given to those group members to whom it is relevant. These rites are more generic, and suggest an earlier authorship or accumulation of ideas. Perhaps information familiar to them all from Everley's group has been repeated here? It may even be possible some of the earlier documents were typed up for Everley's group by Bowers on his typewriter for their use.

To mark its relevance amongst other letters yet to be discussed in this volume, the reader will note a clear distinction in style of authorship, terms of reference, regarding deities, elders, magic, the focus of the rites and how the rites are executed. Terms discuss the five-fold kiss, woman as altar, of decorating her with seasonal greenery, willow wands, priestesses, and many other incongruous references when compared to other letters from within this cache of letters that can, with certainty, be validated as authored by Bowers. *The Theory of Witch Practice, Drawing down the Moon* (long version) & *Dance Forms, their Meaning and Purpose* reveal the clear influence and adoption of styles and terms that may be attributed to Ronald White,'Laurence' or even Everley.

Some of these appear to have been typed on the same typewriter Bowers' later works are created on, but there are particular themes within them that we certainly do not find in his later works, secured and validated as his. It is of course possible that he either acquired the typewriter from the author of those other documents. Or he may even have typed up their notes. He may have typed up his own notes influenced by their extensive input. It is extremely unlikely he composed them himself. We simply do not know who did compose them; there are no signatures to claim the work. All any of us can do is study the works for style and content. To that end, these particular works do reflect a style very recognisable in Ronald White's '*Pagan Handbook,*' which again may indicate his earlier authorship of those other documents. Equally it may express an influence from those early times retained within his own later works. We simply do not know. One thing is certain, the Wican content, style, working indoors and even the term 'coven' (noted by Valiente), were all so abhorrent to him that, even if used by him in the formative stages of his own group, were very soon abandoned for deeper, traditional themes and working rites, held outdoors. The group very quickly began to operate under a Clanship, as a People and those anonymous rites conflicted drastically with his vision for his Clan. They did not configure or feature in the Clan Mythos, Ethos, nor its Rites and praxes.. His own tenacious research and sourced Mentor-ship yielded substantial and notable dividends.

Transcript: Theory of Modern Witch Practise
(Copies to Chalkie, Laurie, Avril, Myself)

This is to be kept in the uttermost secrecy and not any account for public usage. It is not one hundred per cent accurate, but near enough to the real thing to be considered dangerous. On NO account is any member of the Society to attempt to practise whatever is written herein by themselves.

The circle is drawn and charged by the Priestess. The adherents enter after suitable prayers and meditation has had an enlivening effect, and created the right 'atmosphere.' They take up positions and take a slow pacing walk with eyes focussed on a witch tool that has a suitable symbol inscribed thereon. I would suggest each member weave a concentric dance individually, and that such movements are worked within the peripheral path of the next adherent. The music is usually that of the drum, and the whole process of this rite is to cause a mild or deep state of auto-hypnosis. Whilst involved in these perambulations the Words are uttered. For instance, a state of possession is desired so that the Goddess may descend, to do this the Athame is held in front of the recipient and the attention focussed upon the symbol 'O' - 'G'. The edge of the knife is held towards the adherent, eventually the eyes begin to go out of focus and then the Words and Names of Power are uttered in a voice that evidently comes from the diaphragm. The name of the Goddess is uttered over and over again in a monotonous chant e.g. EvoH, EvaH, EvoHA! Blessed be, Wise and Blessed is G......Veh! This is accompanied with the perambulating walk I have already described. I should think that the chant and walk has a rhythm connected with the heart movements e.g. 1234-1234-1234, or 123456,123456, or 1-2-3-4, 1624. The names of the gods are found in the Arthurian legends, and it must be remembered that the real variation is upon the end of the chanted Name, and within the rhythmic structure of the chant and dance itself. Everything is dependent upon a constant form of activity. At a crucial point the rhythm is changed and the 'pacing' gets faster and the chant more empathic. At this particular point the witch has her eyes closed and is busy focussing the total attention upon a symbol such as the Goddess 'O' swinging against a black background. The pacing is anti-clockwise for the Goddess and clockwise for the God (Moon and Sunwise). The tools are useful only inasmuch as they focus attention to begin with, but all these actions must be combined together to produce the effect required. It is obviously upon this count that the Tree Calendar can be pressed into service, or a book of symbols created from ceremonial magic, but it must be remembered that the 'swing' system of thought and visualisation must always be used. For instance a dance to bring down the moon would be proceeded not only by prayer but by a dance to the god. In the Craft everything works to the opposite effect. E.G. First say 'soap' constantly, then say 'water' constantly. They are opposites yet are complimentary to each other.

These symbols are carved or burned upon the Athame. The Staff has carved upon it the symbol of the God. The cord is used to bind various pressure points to cause a change in consciousness. Each tool and I think there may be some thirteen, has a symbol of its particular use or power carved upon it. The meaning of the symbols upon the Athame are:

'This circle is by the Goddess made.

This arrow be the God's domain.

These snakes are the halves of thee.

This triad be thy past and thy birth.

This cross be the element of love.

These four and these five are sacred things;

Let not thy mouth be saying these.'

All magical work, from curing ingrowing toenails to Drawing down the Moon are done in this fashion.

Reverse page:

Hand written note on the reverse of this typed document is allegedly in Bowers' hand, but again is very difficult to authenticate, especially because of the variant spelling here also of 'Chalkie' —note also the inclusion of two endearing terms: 'old' and 'love.' The signature is also very ambiguous and could as easily say Ron as Roy.

Dear Old Chalkie,

Take care of this, it is dangerous stuff. I think that I have broken the Kings. Your intuition was right. It is Gwen and Arthur, Gwen/evo! GWEN/EVE! Had a bad time with the witches, explain when I meet – Can you come down this weekend? I have a lot to discuss with you. I think they may be after me. Love Roy [Ron?]

X............................X

159

(g) Drawing Down the Moon (long version)

Notes: Not Bowers' - Probably Ronald White's?

– used later in The Regency?

The handwritten annotations to the damaged sections better resemble Reginald Hinchcliffe's handwriting? The typed text suggests that it is also not the same typewriter Bowers' normally used which has a distinctive rise on the letter 'T'. However, his machine was used interchangeably by Chalky and George before Bowers' death and so identification is not always so easy to determine. Some of the documents from the Hinchcliffe folder contains a lot of re-typed material, something both Gills and Wilson freely admit to doing with the sections of Bowers' letters and documents they had access to , and which both of them then went on to use as teaching material with their own students. This document specifically, was easily identified by V. Jones as: *very typical of Ronald White in terms of style and content – and certainly not Roy's.* 'Of course it is also very possible that this may have been an example of an early document composed r at least influenced in its composition by 'Everley,' or by persons in the group White was part of. Remember too Norman (Gills) was a one time member there too.

Transcript: Drawing down the Moon. (long version)

This is the basic ceremony of witch practise. It is the invocation of the Goddess to manifest through her devotees. The discipline is strict and absolute for this ceremony. It is the basis of all but one of the festivals and is consummated. At no time is the circle broken, and the pacing and dancing is long and continuous. The aim is to complete a magical circuit and enlighten the initiates as to the Being of the Goddess. In other words, you are opening yourself to the influx of Cosmic energy.

Tools are Sword, Necklace, Phallus, Four Elements, Willow Wands,

Flowers, budding branches etc. Perfumes, Cinnamon and Sandlewood incense. Oils sandlewood perfumed. Symbols the Full Moon and Pentagramic Star, also painted moons upon black background. The moon and star should be made of white metal and highly polished. In some cases, the star is repeated to the number of couples in the circle, that is six silver stars. The normal procedure of purification will be held (water and oil) all tools will be censed and consecrated. A small sturdy table is required, capable of taking the weight of the Mistress as altar. Strictures and disciplines. The Initiate will fast for eight hours previously and abstain from coitus for four days. The Master and Mistress will fast for twenty-four hours previously and abstain from coitus for a week. They will also spend one hour during the previous evening, meditating upon the being of the Goddess.

Procedure. The Coven will assemble four hours before twelve-o-clock and begin at half past eleven, upon the actual preparations of power (dancing). The room or place of worship will be kept clean, censed and purified previously. Talking with be kept to a minimum, the circle will be laid with double lining and with the moon motif, repeated to the four elements, with silver facing outwards (this aspect is bride and young mother). A white bandage, copper wire or silken cord is a good way of laying the circle. The coven will then sit and meditate upon the following seed thoughts for a duration of not less than twenty minutes. 'In thee we live, move and find our being' and as a chaser 'as above so below'. When the period has passed the coven will begin the process of charging themselves with the body of light as shown in the accompanying diagram. This star is designed to open the correct psychic centres and will only open if it is followed correctly, as such it must be learned by heart. When the coven is charged the Mistress will undertake the charging of the circle. She invokes towards the east, then outlines the star, then draws the circle. The Initiates will then see a column of light appear in the centre rising to eight feet, supporting a star containing a chalice from which multi-coloured light pours out and centres the circle and its periphery. (the centre column is white sparkling light shot with glimmering blue, and the pouring out is white with background hues of the colours of the earth. This alters slightly with each different rite).

The Initiates will then enter the circle and be greeted by the Mistress with a kiss, and kneel about the Priestess, she then utters the following short prayer 'Mistress, Queen, thy presence we ask. Thy indulgence we crave. Hear our prayer now for fertility to the earth and to women. And thy blessing upon all things that prosper beneath thy light.' She will then lie across the table and become the altar. The elements and greenery are put upon her. The Priest will then take each circle and lift them towards the sky and towards the east, afterwards he will sprinkle her with water and then symbolically co-habit with her, with the earth, with the phallus. The coven meanwhile will have a joined rapport with the Priestess by 'cornering' her with four willow wands. The articles will be handed out of the circle to the Summoner and the Priestess will come to her feet followed by the females of the coven who will then be worshiped according to the ancient tradition as fertility incarnate (the five-fold kiss). Afterwards the coven will circle the Priestess by their cords and begin outside pace anti-clockwise with the wands. They will utter the following chant and prayer.

'Queen G. Evah, Thy blessings, thy presence we crave.
Fill our souls with thy being. This is our home we offer.
This our land we have prepared for thee.
Our love, mind and spirit is thine to do with what ye will.
O Mother G. Divine Star hear our simple prayer and descend, for

we are betwixt heaven and earth for thee.

The woodland mourns for thee.

Man and women feel thy loss.

O come our Queen, oh come to us.

Or else the land be desolate and the crops undone.

And love will not spring again from the young.

Oh Mother G., woman and star hear our simple prayer.

We guilty children grieve our loss.

We mourn for thy being.

We are but children by thy breast.

Cherish us with your presence.

Bless us with your word.

Thy name we call as children in the dark.

Oh Mother G., woman and star.

Divinity bright hear our prayer.'

After this has been effected, turn inwards and begin the centre rim[sic] which is always clockwise. This takes the form of a simple repetitive chant that I will work out. The Priestess now leads the circle and everyone turns upon the central star and glyph. When she has realised that the pace has built up sufficiently and the necessary peak of power has been achieved, she will deliver the following prayer of Invocation.

Nobody else will speak whilst this is being said.

'Oh Blessed woman. Heavenly star,

Bride of the young king.

Queen of the year. O flower bride hear our prayer.

Ea Evah Geh!

O you who was here before the earth was formed.

163

O you of the soundless bitter sea.

Out of whose depths life wells eternally.

All tides are thine and answer thee.

Tides of the air, tides the inner earth.

The secret silent tides of death and birth.

Tides of souls of dreams and destiny

Thy Priestess pray that Ye answer we.

O That that was before the earth was born,

O arching sky and earth beneath,

Giver of life and bringer of death,

Persephone, Astarte, Ashtoreth.

O golden Aphrodite come to us,

Flowerer of foam, star of sea,

Bringer of dreams that rule destiny

Thy Priestess calls to thee

Eternal woman, Eternal She

Holy Blessed G.

Giver of life, breath of morning

Thy Priestess prays to thee.

Moon, moon that draweth us.

Bride, Mistress, Glorious Dawn.

I am thy Priestess, answer unto we.'

The rite has now taken on its inspirational form it will manifest according to the abilities of the Initiates. Prepare yourselves well!

X................................X

1963: First significant change in depth and of direction.

(h) Letters from Bowers to William Gray:
i - #IX
ii - #III
iii – Mission Statement for the Society of Keridwen
Notes: (1) Not composed by Roy Bowers

Transcript of #IX

Ta everso for the letter. We seem to be gradually extending our range of subject matter until these letters of ours stretch from here to this side of the grave. Occultism, though, is man, so presumably whatever part of it one decides to examine, one always ends up with more knowledge and more detail than one was originally bargaining for. Probably like that old saw of art teachers about the one model who can be sculpted by an artist for his total working like, and still remain undiscovered.

Agreed about the fuller life of the past. I for my part have a distinct impression of being a rough old bastard, but as you say, we all lived then, felt, loved, hated, desired and all for real. This century has had the effect of making everything genteel, clouding the pang of life in clouds of deodorant. Everything is so nice, everything is so grey and completely without taste. We are all Victorian gentlewomen neatly stitched into a twentieth century, that is not really nice or so easy going as the ad man and mass consumer redi-mix culture would have us believe. I feel that one day someone is going to kick over the scenery, then we will all see the bare brick walls of the theater. I have more than a shrewd suspicion that it is this that affects the boys who tore up the seaside towns, it is there that the real mass castration has taken place. Where the desires of millions of genteel people have coalesced into the monstrosities known as sea side holidays, 'getting away from it all' and having a good time. Youth with its good instincts, decided to try and kick the whole sorry mess over by doing everything that is again the mass concept of the good life and the genteel way. When they are more mature and have stopped warring amongst themselves, we may see some interesting things from this generation.

As for the modern artist, he is a poet without a theme, afraid of looking outside himself because it hurts his precious sensitivity, warbling around inside his own head, a delightful little love affair with himself. I was listening to one explain a painting of a woman, and I realised that he wasn't talking about woman as she is, but the pitiful creation of himself that he called woman. One day they must all realise that reality is outside not inside, and that reality hurts as well as teaches. So what if naked truth does kill the man who looks upon her, at least our kind have had the fun of the chase. A little iconoclasm is the best emetic for the indigestion of modern life.My own opinion is that this is the age of the drums, when somewhere from the inner planes a war drum is beating, calling all men of good intent together and to arms before it is too late. Sooner or later we must face the enemies of life and decide once and for all who and what is going to be the guiding light of this planet. Mars himself is esoteric at times, and I feel that there has been a dangerous infiltration from the Firbolg, the children of Dylan and darkness are covering the old human light.

Poverty is a good master, a bad bedfellow though. I was born in a slum, one of eight children. I have had riches in the places where they really count, I have also known genuine hunger though. There is something to be learned from it, now I can look back upon some things with quiet joy, not because they were good at the time, but because I have learned the lesson from them. One thing about poverty is that it teaches compassion as well as anger, but its biggest drawback is frustration, frustration at never having the right things at the right time, of being at the mercy of anyone who employs you, of being constantly misunderstood. I personally would rather walk behind the plough than be in my present job, but this at least is skilled and offers me some escape from the run of work that is open to people like myself.

Destiny .... destiny the one word that means so much and is so very real and unreal together. I personally believe strongly in destiny, but although I can see it for others and sometimes for nations, myself to myself is a closed book. I do know there is something afoot, some force that controls me, not I it. Maybe a son born to some old carpenter somewhere, who is just gathering his wits together to say 'Follow me! I keep on getting the feeling that we are preparing ground for a crop that we will not reap, waiting for a dawn that may never come, but wait we must. We are force for something else that is to occur, the creators of opinion for a new concept that is arising somewhere in the world. The St. Johns the Baptists, hundreds strong, waiting, waiting, waiting. So far the new word hasn't come through, but it will , that I feel certain of. I am also certain of the workers of the inner planes. The one who I see is a man dressed in sixteenth century costume, cloaked and with a cynical smile. I have heard him speak and surprisingly he spoke with a broad accent that must have been sixteenth century English.

It was the very first time I saw the Power we call God, at least a representative of Her. That night both Jane and I were sleeping, and I woke up suddenly to find myself sitting upright in my own body, half in half out. A dark form was in the room with me, and I was genuinely frightened. Protesting weakly, I was <u>hauled</u> out of myself and taken to a wood, where I saw my master for the first time. He was dressed as I described him, and said *Here comes the Lass. Let us worship Her*. I looked up from the ground where I was laying (The moss was so distinct and so real that every individual plant stood out clearly in the most brilliant green) and saw coming through the oak trees a white Light , and I realised that it was a naked woman on horseback, but brilliant pure light also. I have never felt anything like I did then before or since, but then I was shot back to myself with a thundering crash, and got out of bed trembling and shaking. It wasn't for many years afterwards that I realised that what I had seen was the cosmic power we call truth. However since that time I have believed very strongly in the Inner Planes, and have occasionally seen my Master. I also know that when he bends his will to a task, there is no gainsaying , it must be done or else.

Of course all this may be illusion, but like yourself, I have an inner conviction that is stronger than all the psychiatric texts ever written. We do what we are told, protesting complaining, even whining, but we do what we are told, not because we are slaves to something running loose in our own heads, but because whatever it is that writes out the company orders , knows. I seem to remember something about Liz standing with her feet apart, puffing away at a clay pipe in one of the pieces of historical research I take up occasionally. She was an out and out pagan, that is if I am to believe what was written about her by various poets. There is an interesting inscription on a <u>door</u> at Hampton Court which refers to her as Diana, and gives her all the classical attributes of the Goddess of Hounds and hunting.

I would very much like to join you at Glastonbury Tor, since these places are <u>doorways</u> (Stonehenge is a collection of door lintels) . Perhaps we can work our differing patterns together at fifteen paces and see what results we can get. Midsummer is my big night, or the nearest I can get to it. Quite simply our ritual falls into this pattern:

<u>This is the Taper that lights the way.</u>
This is the Cloak that covers the Stone,
That sharpens the Knife

That cuts the Cord
That Binds the Staff
That's owned by the Maid
Who tends the fire
That boils the Pot
That scalds the Sword
That fashions the Bridge
That crosses the ditch
That compasses the hand
That knocks the door,
That fetches the watch
That releases the man
That turns the mill
That grinds the corn
That makes the cake
That feeds the hound
That guards the gate
That hides the maze
That's worth a light
And into the castle that Jack built.

As you can see, it is a child's game, but one that works. We use a skull as much in the same fashion as the Knights Templars, but Mithraic worship is out for us, two differing concepts. The druids, however, were eastern in origin, they again superimposed a different pattern upon the aboriginal gods of the Kelts. They were supposed by the Romans to have more magic than the rest put together, however they were a bloody minded lot. It you want to use nature magic, then you must work outside, preferably by running water, or failing that, as high as you can get. It must be open to the four winds, since they carry the seeds of life and destruction, and they represent your four elements. The earth should be disturbed, and preferably a small sacrifice made of wheaten meal or wine. Working amongst timber tends to put too much wildness in the results, since it is the dark forest of Pan. The more water there is the better, the best sources of all is near a country churchyard, but be very careful of that one since you are liable to disturb the 'watchers' and they are something to be reckoned with .There are no hard and fast rules, it must be played by ear. The sense of power is usually denoted by a sensation of extreme panic, then comes the 'gathering' in you feel that you are being surrounded by hosts of 'watchers'. You may possibly see them out of the corner of your eye, these must be ignored, and the panic overcome.

Then there comes a cold blast of wind, and the power which is being asked for begins the manifestation, this will appear in the form that you expect to see, the main difficulty is in holding it, since (and I speak from experience) it is rather like being hit with a hammer. Usually green, brilliant lights flash on and off in the centre of the working space. Incidentally you will find that a metal sieve placed in a central position gives no end of aid, and acts as a form of working grid for the force that the power is using to transmute its own energy. Once he is established then is the time to ask the questions, and the answers may not come just then, but come they will. Whatever you do, resist the temptation to panic or to feel that 'everything is going wrong' The Farmer has a reputation for affecting human beings in this fashion (hence the words 'panic', 'pandemonium', etc.) Here is a short prayer that may help to consolidate:

'My Lord .....
Here I be stripped of all finery.
No clothes, lover or home have I Excepting by thy Grace

Master, I have descended the Paths towards Thy gates ...

Leaving all but my truthful spirit behind me.

Here am I as naked as the sea , as the sky ,

As grave winter itself.

I pray Thee take pity on me and listen unto my prayer.

The invokation of Earth may help you:

I do conjure Thee, Earth

Now in the secret hour of night Ebb and flow meeting

And as for my place precisely stand centered

By this the mystery of my craft

Entrenched I see the boundary round

And of aught else, naught but the riding moon.

And these possess my thought and soul

Facing my truth to them

For I do desire no other thought but these,

For since long time I do require to learn The Truth of Truths

Yea Verily have I suffered to achieve the life becoming spirit

And know that good and evil will prevail within no forced equality

Circle and moon be gracious unto me.' (1)

Basically nature magick is very simple, it is as simple as doing it , but like all simple things, it has some fantastic fortifications behind it. Witches believe that all things are One and joined, there is no singular (except human beings - Law of correspondence). To create spiritual effect, - one must create physical effect , and to work nature magic, you must first do natural things. There are dangers though, these are in effect leaving anything undone. Once you have achieved your purpose, leave everything as you found it, or else you will spend some uncomfortable nights with nature spooks clomping around your room, taking it out of you for disturbing them.

They are elemental and know not conscience as we know it. However they can be tamed and kept by you as a friend. My family had one for years and he delights in practical jokes. According to how he has been used, so he has become, and I think Tomkins was used unnecessarily for tangle foot work. Once he took an evil delight in appearing before some friends of ours and worrying them silly , but we took him in hand over that one and he behaved himself. There is a possibility that he was responsible for playing the fool and making Bobby make errors in her map. However he is easily seen, and cannot resist making loud thumps and clangs upon metal objects (possibly a left over from the days when iron was taboo to him). He usually is seen as a large black cat or dog , if you do catch him out, tell him off and send him back. But apart from all my personal natter Robin Goodfellow was no figament of the imagination. They are mischievous, unfriendly at times, and completely unreliable unless you twist their tails. They will take a delight in leading you on, and generally making a nuisance of themselves. You will find that once they sense you are out to try and work nature magick, they will fool around all the time, tripping you up , leading you around in circles and so on. Once you begin though, they will be quiet and even help you to achieve your aim. Position five is your best defence against their unsociable side, position six is your best way of making friends with them.

As you say the teenagers are using magic all the time. If they but knew it they are doing what their direct ancestors called 'raising Cain'. All that noise, sexual hysteria and so on is a dangerous force to play with, and that is what the Beatles are doing. I would never be surprised to read that (a) a meeting of R&B had evolved into a fertility rite, and (b) that one of the Beatles has come to a very bloody and untimely end, a la

172

primitive magic as the God of Vegetation. They are obviously tools of older forces that seek an outlet in our age, and what better than the twelve year olds who is basically everything man was at that particular period?

I have no knowledge of astrology at all, since it would be a bad mistake for me to know too many types of divination at once. I base my own divination upon three things , my intuit ion, Tarot cards and my left hand. At this very moment , my hand is telling me about your past lives. The one nearest to you for instance , you were in the occupations of Mars, Venus had too much control over your head, and that you were in the seat of Jupiter which you treated like a fool. Through Mars, via. Venus, you came to an untimely end, and left with regret a life that satisfied the worse part of you. In this life you have gone to Mercury as a counterbalance and have succeeded in balancing the effect of the past. Now is the time when you can step forward, but remourse for your past is holding you back, there is little or no opposition to you advancing in occultism now, you have paid the price. My wrist hurts like crazy, so from this I conclude that in the last life, no, the one before that, you were in some fashion a prisoner or a cripple caused through circumstances of birth, or possibly your parent of that life died giving birth to you. These are only rough readings given as I sit here at the typewriter. However I will do it properly for the next letter.

I write as I speak, that is how I can do so much, that and a few years at knocking off a thousand words a day. We must really try and get our heads together and see if we can work at some piece of nature magic. As I said I would love to work at Glastonbury Tor, it would be ideal. Perhaps when we meet we can compare notes and find out if there is a common way. Regards, Roy and Jane.

X....................................X

ii #III Bowers to Bill Gray

Notes: After some discussion with Bill Gray Bowers sets up a public contact association—'The Society of Kerridwen.' This next document after Bill Gray's letter appears to be the 'Introductory Mission Statement' sent out to its members. It is not known how many this involved. Hoping to extend his networking into other groups practising traditional forms of craft, he asks if Bill knows of any real witch cuveens? He emphasises this naturally excludes those of Gerald Gardner's line. Bowers says he knows of two only that are genuine, one of which he believes is near to Bill Gray. Without further validation, he dismisses them as probable hearsay. Entering into quite a tirade against the excess and frivolities of the liberating forays into sexual emancipation his generation have over-indulged in, Bowers reveals his maturity in stepping away from it, and how his yearning now obsesses in the Mysteries of his Faith and Culture. Disillusionment had crept in and he mourns the lack of similar conviction in the Craft or Faith of those around him. This changed dramatically once Evan John Jones joined his 'troupe.' There is an obvious refinement by E. J. Jones from the rather long-winded invocation expressed in 'Drawing Down the Moon' Doc (g) to:

> "For I am She who is as old as Time
> For I was here before the world began
> For I am the Earth that takes the Furrow
> For I am the Furrow that takes the seed
> For I am the bringer of Life and the bringer of Death
> For I am the Womb and the Tomb together."

Bowers was also to vastly simplify the 'Drawing Down the Moon

Rite' - see doc (y). They speak of Bills illness, of the promise to charm him in to health and of the High Magics of qabbala.

Transcript of #III to Bill Gray

Thanks for your letter. Oh well, so much for J.M.—Evidentally she belongs to the 'wanting' group rather than the 'having'...

Agreed as to the phallic basis of the Qabalists Rod. In spite of all the evidence to the contrary, the witches staff or 'stang' as we name it, is not phallic, but has the same position as the Tree of Life in your system, with Knife and Cord as Father and Mother Pillars. Of course the basic meanings are very similar, but the symbology and the use is very different. The Phallus (a symbolical staff make from Alder wood) is quite a different proposition and is very rarely brought into being. It is in fact the handle of the Broom, and has usually been carved to quite interesting traditional patterns. (See diagrams (pp))

The Broom we have has a carved face and writing all over it. Kether to Malkuth or Malkuth to Kether, what a thorny remark to make. Obviously one has to replace anything that one takes out, but how this is done is usually one of the deep secrets. The Christians use Divine Love as the input and output, but that is rather a matter for speculation, since disinterested service is rarely without pitfalls. The essence of all magical undertakings is balance, without it anything and everything seems to happen. You and I have a basis for some disagreement here, from what I can gather the Qabalists regard Nature as being limited to a cyclic phenomena with limitations upon the actual scope of the phenomena. Witches would disagree philosophically with this concept, saying that Nature Is, and that whatever Man is so is Nature, since Man and Nature, like Beast and Nature are one and the same thing. All known relationships and many 'unknown' ones are to be found within natural laws.

The supernatural never comes into it. The Planes are extentions of the Dark Side of the Moon, where Nature ultimately fails is that Nature is illusion as we see Nature, but not as Nature really is. What a magician of any school would describe as transmutation, is in actual fact, just an increasing perception into the deeper aspects of Nature. All mystical perception is based upon the fact that we go to God, not that God comes to us. There are as many ways of seeing God as there are creations of God, and each individual creation is the Totality, the Hand that Writes as well as the Writing. What is lacking is perception, that is what makes the Path so bloody and so long. Still enough of the Truth department, let us put down the shutters.

Now what are you to do with the charm. I will tell you after the X-ray. One word of warning though, never take anything that a witch says literally, when they have been working on you. We are up to all sorts of psychological trickery, and as I have often remarked, in witchcraft nothing is quite what it appears to be For my money, though, the charm has already worked. You feel better.

Agreed about whooping it up occasionally, and about the high mindedness of Qabalistic magic. It is too rigid a la Dion Fortune standards, and so inflexible that eventually it will fracture like glass. It is not that the Qabalah reccomends this particular attitude, but that some of the practitioners have put unresolved inhibitions and repressions into their interpretation of it. Surely to be good one doesn't have to be constantly moral also? The Vase that is of the greatest beauty is often the one with some small carelessness in its design, rigid design can be the ruination of an otherwise perfect object. The way we regard 'magick' is that it is a fluid, moving, flowing, force, usually started with a laugh and end in deadly seriousness. For my money Violet (Shrinking?! !!) Firth was obsessed by perfectionism, that (a) she has cheerfully kiboshed the chances of anyone finding joy through the practice of her particular interpretation, and that (b) she was sexually out of balance, hence the perfectionism. In fact some riotous living would have made a different woman out of her, much more human and fluid. Quite apart from Violet Firth though, the menopausic state is usually the motive behind much feminine prudism, and that again has nothing to do with 'Nature', but with unresolved catchments of basic energies. Eileen Garret is my favourite femme terrible, she is without a basic problem anywhere, and absolutely truthful. Which you must admit is really something amongst the dun dreary females of the occult and spiritualist world. (Bobbie and Sandra apart). I don't know about 'glamour' but I do know that genuine friendliness can make for more in a group than anything else.

Whooping it up, part two. Orgiastic behaviour. Oh Brother William, Brother William I am in complete agreement with riots, getting drunk, having big scenes , eating too much, sleeping too much, making love to pretty girls, laughing, poking gentle fun, talking too much, going to bed with the woman you love and then sleeping it all off ...... occasionally.I do all these things, but never when I know that they will bring unhappiness in the wake of the general the jolly confusion. Unfortunately the majority of people in our society are incapable of doing any of the above things without being unhappy afterwards. Puritanical inhibition brings some terrible messes in its wake, and the happy playmate of yesterday is quite liable to wake up and brood about hangovers, who said what to him, and lost maidenheads, twentieth century man has no wildness worth talking about and absolutely no spontaneity. He or she is a guilty transgressor once they let things slide for a bit. I personally like the idea of the orgia believing it to be one of the best steam safety valves ever invented by a loving God, but genuine orgies have to be spontaneous in order to work and remain clean. The ones I've been to all wanted (a) sexual performances as a religious ritual accompanied by chanting and words of power (b) as an organised group performance, discussed seriously beforehand, with notes and editorial comments upon performance, endurance, each others sexual deviations, and the partners expectations, 'Who sleeps with who and I bags the prettiest girl'.

Honestly they were the sorriest, most morbid inhibited orgies of any time and of anywhere, and there is always someone who is obsessed with whips or 'servants', voyarism, which makes the whole atmosphere as clean as pig manure. Orgies have to be spontaneous if they are to work, and amongst the types who make a practice of them spontaneity is completely unknown. One we went to had all the usual beginnings , and terribly intellectual it was and all, at last someone actually made a pornographic joke and everyone smiled in that nice cultured way that 'clever' people have. Then it was politely suggested that we should all undress, and get drunk. We undressed and got drunk, then someone else lit joss sticks, put a 'hot' record on the player and began the serious business of having an orgy. Jane and I asked for our pants back and left, but from what I was told afterwards, someone actually got up and changed the record in the middle of it all. All very well if you like copulating on a dusty carpet, but I suffer from hay fever, and get sore knees very quickly. Have an orgy? No thanks, I'm trying to give them up. Used to get through twenty a day at one time .... Happy , happy youth.

I would like to discuss the exorcism with you when we meet, perhaps the second or third week of July. I agree with the need for a magical association. Now, as you say, what do we do? I suggest that we advertise in the N.D. constantly, and let 'em organise themselves. We will have a minimum of paperwork, disorganise any attempt to organise committees and generally run an introductory service, with a possible draft telling of all the services and organisations we can put them into contact with. Let them find their own levels, and the ones interested in genuine occultism will be known by the signs, the old lady brigade will organise themselves into the usual tea party, and just for kicks we will introduce all the sexual cases to the old ladies, that way we will put one variety off and bring untold excitement to widowed mothers and emasculated men (Honestly, there is a place in the other world where one bloody great tea party goes on and on for all eternity. I think they call it 'Heaven' or some such name). We will have to charge fees for hiring halls, but I will back the advertisements until it gets going. One fly in the ointment, though. Publicity, I hate it. Do you know anyone who would be willing to have their name advertised? (Incidentally, tell D.V. to keep the newspaper reporter away from me, or else I will <u>not</u> be responsible for MR Roberts general health or well being). A few wining and dancing sessions will be a good idea also.

Our cats name is 'Jinxie', otherwise known as Madam, very dignified , plump and aristocratic, but she has a tendancy towards gypsy lovers and slumming. Hates my myhna, who hates her. So far the bird is one up, since he got the first bite in. Jinxie wouldn't come in for three days after that event.

Enjoy your holiday. We have got to go to Weymouth, serves me right ... Regards to all.

X..............................X

iii Bowers—Society of Keridwen Mission Statement

Notes: Copy of a letter possibly devised for the contact group Bowers discussed with Gray in **#III**. It describes itself as a Society established for exactly that purpose. There is no other reference or discussion concerning itself with such a contact group, only this one example shown here, discussed with Bill Gray. More and more information begins to correlate a context for the period of transition around 1963 which generates a huge production of material over the course of 1965 to replace all the scant few documents he'd been familiar with from his early encounters with the London people. Early Missives drafted there and for his early coven formed in Slough, largely written for Ronald White's continuing group of less committed associates, and which show White's influence if not direct authorship [eg: Theory of Witch Practice, Drawing Down the Moon and Dance forms] are abandoned and set aside for new works drafted upon an entirely different ethos and mythos. Terms and language used thereafter are wholly at odds with anything prior to it.

Transcript of the The Society of Keridwen Letter

Dear Friend,

Thank you for your letter and interest in us. We are a body known as the Society of Keridwen, named after the Celtic Goddess of poetry and mysticism. We are of recent origin dating from an advertisement entered in the columns of the 'Sunday Observer' last October. The people who responded to the advertisement decided that there must be many more of us, hence the advertisement that you answered.

The Society is a body interested in the structure, practise and belief of the religion of our common ancestors. The aims of the Society are to exchange knowledge, promote artistry among literary groups amongst members who seem to be working with common symbolism, and to examine some of the theological, medical, occult and philosophical that have remained after the persecution. The Society also intends to dispel some of the ignorance and superstition that surrounds the Old religion and promote further advertisements. At some future date we will establish groups of interested people throughout the country, an disuse lists of addresses to such groups so that they may expand also, thereby having a fluid and decentralised organisation. We have no membership or charges whatsoever, although members will be expected to pay for the cost of materials, if they desire information from a central library we intend to establish.

I hope on behalf of the Society that we may have an opportunity to meet later. We will contact you again when a suitable meeting place has been arranged.

Will you please enclose a stamped and addressed envelope with any future correspondence. Yours sincerely, R. L. Bowers

X......................................X

(i) Letters from Bowers to Bill Gray i - #X, & ii -#I

Notes: Bowers offers Bill Gray his birth-date for natal analysis. He tells Bill that he will first discuss the matter of publishing an article on their Cave Rite with the boys (Arthur, Dick & Sean and John), then write it, then post the article onto Bill to deliver to the Magazine editor, commenting this may be best *"since you know the address."* Bill obviously forwarded it to Bowers; in letter **#VI** Bowers thanks him for it, and says he will use it. He discusses Shakespeare, Clans and makes hints concerning the mystical realms Graves hints at, whilst astutely recognising those castles and kingdoms are not the sole domain of a 'Celtic' (sic) based system. He informs Bill that the Clan work outdoors, something quite unique at that time, hinting yet further that he aware of other more eastern systems, and that he knows how to manipulate virtue within the self and how to 'coax' it to manifest form within ritual. He has obvious respect for Bill's knowledge and is keen to engage him on an intellectual level. Bowers is also very keen that Bill does not have the impression that whatever magics and beliefs he holds are not rustic or primitive. He is equally keen in another letter to dismiss Bill's question about that process as 'Necromancy'! Over the course of time he winds Bill over sufficiently to intrigue him enough to join the Clan and attend some of its Rites. He asserts his heritage and how the old clan systems operated culturally in these Isles.

(1) Witch-Blood—Bowers alludes to the peculiar anomaly of the 'call' to blood and bone which often misses at least one generation, becoming an irresistible force of life for the next to be fated into. Brandishing the spiritual banner of the Faith, its survival is secured through the Tanist system of the old clans, wherein the natural selection of succession and continuity falls always to an adult, usually the lineaged progeny of the current leader's elderly male relative.

(see 'Crafting the Arte of Tradition' for a full explanation)

(2) Witch's Compass – the true 'Ring of Arte' and not to be confused in any way with the Magician's Circle. This distinction again is fundamental to the divergence between Traditional Craft and The Wica, which is very much constructed upon the Circle and not the Ring (see *Tubelo's Green Fire* for a full explanation).

Transcript of #X to Bill Gray

Ta ever so for your interesting letter. Like yourself, I enjoy writing. I have even had gear published in the *New Statesman*, but apart from personal correspondence, I never write anything connected with witchcraft. I have to discuss everything like that with the boys, and as such it will be a decision of the group. Thanks a lot for the suggestion, though, very kind of you. I will probably post the article to you, since you know the address.

Shakespeare really knew his witchcraft. I have a wild theory that he spent some time in one of the more advanced clans; and that it was during his service that he first gave birth to the silver tongue. Nearly all witchcraft of the school I belong to, wrap its secrets in blank verse and kennings. Robert Graves in his 'White Goddess' writes a great deal on nonsense about many things, (mainly because he tries to explain everything), but he was absolutely accurate when he wrote that the protean Goddess was the true inspirer of the poet, and that all real poetry must deal with the themes that She is Mistress of. Shakespeare never deviated from these themes, and in many of his works, paganism is far more apparent than Christianity.

His 'Wives' for instance, derives from a very ancient Keltic legend, and gives an accurate description of rural witchcraft at its simplest. The same theme appears in 'Lear' which for me is pure paganism at its noblest and best. The characters of Lear are archetypes of the major legend. The fool is by no means a fool, but very much the simple god. Lear is the old god of death. Even Geoffrey of Monmouth could not quite confuse the issue, and the essential truth still remains in his hodge-podge of mythology and racial memory. The latter day Wica should read Shakespeare, then throw the Aradia overboard.

Our land of the dead, Apple Island, Avalon, Caerochren ... is a place that to the image fixed mind, appears as a wooded countryside, with a bleak sea shore. Across deep pasture, lie hills that rise blue heads to the lowering sky. By the sea and across the woods is a small hamlet;

'There you and I my loves
There you and I will lie,
When the cross of ressurection is broken
And our time has come to die.
For no more is there weeping
For no more is there death.
Only the golden sunset ,
Only the golden rest.'   (witch song)

The woods are dark and terrible, and must be entered by crossing a stream. There the coward withers, the faintheart retreats, for it is there that Childe Rolande must blow the snail horn trumpet, and face the enemy whom no man can ever unhorse. (Browning). The other planes I have no knowledge of, except in the unconscious as all of us do. My mind is almost totally directed day in, day out to the Akashics, where I unravel the silver thread. There has been so much lost, and so very little time to find it again.

To work witch magic properly one must work out of doors, buildings, unless ectoplasmic displays are required, are useless and destroy 'Virtue'. Outdoors is the law for us, and it is also the law of correspondence necessary to the higher ritual. Nudity, although we do not practice it, has a good psychological effect, for the uninhibited types who are the latter day pagans. I understand, although this may not be correct, that they also regard nudity essential as a means to what they describe as power. Obviously scourging is also strongly favored because of this. It again is supposed to produce 'Power'. Probably something to do with the release of adrenaline and its decayed by-products to produce psychological effects. Since they seem to run until they are in a thoroughly suggestive state, the suggestion plays a greater part in this than the scourge. I personally have very little time for such primitive behaviour from subtopians. It is 'all in the blood' as one of them told me. In the past the whip was used because of its symbolic correspondence. The 'Devil' or his summoner chased the others in a grim game of 'Hare and Hound'. It is a good way of bringing home the attraction of death, as well as the attraction of life, and a better way of imprinting a 'party line' I have never yet come across. Once someone has learned the symbology that way, they are very unlikely to forget it again. Forbid that we should use it today though. Nothing can ever remain still. Thought must either grow or corrupt. <u>To retain a primitive pattern is to corrupt minds and souls.</u> The path we have chosen was thrust upon us. (How's that for mangling English). "Thereby," he said, filling his pipe, "Hangs a strange story." "Tell me, Sir Humphrey," she whispered, her china blue eyes opening slightly ... My great granddad was the last grand master of the Staffordshire witches. It has evidently been in the family since at least the seventeenth century, since there are definite records from that period. Even the house my father was born in was between the borders of Staffordshire and Warwickshire, so that when there was danger of arrest, the family moved from one section of the house to the other. Anyway in the arch age of materialism, my grandparents decided to renounce the gods and took up Methodism instead for Sunday afternoons. Thereupon my great grandfather was very angry and cursed them. This curse has decimated my family through the years and generations. Nearly all of them died in misery or violence. Whereupon I was born, which was probably the curse at its worst. My father who was agin witchcraft, took one look at me, and said, "Gawd, the old bastard's come back." (My father was a Guard's R.S.M.) and promptly made my mother swear never to tell me the terrible truth of my heritage. However, I had my first mystical awareness of the Gods at the age of five, and since then have progressed in my career. I am a professional, it is not because I am interested in it, but because it is interested in me. However after I learned the truth from my mother, after my father's death, and then went to see my aunt Lucy, who is a terrible old woman. She taught me the five arts and the tradition. However, the witch teaching official line, is that witch blood must be possessed to gain the ear of the Gods, and that witch blood reoccurs every second or third generation, and in the same pattern physically. (1) In other words only witches can bear witches, and to be without the heritage is the most terrible experience of all for a witch. It is literally slow torture. I personally would rather do anything than face the thirteen years of the wilderness again; but only another witch would understand me.

The information about the nine foot magic circle sounds a bit false. I am very disinclined to believe it as a possible historical event. Everything in the theory points towards a laboured nineteenth century hand, inventing primitive man all over again. No twentieth century man likes to admit the possibility that it has all been done before. But in a different way with different means. However, this is literally what a <u>witch's compass</u> is, a highly efficient and scientific machine, and it requires science to use it properly. The Kelts built in stone and wood, the rush huts that were used until the sixteenth century for milking and cheese making were called 'wiccens,' which is a word that derives from the Saxons, and means [crafter and worker of] salt. It may well be that charms were used in the building of these. Against the simple rural craft it must be remembered that another tradition existed, of which very little is recorded. This is the Key of Kings.(2)

The witches blue band of hope and comradeship has been invented mainly by Mrs. Leek for her own amusement. They sent me a form to fill in which wanted to know all sorts of odd things. I very nearly returned it signed Mathew Hopkins. They would never have seen the joke or the danger. I can only say 'The Unknown God' help them if they ever meet a master of the black art. As it stands I have kept the form as evidence of my contention that they are out to make witchcraft respectable: which will kill it outright. Mrs Bone is the bosom pal of Charlie Cardell who describes himself as Rex Nemorensis, enough said. Incidentally , we sometimes all go out on Sundays for-a run in a friends car. Perhaps with your kind permission we could drop in and see you for an hour.

My birthdate 26.1.31. Time , 3 a.m. Place, London.

Our regards to your wife and yourself,

Flags and Flax, Roy and Jane

Notes: #1 In this next letter, Bowers goes to great lengths to explain to Bill how his understanding and way of working is neither shamanism or paganism, but mystical - crafted as the Mystery Traditions of old. There is a great deal said between the lines of their banter. Bowers speaks of medium-ship, of psi-powers and E.S.P., of the sciences of hypnotism and psychology, and of the Houzle in its true form as a sacrificial and Eucharistic Rite. This is a complex letter. It covers a lot of ground across a considerable spectrum of magical praxis and lore pertaining to magical belief. He does not exclude the Qabbala, but draws Bill Gray out on it. Prior to meeting Bill Gray some time later, Bowers made plans in the spring to meet up with him in Glastonbury in July at the Glastonbury Assembly Rooms for the free evening buffet—held by the Brotherhood of the Essenes as a more open celebration after the formality of their closeted annual Solstice meeting. That year, the BotE held an angelic rite up at the Tor, on St Michael's Mount! Bowers failed to meet Gray here again as planned, confirmed in letter <u>IV</u> in which Roy Bowers presents his excuses for not making it to Glastonbury, '*Sorry we didn't get the chance to visit you when we were on holiday, but the bloody distance was too long, and the buses too short*'. Bowers questions Bill about events that transpired in Glastonbury. He enquires of the nature possession from an 'Angelic Rite' Bill had discussed with him, and the troubles and problems often caused when invoking Michael. Bowers responded there by cautioning him, stating that Michael is not a faithful servant at that level. In so doing, Bowers leaves hints for Bill to enquire further into concerning the nature of the range of 'Otherworld' elementals and spirits as entities of sentience and of contact and interaction with them.

(1)   This chant is a variant of the ones used in Documents (b)-(g) above. Bowers' opinion here is without ambiguity; his disdain therefore does rather suggest he was not the author of those documents.

Transcript: Letter #1 Bowers to Gray

We did not realise that we might incovenience you at this particular time of the year; so we will postpone the visit until you are more able to recieve us. However, we would be delighted to meet you if you have any spare time during your forthcoming visit to London. I dig Jaqueline Murray also, she is quite a cat, man. I have never met her though, although I seem to remember something about the Atlantean Society, and a book published under the title of 'Daughter of Atlantis'. My only conclusion at the time was amazement at the number of books written by women who are interested in magic that either have the words 'daughter' or 'priestess' in the title. The trouble with women occultists as a whole, seems to be that they either have to be a blood relative of the Gods or at least the direct channel. Come to think of it, it seems to work out in mythology also. Still, I would rather have a Sybil for a girl friend than a subtopian housewife any day. About this daughter thing though, I wonder what Freud would have made of that one. I cannot forsee any future catastrophe for humanity as yet.

The bomb, earth tilts, major mutations of the 'flu virus, anything like that is very unlikely to knock Adam off. My only fear for the future is based upon an insidious revolution that is now taking place, the march of the machines and machine man. I had an horrifying experience some time ago, when I had an opportunity to observe the technocratic mind of someone who had very nearly stopped functioning as a human being. He was literally turning into a biological computer, bunged tight with anagramic problems. Every human relationship had to be based upon strict logical control , and emotion was obviously unnecessary, if not positively unscientific.

Love, and he was thirty years old, had not entered his life. For that matter I doubt if he ever felt sex ... This is what worries me. All the bright boys and girls specialising, becoming good careerists, experts upon technology of any sort yet remaining like a rather ponderous child underneath it all. I don't mind admitting that it frightens me, and I have vague fears for the world. I don't think this type will ever destroy the world, but I do think that they will organise it out of existence. I personally can only say to the Julain Huxley's, the Congress of Mathematicians and the thousands like them, 'A pox on 'ee, I'll spite thee yet,' First there was man then man and machine, then machine and man, then only machine. It doesn't bear thinking about.

I found the Akashics difficult to contact at first, then once I found what I was seeking, the information trickled through, then grew steadily into a flood. The whole point about contacting anything I suppose, is to keep on at the one subject, or at least find a link between one thing and another before changing. Fortunatly for me, my subject is one that covers the history of Western humanity, therefore I can afford to change from one century to another without too much loss. (Concieted as it sounds, it is all a matter of opening a channel, and being single minded about what you want. Typical Aquarian doctrine). My apologies for the remark about 'image fixed minds', my intention was to remark upon the conceptual state of the old lady brigade who smother any spiritualist meeting. They appear to think that the next world is absolutely like this one, complete with stocks and shares and servants. Obviously the planes are just the same as this one. We all interpret them as forms and images, since that is necessary to the way we think, but in actual fact, reality is the better word for the other planes, they are all force, irrespective of what interprets them and how. We cannot concieve of force as being just that, our sense of reality will not let us, so we put them into forms and images that appeal to us personally.

Nothing is so unreal than the reality that surrounds us. In certain states of hyper-suggestion, the human mind can and does create anything that it sees fit as its own personal reality. The only difference between the visionary and the schizophrenic is in the emotional state. Even that, if we are to believe the Catholic church's claims for some of its saints, is a negligible difference. St. Augustine was a case in point, capable of speaking of the love of God one moment, and destroying the work of God the next. St. Ignatus (also the founder of the Jesuits) who was the father of the Inquisition, was also another visionary ... When I am dead, I shall go to another place that myself and my ancestors created. Without their work it would not exist, since in my opinion, for many eons of time the human spirit had no abode, then finally be desire to survive created the pathway into the other worlds. Nothing is got by doing nothing, and whatever we do now creates the world in which we exist tomorrow. The same applies to death, what we have created in thought, we create in that other reality. Desire, as you know probably better than I, was the very first of all created things..

Whoa back, Billy boy. Who said anything about contacting the forces of nature? That sort of witchcraft belongs to the Shaman, not to us. Natural forces are means to us, not ends, and that sort of stuff died out with the primitives, Scotch hill farmers and all that. The sort of stuff we practice has little or nothing in common with pantheism at that level. To the best of my knowledge it has been out since the twelfth century at least, along with the group release of the primitive in tribal ecstasies, we have about as much in common with it as we have with Catholicism, for that matter, more in common with Catholicism. That was primarily the reason for me being a little bit uppity about the explaination of the origin of the circle. I suppose I had better tell you a little bit about the history of the craft as I know it .. This may not be necessarily correct, but it has a lot of historical backing. (Assumes heavy and pedantic attitude, clears throat, ruffles through notes and begins ...)

In the twelfth century, the Roman Catholics and the paganism of the country side were well and truly mingled, and each tolerated the other. But just before and during the first Crusade, emmisaries or wandering pilgrims from Persia landed in both Britain and Ireland, and what they had to teach was a development upon the craft at that time. They had been forced to flee from the east by the triumph of Mohammedism and they knew the real mystery tradition of the Greeks, since the Pythagoreans and others went to them after the triumph of the Christians. The druidic and bardic orders of Britain and Ireland were converted to the new order, and it is with this that the Horned God comes into the ascendency. Unfortunately, the Christians saw this new wave of thought as a threat to the established church, and with the reformation staring at Cluny, began the great persucution that delayed the rise of western Europe for another three hundred years. The highest pagan ethic of the twelfth century was better and more defined than the best of the Christians, unfortunately Christianity and ignorance won. It is probably from the same source as the Persians that the Qabbala was derived, since quite a few years ago Waite traced it very nicely to Spain at that period. Hence the real witches and yourself have more in common than is generally realised. We have a tree system that is actually based upon trees, but meditational devices and all that are quite similar in many respects. If you would like to take a really good look at the Tarot, you will see my points about (a) knowledge travelling, and (b) the complexity of paganism at its best. All this stuff about the Great God Pan, nature worhip, Gods of Fire, fertility dances and all that died in the official circles after the twelfth century.

Pantheism still exists, but it is the lesser force for a witch of my tradition, not the greater. We are not people who want to join in the worship of Dionysus, losing ourselves in a welter of untrained emotion, shouting 'Evoh, evoh ha' (1) from hilltops. We have our own disciplines and our own symbology and as much as we can believe it, we think we <u>might</u> be the last to possess the real mysteries of the past. Where everybody goes wrong is in believing that because sex was and still is used as part of an ancient ritual, we must therefore belong to the God Pan and all that codswallop about his ewes. I would advise anybody before following this particular idea to have a very good look at Osiris, and ask why the Pythian priestess sat on a tripod over a snake in the earth. You see, basically a second tradition of thought has been lost, a dual tradition in which nothing was <u>as it appeared.</u> This was the real secret behind the mysteries, and dancing peasants have very little in common with that philosophy. Witches did not die because they believed that their death would fertilise the soil, but to buy time by sacrifice, they did not dance around a circle to imitate the passage of the seasons, but to loosen their astro - physical bodies, and they did not die upon the stake in a belief that their magic alone made the sun come up, but because they would rather die than confess the truth of what they knew. The emotional catharic atmosphere of a modern witch meeting would make them laugh, then feel slightly annoyed, since to a witch silence, intent and will are everything.

Nature worship is a thing that belongs to genuine peasants or to twee old ladies at borderline medicine associations, nature worship to me is a part, not a whole. I was vastly interested in your account of nature possession. For my money I would say that the hand of the Gods is upon you. They have chosen you for something and they will not let you go lightly. Through poetry the Great Ones speak, through poetic inference they teach. The invokation of fire interests me although experts tend to believe that the God of Fire was one of the witch gods this is not strictly true. Like yourself we have the four elements that we evoke, and fire and your Michael are one and the same thing. We use him for purification at the simple level, and for higher symbolic work at the others. I have been in the prescence of fire at an elemental level, and have seen things burst into flame; he is not a faithful servant at that level. I only wish I could tell

193

you how to continue your ritual (but my word forbids me) because I have a feeling that you and I will be one the same side before it is all finished.

However from my point of view, the blank verse is a mantram, not a ritual. Work in silence, treading the mill, will does it all, is the way we work, and we get results. I have crossed the moat and into the spiral castle, and seen and heard some strange things. Last samhuin, all of us had that sense of terror that denotes 'virtue' and strangely enough I could not hear anything except the crying of a baby. It was months before the answer came to that one and when it did come it was quite breath-taking. When you do get your full suit of invokations, remember that the Queen of Spades is the trump. There is also a release of electro-magnetic energy from scourging. That and the decayed adreneline probably produce about anything they want to produce. The peculiar thing about the 'Aradia' though, is the fact that it is a fertility rite, and for human fertility!

The sacrement of bread and salt however, seems to be capable of working up into something like a true rite. Leyland knew a lot about witchcraft, in fact he spent many years studying it in Italy, the fraud laid in the claim he made for sequence, not in the actual subject matter. It was not so much his writing that told me this, but his illustrations to another book 'Roman and Etruscan Remains'. I have come across one of the elementals who disapproved of us everything went wrong and we had some horrible things happen for a while, but on the other hand we have sat quietly and seen physically, small lights appear and move around the room, and Jane once even 'lit up' with a flickering blue flame. Who said that fairies not no how, don't exist?

Thanks for the map reading, my birth date was correct to the best of my knowledge, but, and this is a big but for the Astrologer, I was born for at least three days before the final parting, owing to a mishap during parutition. I was a bit in and a bit out, so this might make some difference to the reading. Basically the reading is accurate, although fire and I are not in oppositon since I was once even a blacksmith in a foundary. However the diseases of fire to affect me. The reason why you keep on sensing this feeling of the bridge, is because it is an essential part of the magical system we practice. Without a bridge, witches of our sort are nothing. The dangers from Pluto are appreciated, this again is something to do with our system. Both Jane and I are supposed to be psychic, been examined and approved for training by a very august spiritualist body, didn't like our religion though so we parted. We can do nearly everything that the sensetives are supposed to do except speak in little girls voices or xenoglossy. I was even supposed to be a good materialising medium, and have a little evidence to prove it. Still enough of myself. My weak point is that I adore talking about me, egocentric nit that I am. I will do a reading for you, ala my own method.

We eat anything, cat and all if you don't put him out of the way in time, but tell Bobby not to worry, we will not be coming for tea, neither will we be more than four.

Thanks a lot for the address, we will use it when the article is finished, that is, if it ever gets written. The group is agin it, says it will have to tell too much in order to prove various points and that they don't like, secretive lot that they are. As far as I am concerned I could shout the truth from the roof trees, and only those who would understand would know it was the truth, and those I would call brother, but the group say NO!, and although in some ways I have power over them, they also have power over me, and this is one of their decisions.

Thanks a lot though, very kind of you.

We must try and meet, since I feel that there is something we will have to do together sooner or later, very vague though.

Regards, Roy

The English peasantry shouted "E.O.I.A.U., EOIAU - poor neddies work is done, EOIAU!! My mother can remember them doing this whilst pulling a plough with a garland round it. Join that tradition to Set and Osiris, read the "Golden Ass" and you will get a clear idea of what we believe in.

X...................................X

(j) 1963 'Genuine Witchcraft' Is Defended
— *Psychic News*

Transcript: 'Genuine Witchcraft' Is Defended

The following article, published in *PSYCHIC NEWS*, NOVEMBER 9, 1963 was anonymously written by Roy Bowers aka Robert Cochrane.

Tired of what he regards as tirades against real witchcraft by uninformed writers in national newspapers a witch requests us to publish his viewpoint. He asks us not to print his name and address, "I have a wife and a small son to consider," he says, "and people still have a tendency to throw bricks at the unusual. His serious comments are in marked contrast to the nonsense printed last week on the occasion of Hallowe'en.

I am a witch descended from a family of witches. Genuine witchcraft is not paganism, though it retains the memory of ancient faiths. It is a religion mystical in approach and puritanical in attitudes. It is the last real mystery cult to survive, with a very complex and evolved philosophy that has strong affinities with many Christian beliefs. The concept of a sacrificial god was not new to the ancient world; it is not new to a witch.

Mystic at heart

Mysticism knows no boundaries. The genuine witch is a mystic at heart. Much of the teaching of witchcraft is subtle and bound within poetical concept rather than hard logic. I come from an old witch family. My mother told me of things that had been told to her grandmother, by her grandmother. I have two ancestors who died by hanging for the practice of witchcraft. The desire for power may have been the motive behind the persecution of witches.

In the 13th or 14th century there was an influx of Islamic mysticism into Europe. This was due to the Crusaders and the wanderings of various mystical societies from the Middle East. There is also strong evidence that this influx of Islamic ideas infiltrated into witch covens of that time.

The king's fear

Since the persecution really began during this period, it is my considered opinion that the extermination of witches was bound up in the conflict of two major faiths, Christianity and Islam. During the Reformation and the decrease of the Muslim Empire the motives were probably forgotten, but the propaganda remained. James I obviously had good reason to fear witches. The witch theology of that period demanded he should die since he descended from a line of "divine kings". The "divine kings", in theory anyway, died for the sins of their subjects and to mediate between man and the evil chance.

It must also be remembered that witches existed probably among the upper classes as well as the lower. These witches possibly desired power like any other lordling. One basic tenet of witch psychological grey magic is that your opponent should never be allowed to confirm an opinion about you but should always remain undecided. This gives you a greater power over him, because the undecided is always the weaker. From this attitude much confusion has probably sprung in the long path of history.

Judgment decides

Nothing about witchcraft is ever stated definitely. It is always left to inference and your judgement. Consequently nothing written about witchcraft can ever solve it or confirm or deny its existence. As for witches belonging to a premature Spiritualist movement, this is a pleasant daydream. Of course there are psychics in every period of history. Sometimes they became priests of the local religion. At other times they died at the hands of priests of the local religion who did not like having their particular theology confounded by spirits, even if the message came directly from the otherworld.

No simple belief

Witchcraft is not primarily concerned with messages or morality gained from the dead. It is concerned with the action of God and gods upon man and man's position spiritually. It is not a simple belief, though many might think so from a superficial examination. Much Spiritualist phenomena would not satisfy the witch, who either attempts the heights or plunges the depths.

There is also a basic conflict between two attitudes. The Spiritualist asks for "miracles" vide the spirit of another world. The witch, or anyone interested in magic, tries to work those "miracles" herself by an act of will with the ordinary "spirit", but it is very doubtful if she would ever allow herself to be controlled by it. It is of course the old controversy between the occultist and the Spiritualist.

X..................................X

(k) Bowers to Robert Graves
i - #I
ii - #II

Notes: These Two Letters to Robert Graves, mention the Menhir of Brittany, the importance of spiritual beliefs and mysticism, the Guiden Corn, the Dark Goddess, the Triple Stave/Stang, the 'Old Man,' the antler of seven tines, mysticism, tribal animal totems, specifically the Stag (to this day, much revered in *Stafford*), and how his system resides in the mystery of Tanhausser. Nowhere does he refer to or discuss an interest in anything 'Celtic' (sic), just the opposite. Focus there had been the preserve of choice for Chalky and George's interest, *not* Bowers'. The Menhir and its mysteries are recorded by the authoress Enid Corrall aka Justine Glass in her book *Witchcraft, the Sixth Sense and Us* where she devotes a whole chapter to Roy Bowers. That chapter discussed several stages of praxis, the three mysteries and the use of a distaff, broom, and sword. Bowers explains to her in concise terms their function. Corrall even attended some of the Clan Rites as a guest in 1965. After his death, she developed a deep and lasting friendship with Doreen Valiente. She also became a member of *'The Regency.'*

> "Robert Graves in his white goddess writes a great deal of nonsense about many things ... But he was absolutely accurate when he wrote that the protean goddess was the true inspirer of the poet, and that all real poetry must deal with themes she is mistress of."

Hence, of Graves' work, Bowers was: *"an admirer and a critic"*

Introduction by Grevel Lindop,
editor of *The White Goddess* by Robert Graves

Robert Cochrane was, by his own admission, an: "admirer and a critic" of the works of Robert Graves—particularly of: 'The White Goddess' launched in 1948 it created quite a stir within academia that has scarce settled since. A work of exceptional poetic vision, it is loosely based upon historic fact, yet elucidates undeniable truths within the Mythopoetic worlds of the mystic, the poet and the mage.

More challenging yet than this, was Grave's assertion that all inspiration flowed by grace of a capricious Muse, an ambivalent ice-queen, worshipped the world over in her many guises and various cults. Yet despite the book's frosty reception by his peers, it was lauded publicly by his readers. Somehow, Graves tapped into a deep-rooted primal need to connect to the intangible and archetypal feminine moumena. Liberation was swift; an overwhelming surge of interest revived this Goddess Muse, elevating her in an unprecedented swing away from patriarchy, affecting the whole strata of magical belief, from folklore to the supernatural, now so firmly entrenched, it is almost inconceivable to imagine a different 'world view.' But, it was exactly this perspective that Robert Cochrane did in fact challenge Graves upon, boldly and quite self-assured.

Ironically, Robert Graves was also in correspondence with Gerald Gardner, who was expounding a very different kind of 'Craft' to that of Robert Cochrane during the 1960's. And although there is a plethora of material assumed to have been penned by Gerald Gardner, we have very few surviving letters and articles of Robert Cochrane's to draw upon. So the discovery of two additional letters expands our understanding of the man considerably. Graves' book influenced both men considerably, but in entirely different ways.

While Gardner used the material as an historical basis for his nature based religion: 'Wica,' Cochrane exploited the resources both allegorically and analogically, allowing him to develop his teaching praxes substantially. Most especially he became very adept at setting riddles based on material from the book to test student upon their intuitive faculties and lateral cognisance.

Cochrane discusses several unusual topics in fact, steering Graves into deeper revelation concerning his intuitive projections, with especial regard for the 'Black Goddess' with whom he is eager to opine some familiarity.

Some of Graves' views he berates and others he commends; but it is clear that whenever these were written, Cochrane intended a long and productive correspondence with Graves. Those familiar with Cochrane's other letters and articles will discern immediately particular themes of importance to his work, which is discussed in greater depth after the letters. The reader is first invited to peruse them carefully, making comparisons with his other works for indications of subjects known, understood and discussed. Collectively, this becomes extremely significant when we analyse to what purpose such scrutiny is served. Above everything, his anarchic passion, frustration, erudition and conviction spill out from the page, infusing the reader with the intense vigour of this most startling figure of 20th century.

Transcript: Letter i #I to Robert Graves:

Dear Robert Graves,

I have read and re-read your book 'The White Goddess' with admiration, utter amazement and a taint of horror. I can see your point when you write of inspirational work, and realise that it must have resulted from quite an internal 'pressure,' since from my own experience, that is the way she works. However, I am just pointing out some other factors that might interest you in the manifestation of the 'Guiden Corn'. There is some evidence to support the theory that the British and French pagans believed in stages of spiritual development and maturity and had incorporated this into thier religious beliefs. There is still in existence a carved dolmen in Brittany that has all the witch symbols and mysteries arrayed upon it, surmounted by a carving in the round of Christ, which archeologists describe as a depiction of the passion of Christ. It dates from 1674 and to the best of my knowledge, (I come from an old witch family and although the family's beliefs were moribund at my father's birth, I know enough to get along) the carving is anything but Christian. In this carving there is the eight circles with death supporting the bell Goddess above them. These, so I was told, represent the eight states or worlds of manifestation, and since they appear to correspond with Jungian psychology which is a rehash of much of the Mystery systems, the rest is quite interesting. Also there are other factors connected with this ninefold unfolding of the spirit. There is amongst many, an old ms that writes of an epic here Libius Disconis who undertakes nine adventures accompanied by Ellen and a dwarf. In these adventures all the enemies defeated are of the true mythological flavour, and Libius evidentally ends by releasing the Goddess in one of her most dangerous forms and marrying her. However it is the progress of Taunhasser in its original form. The damned thing eludes me, since I am unable to make up my mind whether it is seasonal or psychological. I would be interested to hear of what you can make of it. It has the advantage of the various tribal animals and heroes of the Druidical system incorporated in it, and it may possibly be an opening to the mystery that still surrounds much of the iconography of the old religion.

Incidentally, the battle of the trees may also be a system equivalent to the tree system of twelfth century magic. There are many points in common between the Hermatic and Kabbalists meditational system and the trees of Talisien. A friend of mine has claimed that he has worked it out, but until it fits to the endocrine glands of the body, I personally cannot see how this can be so. The kabbalistic tree of life along with the book of Thoth seems to belong more to Apollo than the Goddess. I think that you are absolutely right when you say that she is the prime source of inspiration.

Yours sincerely,

R.L. Bowers

P.S. my apologies for writing but I have found so much of interest in your books that I almost feel that you are an old friend.

Transcript: Letter i - #II to Robert Graves

Dear Robert Graves,

Thank you for your unexpected and very welcome letter. I find your point about the influx of the Islamic societies interesting, but apart from Gerald Gardner's covens and Idris Shah, I have not heard of it before. I have been told that my grandfather's grandfather dressed in skins and horned head-dress for ritual practice Since he was an 'Old Man', (high priest, devil, what you will,) I fail to see that Islamic practice or belief had reached so far, since, as you will know, the Sufi and kindred societies did not enact the part of God; Their aim was to achieve a mystical state vide various practices. To the best of my knowledge, that was not the aim of the Staffordshire and Warwickshire witches. Flags, Flax, Fodder and Frig was their total aim, good crops, healthy children and some power to strike back at the oppressor was the aim, and in my opinion they succeeded. There was poetry, there was mysticism, but these were either side effects or something that belonged to the individual rather than the group. However, there may be a very distinct difference between the witches of the west and of the Midlands. They still used the triple stave or 'Stang', and used deer antlers not bull horns for certain purposes. (Incidentally the stag of seven tines may have a meaning to each of the tines), and to the best of my knowledge they did not use the ritual star, or the binding thereof as part of their ritual, instead they used the death's head and bones. I agree that there has been an influx of Eastern magic and mysticism, but the question is upon the distance that it spread. In my personal opinion there are two distinct kinds of witches (and taking into account the events over the last fifteen years, three kinds) and it may be that they lived in mutual toleration of each other. However, according to some research I have done upon this particular branch, it mayhap that this division was originally social, and there is quite a difference between the peasant and the squires mysteries.

I leave it to your superior knowledge to see whether there is any truth in this statement. But as a sort of interesting side line, there is pretty good evidence that the gypsies infiltrated into the English clans, and for that matter elsewhere. They may have carried various Indian practices with them. The whole ruddy subject gets so confusing that I usually end up with fresh knowlegde about something that I had no intention of examining. Still it is something that once picked up, you can't put it down again. I sometimes feel when I am wandering around in the marshes of the old knowledge, that the dam upstream is going to burst and the whole of humanity is going to be submerged by fifty thousand years of pre-history, swamping the neat neat subtopian conventions of the last thousand years. King Log has already sunk, but they still worship the memory.

I was interested in your description (one of the difficulties of communication—'interested'!) of the physical appearance of the Goddess symptons (Gawd, my spelling). I am not biased towards the poetical aspect but more towards the Black Goddess, so my knees do not shake or eyes run, but I do get a sudden feeling of intense pressure, something like an approaching storm. It is as you say a physical thing, almost a desire to run and find shelter. I have also 'seen' the Goddess, although She was riding a white horse, maybe it was artistic vision, I do not know, but I was genuinely terrified for the following week. At the present moment I have the best of both worlds with the Black and the White... Of course I will pay for it later, hire purchase is no new thing...

Yours sincerely,

R.L. Bowers.

References:

1. When Robert Graves died in 1985 was in Mallorca, his many correspondences were systematically filed and logged for future historic use. Discovered among his many correspondences were systematically filed and logged for future historic use. Discovered among biographical research material, by the esteemed writer Grevel Lindop, to whom I owe a debt of gratitude for his kindness and co-operation in publishing these two undated letters, both poorly typed, and are unedited for clarity (now held by the St John's College Robert Graves Trust), we have another facet of this enigmatic persona to explore.

2. They are assumed by Lindop to have not been written prior to 1963, possibly because Cochrane's subject references in the letters to the 'Black Goddess' had not yet been made public until Graves discussed her within his lectures of that year. Graves' views on the Black Goddess also formed the basis of the book published in 1965: 'Mammon and the Black Goddess.' Cochrane raises this figure with Graves, coaxing further discussion upon the paradox of her contrasting nature with the White Goddess.

X.............................X

1964 Next Stage of his Argosy

(1) Two more Letters to Bill Gray
i - #VI 1964
ii - #VIII

Notes: **#VI** Bowers has finally written up the 'Cave' article for Basil Wilby. He thanks Bill for the editor's address regarding the magazine– *New Dimensions*. He declares how the 'boys were up in arms' making a 'fuss,' being totally against its publication. Bowers also reiterates how he and Bill really must meet. He suggests that he will soon visit Bill for tea, with no more than four: himself, Jane, John and Dick. NOTE! *not* Chalky and George, who do not feature in any of the documents of this period. A later missive to Gills requests a similar visit for 'tea' that includes these people and also Chalky and George. But not here. At this point, Chalky and George had drifted off to pursue their own interests. They did return later and were involved on a more casual basis. Bowers asks Bill if he knows of any real witch cuveens with whom he might then associate, and by mutual encouragement, advance the Old Craft in hearts and minds as a lived tradition. To that end, he reminds Bill that he was not at all interested to learn of a coven associated with Gerald Gardner. Bowers says he knows of two only that are genuine, one he believes is near to Bill Gray. With some sadness, he dismisses this likelihood as probable hearsay.

Transcript of #VI to Bill Gray – 27ᵗʰ May 1964

Many thanks for your most interesting letter.

Do I think that Jesus was a 'born witch'? Basically the teachings of Jesus are very near to my own perception about 'morality'. The crucifixion is a much older story of hundreds, if not thousands of divine kings who died upon the tau cross of the kerm oak, and the supernatural is commonplace legend surrounding such events. It was well known to the ancients that if man draws out power, he must sooner or later replace it with something that is better if the social continuity is to survive. Sacrifice is the key note of survival, and the ancients thought to sacrifice their very best in order to replace the energy loss, Jesus, if I read the legends rightly, literally did die to 'save us all' since he as a developed man, created with his own solitary sacrifice a 'field' that many have drawn upon and added to since. The fault with Christianity lies in the churches and the apostles, not in the founder. The basic law behind the techniques of magic and fate is that nature abhors a vaccuum, and it is with this in mind that mystics and magicians alike attempt to lift the world fate. They replace that which is empty or negative with that which is positive. The trouble lies in the interpretation many casual 'mystics' or divines put upon the word 'love'.

Love is the most divine force, but it is only gained through pain and insight. The Virgin Mary ... whee, what a subject you have given me. Where do I start? The twelfth century also saw the beginnings of the papacy's absorption of the Mother Goddess, since the Marian cult (a Christianisation of the Mother Goddess) gained tremendous power at that time. At first the church decided that the worship of Mary was a rank heresy, but in order to save their own crumbling structure, soon climbed on the band wagon. As for the vision of the Virgin, people see God in basic images that belong to the racial consciousness, not in images that an exterior power has foisted upon them. The racial memory is far more conscious and stronger than people realise. The Kelts for instance are still basically orientated to a Goddess (Queen worship). Concepts of a Father God is Anglo Saxon, hence one of the most noticable differences between Saxon and Kelt. These differences begin with the origin of thought itself, which was probably evolved through the practice of simple magic. (Don't ask me to explain that one, at least three volumes). Again the Keltic mind is strongly addicted to nature worship, although basically God is apparent anywhere at any time, what is not so forthcoming is the alteration in personal perception so that we may see God.

The Christian faith prefers that we see goodness and charity in the Image of Jesus, but in actual fact , the first three aspects of the Mother Goddess are basically more sound psychologically. The aspects of the Virgin, Mother and Compassionate/Wise woman are factors that exist apart from the personal unconscious. Where I find many people fall down, is in their belief that no other aspect of the Goddess exists. This accounts for much of the hoo-ha of modern pagans. Nothing is purely good or evil, these are relative terms that man has hung upon unaccountable mysteries. To my particular belief, the Goddess, white with works of Good, is also Black with works of darkness, yet both of them are compassionate, albeit the compassion is a cover for the ruthlessness of total TRUTH.

Truth is another name for the Godhead. Male or female doesn't really matter, what does matter is the recognition of neither good or evil, black or white, but the acceptance of the 'will of the Gods', the acceptance of truth as opposed to illusion. Once we deviate from the search for truth, then our works are nothing, our lives as the winter winds. Whatever we do we cannot escape from Truth, it will follow us and speak, no matter what ramparts we build against it, no matter what stories we tell ourselves. Truth speaks for itself, outside systems, religious beliefs, beyond and before the grave. The visionaries whether they be Bernadette, Joan of Arc, some of the early revolutionaries or Appolnorius (have I spelt his name right) are all human beings that somehow have triggered off a perception of some small part of Truth, and who have created something from it. Whatever interpretations others may try and give to these 'visions', the explaination is only to be found in the person who saw or felt the presence of 'Truth'. We all have some small particle of these truths in us, man rolls forward, cresting the waves of 'God's will' upon these minute particles. He reached out from the mud and slime of evolution to the stars, and the stars turned back in their courses to help him, and those same stars still gleam brightly for twentieth century man. Become in one with Truth and you must certainly die. Take up works that are based upon truth, and you are a condemned man, for the human race as a whole does not want truth, but the comfort of illusion. We are still babies suckling at a breast whose milk is poisonous, yet we think that we flourish upon poison. Truth, no matter how we interpret it, feeds demons as well as saints.

Saturday I phoned you this morning as you know. We will be working upon your trouble tomorrow night. My left hand tells me something about it, and one thing that comes up is the diagnosis. I feel that the doctors are wrong, you have a glandular infection that is almost gone, possibly the prostate, since I get it very heavily upon my thumb. You will have some further trouble from the same source, but it will not be serious, possible trouble connected with unination. The gall bladder, 'if it is functioning badly, is a by product of this, not the cause.

According to my hand, the trouble has been with you some time (which fits to your description), but it will be healed. I cannot see a knife in it , so surgical work may be out. Your life will end when you are in your late seventies, possibly. You feel defeated about physical things, but there is a feeling of wealth coming to you before two years have passed, but with this wealth will come the necessity to work in a different field from the one you are in now. Surprisingly I get that this money comes in some way through your practice of magic, the Art of Hermes. You will also suffer violence over this, there will be opposition coming from the quarter of fire, but you will overcome it. To some extent this has to do with writing , but getting the thing to come first of all will be a painful process, don't be taken it by a new thing that is coming your way, I feel that someone will try and make a fool of you, possibly something over medicine (sounds like me, won't be, though) . Damn, don't read that last sentance, the power shifted before I cottoned on to it ... It was to do with your health, repeating the same facts again. You will be ill for a short while, but it will not be serious, then your health will improve immensely. That' s all ...

At last I managed to write that article. Basil Wilby has it by now, but you should have heard the fuss, the boys were up in arms. The ritual described is largely fictional, upside down and wrong way up , but the intention behind the article was to describe the feelings that an operation of this kind engenders. 'Impressions of a Missionary Tour in the Darkest Underworld' by the Very Rev. Rapist, Ernest. Vice President of the Society for the Propogation of Original Sin. I hope it gets accepted, I keep on getting the word 'original' but that is too much to hope for. By all means give my very best regards to Doreen Valiente, but I would be pleased if you did not tell her too much about anything I have sent you. I don't know very much about Doreen as a person, (although I get a pleasant enough feeling) but her book rather put my teeth on edge when she described a ritual in which an old man bawled 'Evoh, Evoh ha!'.
It sounds so much like the late Dr. Garnder, that I am terribly suspicious. However, I suppose Doreen has just as much right to bend the truth as I have when it comes to describing ritual, so I may be wrong.

However Brighton is also Mrs. Leek's stamping ground, whether the two are together, I do not know. It is not that I object to them as people, or for that matter, to their religious beliefs, but I do object very strongly to the habit that some of them form of going into press and

211

making the most ridiculous statements imaginable. Doreen seems to be the exception, but even so I remain suspicious until I meet her personally.

What can I say about your invokations except that they are good blank verse. As you know our methods are different, and to me they are meditational aids, builders of atmosphere, not commands to the superconsciousness. We hardly have any speaking at all, since after a certain point it gets in the way. We have chants, series of words and all that, but they are rarely used once things get moving. In fact I would find anyone who insisted upon voicing words of power a nuisance, and probably kick him out of the compass to act as a corner man. Obviously your methods work, you have the feeling of a genuine occultist, but East and West and all that.

Where you would use words to build up an atmosphere conductive to working , we use physical actions to produce the same effect. Where you would use words as a key to the transformation of basic power, we again use actions, (No, not orgies). There is in effect a dual tradition of thought that witches have always used, one part has been discovered by the west and is called science, the other part will never be discovered since it concerns understanding the essential nature of illusion, and thinking at a tangent.   Nothing ever is as it appears. As a matter of fact the Zohar (I have never studied it) appears to have the same basis. Where ceremonial magicians have described the Zohar as being hidden and deliberately confused in certain patterns in order to avoid persecution, and to hide its secrets, a witch of my particular school would regard the verses as an actual method of thought designed to gain illumination. The whole point is that it is symbolic thinking of quite high degree. Unfortunately the real twist lies with individual interpretation of that particular symbology. I know that symbols are supposed to contain the seeds of their own revelation, and that they are appearances of 'force' but man fashions his own interpretations according to his time. Perhaps you would like to consider all the different meanings of a pentacle, that you have heard of during your lifetime. The odd thing is that each of these meanings is basically correct for the group using it. Where the image of virtue really comes into its own, is when a group has formulated an old symbol, then developed it into a 'new' symbol, i.e. Eliphas Levi's 'Goat of the Sabbath'. This is not the original Bran by any means, But Levi in fact made up an illustration that incorporated all the powers that are of the Hermes of the Witches. It is no simple animal God by any means, but a god who is literally Pan.

There again the order and type of symbol used alters with the age. We use a 'tree' system, like, yet unlike, yours. You would possibly find the symbology of our system alien, just as I find the three tree system alien to myself. We work upon an anthropormorphic pat tern to shift virtue from one transcending state to another. Graves, quite knowingly gave one ancient interpretation of it in his 'White Goddess', and also, incidentally, left out a chunk of it;

'I am a wind of the sea
I am a wave of the sea
I am a sound of the sea
I am an ox of seven fights
I am a stag of seven tines
I am a hawk upon a cliff
I am a tear of the sun
I am fair amongst flowers
I am a boar
I am a salmon in a pool
I am a lake upon the plain
I am a hill of poetry

I am a God who forms fire with his head.'

This is Taliesin's riddle, Graves has thoroughly mangled it, and as for the language of trees that he propagates , this suffers from real misinterpretation. It is a high code, and Graves gives a poetic meaning to it.

I was sorry to hear of your adventure with the Essenes. Still they must be fools to play at magicians on one of the most potent sites in the world. Glastonbury is more than an archeological site, it was at one time, the Temple of the High Goddess. If you look at a ground map of the workings, you will see a hand mirror shape, this has to do with two opposing forces that can be called upon there. I would like to know if the Essenes had this Bat' before or after working at Glastonbury. From the sound of it they have attracted one of the 'watchers' that wait for the foolhardy upon such sites, the classical 'fury' which always accompanied the Goddess. These sites are reflectors, doorways by which something enters the world. The old witches used a hand mirror for a similar purpose, but they were well aware that Cain lived in the moon as well as the Museos. Not all the practices of witches are moonshine, some of them had a found realisation in truths that are now known to very few, one of those truths was to do with the reflection of virtue or destiny. Incidentally the Essenes sound like a big brother of the 'Communication groups' which about amongst the pip and peel water brigade up here. The poor dears sit in a circle and unload their neurosis upon each other, then take it in turns to say 'fuck' loudly to release the inhibitions, some of the more wild sort then start a round of pornographic stories in order to arouse their overstimulated sexual passions. Presumably groups of this nature end up with a sexual binge. I can never image them having an orgia. It seems from Gossip that a lot of semi occult groups use much the same methods. One modern 'witch' meeting I went to sat around all evening declaiming 'Eskimo Nell' and kindred nursery rhymes. They would not tell me why they did it, but I presume they had heard somewhere that sex is the raw force that makes magic. It hasn't occurred to the poor boys and girls that this is the best way of <u>un</u>transforming sex. The same group believe that it is a good thing to become purely instinctual whilst working, so much for them. One of their members once confessed to me that he thought Crowley was the only ceremonial magician who bridged the difference between witch and qabbalist, and that Crowley had been misunderstood. Phew!

It is mainly because of factors like the above that I remain suspicious of all the modern, port wine type witches. I must admit whenever I move in such circles I play the innocent for all I am worth, it is amazing how much you find out. Agreed about old ladies and spinster ladies also. They are emotional vampires, who feed upon rumpus, confusion and lost tempers. Incidentally, I agree whole heartedly with folk wisdom in its attitudes towards the average spinster lady. Maybe one day some religious organization will take compassion upon them and found a new brother hood, devoted to helping 'our sisters in distress'. Services three times daily, and absolution afterwards. Extra penances given by dispensation. (I am certain those terrible women are basically sadomasochist).

Reincarnation ... Spain, same period (Elizabethan), small village, cliff top Moorish architecture, vultures and a tall man with wild hair who had a sword cut down one side of his face. Remember me? Wesak Day. Do you go the meeting of the White Brotherhood? I find it a story hard to believe, somehow the attraction of the Himalayas is not for me. I must admit that I regard stories of the White Brotherhood, Masters who are in the flesh, Alice Bailey's 'wog' (what a cruel word) the Count St. Germain and Uncle Tom Cobbly with very deep suspicion and tend to raise my eyebrows slightly whenever I hear dear old ladies speak of them. I'll gladly admit the fact of Masters who are not in the flesh, since I have had that one forced upon me, but the annual meeting, well ... Tell, is it really true? I must admit that I have always wished it was true. Jane is most upset because you think her shell like ears have never heard basic English. We have been married fourteen years, that and being professional bargees once, has given us a deep insight into common everyday English. Bobbie's poems are good material. I don't like her opening lines to Father Image but they keep to the principles of genuine poetry, and that is something in an era where poets display their own entrails for public inspection. I like them.

As you will have noticed, I have written myself out, spelling, English and all that is up the wall.

Regards ,

Roy and Jane

P.S. Have you ever come across a real witch <u>cuveen</u> in your area, not the Garnener's. I would be pleased if you could give me some information upon them. I only know of two genuine cuveens in the country. One of those is very near to you, and I have only heard of them through hearsay.

X...................................X

ii - #VIII Letter to Bill Gray

Notes: This letter is very much concerned with the rituals and charming required to 'heal' Bill Gray. It was heavy work, and required many levels of cunning-craft including elements of psychology, spiritualism, shamanism, exorcism and binding craft. He refers to his ability to manipulate 'virtue' – which is in the gift of the 'Other.' To gain their grace one needs to 'blooded', another gift he alludes to. In otherwords, he is demonstrating further his belief in an ancestral power (virtue) that recognises its own and works through them. Again he laments the lack of true vocation, and the preference for illusion. Remarking on the rarity of 'natural' virtue, he informs Bill Gray that Jane has such gifts in abundance, a view that was vocalised to us personally via E.J. Jones and Doreen Valiente. Answering another question Bill asks of him concerning working sites, Bowers corrects Bill on the rumours of the Clan using the Rollrights in Oxfordshire. He adds that Lois Bourne and other Gardnerians use it primarily for outdoor fire festivals such as May Day (Beltaine).

Transcript for #VIII Letter to Bill Gray

Thanks for the three letters. We will probably meet in London upon this weekend, But I thought I would like to get these impressions down on paper so that the form they have come to me in does not shift. Now about this trouble of yours. I have rarely experienced so much difficulty in working as I did that night. It was rather like pushing the millstone round and grinding sand. It appears to have worked though, since you were put through the patterns of the maze. As we ended (we started much earlier than arranged because of various things), I offered the final actions and words that finish and hold the matter. In the middle of this, a form of words was used that normally constitute a blessing , to my horror I became conscious of extreme interference, that <u>nearly</u> changed the whole operation into a very dangerous curse. I began to use a form that would have reversed the whole thing ... Jane spotted it and took over and finished the job. Now the interesting thing was the feeling of extreme malignant force, we dealt with it then and sent it running, we are certain that it did not have any effect except to cause me to mangle the last and final part of the particular ritual used, but the question arises, WHY? Why should something that exists upon the other side want to interfere particularly with work done for you? Why should it want you ill? Why is it <u>with</u> you?

We embarked upon an analysis of the situation, and made on tuition work overtime. The answers we have found are these. That (a) it is unlikely that you have dabbled in black magic during this life, so there is no fury sitting at your table, (b) there is no living person who holds you a sufficient grudge, as to want you dead, (c) That you are basically a good man, therefore you would not attract this particular malignant force. Therefore we had to look over the walls at the situation and what came flooding through was interesting, albeit painful, since it concerns your mother. We have sensed this, right or wrong, for good or for evil. That the spiritual part of your mother has moved on, and is now well adjusted to the next life, BUT the etheric body has not yet disintegrated , and still contains that original bitterness , and has used <u>you as a supply so that it could survive</u> (hence your sexual trouble). Obviously you are emotionally involved with the image of your parent, and it has used this as a bridge in order to tap your own vitality. It resents interference, and to a certain extent any other woman in your life. It is not aware that it is only a shadow, but believes that it is the corporate whole.

Your mother evidently used some of the methods of the east to project, and as such formed a body of light ...it is this body of light that is now out of control, that is your trouble. It must be disintegrated or cast off to wither away. How you will do this, (and you alone can do it), I do not know. I have an old Italian spell for things of this kind, and know that it works for mental illness, but this one is beyond my personal powers. However before you take any action, I would advise you to get the opinions of other occultists upon this matter, and see what they say. Here is the charm, it can be used by you to form a ritual, and to act as a corner stone in that ritual, but the binding and absorption of 'devils' is not my particular branch.

'Shadow! It is known
When Thou followest anyone,
Be the victim who he may,
Thou art ever in his way.
Shadow! Hear me. If free
Thou wilt leave the road to me,
For better it shall be
If thou will not, then from this hour
I will hold thee in my power.
Shadow! Thou shall learn
That I am a witch in my turn...
All the power of sorcery
So about thee I will throw.
All around, above, below
That thou shalt accursed be,
Held in fear and in agony
And as a dog shall follow me.
Shadow! Thou shalt know what thou art...
Ere thou goest
If ye come here again,
To torment or give me pain.

As thou wouldst make a dog of me,

I will make swine meat of thee.

Shadow! Sorry cheat,

Filled with hate from head to feet.

Be malignant if ye will,

I am more malignant still.

Shadow! For thy own sake,

I pray thee no more trouble make.

To torment me for thy gain,

Will only by thy greater pain.

For so accursed shalt thou be,

I must need pity thee.

Shadow! Now confess,

That with all thy cunning

Thou didst not know of what I now can tell,

That I am protected well

By a lovely Witch ....(Hecate)

And She is mightier far than thee.

Shadow! Ere we go,

If thou more of me would know,

Come at midnight.

I shall be leaning on the standing stones,

And what I shall make thee see,

I swear will be enough for thee.

Shadow! In that hour,

Thou Shalt feel my power.

And when at last thou shalt learn,

That upon the triple stone I stand.

Then to thee it shall be known,

That my shadow is thine own.
 Shadow, Everywhere with me,
These charms I bear,
Ivy, bread, salt and rue
With them my fortuning too.
Shadow! Go away
Unto thee no more I say
Now would I go to sleep
See thou this warning keep
I am not in power of thine
But thou art in power of mine.'

This old charm is murderous poetry, but it works. Out of all the curses and near curses in my possession, this Italian spell is perhaps the most deadly, since it states the witch attitude completely. Will against will, illusion against illusion, eye for eye, life for life and death for death ... When I first started this business many years ago, I cursed someone, they fell seriously ill ... I have never forgotten the lessons I learned from that one episode. Will, sheer malignant will, is one of the most terrible forces in the world. This spell is based upon that very attitude. Whether or not you will be able to use it properly, or whether you will weaken because of the moral training of the Qabbalist I do not know, but once you begin it never leave it or weaken, otherwise it will return to you.

That is all the help I can give you. Remember you will be challenging something on its own grounds, this is against all the training of modern occultism, but for a witch of my school, this is the only way. Rise or die ....In your left eye the power of death and disruption, in your right eye the power of life and growth, this I give to you. Master is a term that we use , and use often. I myself, am a master of a small clan, the devil in fact. I in turn recognise the authority of others who are higher than myself, and that authority , once stated, is absolute, do what we may. Higher plane adeptii, or physical adeptii are terms that sit uneasily upon the witch. Master is the old word for the particular function we all (witches I mean) have to fulfil. My job is to train and organise, fulfil the letter of the law and to function to discipline and to curse, as well as to elevate and expound. To Jane all the men owe absolute allegience, to myself (or rather the law that I represent) they owe duty. We have to train any new members up to certain standards , develop any hidden power that they may have, and finally teach them the manipulation of various images of virtue. We may be the very last of the old school, but we still uphold the old attitudes and expect the same things. Above we two rises another authority whose writ is far older than ours, to that authority we give absolute allegiance, and whose function it is to train us and work with us. I was in the fortunate position of having been blooded, therefore I have some hold on their ears. I and Jane have powers that have been developed over a number of years. I believe that every human being who has at least some sensitivity (by that I mean the ability to percieve others as they are) has also the ability to develop these senses until they are like a second eye. We use various methods to develop latent powers, but unless the person involved is willing to fall, pick himself up, then fall and rise again, we cannot teach them. Unfortunately most people do not basically believe in various things, therefore they do not get results, irrespective of whatever they do. We try and establish a climate of opinion where the miraculous is commonplace, and the results seem worthwhile. I aquired my own powers the hard way, I was not born with them. To this much I owe Jane everything, since it was by her example upon another field, that I began to develop. The surest way of developing power is by observing the path of example, from that all other things grow. It is only in the inter action of man and woman that the will of the Gods becomes apparent, and one learns all from the other, and with it learns the necessary understanding of other human beings that must go with such powers. Our personal ability has not reached its zenith as yet, that will take another five years at least, but we can normally function with nearly everybody. We hate making a show of them since this breaks away from the way of humility, but we do use them when there is a worthwhile purpose.

Doreen Valiente (she seems to be taking up a lot of my time one way and another) As I said I have no objections again her or her particular beliefs, since I am too long in the tooth to cry heresy. You are quite welcome to discuss me, witchcraft or anything else connected with me. I have no worries on that score since it appears we are fated to meet sometime in the future (round August if I have it right) and an offer will be made, considered and rejected. I would be grateful if you did not tell her any revelant matter such as that nursery rhyme, I do not want it in the press. From your account of local witches, I would say we are the last left in Southern England. So be it, we are too old to have lived much longer, and the past is too great a burden for a small group to bear alone. Incidentally the Rollaright stones are the meeting place of one of Gardner's cuveens on May day, there is the source of your rumour. I am surprised that a county with such a history should be so psychically dead, I must liven it up a bit, and throw a wild dance on the Tor.

Sorry about the rambling of this letter. Jane and I were out last night, and we still haven't recovered our proper senses. Honestly, trying to 'fly' around here is like swimming in black treacle. Trying to get over the 'wall' is murder under those conditions. Its all the groups mind round, L.C.C. estate and all that, the inhabitants are the biggest load of monkeys that have been trained since the original ark. If I travel about five miles away, getting outside is as easy as anything. Ugh! Those minds sleeping or waking, they would deflate J.C. himself.

The old chap you saw, I can't place him, except as a man I know as Willum, he was a Norfolk witch and a great friend of a living friend (one of the clan) of ours. He was the husband of a delightful old woman who initiated George (our friend) when he was a young man. George swears by old Mary Maiden and Willum, they were his great friends. I have good reason to thank her also, she has never let us down. I don't suppose you have friends who are interested in occultism a la witchcraft, but if you do I am always pleased to hear from them. The clan is badly out of balance, we number five men and one woman, you try anything that needs a delicate touch with a group based upon those proportions, and it is amazing at what creeps in.

They all get much too aggressive ... Still women have lost the instinct for witchcraft, they are all like little painted dolls today , afraid to do anything which aint all that respectable. Either that they are so bloody inhibited they go to the opposite extremes and play at silly beggars with nudism, tea leaves and dancing a la wild pagan ecstacies. The real witch instinct seems to have gone for a burton ... been trained out of the little dears by too much deodorant, and not enough nature. The ones who do go in for what they describe as witchcraft, all seem to have remarkably well developed histrionic ability, and lose no time in putting on a great show for the hoi polloi, and generally making up for all those years of masculine domination and feminine inferiority complexes. I suppose nearly all of those I have met who belongs to the latter day saints, sorry, witches, have all got a hidden neurosis to do with (a) feelings of inferiority, and (b) a marked desire to handle a mans tools (My God! That is bad imagery. Terrible slip up) with feminine wiles. They never seem to have got the idea that being feminine in its truest form is better than being masculine at its worse, in fact being truly feminine (a increasingly rare quality) is marvellous for both the woman who is like that, and the man on whom she decides to be her lover, husband and mate. Two sides to a coin and all that, today though the coin appears to be standing upon its edge. Regards, Roy and Jane

x..................................x

Compared to document(g), the instructions given in the next document (m), for the preparation of space, bears no resemblance whatsoever. They are as distinct in their theology as they are their mechanics. Even superficially we cannot fail to notice that the former rites are performed naked and indoors, whereas this rite - 'Preparing the Bridge' and those that follow it, are all generated outdoors and all participants are cloaked. There is no mention of the five-fold kiss, no women as altars, and no purple prose evocations to the 'Goddess.' Rather, Her unique presence is now very distinct as the Pale-Faced Goddess, Madam La Guiden (Fate). And there are no remnants of a nostalgic 'Celtic' (sic) twilight world. In this particular rite, and those after it, Bowers refers to himself, or to Jane, and sign's off the work with his name, often accompanied by a sigil or symbol and one of several unique blessings or comments.

Making direct comparisons right here between these two documents allows the reader to better appreciate the implications and consequences Monmouth constructs for his claim that Bowers alone did not write or create all the material for the 'Royal Windsor Coven.'(Being outside the remit of this book, which is to explain the incidents and meanings of matters referenced within the letters, rather than tackle their legitimacy and historicity directly, the disingenuous fiction surrounding the creation and existence for this alleged group is dissembled within *Tubal's Mill,* the book created to address exactly those matters that pertain to the history and legitimacy of the Clan, and its traditions at source). Casting aside therefore the legitimacy of any coven existing by that name, we wholeheartedly agree with the rest of that statement. Within the cache of documents believed to have belonged to George Stannard/Winter, several of them are unequivocally composed by others, hitherto of unknown authorship. These largely appear before this one, within this chronology, and they may or may not have been composed by Ronald White or George Winter. However, Monmouth's purpose in asserting they were, is to claim Chalky and George as the 'eminence gris' the 'tour de force' within the coven he not only claims was named the *Royal Windsor Coven*', but that this coven was established in Bowers' lifetime and which they continued after his death. The entire thrust of Monmouth's tome is to establish his claim that Bowers' was the usurper in their coven, and little more than the front man whose reputation has basked for decades in a glory that he believes should rightfully be theirs.

There is no doubt at all that when Bowers died, Chalky and George took whatever was theirs and used it as a basis for their contribution to the establishment of *The Regency*' and possibly even any works they continued after it ceased its public face in the mid-to late 1970s. But that is a very different thing to claiming the genius of all that rightly and separately belongs to Bowers, as something which was really 'theirs all along.' That there is no point at which those disparate works meet, is precisely why there were so many arguments and fall-outs between Bowers and Chalky & George!

No-one can confuse the content and style of the preceding documents for what follows; and no-one can confuse the articles and letters Bowers' wrote, with anything from within the 'Pagan's Handbook' (composed by Chalky), nor with the works of *The Regency* which were in truth, largely the inspiration and work of Ruth Wynn Owen. Until now, this lady's works have largely been overlooked. Appropriated and re-presented as their own by many with whom she was initially kind enough to share, we should perhaps be re-considering the initial genius of *The Regency*'s works - those rites and festivals everyone lauds Chalky and George for, amongst others?

As an aside there does seem to be a major trend in the history of the craft for its male exponents to become renowned for the works of rather more obscure female writers and creative artists from whom they appropriated their material. To name one other, whose longevity and tenacity singled her out in later life to overturn this pattern, the Mother of the Craft, Doreen Valiente stands exemplary, and is now justly recognised for all she gave to the creation and history of 'The Wica.'

X...................................X

(m) Laying the Compass—Preparation of the Bridge

Notes: Bowers gives George clear instructions on *'How to Lay The Compass'* —Bowers had previously established the basics via a template founded upon earlier works learned from various people and groups he'd worked with or alongside. Forever seeking and pushing boundaries, his enquiring mind sought ever new and ever deeper ways of working. Tired of the circular paganisms those around him freely indulged, he read avidly, hoping to find clues that would lead him to the Mysteries. From magical texts to folklore and legends, he absorbed it all. Inspired by the Muse, he formulated a pattern of magical praxis built upon extant tradition, reworked to make it relevant to his era. Above all, he sought ways to facilitate the truths of occult science to cast light (wisdom) upon the shades of superstition and primitivisms that had haunted and weakened a 'natural culture.' In this rite, each point within the Compass is occupied, placing each member where personal virtue (as described previously) is best suited to its transmutation through a collective virtue, enflaming the very qutub that nourishes it. That point is here occupied by the Magister of the Clan: Roy Bowers. In the North, the source of Clan Virtue, his Maid, Jane holds.

(1). The ground is being dug as a moat and mound – they are working outdoors, on hill tops, creating the old iron forts and stockades of our ancestors, and in some cases the burial mounds and cairns too.

(2). The 'circle' is here referred to as a 'ring.'

(3). Here is a direct reference to the fact that Chalky had made a suggestion for a long expiatory prayer, which Bowers had deemed too long and inappropriate, preferring to use his own succinct declaration within the Rite.

(4). Implements: Stangs and Kippens are introduced along with a host of new tools and terms of arte.

(5). They <u>are wearing cloaks</u>. This is important as Monmouth claims they were introduced later as cosmetic theatrics merely to impress Valiente. However, she was not to join them until August 1964.

(6) Figure on his wall: Bowers refers to an icon of the God he'd forged himself.

(see 'Tubal's Mill')

(7) By 'strip off, Bowers refers to the removal of all outdoor gear, cloaks and boots etc before feasting in comfort after trudging around in the mud, and often rain. E.J. Jones informed us that on the rare occasion they did feast outdoors, it was at another spot outside the working area if the weather was clement enough to do so.

X..................................X

The Midsummer Ritual (m)
Preparation of Site (n) Self (o) Diagram

Notes: Midsummer - These documents are pivotal in the evolution of Bowers' Craft. They example by definition and instruction the 'virtue' Bowers speaks of so frequently and eloquently. The acquisition and manipulation of 'virtue' lies at the heart of his Craft and represent the occulted science the 'Witch' or artificer depends upon for successful synchronicities and overcoming of Fate. Serving as mnemonic analogies, many gods are mentioned, as is the 'Tree' vehicle of the Compass itself, witnessed in Yggdrasil and Otz Chim.

The Midsummer Ritual

Bowers to Chalky and George - Synopsis and the: Ritual For Midsummer
The 'order' of Work follows the magical pattern expounded in:
The Rhyme – 'The House that Jack Built.'

(n) Transcript Part One
The Work To Be Done Before Ritual

A.   Examine the site (1) for faults i.e. heavy mud and exposure to roads, broken branches etc.

B.   The fireplace and ring dug, and firewood gathered for the pot. Jane dances round the ring (2) with the hand of Hermes.

   She centres it with triangle in earth (reference to drawing of circle with six-pointed Star-of-David at centre showing ring and star dug and broom placed in centre of star). Puts in the broom. The fireplace must have a wall of earth surrounding it in order to cut down the chance of being seen.

C.   The cauldron put above the fire to boil. First prayers are offered in silence (meditate the prayer)

The Ritual Proper.

A. Confession. I suggest this should be much shorter than the statement
    Ron suggested. (3) 'Fains I have trespassed' covers it. The word
    'Fains' is in common usage and means 'peace.' It is also a word that
    no philologist can find an explanation for, so it is very likely that it
    came from a secret language.

B. Expiation. I suggest three cuts with a willow wand, the sign of the
    sorrowful lover.

C. Purification. The same series of symbols are used here as in the
    Union Jack, but put the finger on the forehead in oil previously
    consecrated. During this, members should hold their thumbs in hand
    and cross arms on chest. After which they rise and assemble before
    the skull in the triangle with three sticks of incense. Kneeling, they
    offer it in triple homage. Bowing as the bell rings, then rising, proceed
    to the cauldron, where all walking around it plunge their knives into
    it five times, then laying knives upon the floor, proceed to dance
    around nine times holding hands. From this, led by Jane and I,
    proceed to the circle which is finally closed by the Summoner with
    Stang with a Cross. (4)

Previously to this, Jane takes water from the Cauldron and throws it
three times upon the circle with ladle. Once in the circle the Elements
are shown, at this point, bang stangs three times upon the ground. Then
I pass the Staff through the sickle followed by you and the rest of the
Coven. Cover Stangs with Cloak (5) and dance around willing the
appearance of the God in the centre. If possible once there is a build-up

do NOT chant or make sounds, but keep the hood pulled over the face. I suggest that we all have a common image of the God, that is like the figure upon my wall.(6) Hold this image as firmly as you can, and will it to the centre of the circle along an image of white light. This point may lead to definite possession in which case symptoms may be noticed. The person possessed will be icy cold to touch and breath. His voice will alter and a sensation of energy will be felt from him. If this phenomena happens then the possessed person will know what to do, since within the broom which is thrust upright in the centre of the circle there is a phallus.

Notes. I suggest that when we have all achieved the necessary state we commence our homeward journey. Having arrived home, strip off and have our feast indoors. (7)

Note. No salt if possible in food one week previously – pull hood down over face so as to cut out all external stimuli – No other magical work is undertaken except the above. Concentrate the week previously upon the image of the God and get a very clear picture of him in your mind. We stand or fall on this so get it perfect. Concentration upon the God image for the previous week is absolute, essential. Love Roy

x..................................x

Transcript: The Tools

<u>The Tools:</u> These are given magical properties instead of more conventional properties of the simple rural craft. Incidentally, it is from the failure of witches to develop their ritual that the failure of them to work any form of magic in recent years stems from. As much the tools are incorporated into magic rather than religious usages.

<u>The Knife.</u> This is the masculine Tree. It represents Intellect, Will, and is

symbolic of the search for knowledge and experience. It is also Choice, Love Physical, Mercy and Generosity. It also represents Craft or Skill.

The Cord: This is the feminine Tree and should have five and three knots with a noose at one end. It is representative of all FATE. The Noose formed properly is (a) subjugation to Hekate as Moria. Hekate, the 'Strong Fate.' At a different level it represents the End and beginning of Life.

The Knots represent:

(a) The Round of Life,

(b) The Spirits of the Moon,

(c) The Horn, and the Noose and a Third knot depicts the   power of the Goddess over these things.

It is from this Cord that the practise of Witches of repeating a

Magical action three times came from.

Staff or Stang: This is the Supreme Instrument. It represents the Middle Pillar of Ygrassdraall. It should be forked and bound at the base with Iron. It is the Gateway, at the base of physical experience. The Chariot at the centre because it is the power and the treble. Horns at the top, the High Spiritual endeavour. Then from the base upwards it represents these factors: The Stone or Gate because it is phallic and because it represents the Guide. Next position is the Moon because this is the path to the Mysteries. It is the Foundation of Wisdom. Next. It is Love, because it represents the Union of Male and Female, therefore Attraction and Counter-Attraction. Next it is Beauty, the Child of Wisdom, then at this point it becomes the Chariot or Power. Its next attribute is Death and Destruction. In this aspect it becomes Lethe, Chronos, in fact Mercy and Chronos in One. The next attribute at the Horns is mystical and may not be written.

Sword	Truth
Sieve	Judgment
Stone	Mysteries
Pot	Inspiration, Rebirth
Fire	Passion
Sickle	The Cruel Mother, Death
Cross	Elements (drawings here) Resurrection
Platter	life forthcoming – Choice, The World
Cup	Abundance
Cords	(Binding twine) Power over (red) Od, Power over (blue)Helas
Broom	Conjunction of Heaven and Earth the Cord of the Mysteries, Love Fertility.
Herbs	Birch (Life) Vervain (Love) Apple (Maternity: and Maturity)
Fennel	(Wisdom), Willow (Death)

x..................................x

Transcript for Midsummer Ritual (partial)

Dear Chalky and George,

The ritual purification and preparation for Midsummer. Here goes.

The tools used for this ritual are these:

Hempen Cord with five.... 3 knots.

The Five represent the feminine star, or the Round of Life.

The Three Knots represent The Triad, or the practise of power through the Moon Goddess as Her Virgin Mother, Wise One aspect.

These Knots are meditational devices and should be used to form a personal chant, invoking each aspect of the Triad, and climbing beyond the Round of Life. The Cord should also have a noose in one end and a thong on the other, so that the Hangman's noose should be present when the whole thing is finished. This noose, in one aspect only, represents subjection to the Power of the Goddess. It is feminine in its purpose and represents basically the Power the Protean Goddess has over us. This is many more interpretations to it, but it will be found that each of these tally's with the above definitions (umbilical cord, cords of binding). The Round of Life as agreed upon represents not the actual aspects of the Round but the Power the Goddess has over them. Knife: This is the masculine Tree, and such represents Intellect, or the actual search for wisdom, experience and knowledge. Basically then it represents these aspects. Wisdom. Love physical. Mercy and generosity. Victory and conflict. And as such when sharpened against the Stone of the Mysteries (the Gateway….Malkuth) it represents our passage through time and space on our search.

Staff: The Staff is the Supreme implement. It represents the Middle Pillar or Yrgrasddall the Ash and the Rowan in one. In roots are in Earth or the Gateway that is physical experience, and its main attributes are: The Gateway since it is phallic and represents Hermes the Guide. The Moon because it is the Path to the Mysteries of Magic, and the Formation of the Wisdom, the Foundation of Spiritual Experience, it is Love because it represents Union of the Masculine and Feminine, therefore it is also Attraction and Counter Attraction and it is Beauty, the Child of Wisdom and Experience. Its next attribute is that of Death and Destruction, since to achieve the Highest, one must pass the Lowest the Passage of Time, in fact Chronos and Mercury in one. The next attribute is The GODDESS or the primal movement. In other words, it is a combination of the Masculine and Feminine up to Death. Then it becomes the Pure Path of

Enlightenment. The Goddess and the GODDESS are lower and higher aspects of One Source.

Stone: Any stone will do providing it is square and natural. The Stone represents the Stone of the Mysteries and it is three-fold. I will not explain in the letter, but examine the Triad at its highest level.

The Cloak: The Cloak represents:
   (a) the Concealment of Spiritual Knowledge
   (b) Night the Coverer of Mystery
   (c) Humility.
Through these lower case interpretations it goes again higher too
   (a) Charity or Love
   (b) Hidden Wisdoms
   (c) Magical Power.

I can keep on explaining but I think you find everything interlocks and forms One Whole. I know it is a lot to remember but I have a career and considerable responsibilities external to Witchcraft. Incidentally, before anyone starts to say that I am complicating things have a look at my original letter. You will find that we all agreed to a common symbolism, and these symbols are historically valid and correct. It was what the true witch used to believe in, no simpleton by any means. Now work before the ritual. Each night a small amount of time will have to be spent upon these things.

(a) Consecrating each of the tools.
This is done simply by imagining yourself filled with the highest power from above, bringing that power down to the base of the spine and

236

lighting the basic fires there, bring it up to the RIGHT hand, externalise it and bless each tool in the name of the GODDESS (anyone will do) in its particular aspect. ie. The Knife Hermes. *"Hermes. Hermes. Thou Bright Light leading us through the Gateway of Death. Thou Guardian of the Portholes, Fashioner of all Skills and Knowledge. Torchbearer, here me! I pray for Thy assistance in my trade. Thou who burnest as Love Physical, Thou who bearest the entwined snakes, Thou who knowest all things, who was born from the Union of the North Wind and Darkness. Here me. Here me. Here me. Hermes bless this Knife make it all Thou Art. May it fashion my art for me may it protect me from ill doers, may it lighten the way for me…. Amen."* And so on. It should be simple to prepare a personal consecration for each tool. The Goddess is the Highest aspect, image Her transformed into each of the Forces you invoke.

b) Consecrating yourself.

This done by appealing to the Highest Source and by trying to get out of the physical to go to Her. Lay flat on back, will yourself outside your body and constantly keep invoking the Highest aspect. You will probably notice no difference at first, But you will find that just immediate to sleep, you will float upwards. Now if you want to see what it is like outside, imagine a circle around your bed charged with a command for yourself to waken immediately you pass it.

(c) The Rub. Sex…..

Keep continent at least three days and nights before the ritual. Fast one day before, only water. Now the last night before the ritual, take your sexual power and transfer it around your body, stopping at all the extremities, charging each one according to the Mask of God then bring it up to your head and transfer it outside to the GODDESS, transmuting it of course to the Power. Then bring it down the body and back to the original source again. You will have to do this at the meeting but you will find that once it is properly done that it will make you sexless until the following day. This actually more important than anything else, but it has a penalty attached. It is the source of all magic. This transmutation and once the banishing has been done, it can be transferred to the ritual in hand.

These are the Preliminaries. I am sorry if they are complicated, but there is no simple way to do them. It is all time and will day in day out.

Transcript: The Ritual

Firstly this should never be written down. I had the notion that perhaps you would be far enough advanced in symbology to understand the nursery rhyme, but experience has proved me wrong. Now get that nursery rhyme out and look at it. you will notice that it contains considerable chunks of philosophy: for instance, why should the cord bind the staff, and why should the knife cut it? There is a lot more in it, and basically it represents both Jane's and my total knowledge upon witchcraft. Still, here then is the ritual in basic and formal terms. The work first required is that we cut the circle out. This is Chalkie's job, and the three boundaries are laid out as per instruction. In the centre is the sword with the mask fixed upon it, and Jane will then mark a triangle a square and a crescent in that circle. I then consecrate it from outside and leave my knife across the boundaries as the Bridge. Once this is done, we are ready. The consecration is as follows. I proceed widdershins around the circle with the platter muttering something under my breath, then Jane will sweep round it three times, a la riding. Incidentally, Jane before marking the three symbols of the ritual will sweep spirally in the circle, towards the centre.

Preparation of Self - The Basic Ritual

We then kneel in a crescent facing East and the Invocation of the Highest GODDESS is begun by Jane. To do this we will work as a group beginning by all blessing ourselves in this fashion. We must consider our own bodies and our own faces as the Mask of God, and bless ourselves accordingly.

Top of Forehead.

'Divine Goddess! Fount of all Life,

Thou Who Art the Staff of our mortal round,

Supporting all Life bearing ever anew,

Bringing forth from the Unknown,

Life….Love….and Beauty.

Thou Who Art First -born,

We pray to Thee.'

Right Side of Forehead.

'Transformed Being Sun of Suns,

Bringer of glad daylight, of Dawn

And the Vanquisher of Evil,

I Salute Thee.'

Left Side of Forehead.

'Master of Death, Lord Who Judges.

Redeemer of the Soul. I salute Thee.'

Left Ear.

'Thou Bringer of News,

Messenger of the Gods,

Inspirer of Spirits.

I salute Thee.'

Left Eye.
'Time, Decayer of all Things,
Blaster of the Flesh,
I Salute Thee.'

Nose.
'Wisdom, Thou Light of Life,
Comforter of the Poor,
I Salute Thee.'

Right Eye.
'Splendour, Thou Growing
Being Inhabitant of the Knife,
I Salute Thee.'

Right Ear.
'Thou Who Art Generous,
Beneficent Being,
I Salute Thee.'

Lips. (Tongue)
'Thou Who Art One in Two,
Love, I Salute Thee.'

Left Side of Chin (Beard)
'Thou Who Art Mother of Creation,
Womb of the World, Nature,

Divine Goddess. Hail.'

Right Side of Chin.
'Father. Old Pan, Earth God
Who has Shepherded Life
From its Beginnings,
I Pray unto Thee. Hail.'

Centre of Beard.
'Root of all Life that
Stretches from Heaven to Earth.
I Greet Thee.
Vouchsafe us deliverance this day.
Amen.'

(Jane will then speak the prayer)

These are meditational devices they can be spoken aloud, but it is not necessary provided the meaning of each aspect of the 'Mask of God' is understood. The main thing is that the feeling of each of these Powers should be there. I have tried to create a meditational seed form, It must never be spoken aloud, but always muttered since this is the Witch system, think you will find that the trees of Robert Graves correspond with this, and Magic can be performed by its proper use. Sex is the power employed.

Upon the personal consecration being completes, Jane will lift the Grail and empty it into the Pot as per normal ritual. Proceed around it chanting if you like, Words we can agree upon for meeting. Dip knives into the pot proceed nine times about, then be fed by Jane with the contents of the pots. Proceed to the circle but do NOT cross over yet. I will cast cake upon the ground then go in myself, followed by Jane who will greet each of you as you cross the bridge. Offer to the Mask of God, the tapers or sticks of incense, bow three times then proceed to pace around the Compass I want everyone to will the appearance of Hermes, otherwise known as Odhin, and he will lead us through the Underworld. Try and visualize in the centre the figure of our God, the Conductor of the Dead. He should be in 16th century costume with a hat, and cloaked.... Medium build white stockings with garter, cloak across face, hat over eyes (hat incidentally means secrecy). The purpose of the ritual is WISDOM, this is the Aspect we must focus our power upon. Once He appears greet him then ask him to lead the way.

The usual procedure of confession expiation and purification to be used at the beginning. Cauldron and Tripod Grail and Herbs. Sorry about the amount of work, but we are working twice as hard since we have that much more to remember. This paper and the two others will explain everything now. Whilst pacing place the Knots of the Cord between fingers and meditate upon them in the wisdom aspects, it gives the physical body and the ordinary mind, something to do so that superconsciousness can take over. Now tell me where I have changed my mind, all that has happened is that the path is that much clearer for you.

Once this particular letter is really and thoroughly understood, destroy it. This is not a suggestion but a command. The basic knowledge written in here can do terrible things in the wrong hands. Take notes if you wish, but the actual workings must be remembered then the letter destroyed. Incidentally it does work, we have been 5using it now for some time and my original intention was to tell you the same thing as I was told, so that you could draw your own conclusions. We have had results from it. And have got letters to prove it. The Mask of God is fitted to the Body and charged by the use of sexual energy. Roy and Jane.

(0) Diagram of the castle and the moat and the mask

~2~

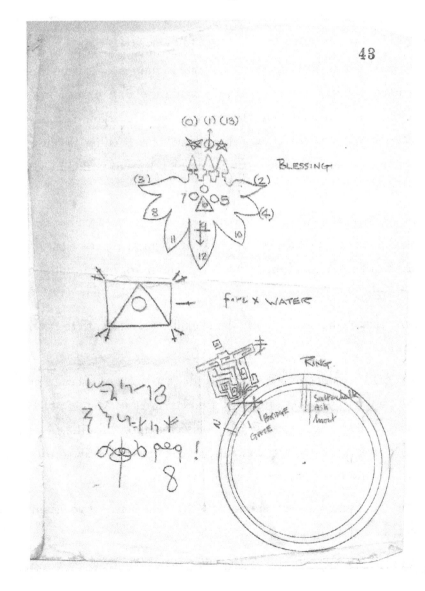

(p) Failure in Communication: Finding the Bridge.

Notes: The Ritual & Assumption of 'Mask' & Maze.

This documents highlights very neatly, how even at this stage, they failed to achieve a group harmonic, and were constantly trying to form a group mind fuelled by compatibility. Bowers' desires for his work through his Clan, never reached fruition. The disparate and diverse principles within the tenets of the beliefs held by Chalky and George created continual friction, as noted by E. J. Jones to ourselves.

(1). Bowers' asserts his intention to separate all future works from those worked previously. He has already made the shift towards more traditional methodologies. He explains that what came before no longer serves and has little or no validity. This is either because it pertains to outmoded ideas, or because it relates to nothing real or tangible.

(2). Bowers here emphasises the imperative of silence, and the unreserved need for disciplined focus; for everyone to know exactly what they are 'working' for, and the image they require for manifestation of 'Virtue.'

(3). Love agape - the beatification, the worship, - the cake offered to the Hound.

(4). The Stang has become the Altar as the true point of sacrifice and the Cauldron is where the Moon now infuses its Virtue, <u>not</u> the naked body of a Priestess. Each tool is a mnemonic for the pattern woven in synchronicity to build the matrix that will 'draw' through into manifestation, the god behind the Mask.

(5). The Tree System Bowers speaks of is the Rune-staves as vowels and as calls.

(6). A theme Bowers returned to often was the need to make everything relative to the 'now,' be that an idea or a symbol. The Faith itself required overhauling to mean something to the modern mind, one no longer processed through the paganisms, life-styles and beliefs of our ancestors. He is not saying of course that we should abandon their values, or their Gods; he advocates only that we seek a better understanding of their abilities and a better appreciation of their wisdoms. All of which we need to apply to our own lives and evolution as a collective humanity upon a planet, within a Universe that thrives on symbiosis.

(7). A very animistic and highly sophisticated form of shamanism in which the virtue of the animal invoked imbues the Compass point and the Knot worked.

(8). Bowers explains how these ideas are something he and Jane have already put into place for themselves. Having discovered them, they have moved on and wish to share theses workings with the the others. He appears to be giving them the option here of working in the new style with Jane and himself, or continuing without them.

Transcript: Failure in Communication: Finding the Bridge.

Dear Chalky

Reference our telephone conversation. Obviously the real fault lies in communication and not in the alteration of the ritual. Since we have decided to follow strictly traditional patterns, we have had to scrap nearly everything that was valid previously.(1) During the formation of traditional practise, it must be remembered that nothing has come to us as a bulk commodity, but a series of small but increasingly interesting information. Therefore let us agree to what are the actual limits and practises which have been proven and disproven. I obviously cannot go into why various energies are used, or the production of these energies, but I can go into some detail of future projects and their direct continuity with past practise. First then the philosophical structure of the circle. We must first consider it as apart from religious belief and as an area designated for working in. the style of work falls in to three major categories. First is the ritual of manifestation, in which absolute silence must be maintained (2) a common image rigidly held, and the group discipline at its highest level. All this is not only dependent upon the actual procedure at the time, but upon preliminary procedure to a meeting. It is also subject to a preliminary 'build-up' of energy through an associative chain of imagery and various mental and physical devices. The second structure of the circle is dependent upon the success of the first. If we can manifest out Lord, then and only then are we capable of working magic in the circle, since it is not dependent upon how much energy we can personally produce but whether or not it can live upon the planes external to our area of operation. In other words, we must establish a strong bond of communication between us and the forces we try and invoke. As such it is a matter of indifference how many times we run, pace or crawl round a circle. In true witchcraft the operator runs around a ritual number of times to work magic, they do not run around until they are in a hyperaesthetic state. This of course is the basic difference between the pseudo witch and the genuine article. The real article has contact that certain words and actions can bring into communication. Without this, we are limited to the tea party kind of magic in which fortune telling is our highest aspiration. With it, our only limits are those imposed by our own lack of intelligence. It really doesn't matter whether or not these forces we try and invoke are external or the deeper reaches of the superconsciousness, what does matter (is) that we have a common image of what we are trying to produce and a common source of original inspiration to induce the current to flow. The third state (3) of working in a circle is the one already known to us and its final product is happiness at the time.

All this then is dependent upon whether or not we can find the bridge. As you know we have got near to that point before but each time we have been defeated because everybody wanted something different. The case in point is that you for instance saw a decaying corpse, I saw a 17th century man beginning to appear in the centre George saw someone standing to one side and Jane felt a distinct lowering of vitality. If at that time we had all agreed to see one thing and one thing only, then than one thing could have been strengthened until it actually could be seen or felt by all of us, and then would be the time to begin communication. But as it stood, we all had different ideas about the what the circle was, what magic was and what we all wanted out of it. Obviously it is like the magic grail, you get out of it what you most want, but that is only applicable to yourself and nobody else. If we are to succeed then we must agree upon a common image to work upon and a common philosophy, even if we do not think too highly of it since it does not fulfil some personal theory.

Therefore, both Jane and I suggest this as a common belief as to the origin and structure of the circle. We do not intend to put it in modern technical terms since they have little in common with the area of spirit that magic proceeds from. As far as we know these symbols and this system are the direct descendants of the 'Keltic' tradition, and you will no doubt find many things in it that parallel with your own experience and with your own knowledge of 'Keltic' belief.

Since we worship Hekate or Keriwidden as the Wisdom aspect, then in accordance with all esoteric systems we will find Her only by crossing the Lethe, a common enough story from the past. Therefore the circle as such represents the Underworld or Spiral Castle (this is something we all agreed upon many months ago). Now then, how do we create an image of the Spiral Castle? This I would suggest consists of these symbols. First a layer of salt to represent Life and agitate the Dead, then at an interval of three inches, a layer of Soot or Ashes to represent Death, the principle of universal decay, then a channel dug to represent the river Lethe or Time that separates the Dead from the Living. In the centre of the Circle a sword embedded in an oracular head, this represents Truth, in the sense that Pluto or Persephone as the Guardian of all Purity and Truth as well as the Ruler of the Underworld. To this symbol is offered the Taper representing your own life. To enter Spiral Castle we must first cross the Bridge of Knives which are the lesser truths or experience or knowledge. Now previous to entering the Castle there must also be other things. The minor Ritual of Expiation for instance to purify and it is worth while noticing that the best results have always been found this way. There must also be the assumption of the spiritual body which is basically that of the greater banishment ritual in Cabbilism. Upon the Ritual of Assumption there is a necessity to drink from the Cauldron of Inspiration, which is a necessary preliminary to the finding of Truth. As such I would again suggest the ritual that we normally use for this, that is the Fire of Masculine Intellect boils the Cauldron of Feminine Inspiration into which we plunge our knives (knowledge) then dance over them to achieve power over Wisdom.   Then and then only do we proceed into the circle where we offer the Taper of intellectual awareness to the Banner of Truth. Then and then only do we begin to pace the circle round. Obviously there is purification of the circle, the Drawing of the Moon into the Cauldron, but these are minor details. (4) There is as you can see a pattern emerging from all this, a pattern of religious philosophy and this is what we should try and achieve, since it will form to link. Also against the basic ritual can be set the fact that it will accommodate any other ritual or development in the future, such as the greater ritual at

248

Halloween. It will also accommodate itself to a tree system that we are working on at the present moment. (5) In other words both Jane and I have been working upon a development of Witchcraft. We are in the 20th century, therefore our needs are different from those of our ancestors. What they practised worked for them, if we practise the same thing, it will not work for us, since our framework of reference is very different. Obviously a simple pagan ritual will not work for us, this we know for fact since our intellectual needs were greater than the thing offered. (6) Truth is our aim nothing else.

Now about animal (s)kins. Heat is a necessary ingredient in the working of magic. But how do we translate animal magic for the fertility of herds from the 20th century, into a modern idiom of a high philosophy? I would suggest we reference work upon the symbolic meaning attached to animals, and refer to animals of this nature as symbols of the spiritual forces attached to the basic interpretation. In other words that if a Hare represents Life, then we look upon the wearer of the Hare symbol as the Priestess. If the Bull represents spiritual and physical Strength, then the wearer is not a Bull but a representative of that force. (7) This I think will answer Graves' question when he asked what Anne Armstrong meant by the Witch Song 'I shall go into the Hare', and also explain the esoteric meanings behind animal transformation. They did not transfer into an image of the animal, but into a possession of the God the animal represented in the old philosophy.

Anyway, I am not bulldozing you into anything, but this is the way both and Jane and I have been working, and will work in the future. Let me know what you think vide letter. (8)

X...................................X

(q) Bowers to Bill Gray:
i - #II
ii - #IV

Notes: Bowers finally meets Bill Gray in 1964. Charlie Cardell had begun to seriously attract negative attention. Bowers describes him as a 'naughty boy,' caught out in his misdemeanour's. He relays to Bill that someone from St Albans phoned to inform him of their intention to curse Cardell (Valiente's note-pads cite Lois Bourne & Eleanor Ray Bone). This would be a very strange thing to do, only if Bowers was an impartial or objective person with no interest or even knowledge of the persons concerned. He obviously knew both parties well, and on both sides. Bowers continued to correspond with the 'Old Man' whose mysterious identity has allowed for much speculation; and almost all of that is absurd in the extreme. No-one has yet been able to assist in any reasonable estimation as to who he was with anything even remotely sensible, less still provable. In like manner of the greater portion of what is 'known' beyond the remit of The Clan itself, it remains gossip and speculation. Anyone able to come forward with anything beyond an intuitive 'guess' will be most welcome, though they should of course always secure sound reason for all suggestions put forward. {NB: *we do make an informed suggestion regarding his identity, ourselves, based on considerable evidence. This is explored in 'Tubal's Mill' 2016*}

Far better candidates exist to en-flesh into manifest form, this hitherto enigmatic figure, than any previously suggested or hinted at. In lieu of the manner in which this information was first sourced and later disseminated, there is absolutely nothing anywhere to hint at George Winter, whose own ill health was beginning to seriously hamper his activities and life-style. In fact, very little is noted of or about George Winter, he is almost always an obligatory appendage to Ronald White

250

whose works are now accessible to the public or study for style and content. This is strongly encouraged. But of George, no works or writings are known.

Whoever this 'old man' was, he supplied Bowers with solid traditional craft material of such incredible significance, it is still being realised today by those of us working his tradition. Prior to receiving these instructions from Bowers, Chalky and George were obviously unfamiliar with this knowledge. The chain begins with the 'Old Man' through Bowers, to those people he shared his time and knowledge with—the actual working members of his own group and those of his Clan. That is again highlighted *as coming*—from *The Old man, to Bowers, then to Chalky and George. NOT,* the other way around. All documents within this cache from Bowers, assist or instruct them regarding essential ritual procedure, giving them the authority needed to not only perform requisite duties, but to aid and assist their establishment of another group within the Clan.

Chalky received many instructional missives from Bowers. So it must be noted that *nowhere is the reverse true. Not a single missive exists where Chalky advises Bowers on any subject or matter of life or ritual.* Even so, despite this, their methods and opinion continue to be very much in opposition. Bowers is required to periodically assert his authority as leader overall, making it very evident that Chalky is quite grudgingly subject to Bowers' instruction. And, though he does acknowledge the increasing tensions between them, Monmouth suggests that Chalky and George had sufficient 'strength of character' to take a passive back seat, allowing Bowers to usurp an authority neither they nor Monmouth believes was his by right to exert. In fact, somewhat ironically, Monmouth confirms how unlikely this was, given that they, *"were not easily led."* But does this not mean then, that they actually were led? Just not easily!

Bowers offers them these specific instructions from that information to make the activities of that second group compatible with...*his own group, the founding group and Clan.* Bowers' Clan, consisted of Inducted members only. That policy remains rigorously enforced within His Clan today.

(1). Again an exampled expression of Bowers' increasing frustration and constant battles to bring those members of his group further in their understanding of the mysteries and to gain an understanding of the craft as an occulted science. Chalky and George did not share his vision.

(2). This comment refers back to the first coven he set up in Slough after leaving the group in London. This may have been the *'Thames Valley Coven.'*

Transcript of #II Bowers to Bill Gray

Thanks ever so for the missive. We enjoyed meeting you, and as you say, it was like renewing an old friendship. It definitely was Germany, the moment I saw you I started to remember something but then it vanished. I wonder, did we leave a kettle on the boil in our last round? It was a bit like that feeling ...

I will try and get to the lecture given by Sandra, I am not certain but I think that I will be required to drop down dead as a demonstration of her magical powers. Easily enough done for a joke, but the old lady brigade will certainly faint if we tried it. Incidentally, J. Murray appears from my gentle probing to be a case of potential hysteria, I wonder if we can straighten her out a bit, before it gets too big a hold? I honestly felt the approach of a mental disturbance, not actually mental but emotional to be more specific. It worries me a bit, I will have to run around in circles to find out more. Anyway I will be there for the lecture.

I think we have been brought together again for a purpose also ...

The way I see it is that you are children of the sun, we are children of the moon ... you are light ... we are dark ... you are open ... we are secretive ... your brand of magic deals in intellectual truth, our brand (sounds like a bloody detergent advertisement) deals with the essential nature of illusion. Yet above all this we seek the same final truths, the same finality of expression and experience. It is really amazing the way our rituals come together at so many points. (been reading 'Mystical Qabala) and then wind off again into our respective worlds. There must be a middle pillar that we can both ascend , a place where the moon and the sun can both shine together in the miday/midnight sky ... sounds as if I might have unconsciously discovered it, a very good description of the real Inner Planes.

You know then why we are reluctant to do anything about disintegrating the image of your mother. If it was me, (and I have walked the lonely path of near insanity at one time), I would use the same process now as I did then, look outwards, love everything and everybody, get as near to the earth as you can, and achieve equilibrium with your past. Ignore what is going on, and force yourself to get out and meet people, accepting them for what they are. The power that possessed me vanished with this treatment , and a terrible power it was ... violence, death and destruction possessed me, and I was a walking threat to anything or anybody. If it hadn't been for my beloved Jane, I would have eventually really tangled with the Law and gone down fighting rather than be taken prisoner.

The broken nose and the scars upon my face are constant reminders of the time when it was easier for me to kick out and fight about anything in order to avenge my outraged sensitivity. There seemed to be nothing but horror and destruction in the world and it was pure anger at war and the bestiality of war that made me a wild animal myself. There is always a path back, my love for Jane was my path back. I think that your love for your chosen field will bring you back, and Bobbie will hold the torch that will guide you. We will try and give you all the power we can in your lonely fight.

Surprizingly enough, someone from the St. Alban' s mob phoned me just after I had recieved your letter and news about Charlie Cardell. They apparently have cursed him formally and with intent, but for my money he will go from strength to strength on that alone they havn't got any power worth speaking of. I have heard from various sources that Charlie is quite a naughty boy in many things and is well on his way to becoming the Tarot fool at its lowest representation. I think he will destroy himself eventually, but before he goes down he will try and drag everybody that is around him down with him. Still the Watchers and the Hounds will be after him soon, and they when the Horn is sounded are truly terrifying. I honestly feel sorry for Doreen Valiente though, she is getting the blame for events that took place a few years before she appeared upon the scene. Gardner was, in my estimation, and in the estimation of other people who are in the possession of the apostolic 'breath' an out and out fake, who through various degenerate habits first came into this field. He was in various occult movements around London before the war and is reported as asking around as to the whereabouts of the 'witches'. Nobody could help him, and then after the war he published a crude novel 'High Magicks Aid' which was absolute nonsense with a strong flavour of sexual deviation. From this novel he went on the game of writing books about witchcraft, and became an 'authority' who in turn started his original group somewhere in Southern England, then came the St. Albans people, then various other groups. No real authority except maybe one, ever accepted Gardner as being the genuine article. However according to my information dating some years ago, Cardell was initiated himself by Gardner, then quarreled over something or the other (presumably inflated ego) and they parted. They have all made the one fatal mistake of believing that witchcraft was the relics of a fertility religion, and misunderstanding the phallic rite that the puritans were so horrified by. I am not supposed to explain this to anyone except a female witch, but for this purpose I will consider you as a witch and as a female, either that or Bobbie will have to read this explaination. Here goes the, the real explaination behind the apparent phallicism of the witch cult.

To begin any work , like yourself, we go to Kether, Tiphareth, Yesod and Malkuth. It is with the Malkuth however that we walk the bridge and open the Gate. Hermes is the Guide at this point. Now in spite of 'historical' evidence, Hermes was NOT a God that was phallic, but essentially the Guide through the Underworld, Kay of Castle Arianrhod. Phallicism does come into it, but historians, antiquarians and foolish would be witches have misinterpreted it. Remember I have always said that in witchcraft nothing is as it appears. The rituals in which the male and female generative organs were used were rituals of (a) Magick, (b) Death, (c) Ressurection, in the sense that virtue, our word for power, can be passed from one person to another (now you know why witches must pass from male to female). This virtue originally was given to 'Hecate' by union with Saturn. They between them produced a Son 'Hermes', now he by combining his function with that of the Guide, generated in the female witch virtue by the same process, she in turn passes it to the male warlock. Now remember that each piece of witch philosophy has many different interpretations, and is never quite what it seems to be, and I will leave you to work it out from there.

They in spite of their many names, are all aspects of the Two Pillars, or as we call it, the knife and the cord. This ritual can be actually carried out with certain reservations, or else it can be transmuted into another

<u>form</u>, which is the process we use. Obviously the near savage villagers of the past used the most obvious form, we are of the twentieth century and we do not. But from this piece of esoteric knowledge, you will find many beliefs about witches and their attributes. I for instance, cannot die until I have passed my virtue on, I carry within my physical body the totality of all the witches that have been in my family and their virtue for many centuries. If I call upon my ancestors, I call upon forces that are within myself and exterior, now you know what I mean when

I speak of the burden of time. This is why witches lose their power when blooded by an outsider, why they float when others sink (virtue is supposed to be the force that lets us fly) Why iron is a good defence against it, since it earths it, why this and why that.

However, now to bring you back to male form again ... Before we return from our excursion from the underworld, I would like to say that Hermes, Hecate, Saturn are only approximations of what we really mean. Enough said. I am seriously considering leaving my group and working alone. I may sound dreadfully <u>un</u>-humble, but Jane and I have reached a stage when we can go faster by ourselves.

(1)The group is beginning to pull us backwards, and I for one would like to establish a new leader and move on myself. We had a brilliant 'flash of light' recently that may lead to the end of an old era and the beginning of a new for us. The Gods seem to favour us leaving also since they are going their hardest to stop new blood from coming in. We shall see whether it is meant that way or whether the Gods are just saying 'This is what it is like. See! you bumbling little worm'.

That article I have written for *New Dimensions* has been accepted, and I recieved the magnificent sum of three nikker ... well, well ... I suppose now that I am considering moving on, hundreds of very suitable people will want to come crowding in. We have had trouble in the past with various unsuitable types, I once was in charge of a full and balanced cuveen, but they wanted to play silly beggars, so I let them (we moved on).

(2) Net results broken hearts and broken heads, but they still don't seem to have learned. The last I heard from them was that they had gone over to the Aradia 'since it is so exciting' and have taken a vote to share the women out. Sex and Witchcraft, whee! The messes some people get into over that little bit of flesh. I suppose one cannot make silk purses out of sows ear'oles.

My cat, when waiting to be fed, dances around Jane widdershins with tail up and meowing. Jane suggested that she was chanting 'Eko, Eko Azarack ... Eko ... Eko ... Kiti-Kat! '

Blessings, Roy and Jane

x...................................x

ii - #IV Bowers to Bill Gray

Notes: Looking again at letter #IV a little more closely, Bowers informs Bill Gray how that *second group* is now firmly organising itself around him. He is eager to inform Bill how his two apprentices, the new members to his group, mentioned in #VI (as Dick and John) now enthusiastically seek others. This drew the interest of Chalky and George to draw more closely once again to that 'second group,' noted as 'gathering around him'. They were to have their own members and guests just as Bowers did. But more frequently than not, they did all work together in Bowers' newly founded *Clan of Tubal Cain.* Spurred on by the info from the '*old man*' (of Westmoreland) he began to operate a more traditional craft system, as opposed to the more magickal fraternity established with Bill Gray's assistance, expressed through the '*Society of Keridwen.*' He bemoans how the *New Dimensions* article is not yet printed. Doreen Valiente is writing still; they have yet to meet. Bowers sends Bill Gray a lure, he mentions to him that they will be caving in October specifically, he describes again to him the stone-age temple in one of the caves they wish to investigate. He apologies for not making it over to see Bill whilst on holiday.

Transcript of #IV from Roy Bowers to Bill Gray

My apologies for not writing before, but events, lethargy and holiday' s caught up with me in no uncertain fashion. I hope you will forgive me, otherwise I shall have to charge a damned circle round my bed each night, and ward off your thoughts of indignation (joke).

The second group seems to organising itself around me, people are coming in quite happily from all nations and walks of life. My two apprentices have found others, it would seem, and I have aquired an American who confesses to more than a passing interest in paganism. Factory workers, rough diamonds, schoolteacher, artist, mechanical genius, etc, it looks as if we have the basis for a working group at last. All different types, stars and personalities, but all interested in magic and the God. If we fail to get more women, I shall have to start calling myself a sort of Robin Wod and his merry men, with Jane as Maid Marion. However I cannot see myself taking up archery in order to do the ritual properly (shooting an arrow through a garland of flowers at a distance of fourty nine paces. Sun and moon marriage) .

Still, see what the future will bring. When 'New Dimensions' eventually get round to publishing that article, who knows, a couple of females might get brought in by that. Anyway that is what it was designed for, very tricky, calculated to influence the female rather than the male. See what Bobby picks up from it, and watch reactions for me and I will be your eternal friend.

Sorry we didn't get the chance to visit you when we were on holiday but the bloody distance was too long, and the buses too short. They did a day trip to Glastonbury, but with only a twenty minute stay, and two buses a day to your home town that were distinctly unreliable. So we scrubbed round it, and held a private little ritual on top of Chalbury rings (and very nearly had our heads blown off for our pains - - wind and more wind). Doreen Valiente is still writing to me, but the last letter was so full of questions I had to cry aloud. I wrote and rewrote the bloody answer three times, then scrapped them all and wrote a fourth.

I man what or how can you answer a friendly letter that asks you to explain Arabic influence upon witch thought during the twelfth century, Leyland's inferences from the 'Aradia', the explaination of the four stones of the Universe, and a side question as to the meaning of the Maze? Apart from this, other questions cropped up as to the interpretation of the Sword and Graal, Cauldron and Cup. Jesus Wept! When Doreen goes to town, she really goes to town, and I wrote a short and fusty treatise upon Arabic influence upon modern 'witchcraft' with quotations from a discipline of the Ka'ba which covered about a thousand words, whizzed round the other questions as briefly as I could without actually answering any of them, and prayed for a fair wind to the coasts of France. I shall leave England, I really shall, and flap my way to somewhere that will understand me.

Yours sincerely, 'Blue Eyes'.

As per usual, I have quite suddenly dried up on the writing side, so the stream of ideas that would have got both of us out of our respective bug holes, has petered away to a mere barren trickle. I expect the full flush of new ideas will come crowding in when I start work again on Monday, and I aint got any time nohow. She always does this to me, write poetry she whispers, I write poetry, write a great novel she whispers, I write a novel, then I turn round, get hold of her by her doves wings, and bawl in her ear'ole, 'Whatta 'bout the lolly, spondulicks, paper nickers, eh?" and she looks at me with a pitying smile, and sweetly says, 'Art, Dear boy. ART! Is greater than mere material wealth'

At that point I wring the muses neck, and have her for dinner ala capon. Well, I either eat her, or go on national assistance. I mean what would you do Guv'ner? No! The bitch has just come to me again and in best blue stocking has said snootily 'Emancipation for Muses, fourty hour week, and three weeks paid holiday. Sorry old chap, but the Muse holiday roster coincided with yours.' And with that she has just marched away, bearing a banner with the inscription of 'Votes for Muses. Muses of the world unite! You have nothing to lose but your brains.'

We will be caving in Wales round about October, so we will possibly drop in and see you on our way through. Incidentally we have found a stone-age temple in one of the caves very difficult getting to it though.

Regards, Roy and Jane

x................................x

Anchor Points for cross-reference: 1964

Due to the death of G. B. Gardner earlier in the year, in February 1964, Lois Bourne left Wica (coven in Brickett Wood) to explore her desire to become an independent Traditionalist in Norfolk. (see *Tubal's Mill*.)

1. Leslie Roberts chases up Black Magic activities that occurred 61/62, then another brief spate in 63/64.

2. Article on Esbat that occurred in 63, is written up and accepted in the spring of 64 then printed later that year in the Autumn of 64.

3. Bowers discussed caving to Bill Gray, planned for October that same year.

4. Valiente continues to write to Bowers. They have not yet met. So again in the time period prior to late summer of 64.

5. Bowers mentions the 'late' Dr Gardner in #VI. So we can safely determine this to be written post February 1964.

(r) 1964 Letter to *'ickle deric'* [Deric James]

Notes: An unusual exception to the style and tone of all the other letters in this chronology, We see his acid wit and banter, but also his genuine desire to encourage those who are true seekers in the Craft. He admonishes 'Deric' for his errant views, but explains where the root of those problems lie. In this very interesting letter Bowers again refers to his Clan. He also refers to himself by his published alias Robert Cochrane. Already he declares to Deric that his supreme deity is 'Fate.' By way of encouragement, he offers Deric the 25+1 riddle of the winds and the vowel dance of the Mill. He also mentions his Tradition as 'Craft,' having specific family connections in *Stafford & Windsor*, and that women do not 'lead' in the Clans. That duty and responsibility resides with the Magister. This is not at all to say the role of woman is inferior in any way, quite the reverse in fact, a point so easily misunderstood. Significantly, both Stafford and Windsor are the two dedicated regions of the Frisian Tribes peoples— *Gerwisse* and *Wicce*. They'd settled in both these regions of the Upper and Lower Thames Valley, establishing the blood-group and folk tradition of cultures that enriched their ancestral, regional praxis, layer by layer. The fact of that ancestry supports entirely Bowers' claim to a combined Tradition of 'Two Admissions.' Other connections are explored in *Tubal's Mill'*. Note also that he does not anywhere refer to *Royal* Windsor, simply 'Windsor,' a point of extreme relevance to bogus claims regarding his tradition. Again, these matters are properly addressed in *'Tubal's Mill.'*

Transcript for Letter to 'ickle deric'

Dear 'ickle deric'

Ta ever so for yours. There are wrong, all bloody wrong. I have no intention of telling you what things mean what and how and why, but just for the record. I couldn't care less what Mrs Leek, Pat Crowther, Bill Gray, Uncles Gardner and Cardell, Mrs Bone, Mr McKay, Mrs Wilson and Uncle Tom

Cobleigh and all, say and have taught you, about the 'secrets' of thier 'art.' Your answers are bloody wrong.

I suppose I do know a little bit about the Craft, and having descended form a very old witch family, that had connections in both Stafford and Windsor, I suppose I do know a little bit about what I'm saying and doing. Witches don't, no how tell anyone the secrets of their Craft, once they do, they have to pay a price, and what is more they make sure the receiver of that knowledge also pays part of that price.

Now to go through your letter, so my knife means air, and it is a weapon of defence. Gawd. I shall choke on my soul-cake. The knife is something quite different, and it doesn;t really matter what colour the hilt is, we leave that sort of nonsense to Qabalists, and that is where the modern belief began, in a pre-dash war Qabalistic circle.

I am interested in my religion, because it is applicable to me, and because it is my way of life. I really couldn't care less about anybody else finding out about it unless they too are members of the Congregation and true believers. The <u>genuine</u> Craft has a lot of power, it would only do harm to unlease such things upon the crank fringe, sine the poor dears always want something for nothing and the basic law of the Craft is 'what you wants, you pays for.'

I am also a practitioning pellar because I have no choice in the matter. One doesn't take up the Craft, it takes up you and can reject just as rudely. You, my bucko, are making a fatal mistake. You are trying to bend the Craft to your will and desire, be careful. The Craft is a vortex that can draw down and destroy and well as bring light and love.

You, from your letters, I would suggest are in the first throes of a love affair with Old Night, and it will develop into a life-long passion. Your hooked laddy. She's cast her net and caught you. You think about drink, eat, and fret over the Craft. Hoping that you had the answers, since they really mean something to you, the book you are going to write is merely an excuse for something you do not understand within yourself. It will grow, give it time, food and devotion and it will grow. But don't try and use it, or else you will get badly hurt, the Craft will use you.

You most certainly do have half-baked ideas about witchcraft, and what is more you know it, but your 21 year old pride will never let you say so. Never mind.... you have the desire to learn, that at least is better than having the knowledge especially when it is half-baked.

Of course, I run around and so does my Clan loving everybody, we have a glorious time behaving like little Christians. Luv is all, and after the first two or three days we all get heartily sick of being so spiritual, a sort of soul-ful gentility and degenerate back into ordinary people once more. Witches are good honest people, didn't you know? In other words, the way we live our lives is just as normal as anyone else, and all that soul-ful clap-trap is just ordinary clap-trap.

No man can be 100 percent moral and normal at the same time. A little wickedness goes a long way, and I and my compatriots always feel a little better for it. Whoever preaches that sort of rubbish has very little insight into the true nature of the spirit. Love is the Law, Love under Will, and the net results is Love underpowered, since there is no contrast, an essential to human insight.

Whoops! Tra La ala, so we bind people, sigils and thingmebobs do we, and a Stang is blasting rod, which one do we blast with – the fork Kippen, the hawthorn Stang, or the Bone? And the sword that is used by the High Priest-ess - Well, well. The day my mob and there are quite a few left, have a High Priestess, the Master is going to be annoyed since apart from the groups which originated with GBG and a passing reference to Eliphas Levi, I ain't no how ever heard of a female leader in Britain, least-ways not in the Midlands or in the South.

Another group I know of by hearsay, and they have been going a long time (centuries) also have a male leader. Someone's been telling you a load of claptrap. And Jesus turns up in the foliate Mask. Well, well.

Where on earth do you dig up these atrocious sayings, bits of inferior poetry and supposed gems of traditional wisdom from? They make me feel quite ill. The prose of 'thou art that which thou chooseth to think of thyself' is from Mrs Leek. How do I know that? Son. I recognise the line, it is part of something I wrote once to her but read 'thou art that which thou think to be.'

'I am that which thou art thyself,' a very different thing. Mind you I have gorn upon my lickle old intuition for the answer and I may be quite wrong. If I am not though, let me know and I will send you the rest of the poem, and you can compare notes. If I am wrong my sincerest apologies but I reckon I am right.

Anyway, I am enjoying myself talking to you, and on this side I have got some really vicious bites in (well, you gave me an open invitation to bite. Now look at you all steamed up, and you don't know how big I am an all.) Just for the record I am 30ish, married, have a son and belong to traditional mob as a sort of conceited Sir figure. I would not claim to be the leader by any means, but I am a sort of mouthpiece of the Old Man. To the very best of knowledge what we believe is traditional handed down form very old. Various relations are also in the Craft or have been connected with it. At some time or another, and my Great-Grandad was the Supreme master of two counties. You sound like a potential, once you have got rid of the qabalah, Budhism and paganism out of your system, I would like to meet you. Perhaps you could come and stay one weekend. One other point, Witches do worship the Devil, but not the Christian one, wouldn't be seen dead with him, we have our own.

We have but one name for our supreme deity – Fate. The questions were absolutely genuine, I was finding out how much you knew about traditional witchcraft. How many beans make five, how many steps to a ladder, where do I wear my garter? And another for you, I send you five arrows, tell me what they are. There is one more—4+1+7+1+12+1 E+I+O+U+A.

Still you have tried, and that is something, But don't try and bluff, we knows, we does. Now I have finished playing about and got you into a state where you are probably going to write a very rude letter to me. Half-baked I said. Anyway, I hope after the inevitable battle of wits and ego, we shall become friends. See you.

PS. There ain't no age restriction. You were being prodded to see you would blow. Nothing like being brushed against a pompous Elder to make a young man get on his high horse.

Robert Cochrane.

x..................................x

(s) Bowers to Bill Gray:
i - #V
ii -#VII

Notes: Another very interesting letter and written around the same time as the missives from the Old Man; Bowers had shared many gems over the Summer with Clan members relating to 'The Ritual of the Mask and the Maze.' (m)

Note in particular how excited Bowers is that Gray knows something of the 'Maze' and was able to share an in-depth discussion with him. He queries Bill's wish to join them at Hallowtide, stressing just how gruelling it is. He caution's Bill on matters of procedure, remarking how, *"discipline is absolute seven days before the knot."* With confidence, therefore, we may date this as circa Autumn 64 as it refers to an entirely separate trip from the other caving expedition planned for October mentioned in letter VII.

He also speaks of having straightened out John's neck and how he was only a little bit off his timing regarding 'Mrs Bone's predicted invitation through a friend. He assures Bill that he will write to 'GN' (Gerard Noel aka John Math) that weekend.

Transcript for: #V Bowers to Bill Gray

Thank God someone has at last understood what I have been driving at in this Troy maze of witches and wizards. Hooray! Paganism is a religious pantheism, a comprehension that Nature is a reflection of the Hands of God, and that God is in Nature complete. Witchcraft, on the other hand, is a science, an occult science with it's own distinct traditions and philosophy that in its lower stages, can be confused with paganism, but in its higher stages can no more be pagan than the Qabbalah. Its origins lie in Paganism, but for that matter so does every other philosophy that is genuinely concerned with the spiritual. For instance the Old Testament's

JIEVOAA, is A.O.U.E.I or to put it closer, II.I.E.U.O.A.A.A. which are the sacred vowels of witchcraft. Read them sunwise from Hebrew to Latin and they become the Sacred name of the Sun King, (Jah1 I IO. miss two). But apart from this display of erudition, the vowels are the sacred tree sequence of the North, which amount to a statement of the mysteries of witchcraft as opposed to paganism. All this points towards a common magical tradition based upon a transcendant God, not a God of the Sun or the fields, but a God that represents the transcendant spirit of Man <u>the unknown God in fact</u>. The Jews had no actual vowels in their language since to write the sacred Name was blasphemy. The witch holds up five fingers. Now then what is a witch? A witch today is an unlicsensed practitioner of the mysteries of witchcraft since there is no longer (apart from one clan in Dorset an unbroken tradition of discipline.

What do witches call themselves? They call themselves by the names of their Gods. I am Od's man, sincein me the spirit of Od lives. Now you know how that old country dance 'The Goddesses' got its name. Want to argue 'simple old pellars' now? In other words there is only one way of finding the witch, judge them by their works , and their silence. If one who claims he or she is a witch can perform the tasks of witchcraft. that is they can summon spirits and spirits will come. they can turn hot into cold and cold into hot. They can divine with rod. fingers and birds. They can claim the right to omens and have them above all they can tell the Maze and cross Lethe (all this and many more in our surprise bumper packet). Now what do I call myself? I dont't. Witch is as good as any, failing that, 'Fool' might be the better word. I am a child of Tubal Cain, the Hairy One.

Bald mountain and Halloween. Are you sure? The ritual is our hardest and the pace is killing. It is also our most rewarding , the one with the objective phenomena. Last year I sweated fearfully as I heard the crying of a baby, it prophecied a death which came true later that year. Since I do not normally have eyes that see I have to give you others descriptions of some of the things observed. A woman dressed in white pacing with us, a skull from the North, and the many others all seen by the group. Necromancy? Never, just the opening of the castle's gates, these things appear for a short while only, then the big event begins. One cannot cross the Lethe without some heart searching and nail biting. It is hard like this until our Guide appears, then we are through. If you really want to join in with us then I will give you these warnings. Discipline is absolute seven days before, and it means fasting, simple foods without any form of salt, and considerable preparations that concern the bringing through of various images in a sequence.

Really to do it well, I would have to tell you the master keys since I do not think your own will work on our myth. The sequence is Keltic, and since I have been thinking of holding it in Wales instead of the Mendips, we will be in Dylan's territory, which for me is untried. Anyway I have shot over it as quickly as I can, and will leave you to make your own decision. I would prefer that we get together and work out a mutual arrangement beforehand, so that neither of us tread on the other's toes in the process of working. God help us if we do. Will any of your group be joining you? I cannot whisper sheep, cats or birds (except chickens which are dead easy) But I can make a dog do practically anything. Horses need two mechanical aids, fennel and the issue from a mare in heat. Basically it is based upon two things, Love (sex and pure) and overlooking. If you can transmit a strong enough desire to the animal it will respond. Try getting into Selina, transferring your motive desire to her motive energies and you will probably make her do anything. I can't touch cats at all, too independent. My one waggles her ears when I waggle mine, but that is about all. I have tamed ferocious dogs, in fact I have sent them crazy also by a bit of extra knowledge that concerns itself with their language.

I can stop burns, bleeding is another matter since I have never tried a severe case. Aches and pains are relatively easy. Incidentally I have straightened John's neck out, he now has no hump on his back and is an inch taller.

Recieved an offer from Mrs. Bone through a friend of mine , to make contact with her group. She knows nothing of me except that I live in Slough. I had a feeling that an offer was coming from one of the "others", but I wrote it down as August, I was six days out.

I will write to Gerard Noel this weekend, I doubt if he will answer though, which is not a piece of forsight, but an intellectual guess.

I have no intention of selling my soul to 'sperritts' merely a piece of mutual aid. Even God can't do everything, in fact He has left more than enough for us to do.

Regards and Briget Bardot (I reckon that's a better wish than Blessed be.) Roy and Jane

P.S. See you on Saturday at approx 2pm.

PPS Reading another authority, he claims the bardic tradition during the 11th and 12th centuries was based upon the O.T. and not upon Paganism. Robert Graves states the same in "King Jesus", and Graves is an ardant Ladies man. It apparently works out much the same as we were tending to think. Influx of Semetic (Arabic) influence lead to the O.T. being taken up by witches.

Notes: **#VII** The invitation is cordially extended to Bill to join himself and Jane only for *'a callin'* down the valley at Crickhowell (there being no others to accompany them at that time. He says that by his estimation, there are, "*no boys, as they are not yet up to scratch*"). The boys he refers to are of course, John and Dick. They plan to go exploring down in the valley below at Llangattock, in a cave he names 'Fanny.' It is near to, but is not 'Aggy Aggy Aggy.'). This was a rite in which Bowers hoped to engage the attention of his distant ancestors across the sea.

Transcript of #VII Bowers to Bill Gray

Many thanks for your letter and copy of the magazine. Sorry and all the rest of it, but I view some of the statements in it as rather naf, not so much the editorial but the article by Ariel. I do not think that I can ever cross the line between them and myself, since the basic philosophy is so very different. I really think it is time that a distinction was made between witchcraft and paganism. One can be an ardant Christian, and practice witchcraft. One can be a raving pagan and never touch the stone or cord. The real trouble lies in Victorian interpretation of the Mysteries and the philosophers who have foolishly accepted such writing as being the last development of thought upon paganism. Witches existed during the pagan reign, and were recognized as such, and the mysteries of witchcraft were also recognised as different and distinct from the mysteries of paganism. The nineteenth century attitude that lumped them quite cheerfully together, was refuted before the advent of folk- lore, and refuted since by such authorities as Carl Jung etc. Even Shakespeare made a difference in 'The Merry Wives' in which he refers to something very similar to modern witchcraft as 'rustic games'. The magazine still seems to make this basic mistake, and cheerfully asks that we should all join together and be friends. Ariel may as well asked that Catholics and ceremonial magicians should all join together and practice the Mass in joint harmony. It just would not be possible there is too wide a gap between religious faith and <u>religious science.</u> Like you, I despair of ever finding people who can accept the discipline of thought necessary to achieve magic, and this is what drives Jane and I apart from the others. Apart from that gloomy outburst, the presentation of the magazine is excellent, and the editorial hand is light but firm, and you have my sincere and grateful thanks for sending me a copy. Noel sounds like one of my type, I would like to meet him, and discuss more fully what he thinks the mysteries are. There is something about modern witch thought that makes its adherents intellectually incapable of going further than the last variations on fertility, pantheism and rolling in the dew. Noel sounds as if he has begun to inquire further, and examine something of the faith he practices.

I definitely would like to meet him since both he and I might be upon the same track through a very devious and difficult passage, and we might have something in common. You sure you want to try your hand a caving? The caves are at Llangastock by a quarry over a gentle drop of about a hundred feet. The one which interests me is fondly known as Fanny, and is a triple layered cave big enough to take a double decked bus in the entrance, and small enough to squash me flat at the end. A crawl followed by a transverse bedding plane, opens out on a stream tunnel that is horribly low. It is the end of the passage that the interest lies, since I felt the living rock move when I sat on it. I think there is another system underneath this point, and we will be digging down to find out this trip.

The part where the mound and stone is, is at the back of the cave in a very tight spot. I could not manage the whole crawl myself since it was very low, but according to reliable caver's report, there is a recent rock fall, then a chamber where the stone is. The crawl to it is our own discovery, since it is not marked upon the reference of the cave. Since Aggy Aggy, the longest cave in Britain is only a few hundred yards away (Aggy is thirteen miles long), it may be another system that extends for a few miles on. If you would really like to try your hand out, and incidentally work on top of a Welsh mountain the previous night with Jane and I, we will be setting out a fortnight from now and passing through Cheltenham about five o'clock on the Saturday.

You will need a good pair of boots, a tent and bedding. We can arrange for a helmet and light, but wear old and warm clothes since the caves are dirty and very cold. Fanny is a fascinating cave, with many water markings that are very beautiful, plus a small cavern that could be possibly used for magical work on the right. It is well worth the ride just to feel the atmosphere, it is very Keltic and green, and the mountains are all around the site. We will camp overnight since the nearest inn is a Crickhowell, about four miles down in the valley. Jane and I intend to hold a meeting on top of the mountain, which is a moor about twenty miles square without any human habitation.

It is only a easy scramble to get up the rock face to the top, and we will be working out that Saturday, just the two of us, since John and Dick are not up to scratch as yet. As I said, you will need good boots with the maximum of nails and a tent (or if you feel like a long walk, Crickhowell may offer some possibility of accommodation. The main entrance is very easy, Adrian has done it with knobs on, but the floor is slippery and strewn with boulders. If you would like to come, you will be very welcome, and to add some sauce to the meat, you will also be welcome to join us on the mountain that night. I am preparing a 'callin', that is, I am going to summon 'spirrits' from the Netherlands , since I need some help in the next stage of my magical argosy, and I am going in for some bargaining with the powers that be. Perhaps we can work out something between us and try to get some react ion from the other side, even if it is only a loud rasberry. In spite of everything, Jane and I are still fighting on. I reckon we will be working by ourselves before long.

I am very inclined to agree with you about apprentices. People either have the desire to learn or they haven' t. If they want things easy, then it is no use. I find that the most difficult job is teaching them the first. basic steps in abstract thought. They all appear to think that physical actions will have spiritual results, and they can take an untidy and undisciplined mind and work miracles with it. Witchcraft generally seems to be cursed with types that want nudism, sex and free beer as a religion. Try and teach them the next- stage beyond desire and the howl of anguish is fantastic. I have definitely got beyond the point when I am willing to teach someone who just wants an excuse for senseless blathering about his particular fantasies, and I really do sympathise with you trying to teach ordinary disciplines of the path, since I have tried it so often myself. 'Magic' is all science fiction to the average inquirer, and they bloody well expect miracles with two penn'oth of action and thought.

As you know, magic is blood and tears all the way, and with no let up. I suppose a strong instinct for self preservation of the personal ego is responsible for most of the errant and erratic meanderings of the student, because when the first light does come through, it is so bright and clear that what little we have is so very small in comparison. I think I will ask only one question in future, that is 'Do you really want to die?', and if the answer is positive, then I will have someone to learn from and teach. To practice genuine magic is to literally throw your life away upon imponderables and half apparent truths, that you know will never become clear until death overtakes all of us. Magic is the rejection of illusion in favour of what may be a greater illusion still. Still somewhere, somehow, someone will listen and understand.

I am pleased to hear that you have one in N.D., Doreen V. wrote and told me that she has a poem in also, both your letters arrived at once. I just cannot get to any understanding with D.V. We seem to be circling each other and then she asks a key question, I counter, and code up on for her, so far we have missed in the middle and shot off to our divergent paths. I shall have to work with the woman so that she will understand. Up to date we sound rather like two Dons trying to outbid each other with snippets of academic knowledge. Not my game, but each time I start fooling it up a bit, she takes me seriously. Oh well, love will overcome. So help me if this keeps on, I shall go out of my way to either make a really wild and fantastic statement with suitable cooked up historical backing, and invent a totally new mystery, or I shall work moon and birch upon her and so fascinate her, that she will get all coy every time she writes (Joke.) Talking about fascination, I did a bloody silly thing when I was on holiday.

I was demonstrating to a friend, rather talking about whispering animals, and they looked rather sceptical, so I did a live show on the spot with a couple of chickens that seemed to be hanging around. About ten minutes later I realized that we were being followed by not two chickens, but a whole bloody chicken farm, thousands of 'em, 'ollering like mad at me, evidentally thinking that I was the biggest and best rooster that they had ever seen. My friend is now convinced, that is the evidence of three thousand hens takes some beating, and the farmer gave us a very old fashioned look.

We will see you on the twelfth, God willing (if 'E ain't, I am) and best wishes for you group.

Three F's , Roy and Jane

P.S. I will give you a telephone call the night before we move out to confirm arrangements - Bloated Capitalism - how nice for you. I can't even get plump on my money. 'Break a leg' for your opening performance. Roy

X......................................X

Anchor points

A.M. joins Roy's Group. A. S. joins Chalky's group, briefly only in the Autumn

<u>Witchcraft .Research .Association.</u> October 1964. Established by Valiente and Gerard Noel (aka John Math) primarily as a vocal body for all members of The Craft.

The Pentagram is the Journal for that association. It ran for five issues only before it collapsed under the furore of controversy in 1966.

Notes: A.M. joins the Clan directly, and A. S. through Chalky's group, she attended a few only of Bowers' Clan Rites as a guest, leaving to pursue other venture. Guests still occasionally attended either or both groups, but less often now, but the Clan continue to meet for certain rites where members only may attend. It must be made clear that Chalky and George were Inducted Members of The Clan, albeit as Evan John Jones asserts, the groups they formed 'were kindred only.' They'd worked together for many years in Companie, drifting further apart as their paths diverged. They began to part 'Companie' when Chalky and George began expressing their preference for Gardnerian ritual (they were after all, Initiates of Lois Bourne), which led to the rapid disintegration later, when they struck alliances with others to form their own group within The Clan. Very few people were actually Inducted into the Clan, fewer still became members of Full Admission to it. Bowers conferred the Rites of Admission to his own group within it. Early in 1965 A.S. aka Marian Green, was also a pupil of Bill Gray for a time. Commenting upon her time spent with Bowers, leaves us with no doubt how the rituals were wild, unscripted, unrehearsed events that revelled in the impromptu, the spontaneous fervour—the atavistic dance, primal and pure. Around 8-12 people were in regular attendance. She affirms the total lack of scripts or board prompts used in these rites, though they were used by the later 'Regency.' [48]

Again this adds increasing weight to the improbability of another letter's validity (**ooo**), especially based on the estranged subject matter within it. In that letter, 'Joan' describes her plans for seasonal scripts, instructing them to learn their lines. Anyone interested in the history of Roy Bowers and his works will already know that he never worked in this way. It represents everything he considered anathema within the occult world of his day. Evan John Jones, Marian Green, Bill Gray and Doreen Valiente have each recorded in numerous places his working praxis and though utterly idiosyncratic, for his era, those processes were totally unique.

This curious letter describes exactly the opposite of the aforementioned experience Marian Green recalls as the most outstanding and profound method of praxis she'd encountered then, and which has not been matched since, noting how it was completely at odds with everything formal and dogmatic typical of late 20th century occultism. This method of working was however very familiar to and indicative of someone who would spearhead its format during the following decade after Bowers' death. That person is of course Ronald White. But who was he working with?1965 Opportunity not of this time or place.

(t) 'The Craft Today' — *The Pentagram #2 - 1964*

Notes: Bowers sets out his views on why The Craft is not pagan, and what it must become to remain relevant to the needs of the 20th century. A perennial issue which has only worsened and is far from resolution. It is quite a powerful rant against apathy, dogma and out-moded ideals.

Transcript: The Craft Today

Witchcraft, according to those who are modern witches, is the Craft of the Wise. A simple pagan belief, full of old traditions which are appealing, simple virtues, and—if we are to believe their detractors—some ancient vices. According to further information it is a traditional religion based upon an exceedingly simplified concept of the works of Nature.

It is by inference from their rituals as reported, an attempt to bribe Nature by various actions and beliefs into a malleable state, so that Nature will function according to the needs of the coven, and what the coven believes to be good for society in general, rather than Nature carrying on in her own sweet way. If we are to believe various interviews carried out by television and newspapers, this has an effect not upon Nature but upon the witch, since there is a report of a witch who claimed that she believed the sun would not rise again if she did not undertake her rituals.

The interesting facet to be gained from such blazes of publicity is that it would appear the Craft has rapidly become an escape hatch for all those who wish to return to a more simple form of life and escape from the ever-increasing burden of contemporary society. In many cases the Craft has become a funkhole, in which those who have not been successful in solving various personal problems hide, while the storm of technology, H-bombs, and all the other goodies of civilization pass by harmlessly overhead.

Modern Witchcraft could be described as an attempt by twentieth-century man to deny the responsibilities of the twentieth century. It is a secure and naïve belief that Nature is always good and kind. It is also a belief, or so it would appear, that if you personally can go backwards in the evolution of thought, then perhaps the rest of the world might follow suit. Good enough, the Craft is all things to all men, if it is a simple pantheistic belief to those who think it so, so it has become, since the Mysteries were evolved for all men, and Man was evolved for the Mysteries. Which of necessity leads one to ask what the Mysteries are. All mystical thought is based upon one major premise: the realisation of truth as opposed to illusion. The student of the 'mysteries' is essentially a searcher after truth, or as the ancient traditions described it, "Wisdom." Magic is only a by-product of the search for truth, and holds an inferior position to truth. Magic, that is the development of total will, is a product of the Soul in its search for ultimate knowledge. It is an afterthought upon a much larger issue, the ability to use a force that has been perceived while searching for a more important aim within the self. No genuine esoteric truth can be written down or put within an intellectual framework of thought.

The truths involved are to be participated in during comprehension of the soul. Truth of this degree is not subject to empirical thought and is only apparent to the eye of the beholder, and to those who have followed a similar path of perception.

Throughout the history of humanity there have been myths, schools of wisdom and teachers who have shown a way to attain a working knowledge of esoteric thought and philosophy by using inference rather than direct method to teach the approaches to cosmic truth. The secrecy of these Masters has nothing to do with protecting the Mysteries, since all that can be said about the Mysteries has already been written into folklore, myth and legend. What is not forthcoming is the explanation. It was recognised that these legends, rituals and myths were the roads through many layers of consciousness to the area of the mind where the soul can exist in its totality. These and their surrounding disciplines and teachings became what the West describes as the Mysteries.

The Mysteries are, in essence, means by which man may perceive his own inherent divinity. During the persecution the adherents of the Mystery system went underground and joined forces with the aboriginal beliefs of the mass, and so became part of traditional Witchcraft. Centuries passed and the meaning behind much ritual was forgotten, or relegated to a superstitious observance to elemental Nature. Much of the old ritual that has survived became ossified and repeated by rote, rather than by understanding. Consequently it has become static and remote from its original purpose, which was to enlighten the follower spiritually. In what generally passes as Witchcraft today there is as much illusion and unresolved desire as there is in the outside world. In the closed circles of some covens there is greater bigotry and dogma than there is in many sections of the moribund Christian church. Many witches appear to have turned their backs upon the reality of the outside world and have been content to follow, parrot fashion, rituals and beliefs that they know have little or no relationship with the twentieth century and its needs. There has been no cause for a fertility religion in Europe since the advent of the coulter-share plough in the thirteenth century, the discovery of haymaking, selective breeding of animals, etc.

To claim, as some witches do, that there is a greater need in the world for fertility of mind than before is understating general facts, since Western Europe morally and socially has advanced more without the Old Craft and its attendant superstitions than it ever did with them. The value of the Old Craft today is that in it lie the seeds of the Old Mystery tradition. Through this the witch may perceive the beginnings of that ultimate in wisdom, knowledge of themselves and of their motives. The genuine Mysteries are open to all, because anyone having experience enough can understand that basic Message. To close the human mind in order to protect it from outside circumstances that are hostile, is not a way to discover that within oneself which is most profound, but a return to a claustrophobic mother who will eventually smother the child. If, as is claimed, the Gods are kind and They are all things, then why does the twentieth century witch run so rapidly away from them in the practice of the "age old Craft"?

In fossilised superstitious tradition there are profound secrets hidden, secrets folded within the most mediocre belief and action. These great secrets, secrets of the soul and of destiny, are only apparent in the open light, not in the illusionary world of Ye Olde English Wiccen. If the witches are to survive then the religion must undergo some violent and radical changes. Changes that will open the ritual for examination, so that the spiritual content may be clearly seen. Changes that must kick over many sacred cows to see whether these old cows still give milk. The inherent philosophy of the Craft was always fluid, and fluid it must become again before it gasps its last breath under a heap of musty nonsense, half-baked theology and philosophy. Witches cannot retreat from the world any longer, there is no room for us in this society unless we have something valid to offer it, and participate in its social evolution.

X...................................X

(u) 'Witches Esbat' - *New Dimensions* : November 1964, Vol 2, No. 10

Notes: Cave Rite finally published from a former working late in 1963 involving John, Dick, Jane, Roy, Arthur and at least one other present, possibly the person known as 'Peter.' John and Dick are the new apprentices mentioned as the boys drafting in new members to the Clan. Bowers was to state that this rite is much embellished and altered in order to make it acceptable for those involved. This is not the Cave and the Cauldron Rite which is not an Esbat nor one of the Rites held on the Knots. The C&C is one of the 'Tetrad of Rites' reserved for Elders only willing to commit to a three year cycle of Observances. (see Tubelo's Green Fire)

Transcript: 'Witches Esbat'

IT IS COLD, the damp grass steaming mist upwards to the moon as we walk across the fields to the caves. Across the hills, somewhere towards the west, a dog fox barks defiance at we intruders of the night world. In the silent world of Hecate, a billion insects spin their small webs of destiny. We feel like invaders from a more brilliant age, treading carefully, threading our way in silence past the still hedge rows. The cauldron in Peter's haversack rings faintly as one of the knives strike against it. He stops and shifts the weight slightly, then points upwards towards the looming hill. The wind clatters a few leaves upon the trees as we begin the ascent to the caves. Seven of us, six men, one woman, feet slipping upon grass that feels slimy with night dew and unmentionable insects, sinking in the sodden ground under our own weight. Down below in the valley, the representatives of the twentieth century shoot along dark roads, headlights slicing the night for a brief minute, then vanishing with a flutter of mechanical life. Standing bleakly against the moonlight we can see the tumbled rocks that hide the caves. Our lead man stops then turns round and comes to us. "Be careful here, the hillside falls away pretty rapidly". His face is anonymous in the moonlight. Joan reaches out and takes my hand, and we walk forward carefully in the gloom.

Gusts of wind buffet us, a sensation of space to our left side grows more definite; then we are out of the wind and into the lee of the rocks. Arthur, the lead man, seems to vanish suddenly from sight in a flurry of white torch light, then his voice comes from beneath the ground muffled and faint. "It's all right, come on down". One by one my companions slide through the entrance of the cave, slipping on the wet chalk. Joan sits down prettily upon her heals and follows them, still holding my hand to give balance to her impetus. I slide down after her and into the cave. We straighten ourselves out and stand up, torches on for the first time in the hour-long walk, the light gleams from the wet sides of the caves reflecting into the lime water pools on the floor. Out of the wind and underground the silence is suddenly oppressive, then everybody begins to talk at once, unloading themselves from the tension of the walk and the fear of discovery. I shrug the haversack from my shoulders and note with some disgust that it has become covered with wet chalk.

Opening it I search for my compass, looking at it carefully until I find true north. The rest begin to pull out the equipment from their haversacks, throwing firewood over to me as they find it. I begin to build a fire, soaking it with paraffin bought specially for this purpose. The caves suddenly become alive and friendly as the yellow flames soar to the roof, a million drops of water reflecting the light like a million individual diamonds. Piling more wood upon the fire I stand back and the flames descend to eat the fresh fuel. Smoke coils around the roof and the boys put out the torches. We stand around the fire warming ourselves and begin to undress. "Dig the circle out," Joan says to Blackie. He is in the process of removing his trousers, and stands stork-like upon one leg as he considers what she has just said. "Right, as soon as I'm changed."

He hurries to stretch and moves nearer to the fire as he puts on the garb of the witch, and wraps the cloak about him. He goes to the center of the cave and begins to cut the circle out with his knife. The others all go about their appointed tasks in silence. Joan and I search out the implements from the haversack, fitting them together and wiping them carefully, laying them upon the ledge that acts as a serving table. John and Peter fit the banner together, facing the mystical symbols inwards at the four quarters of the compass, throwing up the chalk as they thrust them into the wet earth. Blackie straightens up, his face dark with the effort of digging. "What do we say if we're caught?" he asks generally. "That we're bloody archaeologists of course", John answers. Blackie laughs then bends down and continues digging. We work steadily creating Caer Ochlen in the cave until at last everything is ready. The graal and cup reflect with silver the red flame of the fire.

I build up the tripod and hang the cauldron. It swings gently in the heat. Joan brings over the wine in a thermos flask and pours it into the cauldron. Fragrant steam rises as the cold wine meets the hot brass base of the pot. "Smells nice, mum, what's for dinner?" Peter asks, smiling at his own humour. Joan laughs as she ties the girdle around her waist and arranges her shift, placing the seven knots carefully. We are all dressed now in our black garb, adjusting our cloaks as we stand now in humility and poverty; the beginnings of all magical power. Some more work, then I take up the skull and thrust the sword through it, tying the skull carefully to the carved hilt. Holding it aloft I go to the centre of the compass and thrust the blade deep into the earth.

It is time to begin.

Joan casts grains of incense into the fire, then blesses herself, first her left ear, then her left eye, up to forehead, then down to right eye and ear. She turns, outlined by the flames, touches her mouth, then her right breast, then finally her left ankle. We have grouped ourselves into a crescent about her, following the blessing, each action accompanied by buttered prayer to God. The old words reach out into the shadows of the caves, and echo faintly to the basso profundo of six male voices, with Joan's voice threading in between. The fire leaps up, and Joan reaches forward taking the graal from me. Holding it aloft she presents it to heaven and the moon, the herbs and apples floating gently upon the water, the darkness of the cave seems to surround it. I begin the words of the great chant, and the silence of the night suddenly breaks into life. Joan lowers the graal and breathes across it, then empties its contents into the cauldron. We stand up and walk towards it, still in a crescent, our hoods thrown back, and follow her as she begins the weaving dance of a maze in front of the boiling pot. Then the pattern changes and we dance around the fire. We stop, and she dips into the pot with the ladle and passes it from one to another, as we eat of the fruits of life.

Whirling the ladle furiously Joan alone paces round three times more then plunges it back into the pot. We draw our knives and thrust them into the earth, then dance furiously around the fire once more. I, leading, dance off until we all surround the circle. The summoner, who is last, takes the cauldron off the fire and pours its contents into the ditch which surrounds the circle. Steam rises around us and the red liquid floods through and forms a completed circuit, washing the ash aside, swirling round the willow and rowan twigs. I step forward over the ditch and stand in front of the sword and skull. Raising my left hand I run the signs through with my fingers, then quickly go through the traditional gestures that mean so much to a witch, hands slapping upon my legs and body miming the old legends. The rest follow suit. Joan casts the cake upon

285

the ground just by the door of the circle and at last we all step over the barrier which divides the quick from the dead.

"UEIOA", five fingers held high. UEIOA", slap upon the left thigh then forward with the wild horses and through the silver ring. We began to pace the compass round holding the ring in the air, then finally lowering it upon the skull. Turning, we place our staffs upon the ground fashioning the pattern of the ritual and begin to tread the mill. Round and round in absolute silence, fingers following the pattern that the seven knots make in the cord. Willing, thinking, concentrating upon our work, the hoods of our cloaks down over our eyes, thinking, willing, visualizing the image of virtue shifting from one part of our bodies to the other, the sensations of changing like colours upon our minds eye.

In the brief glimpses we get when our concentration lowers in its intensity the cave seems to be spinning around us, then back to the darkness of our hoods and our compressed wills. The smoke thickens as the fire lowers...and we all seem to have some difficulty in breathing, almost choking in the turgid atmosphere. Then suddenly it is like breathing pure ice, cold clear. The virtue has been transmuted. Immediately following this sensation a cold wind seems to whip around our ankles tearing off the physical power of the flesh. Fear suddenly descends like a clammy blanket and everyone receives the impression that we are being watched; it is the gathering of the force we are invoking. The sensation of fear deepens until we need every bit of our will to stop ourselves from running away.

Knocks and taps seem to come from everywhere in the cave, and I give a start, coming back to complete consciousness for a brief second, then catching myself return back to the dark path of the will. I am no longer walking the floor of the cave, but treading on air. My body is in many different places at once, an incredible sense of disorientation fills me and I am no longer conscious of my body. Darkness rolls in upon my consciousness and I float in a void around the circle, my body stumbling mechanically on and on. I become aware of everyone else in the clan as if they were in me. I can feel them all. A strong feeling that someone is standing where the skull is impinges my mind. Immediately we begin to thrust our will towards it probing, questioning, a sensation of the stranger increases immensely. We know who he is.

My heart gives a bound of fear and joy together. We intensify our will until it is like a bridge of iron, our total concentration is upon him. We can actually see green lights flashing on and off around the skull. "Master, Master" I can feel the group calling him. Blue slight twists and spirals in the centre. We work harder and harder still, our minds hurting with the intense effort. The light coalesces into the shape of a man, cloaked like ourselves. Wave after throbbing wave of power pulsates us. A feeling of exhilaration erases our tiredness, he exudes strength and wisdom. We greet him.

We come to ourselves again back in the dank cave, the fire almost out. Pins and needles stab at our limbs, we feel very tired, we stop pacing, the air of the cave flat in our mouths. Joan offers a prayer of thanks, and we break up the compass, returning everything to where it was. It is all over now, we sit listlessly for a short while getting warmth from the dying fire, for we are both cold and tired, our minds numbed. Blackie throws more wood upon the fire, tending it, blowing upon it until the fresh fuel catches and throws a cheerful warmth upon everything. We look for food and drink in the haversacks and begin the feast. Gradually we feel refreshed, then full of energy. Talk rises with the smoke, there is a lot of laughter, and we stretch our limbs luxuriously in front of the glowing coals. Six men, one woman, all devoted to each other, and above everything else, to our Gods. The conversation increases, various things are discussed.

How to do this...how to do that ... women, how to get them in, but they have no interest in witchcraft today ... the group remains unbalanced, no women, no balance.

We talk and eat, then finally clearing up, begin our journey home. Tired yet refreshed, dirty from the caves, but pure in heart. We walk across the fields shivering in the dawn air, back to the cars. A policeman steps forward out of the shadows. Excuse me ... parking ... dangerous place...what have you in the haversacks? We empty them and explain. You can see by the expression of disgust and horror what he thinks. Questions and still more questions, misunderstandings, always misunderstandings. Gods, the things we poor witches suffer.

X.................................X

(v) Introductory Letter #1 To Norman Gills & Letters #2 & #3.

Notes: Bowers and Gills appear to have developed a very stilted and curious friendship. There is often a slight undertone of sarcasm to the exchange, and he does not often extend the warmth he shows Wilson, nor always the respect he exudes to Bill Gray. Though, in the end, his final letters issue a desperate reliance.

Bowers, anxious to meet Gills, formally introduces himself. Cross-referenced via two events noted in contemporary letters to Bill Gray, regarding Gerard Noel and a caving expedition, we may secure this introduction as late *64 at the earliest!* He had given Gills his wedding anniversary as 14 years. We have documentary evidence for the date of their marriage in 1951, so we can date this very accurately. When Bowers offers Gills his consolations for the 'loss of his girl,' he ask after her name. Had he known and worked with (*Jean*), he would not need to ask her name, nor would he need an introduction through Gerard Noel, via Bill Gray.

In this introductory letter from Robert Cochrane aka Roy Bowers to Norman Gills, he asks if they can meet up. Brief references of common interest in life, in art and in the Craft. He laments the general lack of experience and of basic historical knowledge that should be fundamental to all praxis. It is highly unlikely they met up before Spring of the following year. This confirms Bowers did not know Gills personally until late 65.

Transcript of #1 Bowers to Gills

Dear Mr Gills,

Gerard Noel[49] has given me your address, and correspondence, since we live near to each other, and it will be easier for us to communicate or meet.

I understand from Mr Noel that you are interested in the Craft and have met people who are adherents to the old ways, and have had some experience of their ways. I have an interest also, and have spent some time in the past doing research upon historical aspects of the craft, and come up with a few answers, and that interested me considerably. Perhaps we may be able to discuss them in the near future.

Gerard also tells me that you are interested in art, so am I and I work as a typographical drafts-man. Anyway, I hope to hear from you soon. I am sorry I have written such a short letter, but today I am rather a rush.

Yours sincerely, Robert Cochrane

x...............................x

Bowers to Gills - #2

Notes: Consolation letter for Gills' loss of 'his girl.' Bowers offers a beautiful poem and help where possible. This curious inclusion suggests this may well be a very different 'Norman' and not Gills at all. Valiente confirms Gills as a bachelor living alone with his Mother (see *Tubal's Mill*). Bowers freely expresses his philosophical perspective regarding the societal mores of his time. Bowers gives his opinions of the Craft, and of his preference for the Rowan and its native gods to those of the walnut and the east. Bowers then consoles Gills about the loss of his love with a profound poem. He mentions his recent visit to Wales, referring of course to his *'Callin on the Sperrits'* at Crickhowell with Bill Gray. So this anchors another date circa October 1964. Comments too of the harshness of his mistress—Alba Guiden, the Pale-Faced Goddess. He suggests arranging to meet up one day, and provides a brief description of the Britwell Housing estate where he lived. Offers Gills his real name. Bowers relates his own Craft family background, remarking that his great-grandfather was Grand Master for Staffordshire and Warwickshire, and that his mother had been a scryer for Mrs Blomfield when the last of the old Windsor coven was still alive back in the reign of Queen Victoria, indicating that coven had long since become defunct. (see *Tubal's Mill* for a full and complete history).

Transcript of #2 Bowers to Gills

Dear Norman,

Thank you for your very prompt reply and interest.

I agree with you about the artists and poets, but so very few have ever produced their best when fat and comfortable. I think a certain amount of physical discomfort is essential so that the 'Muse' or to give Her proper Name, the 'White Goddess,' can descend and inspire. Likewise the (Alba) Guiden is a harsh Mistress in return for Her gifts. I don't know if you have read the old very wise Bardic poems to Her, but there they sing that Her nest is lined with the bones and the skulls of artists and poets. One only has to look or read the greatest works of any artist to realise just how true this is. Still I keep my faith with the Mother, even if Her third face is dark and terrible. To be born an artist or a poet in a way is to foreswear all normal life, and follow the primrose growen footsteps of our Lady of White. Therefore, although we do not succeed in the material world, but at least our eyes, our hands and our voices are raised in inspiration, to honour our Lády. For that, I would foreswear anything of the flesh except love, and that is what our Lady gives to us.

I am very sorry to hear that your girl died, I can think of no greater loss that the person one loves. In the Craft maybe, love is even deeper than it is amongst others, since the two walk such a close path together in that strange half world that only the Crafters can know or understand. The Craft is something born or something given in love, once the gift is received there is no going back, once a "witch" always a "witch" and it is there forever. I am sure that your girl often comes back to you, as only "witches" will, there is an old story in my family in which it is said that the "witches" heaven is in the setting sun, and as the old song ends:

"There you and I my loves,

There you and I will lie,

When the cross of resurrection is broken

And our time has come to die,

For no more is there weeping

For no more is there death

Only the golden sunset,

Only the golden rest."

I am interested that you mention 'occult schools' do you mean the colleges of witchcraft that once existed in the country, where the seeker after wisdom could learn, or do you mean the Teachers who come from the otherworld, or perhaps you mean people here and now who teach occultism, such as the school founded by Violet Firth? I would be grateful if you would tell me more.

I am a member of a cuveen, and come from a Craft family in which the Craft has been practised for many generations.

The local coven[50] is small, consisting mainly of men of recent making since the last of the old Windsor coven died. When my mother was a girl, back in Victorian time. My mother helped her occasionally, as a 'Maid' for scrying but she did not tell her too much and you may know her through reputation, her name was Mrs Blomfield, and was of high degree. As for my own Craft, it comes from the Midlands, where my people originated. My family tell me that my great-grandfather was Grand Master for the whole of Warwickshire and Staffordshire, with some sixty witches under his care. How true this actually is though, I cannot say, although my aunt swears it is so, and she has a very impressive collection of witch things inclusive of a Maze that must be centuries old. It seems to work out in The Clan I belong to since we are interested in the old high magic. There are very few genuine cuveens left in Britain, most of the people who appear on television or in the newspapers are fakes, and seem to originate from a man who lived on the Isle of Man, and who made the whole thing from his own head. I personally have little time for them since they seem to be more interested in dancing naked than the real Craft, and as you know those sort of lies do nothing to help the real Craft.

I agree with you about the Gods from the East, but as you know not all the Craft accepted the Eastern Gods, many still preferred the Old Ones, and continued the ancient observances. I for one do not like the Eastern Star, but prefer the Mill as did my ancestors. I must confess that I am very interested in that you mention it, since I thought the wisdom about that was almost lost, and it was only through mere chance that I heard about it. It seems to have begun at the end of the twelfth century and ended by the Craft almost being wiped out by the Church at the end of the seventeenth century. I honestly believe the old ones of Britain did not like their people taking up with foreign gods, and I have never heard of anyone getting results from them that did practice the Eastern system and who followed the walnut and the Almond, rather than the Rowan, The Oak and the Blackthorn. Agreed that we still need to be careful, but this time even more, there are enemies within as well as without the Castle, and we do not trust anyone who cannot give the true signs today. I think that the Craft will come back, but as you say in a very different form. I was in Wales last week, and you could feel the Old Forces stirring in the mountains. I think that maybe Our Lady will come down to earth once more and we can begin all over again.

Britwell Estate is a big housing estate outside Slough, towards

Farnham. It stands on one of the old meeting grounds, and although it is hard to work there, we do get good results.

Although we do not have a car, we will arrange to drop in and see you before the Hallows and talk about the old days with you. Perhaps we can get you to a meeting we are thinking of in Sussex, tell us if you would like to go.

Flags, Flax, Fodder and Frig

(a roof over your head, a shirt on your back, food in your stomach and someone to love)

Roy Bowers (my real name,

Sorry to be crafty, but I was being cautious)

Bowers to Gills - #3

Notes: Bowers informs Gills that Jane is also in the Craft and that his son, shows keen potential. He again relays his frustration with other practitioners whose lack of wisdom lowers the bar, effectively jeopardising the legacy of the Craft. He emphasises the distinction between a witch and a pagan. He mourns the old high magicks, and their place in the schema of Craft, and distinguishes his role as a pellar–an advocate of the old craft, plain and simple, no title, no label, not witch, not pagan, not anything but a simple pellar. Informs Gills he has been married for 14 years [since 1951] and ask Gills his late wife's name, offering a 'lily' and a 'mary' as possible insights. He tests Gills knowledge of the Craft by posing questions concerning the Mound and The Maze, and how to call the Raven, and what relevance the skull has.

Transcript of #3 Bowers to Norman Gills

Dear Norman,

Thank you for your letter, and the question you asked in a round-about fashion. The answer is enclosed, you will be able to read it as clearly as any book.

I am married, Jane, my wife, is a crafter also, and my son A, has all the markings of a pellar. Typical Craft, Jane and I met, fell in love and were married three weeks later. We have been together 14 years.[51] We always work together, and I have found that from this, we always get good results. Men and women are mirrors of each other, power cannot flow from man to man, or woman to woman, it must flow together and mix. Not that we use power all that much, but when we have too, it works between Jane and I.

Was your girls name Lily, born a Mary? [handwritten line]

I am pleased to read that you know something of the old high magic, not many do, although many claim to. Can you cast the Mound and the Skull? In fact thinking about it, I am more than pleased since you are the first person I have met for many a long day who knows something about the Craft.

Nearly all the others have their hearts in the right place, but are inclined to use their brains too much and not their wisdom. The small group I belong to falls into this trap, I can very tired with trying to show them what is under their noses all along. A crafter is born, not made, or if one is to be made, then tears are spilt before the moon can be drawn. What I can make of it, and I have been looking hard, the old craft is nearly dead. Various groups of people call themselves witches, but this in many cases, is an excuse for high jinx, and tawdry orgies, rather than genuine craft, although some of them are genuine enough in their beliefs. The real pellar wisdom is almost lost, and the gods are almost forgotten, yet today, for the first time since the Christians came, more people are genuinely interested in the Craft, from the religious and devotional viewpoint. I suppose the industrial revolution and two world wars are to blame really, but I think nearly all pellars today work alone, or nearly alone, with just or two clans still surviving, the real old ways are past, and it seems to break my heart when I think about it. Still enough of my miseries, you no doubt haver enough of your own. I am trying to bring up what I know of the craft, and apply it to the way of thought today. To do this I have had to read a tremendous amount about the old pagans and see what fitted and what didn't, and shape the religion as it was originally. To do this, I have had to break away from the knife and horn, but also keep them and make them into something slightly different. The Moon and the Mill I have managed to bring back to its original shape and symbolism and ended up with the Castle, which seems to me to fit the old legends more correctly, and it works very effectively, but to do this I have had to alter, and this by Craft standards is terrible, the old ways quite a lot, but as I said, high magic, and its attendant philosophy is what we are interested in. Many of the old craft ways were good and effective, but nobody knew why they worked. We do now.

Jane and I give you our word on our thumbs that we will help you as best we can, and however we can. Wise and Blessed Be, Roy & J. Bowers.

Letters to Gills #1, #2 &#3 listed above at (t); #4 at (aa); #5 at (dd) #6 & #7 at (ll) #8—#14 at (oo-uu)

X..................................X

(w) Bowers to Gray: #XI;

Notes: Bill and Bobbie Gray join The Clan as brief members. But like Doreen Valiente who was soon to join them just before Yule, neither of these three stayed for long, in fact less than a year. Bowers notes his receipt of a letter from Gerard Noel and shares notes on the Castle Rite for All Hallows with Bill Gray, and all the preparation needed for that. Instructions include fasting instructions and other things that indicate their planned arrival over at Bill Gray's for this knot. Briefly he explains the science behind the Witch's Compass, knowing that Bill would pick-up on those things he alludes to here. Bowers emphasises the intensity and importance of this Major Knot and Sabbat Star. This was probably the closest he ever came to working with his ancestors of the Craft.

*On Salt.

Salt is the key of kings. Saxon word is *'wiccen'*

"The sacrament of bread and salt however seems to be capable of working up into something like a true rite." Roy Bowers

The contents of *Aradia* and also of Leland's 'Roman and Etruscan Remains' and its illustrations are given to Bill as recommended source material to grasp the tenets of this Rite. Abstinence from salt is also mentioned in #V.

The circle's outermost ring or moat, representing human labour, is formed with *salt*. Strange though it may seem in an age when people are often encouraged to use less salt in their diet than before, salt equates with life and work. Yet some amount of salt is necessary to human life, and its importance sticks in our language: the word 'salary,' from the Latin word for salt is one example. Another is the saying: *"He isn't worth his salt,"* meaning he is worthless and not earning his salary. At one time much of our food, be it meat, fish, vegetables and even pickles, could only be preserved though salting. Electricity made refrigeration possible and was an invaluable process that largely replaced it. Since salt is primarily sourced inland and was once dug from the earth (at sites such as Salzberg– 'Salt Mountain' in Austria), it has long been associated in magic with the earth, through the 'sweat' endured in the simple toil of existence. Thus, by making the outer circle of salt, we consecrate our efforts to the giving Goddess of all bounty.

Transcript for #XI Bowers To Bill Gray

Dear Bill & Bobbie,

Anyway, we managed to meet up on the phone. Now I am trying to arrange for a meeting at my house, and from there to proceed to Wendover Top, which is an ancient ley site complete with Barrows. It is our common working site in this area, since it has all the trees, the height and atmosphere.

Now I have included a ritual that you can use if you like, it is traditional to Warwickshire, and I have seen a Grecian vase decorations with a very similar ritual depicted, only they seem to use a vase. The mirror and the horn and the knife are all old and possibly part of a far more complex past, in which force was invoked mentally, on physical levels, since the structure of the ritual is so close to shooting the sun in navigation as to be hardly believable. The nearer I grow to the original old craft, the more it points towards a science that knew all our answers, but solved them in different ways. In spite of all the archaeological evidence which says that Atlantis was a place of myth, it certainly seems to occur with illogical frequency in anything connected with the old craft. I often wonder if the myth was derived from some other planet, and that the ones who escaped found life on a primitive planet too much for wide-open minds.

We will try and congregate upon your place come December and hold the second ritual near there, if you can think of a suitable site, it will make a lot of difference. The usual indications being it should never be near modern civilisation, that is it should have timber of the old sort about it, and that it must be near water or on a high place. If it is permissible, we would like to sleep upon your floor since as you no doubt now appreciate, sleep is number one essential after a meeting of any sort. We all suffered from the lack of sleep last time. And I think this has something to do with the flux of colds, aches and pains. I suppose we will have to accept it we ain't so tough as our peasant ancestors, and a night out in the woods a conjuring... [rest of letter incomplete—damaged/missing].

(x) XII Drawing Down The Moon [short version]

Transcript for Drawing Down The Moon.
(short version)

Equipment needed. Cloak, Cross Straps, Girdle, Cord, Knife, Horn, Consecrated Wine, Consecrated Wafers, Mirror, Apron, Stone, Five Candles.

Woman holds mirror in right hand and horn in her left hand, reflects moon in mirror to surface of wine in horn. The others pace deosil about her nine times.

Man steps forward with lantern in left hand, and knife in right hand and says, "Lady, I am between Heaven and Earth for Thee." Woman answers, "Sir, take Thy fill, but drink the cup to its bitter dregs."

Man plunges knife in cup stirs 3 times and splashes it to 4 quarters, kisses woman, drinks from cup and passes it round the circle deosil. Another woman hands around the wafers.

In a group 2 men and 2 woman should quarter the couple with lit tapers that are bound, for the man red cross straps ties, and for the woman, blue cross ties.

The whole purpose of this ritual is that the reflection from horn should reflect back to the moon before drinking.

END OF CEREMONY

The Circle in this case is the wheel of life and not the Moat.

This should be done at Full Moon each month even if one is alone, by simple adaptation. Quarter to Twelve Saturday Night.

X..................................X

(y) #XIII Covenant for All Hallows & (z) - #XIV

Ritual Format For All Hallows

The **All Hallows Rite** that follows this poem, can be shown to adhere to its magical and mystical mysteries: This chant is mentioned by Bowers within the Rite below, and begins its correlation sequence after the preparatory Confession, Expiation and Purification have been accomplished and the Ritual 'proper' begins.

> This is the Taper that lights the way.
> This is the Cloak that covers the Stone,
> That sharpens the Knife
> That cuts the Cord That Binds the Staff
> That's owned by the Maid Who tends the fire
> That boils the Pot That scalds the Sword
> That fashions the Bridge That crosses the ditch
> That Compasses the Hand That knocks the Door,
> That fetches the Watch That releases the Man
> That turns the Mill
> That Grinds the Corn That makes the Cake
> That feeds the Hound That Guards the Gate
> That hides the Maze That's worth a light
> And into the Castle that Jack built.

Transcript for the Covenant of All Hallows
The Ritual of the Covenant of Hallows

1. <u>Confession</u> This applies only to my personal group

    <u>Expiation</u> Others must make their peace with the gods in their own

fashion, but since it concerns the transference of authority, you may join in if you wish.

Purification

2. Renewal of the Covenant. This is Traditional and consists of an altar comprised by a Stang, a sickle and a cross made of arrows. The witch is expected to bow before each aspect three times and then go on to the...

3. Blessing see diagram.

4. The Charging of the Pot. Sharpen knife upon stone, plunge into pot three times, place about fire in accordance with the diagram. W. usually undertakes this part whilst pacing around the pot and fire. \there is a chant for it.

5. Three women elevate platter to the dark moon, after the old woman has bound the contents with red and blue twine. It is then emptied into the pot. Women retire to out perimeter. All the men clasp the hand that holds the sword, and then plunges it into the pot. The sword is then passed deosil to four men who cast the drops on the blade to the Compass. The sword then is taken by the Summoner who fashions the Bridge. The Maid steps forward and taking the ladle from Server, whirling it rapidly dances around the fire widdershins. Then takes a ladlefull out of pot and poutrs it upon the ground, then proceeds to fill cup which is passed round deosil.

6. The Tipping of the Cauldron. Summoner does this, left heel from the South.

7. Everyone enters the Ring by stepping over broom and sword. Women first. Devil Hindermost. The Bridge and the Gate is left open facing North.

8.   The group stand in crescent, Devil centre, and the Summons and Word are said three times. This needs teaching since it cannot be explained in a letter. After the word has been breathed each time, the Stang should be struck smartly upon the ground, with a particular cry. Afterwards, stand Stang upright upon the perimeter of Ring. Cords should be worn about necks, with monkey's paw dangling free.

9.   <u>The Mill or the Grinding of Fate</u>. Pace widdershins. Summoner leading, as afar as possible male and female. Silence is the normal chant used, but if it pleases the group, a chant may be useful (Doreen?)

10. <u>Inspirational</u>. This begins with the devil, and cannot be explained since it is a major trade secret.

11. <u>The Manifestation and Worship.</u>

12. <u>The Blessing</u> from ten to twelve are not to be explained, proof will be given that it happens upon the night of the meeting. It either comes or it doesn't.

13. <u>The Feast</u> as already understood. Anything goes. It is a time of complete relaxation from the discipline of the ritual.

     Time of beginning, quarter to twelve. Dress optional.

X..................................x

(z) XIV Round Robin

Notes: Additional Letter to 'Clan,' which now includes Bill Gray.

Bowers defines an Esbat as one *"normally held to discuss business matters and to hold a minor ritual and prayer meeting,"* where Elders may mentor their neophytes, and matters pertaining to other members and outsiders may be discussed. Attendance is required but *"not compulsory unless [summoned by] the 'calling of the cord,'"*

Clear notice is given in this document for all due preparation incumbent upon all members prior to each Sabbat, where the same disciplines from the Esbat apply here. Of particular note is no17, which states *"that no detail or information as to the place of meeting or nature of the rites be expressed to 'outsiders.'"* This totally refutes Monmouth's assumption of what criterion determines an Esbat and a Sabbat, ergo what qualifies the meaning of 'Clan' and Clan workings, group and coven workings and those where guests may attend, being quite distinct altogether, and are as noted by Bowers himself! There is clear instruction headed on this document for the rules pertaining to Sabbats and Kindred Festivals, citing rules for the behaviour of members. This confirms both Esbats and Sabbats were primarily for members of Bowers' own group, and that the Sabbats extended the workings through a *larger mix of people from kindred groups, though still 'members.'*

This illustrates perfectly Bowers' later and consistent use of the term—Clan, as correct, in referring to and including inducted and affiliated members, directly from his own group and through kindred groups. It does *not* refer to guests, though they were known to occasionally attend as Valiente had remarked upon. It is why in several documents, he makes distinct directions to members that he clarifies *do not apply to those present as guests.*

Transcript: The Clan – 'Round Robin'

Clan

Thank you all for your comments and reports. It would appear that we have had a successful meeting with better results than could have honestly been expected from a scratch meeting with a scratch group. To date, all reports indicate the recorded phenomena was shared by other people, and that no one person has indicated anything that was confined to themselves alone.

Three people gave a description of the Castle, two others felt the sorrow that indicates the approach to the Castle. Each of us has indicated that we felt or sensed the presence of a Watcher and saw various lights etc. therefore it can only be concluded that the phenomena was of the group and not of individuals. This in turn has raised an interesting problem since we have had the occurrence of both objective and subjective phenomena, which to say the least is very unusual. The organization of the ritual was at fault in so much that it lacked rehearsal, and that a previous telephone conversation between two of the leading lights led to utter confusion, as to who was to lead the ritual from the beginning onwards. However, the general feeling from this end is one of amazement that the bloody thing worked at all, and a feeling of caution for the future of the group. We have maybe gone too far too quickly and this will result in a period of confusion as to our actual purpose.

<u>Bill</u>: It is common for any witch group to share a group luck, or thought. This is Robin the Child of Art, an over-mind that is shared by everyone who participates in witchcraft of our order. Will someone please win the Football Pools now. Basically the formation of this group-mind is of the uttermost importance, since the addition of a disturbing element, or the unbalance caused through the lack of one sex or for that matter the failure to complete the cycle of witchcraft (as opposed to other forms

of magic) results in an over balanced Robin. Whatever energy is put into the Robin (and that energy should correspond with the totality of any normal healthy human being) results in the input energy being stepped up to the power of three at the output. Therefore a witch cuveen should be comprised of many different types of people with different energy ratios, who must fulfill a normal cycle in their lives as well as a magical, intellectual or spiritual cycle. When this is achieved the Robin is a completed and mature power principle, and has a balance and effect upon the group. Many modern cuveens have failed to appreciate this one basic factor and consequently are putting in power of one order only and getting out power three times that amount in the form they are putting in. Obviously feather dusters, fertility rituals and anything like that is out, since we live in the 20th century and our human needs are complex, but the roots of the ash tree called witchcraft are always in the earth, no matter how the branches touch the stars and unless the earth is fertile and the roots strong the tree is not healthy. That is the reason I said many months ago to you that witchcraft is something like gardening, something like cooking, it is a little bit of everything starting with the basic ingredients. We are the stew or the postage in the Cauldron, the roots, the Trunk, and the Leaves and the Tree, it is dependent upon ourselves how we flourish or wither with Winter storms.

The next meeting, an Esbat, is on the 21st of this month, purely business and a get together. We may do something outside, I am not certain yet. The place of gathering is Anne's home on Walton-on-Thames. Will everyone please indicate if they are coming. Anyone who wants to sleep at my home for the night.

[Hand written on the back]:

Pleased to hear that you have written to Doreen and found your working partner at last. What do you think of Bill's bit of nonsense, wish he knew what he was talking about. Our lady will take a bite of him sooner or later just to remind him that she really exists.

Affectionate regards Roy and Jane.

You have Anne's address, let her know you are coming and she will give direction.

x.................................x

(aa) Letter #4 to Norman Gills

Halloween that year was an awkward affair. An apology is given for being unable to have Gills present at the *Hallows Rite,* revealing the nature of Gills' status as 'guest', an occasional attendee and *not* an Inducted member. It has been popularly believed by many, especially in America, that Norman Gills had been a member of the Clan. He was not. He was already part of his own Clan, as Bowers reiterates. Guests clearly unsettled his own members who were already experiencing internal traumas. Bowers discusses with Gills the Kings and Queens of the Compass. He enthuses its success, despite the presence of guests. Speaking of the magic of Long Compton, Bowers also refers to the summoning of the Hound and the Raven and his vision of Old Tubal & The Old Queen. Refers again to the usage of mirrors and of symbols. All in all, very vivid description of the Hallows knot. He reminds Gills his group is an 'Eight' clan, that is, it consists of the Luciferian and Sophianic formulae of seven + 1.

Transcript: Letter 4 to Gills

Dear Norman,

Many thanks for your calendar, and especially for the crossed owl feathers upon the back, a blessing only a "witch" can understand Life ... Love ... Wisdom, or as we're taught to say, 'Flags, flax, fodder.' I return them back to you with my good will. Different traditions, but the same basis. I noticed that you wrote to us in Theban script, which I translate as "Three hundred and sixty-five days of happiness," Ta, ever so.

We have been pretty busy recently, organising a magical group along the Seven and One basis, as opposed to the old rural, Twelve and One. The Clan seem to be responding, and our ancestors are appearing to give their approval, the only approval that counts for us. The Hallows of the Covenant went off all right, had to cover up some things since strangers were present, but we got through a few results. Sorry about not bringing you along, but since it was already overbalanced with outsiders, there was not very much else we could do. We could not have helped you under those circumstances at all. The summoning of the Hound and the Raven had to be done symbolically as it was, and there were only four of us who knew what we were about. Still one of the outsiders said she had a vision of the Old Queen, and Old Tubal was definitely there. Not a bad night out all in all.

Concerning your magick mirrors, with or without the horn? Or do you mean a scrying glass … I know of two mirrors, one the lady holds, by a very old piece of wood, and the other that is between my eyes. One mirror speaks of the trees of the forest, eight in all, the other speaks of Tides that is still to come. My question to you as to where the witch wears her garter … needs an answer. However, lets leave these things for the future. Perhaps we can meet sometime, in the New Year. Perhaps your Clan and mine could meet one day and discuss things. Staffordshire and Warwick don't come to Long Compton. Maybe they went to another Well.

May the hare, owl and pussycat, Roy

X...................................X

(bb) Hand-written letter from Bowers to Chalky - Twelfth Night

Notes: Hand written note about a meeting at Doreen's House. Off to Newtimber for their *TWELFTH NIGHT RITUAL* (previously noted by Valiente where she references the Wild Hunt). Pay particular attention to the diagrams drawn in this letter. They demarcate the 'bridge.' Again we have Chalky receiving instruction from Bowers, and on quite a challenging rite, one asserted by Monmouth as a primary rite Chalky and George must have shared with Bowers. Yet here he is, reminding *them* exactly how to Construct the Bridge with the *'Broom & Sword,'* and how to prepare the *Moat and the Mill.* These are direct instructions for the Laying of one of the Rings of the Compass.

Another group separate from Bowers' is again hinted at in the title below. There is no reason given, nor clue hinted at that directs us to assume the title refers to any wild notion of a single group (ie: Bowers') plus 'guests.' Again, the language determines for itself the presence of *more than one group as constituent parts within a 'greater' body—the Clan in fact.* Members would therefore make up that *'Greater Congregation,'* occurring on a major knot. The presence of any others, for instance 'guests,' are not noted, but some may have received special license to attend. It was a term adopted and very much favoured by *'The Regency.'*

Notes

(1). Note spelling of Ronald White's name as the variant of Chalkie!

(2). This usage has historical precedent. It is recorded that the barbarians would hold their shields to their jaws, and would breathe over them, chanting their battle cries, building to a fearsome crescendo as they fell upon their enemies. This fear this induced would often break open the Roman Lines.

(3). Gestures are indicated in the drawing for the 'Building of the Mask' upon the face, the prose for this differs from that given in doc (m)

Transcript for Twelfth Night

Dear Chalky, (1)

All is well! We meet at Doreen's place at approx. 10pm. Here are some matters to clear things enclosed. We will have your cloaks etc with us. See how we dress and copy us.

Fashion Bridge by binding sword and broom together with eight three times on North gate of circle in forming X (followed by sketch showing bound sword and broom)

After cauldron ritual, take the pot off the fire and kick it over into the moat with left heel facing towards North. You lead circle with a steady pace increased slowly Jane follows behind. Male then female. The opening chant is Master: Hoggan amai Clan: Henne! (say it (whisper) like the sea breaking upon the shore). (2) Then as you say it raise Stand and strike butt upon the ground with a sharp cry of Hoi! This happens three times. Then Master begins vowel Chant :U:I:A:E:O: Count 9 then take it up [Stang] and begin pacing Widdershins. Will the god to descend into me with everything you got. Keep a steady pace, don't go too fast and make sure the circuit is complete, that is your arm joined to the last person. Make sure your cord is well tied around your middle (waist), Cord of Fate (Hempen One) About neck.

George opens the ceremony with four blasts of Horn to elements (got a real horn for this job). Doreen has chant for cauldron all we say is A aha eveaveava! A, AHA Eveveva.

Statements to master for purification is 'Magister, Fains I have Transgressed' followed by the stroke from a rod, then a blessing (sketch of St John's Cross).

Prayer for Mask 3

"Goddess,

Thou who created Heaven and Earth,

Who brought forth Order from

chaos, Time from Eternity

– I pray to Thee.

Thou who listens to our deepest desires,

Who shines forth the pleasing lights,

Who inspires our inherited wisdom

And protecteth us from the

Baleful might of the Destroyer.

I pray Thee,

Grant us the inner voice of angels

Speaking of things spiritual

And let Love be our guiding light.

In the names of the Father, the Mother,

And the Spirit that moveth all."

Cross arms, bow, stand up, go to cauldron.

Transfer masculine power to sword when plunged.

Regards Brothers

Roy

MEETING PLACE:

NEWTIMBER HILL 12-13 X 26-27 O.S MAP 182

ASSEMBLE DOREEN'S PLACE – 9.30-10PM

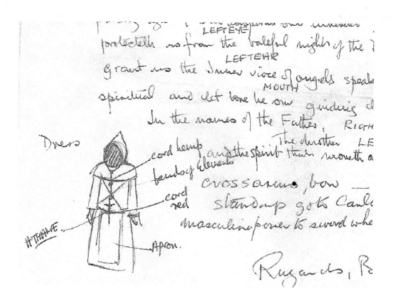

~3~ Diagram of Cloak with Apron

Justine Glass–Article written for her book *Witchcraft, The Sixth Sense and Us*, in which Bowers instructs her on the Old Craft using the Breton Menhir as an allegory of its Mysteries.

Norman Gills would eventually guest at the Hearth of the *Thames Valley Coven*, but through extant familiarity with Chalky and George, he may have joined *their* group slightly prior to that.

Anchor points

Solid confirmation validates the meeting of Bowers and Gills no earlier than the end of 1964. Based on info Bowers secures regarding his marriage, 1965 offers a more certain date. This is verified where Bowers informs Gills of his 14 years marriage to Jane; an official civil event we know is recorded in 1951. This allows us to securely date their initial association on those grounds alone. Valiente's named presence in the February Rite of 1965. She had left by September, 1965.

X...................................X

(cc) Documents 'as enclosed' concern: February: (i) Gathering of The Greater Congregation & (ii) 8 Spirits of the Moon - 1965

Notes: Animal Totem spirits denote the 'Masked Rites of Tubal Cain that E.J. Jones explored further in the mid 1990s.' Their Virtues and associations are noted here. A Clan Rite for any and all groups of kin to meet up, quite literally as 'The Greater Congregation.' Bowers' mentions: Chalky, Doreen, Jane and Roy specifically to bless the crossed horns. These Rites discuss the Totemic masked beasts of the Compass. The letter to ickle deric' mentions the 'Congregation.'

Transcript of the Gathering of the Greater Congregation 1965

February - The Virgin Queen – Life to Death
Code:Northern Twin, 2 Owls, Southern Twin, 2 Owls, Chariot.

2+5 New Moon. Rings, Greater Wheel, Fire, South. Moat, Stake North. Animals Hare and Horse. South. Hound and Raven, North.

Equipment: Skull, Stake, Tapers, Knives, Cords, Ribbons, Cloaks, Arrows, lanterns, incense, Treble Horn, Wine, Bread, Wreath, Mirror.

Preparation of Site. Greater Wheel prepared according to Sabbat, Fire centre. Greater Wheel invoked South. Treble barriers. Chalk. Moat, thrown up facing North. Stake centre in Pentacle 3.
Snake of Upper branches centre between two Rings.

Rulings covered by Cuveen Writ.

Ritual.

1. (A) Confession (B) Expiation (C) Purification

2. Blessing. Mask symbol. Assumption of the magical personality.

3. Gather in the Moat. Drawing of Moon in to Left Horn

Invoke the Twin of the North. Sacrament of the Old 'Un'.

Offer Tapers to Skull. [hand written - *Bread to Earth*.]

4. Greater Wheel. Invocation of the Twin of the South.

Sacrament to our Lady. Cast wine upon the fire.

N.B. Horns Crossed Thrice and Blessed by Chalky, Doreen, Jane, Roy.

Dance round fire. Lead off into Moat.

A Woman for Trance, under the Skull, facing North.

5. Feast.

Further magical work to be undertaken after.

[Hand-written on the front -bottom of page]

Ron as marshall. Fashion bridge into moat with this pattern

W

       Roy

[Hand-written on the bottom of copy]

Dear George.

We will have a look at that foot of yours.

       Roy.

x...............................x

Transcript for 'The Spirits of the Moon'

New Moon

Dexterity, Science, Action, Marriage, Realization, Religion, law and Temptation.

Animals:-

The Hare:- represents Life, movement, skill, speed, significant of study, and healing, and writing and travel. Higher aspects. Absolute Being which contains infinate possibilities.

Tree: Birch. Gem: Quicksilver

The Cat:- femininity. All seeing, secrecy, action, inquisitiveness, realisation, power, sight, power to see past and present. Projection.

Herbs: Valerian, Nightshade, Woodbine. Tree: Broom. Gem: Jasper

The Owl: religion, law, teaching, knowledge, germination of acts, covers partnership, public image.

Tree; Rowan. Gem:White stone Diamond etc.

Full Moon

Truth, Force, spiritual power, strength, will, victory, balance, philosophy, travel, poetry. The central figure.

Tree: The Ash

The Ram or Bull: Sacrifice, fertility, fecundity, strength, determination, rulership, growth.

Tree: Oak. Gem: Ruby

The Goat: Love, Lust, Life physical, Power over animals, Magic.

Tree: Blackthorn. Gem: jet and iron

Dark Moon

Serpent: Supernal wisdom, there are twin dragons or serpents, earth and air. Represents the heart of the mysteries.

Gem: Emerald. Tree: Quince

The Bitch-Hound: Vengence, Retribution, Nemesis.
Tree: Elm. Gem: Opal or Pearls.

The Raven: death
Tree: Alder, Willow and Yew. Gem: Onyx or Porphyry.

x..................................x

(dd) i 'On Cords' – Pentagram March 1965 & ii Typed Letter to George from Jane

Notes: Typed letter about the Pentagram article on mushrooms. It is known that at this time, George Winter was beginning to suffer from a heart condition. (ref: Valiente's note-pads)

Transcript: On Cords – *Pentagram*, (3) March 1965

Mrs. Basford has raised an interesting point about the real purpose of cords, harvest twine, string dolls, etc. They appear to have originated from the woven strands of Old Fate, the major deity of all true witches. They are, of course, the origin of such descriptive terms as "spellbinders." When worked up properly they should contain many different parts— herbs, feathers and impedimenta of the particular charm. They are generally referred to in the trade as "ladders," or in some cases as "garlands," and have much the same meaning as the three crosses. That is they can contain three blessings, three curses, or three wishes. A witch also possesses a devotional ladder, by which she may climb to meditational heights, knotted to similar pattern as the Catholic rosary.

The Celtic practice of binding the dead, used now as a devotional aid by some modern groups, was originally an indication that the dead person had undergone the necessary stages and purification towards the final judgement and redemption. The actual pattern of the knot was considered to be the important thing; the pattern formed by the lines of the binding being a symbol of secondary importance.

Alexander the Great, by cutting the Gordian knot, announced to all and sundry that he was going to cut his own fate with the edge of a sword. It was the action of a truly brave man, since the knot was bound upon the yoke of the Twin Bulls, the Masters over Life and Death. It may be that when he later built a temple to Nemesis he was attempting to buy off the terrible fate of his former action.

The art of binding is to be seen in one of its best forms in the old craft of thatching. The pegs and binders are traditionally put into a crossed shape, held by a final structure over the roof trees that also has a very close connection with Witchcraft.

The so-called "sacred object" held in such reverence by some witches was in fact a weaver's distaff—and could easily be mistaken for a phallic symbol.

The weaver's distaff, bound with reeds or straw, appears frequently in rural carvings and elsewhere. It again has reference to the Craft and supreme Deity.

It would appear that the witches were not in the least influenced by Freudian concepts.

There is good reason to assume that the nursery game of snakes and ladders originated in a much older pastime connected with binding. One aspect of the snake is that of the Tempter or Destroyer, and the game remains as a lesson upon life: one either ascends by the aid of the ladder, or descends via the snake. The action of the game is still dependent upon the throw of a black and white cube (dice)—a symbol of Fate from ancient times.

Basically the cords of binding, as used today, are worked upon with mistaken enthusiasm. Originally they were cords of Fate, woven and bound into a charm for a defined purpose. Sometimes shaped into a semblance of the object or person to be influenced, they were also hung on a gatepost or nailed near to the object or person, preferably in a public place, as an indication of intent.

In an Italian spell, the ladder is actually placed in the bed of the person to be enchanted. A beautiful witch ladder, incidentally, was once found in a church belfry: presumably one of the Old Craft could not sleep late on Sunday mornings because of the racket of the bells!

"Cat's cradle" as a game is interesting enough but as a form of witchery it becomes an interesting indication of the complex nature of the Craft. Each of the fingers on the hands of a witch has a defined meaning and purpose. It would be reasonable to assume that, to the knowing eye, the crosses and planes formed by the strings would tell much of a particular ritual.

Transcript of Letter to George From Jane

Dear George,

Sorry I didn't see you before you left. I didn't know you would be going so early.

We all sat around nattering all day Sunday as usual. I hope you are feeling better now. There was a little article about Louise in the 'Sun' today. Did you see it? We received our copy of 'Pentagram' today, written almost entirely by Roy, or rather this fellow Robert Cochrane. Also a very interesting article by a Witch from the West Country, about the mushroom eaters. Evidently they use this as part of their Rite. Roy has written to him. He has divided the witchcraft movement up between the ancient and the modern and equates Roy with a sort of Kier Hardy. I hope this time we have come across someone who is really genuine. At least the encouraging thing is that he is definitely not one of the Gardnerians. Do you realise that it was us who started using the term Gardnerians, and now it seems to have spread. I don't know how, but it's funny isn't it?"

Love from, Jane

X.................................X

(ee) The May Game

Notes: A Rite that also incorporates the Animal Totems. [in like manner—after Gowdie] Isobel Gowdie's famous chant and folktale is here given manifest presence in a sensory form. These totems are very similar to the spirits of the moon. These are the first evolutions in developing animal totems as spirits of the moon. Their associations with the *aetts* of the compass are clearly obvious. Moreover, in providing a clear description of these 'masked' rites, they inform the fundamental premise that is the very basis of the atavistic journeying, of transvection through the form of one's totem animal. This precedent exonerates our mentor, E.J.J. for his continuity of these rites within The Clan.

In bringing these rites to the attention of the craft community within *'Sacred mask, Sacred Dance'* he was much criticized by those he had sought to share these sacred rites with, first hand, and by his peers who raised considerable publicity denouncing them as his own invention, declaring they has no basis in the works of Bowers and his Clan. So, here for all those detractors of the sterling work of Evan John Jones, proof positive they are everything he claimed and more besides.

Transcript for 'May Games'

This is a pursuit game of 'Hound & Hare,' in which All are one and ever more shall be so! Each member of the group 'becomes' their own totem spirit part, snaking rapidly round the circle in an exhaustive chase of union. The following animal attempts to catch the preceding one, but always the female avoids the Male until the Last verse.

The lines "Alack, alack, my love is gone" is spoken by all the men, each time, and the response "Devil a damn does she care" by the woman. This creates a form of two word music, and the whole thing ending up in the 'Sacred Marriage'.

"I am a Maid all dressed in white.

Alack, alack, my love is gone   [males]
I am a Maid all dressed in white

Devil a damn does she care   [females]
I am a Maid all dressed in white,

prepared for marriage this very night.
Devil a damn does she care   [together]

I am a taper burning bright,
Alack alack my love is gone
I am a taper burning bright
Devil a damn does she care.
I am a taper burning bright,   Lit for my lady as her right.
Devil a damn does she care

I am a Hare a running fast.
Alack, alack my love is gone.
I am a Hare a running fast
Devil a damn does she care.
I am a Hare a running fastened,   N'er will the hound get past.
Devil a damn does she care.

I am a Hound chasing the Hare
Alack, alack my love is gone
I am a Hound chasing the Hare
Devil a damn does she care
I am a Hound chasing the Hare,   Red of eye and white of ear
Devil a damn does she care.
I am an owl in aik woods
Alack, alack my love is gone
I am an owl in aik woods
Devil a damn does she care

I am an owl in aik tree, It was I that set the grey Hare free.
Devil a damn does she care

I am a Raven of the dead
Alack, alack my love is gone
I am a Raven of the dead
Devil a damn does she care
I am a Raven of the dead,
I will peck the owl's eye from her head
Devil a damn does she care.

I am the cat come to save
Alack, alack my love is gone
I am the cat come to save
Devil a damn does she care
I am the cat come to save,
To catch the Raven and Eat the Knave
Devil a damn does she care.

I am the Ram all strong and proud
Alack, alack my love is gone
I am the Ram all strong and proud
Devil a damn does she care
I am the Ram all strong and proud,
This is my ewe I say it loud
Devil a damn does she care

I am the Goat all crafty and wise
Alack, alack my love is gone
I am the Goat all crafty and wise
Devil a damn does she care
I am the Goat all Crafty and wise, I will get the proud Ram's Bride

Devil a damn does she care.

I am the serpent that made them all
Alack, alack my love is gone
I am the serpent that made them all
Devil a damn does she care
I am the Serpent who made them all, this is my ancient rule.
Devil a damn does she care"

All: Maid, Man, Hare, Hound, owl, Raven, Cat, Ram, Goat and
Snake....

[Old Woman, centering Ring. Hands held above her head left foot
forward, her fingers touching making the bow of the Night.]

I am the Mare nine-fold born.
The glorious Star, the wondrous Dawn
I am the Mare that bears the Moon
All: Devil a damn does she care.
The Fate that cuts the Thread of Doom
I am She that walks in White
The One that Meets Her Love this Night"
[Magister comes forward and kisses her.]
The Feast begins.

X..................................X

(ff) Bowers to 'Ron and George'
- Re: 'Old Man's' Letters

Bowers made no secret of the source of his information, of who inspired him and mentored him. In his #2 to Norman Gills, he confirms his mentor to be 'the old man,' he even draws a tiny stick figure among his symbols on the last page holding a broom and a sword, which strongly suggest the *Broom and Sword Rite*' noted previously at (m) Throughout his letters, Bowers quotes 'The Old Man' and Robert Graves as the two main sources of his inspiration. As with so many examples given already, Bowers firmly impresses his authority as leader in this document too, making it very evident, that Chalky is not only subject to Bowers' authority, but that he is certainly not, as Monmouth attempts to project, merely taking a 'passive' back seat—allowing Bowers to assert an authority Monmouth feels is not his by right to exert.

Bowers re-iterates that information here in this document, giving strong instruction on: 'How to fashion the Bridge.' And how to use the Kippen. Diagrams are drawn onto the back of the Document. Bowers here again makes firm the point that everyone needs to pull together, sharing the same view in developing their Mythos, if not, then all is doomed to fail. Their methods and opinion are evinced with opposing clarity.

"It is not a matter of great importance what each of us believes, but what is important is that we should examine the contents of his letters, add our own concepts and comments, and pass it back so that the whole can be absorbed by the group 'Will'"

Transcript for The Old Man of Westmoreland

Dear Ron and George

Herewith is enclosed a copy of the old man's letters to me over the last few weeks. They deal with various matters that range from magical thought to the correct way to approach an altar. The art of Kundaline as described by him is strongly associated with riding the staff. Combined with an anointed staff it would undoubtedly bring about a state of mystical knowledge.

(1) Upon approaching an Altar properly. "have you ever experimented with cows? If you approach a cow so that they do not see you, you will find that more than one of them will have its rear towards you, but the head turned to face you completely.

Now if in a state of Kundaline (snake) you face the altar with the moon's reflection upon one side, the left giving a different result from the right, a state of realisation will come to you if there is no interruption until after the first stage is passed, afterwards Samahadi is apparent, and this state cannot be broken until its own time is fulfilled. The time is about one second but enough happens to impress you with the everlastingness of time."

(2) Upon the use of the Kippen rod [Stang] "Starting (f) gaze steadily moving up to to (e), at about (g) a cone of light is seen at (e) not moving your gaze in anyway. (G) can be seen without moving your eyes in any way. Now if the rod is coloured the cone changes colour, if the rod is directed a freely moving pyramid the pyramid will revolve. The power of the rod is illustrative of elemental power and kundaline. The snake begins in an area which will be considered sacred, as it is the site of a power that is final in itself. This power, when fully developed and usable must be used with the elements. As water into a tank – a tank fills and when full is static. (Lewthwaite maintains that the seat of power in the area between the anus and sexual organs...correct)" Diagram of rod entered separately below.

(3) Upon the use of drugs. "Consider the potato, the tobacco, belladonna, all related and possessing characteristics which are ideal for visions of

327

the past and future, remember always that there is no present. If these plants are used wrongly there are periods of false pasts and futures, these are always with you unless the user understands the proper use of the elements. Certain of the herbs can be used in regards to the angels. Poppy seeds are essential, use them in incense, or boil them and drink them, or rub it all over you."

(4) Upon the Elements "There is no better method of beginning or strengthening a ritual than by using that ritual (the invocation of elements). Here once again the operator if ignorant can proceed too far and find himself in an elemental hell. The four elements can solve all problems, but not by themselves. They must be used with other forces as follows. Earth with the language of Trees

Air with clouds (dukkering?) Water with air and earth. Air at times by itself (these counterbalances are presumably opposites to stabilise a power)."

(5) Upon the powers developed "Telepathy to a developing sense. Double thinking (dream voices). Bell Tone (getting out of the body). Trees, etc, projection of self and will, transportation in astral conditions, and with the sense in operation. The Serpent with instances capable of demonstration. The Rod... the development of all faith. All this brings into use other powers such as an anticipation and an expectancy. The only books worth reading and learning from a witches point of view are: the Qabbalah in full. Three Volumes of Hermetics by Bardon. Magick by Crowley. The Rumbleston which is old time Swedish. Runic and Hebrew aught to be learned."

(6) Upon the Devil. 'The Tree of Life' is as you know paramount. This is the method of directing Kundaline. It is liberated to travel on a guided and controlled route at first upwards to Tippareth and Kether and at both sides at once. To stations Binah and Chocmah which both being

minus, and Kether being positive. The two forces where they meet do not mingle because they repel each other, but with a suitable meditation they bring about a state of Samahadi in which All is made known. Kether is an area at the back of the head which is receptive, the front of the head being transmissive. Now when the two powers meet)ab. CB being the throat) control over the arch angels can be obtained, but the state of obtaining is so narrow that the obtaining can be lost and often is, and the spirits are loth to help you regain it.

(7) Upon the past "I can remember something about the Witches Charter, which is the Bible. I am now writing it down."

~4~ 'Cleft Stick'

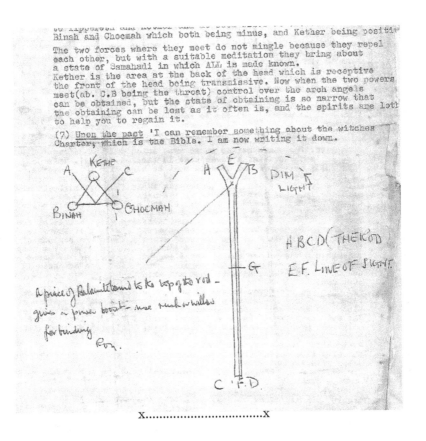

(gg) #5 Bowers to Norman Gills

Notes: This tackles the ever thorny subject of Lucifer, his virtues and form, Bowers also cites a profound and powerful poem by Jane entitled: 'I am She.' The content in this letter lays to rest any question as to the ethos of this current within the Mythos of CTC. He explains to Gills, the dynamic of Death, and of union through love, with the Grave. How that virtue holds the guard as Champion of the Glass Bridge. Requests a meet-up. Includes a brief hand- written note on the back page. Bowers presents a symbol for Gills to decipher, adding that it should be easy if he truly knows his stuff.

Transcript for: Letter #5

Dear Norman,

Thank you for your letter which I read with great interest. I take it that you write in symbols, and your description of the Two Kings and Two Queens are purely symbolic, since we have something similar in my own branch of the Craft. You also ask me whether Lucifer the Angel of Light is winged, it depends of the ritual you are working. Sometimes he comes as a tall golden man, moving rapidly.[52] Other times, the wings of fire surround him, but few can face that vision without aid from an even Higher Source. At times, he is winged at the feet, others at the head, behind the glorious hair. You also speak of Toutes, Lord of the Mound, dark, unpredictable, the true God of the witches, magicians if they are working at any decent level at all. A cold wind flows from Him. Dark is his shadow, and he bears a branch of the sorrowful alder, and walks with the aid of a blackthorn stick. Sorrow is printed upon his face, yet also joy. He guards, as a rider upon an eight-legged horse, he approaches the Castle of the Night. He is also the Champion of the Glass Bridge, after the Silver Forest. Cold is the air as he passes by. You say tall and dark, I say small and dark, speaking in faint voice, which is as clear as ice. They are the Twins, the Children of the Night and the Serpent, brothers and some say one and the same person. Fire and air, growth and decay. One looks forward, the other backward. One creates, the other destroys, Caster and Pollux.

The waterfall, a secret place where a great river winds back upon itself after coiling four times through air, fire, earth and water. It spouts outwards, downwards and upwards, for ever and ever. Behind the waterfall, there are three stones, upon the stones there are three signs. One winds left, one winds right and points straight up to the stars. The water pours down into a mighty and some say bottomless, chasm, but I know different for I have seen the Hunter ride out, chasing the Hare back to life again. In the darkness of the chasm, Night still is and is still creating, bringing forth.

Sister, sing a song about Night:
"I am what they think me to be
I am what ye consider of thyself.
I am myself and thou as thou art
And will be... time come.
I am that without form
I am that without force,
 Yet force and form I be.
I am the loved and beloved,
I am the whole and the part.
I am compassion healing rift
I am diamond cutting stone hearts.
I am a mirror without reflection.
All eight of those I be.
I am the well without water,
From which all must drink and die

331

I am words, letters if ye understand me

I am words without sound, listen to the wind.

I am pain, grief, sorrow and tears,

The rack, the noose, the stake.

The flayer and the flayed.

The hunted and the hunter,

The head without a body

Thrust upon a Stake

The body without a head

Hung upon a tree

Yea! All this and still I am whole.

I am night and sleepless dream, I am …

Thou must overthrow me to release thy soul (between)?

I am the Watcher upon the Hill

The Keeper of the Gate, all keys I own.

I am peace, now understand thou thing of clay,

A rose amongst the living dead

I am turned about, and turned again

I am a root, a leaf, a tree

My tap draws strength from eternity

All things be mould for me.

Few know me at all, and that secret be

Yet woman is my name,

A plated host marcheth at my skirt

For I am mighty as the Dark one knows me

My nostrils smell the food of the slain.

I am weak as woman knows me. Yea! Be that my truest strength

I am desire

I am the first created.

The first Sin. Behold!

For I am She!"

Also named, The Ash Tree, on another document written after a meeting in 1963, by Jane Bowers under the mask and guise of the Ash Tree, the Asherah pole and totemic altar and tree of sacrifice upon which the horn-ed god is hung in suspension, a becoming through Her.

X...................................X

(hh) Bowers to 'All Members' Entheogen Experiments

This Document is completely self-explanatory. No comment is required. The reader will conclude their own thoughts from this. The student may ponder more deeply into these mysteries. This entire cosmogony and cosmology combined forms and informs the Clan Mythos via its lawful tenets, prescribed throughout as: *The Basic Structure of the Craft.'* Needing no explanation here, its tenets form the 'Mystery Tradition' proper. But it is for seekers to discern as individuals, through the establishment of their own vital contact within their singular endeavours to attain that graal. It is however, alluded to in the many works and missives within this publication. All of them are dedicated to the illumination of the 'Faith,' the veil through which Bowers viewed his Craft. The true seeker will discover these, recognising the keys to the path. These are not secret, they are known throughout time. But their purpose is sacred, as is the unfurling of the process of realisation for those who traverse this path in Truth.

Battles over Wica & Gardner escalate.
Hostilities within the *Pentagram* erupt.

Inevitable breakdown of working relationship between Bowers and Valiente largely due to what she referred to as his obsession with drug experimentation (a practice she was utterly opposed too). She leaves the Clan.

Transcript: 'To all Members' Re: Ethos

There comes a time when we all must take a flying leap into the dark hoping that we can reach the other side. We have discussed the four castles and their meanings. Before we can go any further as a group we must learn how to explore these castles. The exploration can be done by an effort of Will and Will alone but this takes a considerable length of Time. Therefore I now suggest that we proceed with a series of controlled experiments, involving the use of hallucinogenic plants and fungus. Properly controlled and directed these experiments will not be harmful. As such I shall be the first guinea pig, and nobody is obliged to follow me.

The Castle seven worlds, Kingdoms, etc are descriptions of Unworlds that are the keys to power. By careful symbolic description it is possible for a human to explore them, and make contact with the inhabitants under the influence of certain drugs.

These drugs can be found in:

(a)   Butonin, Toad venom.

(b)   Fly algaric, spotted toad stool, a piece of skin as large as one's own thumbnail is sufficient.

(c)   Henbane, the smoke thereof.

There are many other plants all of which have a property. I am fully aware that Chalky and George are conversant with these plants and their properties, therefore I lay in preparation and research into these plants in thier capable hands.

The reason for going round the Ring is strongly associated with the use of these plants and their quick disposal throughout the body. I recommend that myself should be the first to try any new drug, and I would like to emphasise that these drugs are not habit forming, although all of them are highly poisonous. On no account is anyone to attempt their use without the presence of the group.

This action has been precipitated before its time by a forthcoming article in the 'Pentagram. It was to be made the final end of our teaching since the symbolic framework which contains the use of these drugs is of extreme importance. Hence the reason for the intense secrecy which surrounds our symbolism.

However, once contact has been made or successful flight the need for these drugs is considerable diminished, since the technique can be learned by personal experience. Therefore once techniques are developed, the only time these drugs will be used is in major work when we want to function as a group and not as individuals. I would like to emphasise that the correct use of these drugs is of major importance and may not be divulged even to the death. Regards, Roy

X...................................X

(ii) 1965 Bowers to 'All Elders' -
Info On BSoTC - (Final Shift)

Notes: Bowers goes on to explain at length why their work is not of a cuveen (sic), nor one that works nature/seasonal magics, but one that strives to access the higher magicks of its mythos through a directly mystical approach. Most Significant of all, he lays great emphasis upon the fact they are an 'eight' Clan, in contra-distinction to anything a group or cuveen may be. It has therefore a completely unique duty to its cause aided through a *bestowed egregore*, assigned to it, and maintained by the vigor and valor of its people.(3)

Note too, there is no compulsion upon Clan Elders to accept this view, but they are told, with equal clarity, that he and Jane intend to work in that manner, even if they do so alone. This demonstrates without doubt or ambiguity the status Bowers assigned to the Clan, as a separate entity to a group or cuveen (sic), and also, how he viewed that as having a unique aegis, and trajectory. He makes a final plea for them to grasp this premise, agree to its demands and work towards that same goal.(1)

That events and friction worsened yet further, is testament to the failure of this missive to hit its target. Therefore, when Bowers died less than a year later, this ideal of a Clan, along with its Egregore, Aegis, Mythos etc was held by his Maid and widow until it became the responsibility of another to guard, and until such time arose in the future when it could fulfil the desire of its founder, Roy Bowers. Hence, Chalky and George parted company, with the Clan taking with them only what was rightfully theirs to take—all they had first brought with them, no more and no less. Their lore and preferred practise was then channelled into the formation of The Regency. It is to be noted how this information, shared by Bowers as 'Priest' amongst his Clan's 'Elders' only,(2) was obviously also shared in part with Norman Gills as a member of Chalky and George's group. [Though some, in part, had been shared by Bowers in one of his own letters to Gills.[53]] Then, after his death, Gills and others were given full access to what remained in their possession of Bowers' works. Some of this was later shared by these men with Joe Wilson in turn, during his visit to England circa 1970.[54]

Prior to John of Monmouth sharing these completed documents with ourselves when compiling information in consultation for his own publication of those early letters, circa 2011/12, we had not seen an extant, complete copy of the original document (ii). A partial copy, missing its first and last page was sent to us with an enquiry regarding our knowledge of it.[55] Over the course of time, E.J. Jones had discussed with ourselves selected tenets from that list, albeit as natural methodological teaching mechanisms, being intrinsic, rather than distinctive. Naturally, we had not 'seen' those tenets so formally listed as they appear in that document. Sometime later, after E. J. Jones's death, we were offered an opportunity to study selected pieces of those documents, the property of another good soul in the Craft world. These were kindly shared with us by Iain Steele (sadly now, deceased).

Thankfully, with the very generous help of Mr Steele, we acquired access to other documents relative to it. These have collectively facilitated solid research on all pertinent matters relating to the cosmology of the Mythos relayed within those documents. This further inculcated important validations, thus confirming a working knowledge in continuity—A lived Tradition. More importantly, however, the inclusion of those first and last pages has provided an unequivocal affirmation that it *had not* failed to address its Members and Elders of Bowers' group and Clan. On the contrary, it asserts a dynamic, *communal imperative*.

And so the happy existence of those vital pages within that original document completely refutes an opinion asserted in the introduction of

The Robert Cochrane Letters that knowledge of its tenets and principles were withheld from Members of his own Clan, whilst 'sharing' freely of them with others, namely Gills. It is too often the case that false information, once established, asserts a resistance and prejudice to truth.[56]

Transcript: 'To All Elders' Re: Mythos (BsoTC)

We hope that everyone has settled down after out last meeting. Whether we received any tangible results, well we do not know as yet. The signs are that very little is coming through. But at least we all showed willing and made the effort, which is a Prayer in its own right.

In the beginning we decided to confuse the issue deliberately, since we were uncertain of the people we were working with. (1) In the course of time, it became apparent that this course of action was wise, and when dealing with newcomers remains wise. However we are now beginning to work as a group, and I think everyone has shown their honesty and sincerity of approach. But the confusion of the beginning seems to have carried forward into the group now, and consequently few of us have any clear idea of what, and why we do certain things, and what we believe in. To clear this matter up, Jane and I have decided to write down the very Basic Craft and post to each member for study and comment. (2) The real fault at the heart of the group seems to be a lack of understanding of these basic principles. As long as this misunderstanding continues we cannot create a group mind, therefore we cannot expect to work a group magic, irrespective of our personal power.

Whether our interpretation of the basic Craft agrees with what each of us believes, is not a matter of great importance, but what is important is that we should examine the contents of this letter, the whole may be absorbed by the group Will. It is a great temptation to add bits and pieces garnered form years of study but the main issue is whether they are relevant to our purpose, which is the re-creation of the Old High Magic. As a group we all have to step down from some of our previous ideas and use those which are most suitable to the group. In a simple Cuveen working with seasonal magic, it is possible to bring many wines to the feast without becoming sick, because there is that much more freedom of choice, but we are an eight Clan, which means we work the Castles and the Seven Stars, (3) a very different thing. Therefore for the sake of coherence, we must establish a group thought and opinion. As such was is written here is not absolute, but open to suggestion and comment, so that it that can really be a group opinion, and not an opinion forced upon the group. Therefore we ask for you honest comments upon these matters. These opinions will be considered and accepted providing they form a coherent pattern and are related to the truth of the Living Mysteries. In other words, only matter which is capable of being developed to a very high level should be forwarded.

We would also like to make it clear that we are trying to avoid the trap of intellectualism, and the curse of academic study. Herewith is the basic structure of the Craft.....

In the beginning there was only Night and She was alone. Being was absolute. Movement was there none. Being force without form, and since She desired that form was desired. Woman being woman, She desired union, and Created Man from her North side. Having Created Man, She discovered Love and so all things began. Here was the first of all sins, Desire. From Desire sprang all movement, all Life, all Time, all Death, all Joy and Sorrow alike.

From the Gods came seven children, who Created Seven Worlds to Rule over, and they formed a Great Halo about the Great Gods as Seven Stars. They also Created Earth, Air, Fire, and Water, and gave these lands to four of the Seven Gods. These Gods each lived in a separate Land, bounded by the Great Gulf Anwen which is the Land of Chaos, and unredeemed souls.

The Lands of the Gods are then, a Castle surrounded by Fire that lies upon the East, ruled over by Luci, a Castle that lies under the depths of the Sea, laying towards the West, ruled over by Node, a Castle in the Clouds laying towards the North, ruled over Tettens. A Castle builded upon the Earth and surrounded by Trees, laying towards the South ruled over by Carenos. To each of these rulers was given a wife that sprang also from the Love of the Gods. Each of these lands had Power over human endeavour. Luci is the King of Light, Fire, Love and Intellect, of Birth and Joy.... He is visualised as a Bright Golden Light moving quickly, with wings. Thieving and mischievous.

For thy Kingdom is passed not away
Nor Thy power from the place hurled.
Out of Heaven they shall not cast the Day
They shall not cast out Song from the World.
By the Song and the Light they give
We know Thy works that they Live
With the Gift Thou hast given us of Speech
We praise, we adore, we beseech
We arise Thy bidding and followed
We cry to thee, answer, appear
O Father of us all Paian Apollo
Destroyer and Healer here!

In The North lies the Castle of Weeping, the ruler thereof is named Tettens, our Hermes or Woden. He is the second Twin, the Waning Sun, Lord over Mysticism, Magic, Power and Death, Baleful Destroyer. The God of War, of Justice, Kings, since all pay their homage to Him. Ruler of the Winds. Cain imprisoned in the Moon, ever desiring Earth, He is visualised as a tall dark man shadowy, cold and deadly. Unpredictable, yet capable of great nobility, since he represents Truth. He is the God of Magicians and Witches, who knows all Sorcery.

In the South lies the Castle of Life. The Ruler is named Carenos. He is Lord of the Animals, of Joy and of Passion. Ruler of the Woodlands, a Wild Hunter yet the God of Happiness, Fruition, Fertility, equivalent to the Young Dionysus. Shown as Horn-ed figure wit curling ram's horns. He is the God of the Fertility Cultus, and everything about Him is connected with Life, Growth and Strength.

In the West lies perhaps the most complex and the greatest figure of them all. The God of Paradise, Node He is the God of Rest, Sleep, Achievement, Fruition of labour, Spiritual Growth, He is also Noble, ever fighting against evil, and is equivalent to King Arthur. He is also God of the Sea. He should be seen as a mature man with golden light playing from Him and a Lion at his feet. Eyes that are wide and sad. He is the King of all true Wisdom.

These Four Kings are the reversed pentacle, thus and the fifth Ray is turned into six points, or three and three, which in part represents Old Tubal Cain, or the All Father Himself. Herne. Above the Head of the Moon as shown in the diagram lies five other stars known as the Goddesses, that is they are to be seen in the Plough of Haywain. They fall into this sequence. Life, Love, Maturity, Wisdom and Death. (4) Since I maintain that Knowledge is understood more fully if one has to work for it, I leave you to fit your own interpretation upon the Five Stars and how they fit as Queens within the Castles. By looking at the diagrams of both Moat and the Mill, it is possible to see how they become Queens, and also why in ancient mythology why the Queen was also considered to play the Harlot, or fallen woman. In other words, by the juxtaposition of King and Queens, it is possible to work out the magical formulae concerned with (a) aspects within the Mask, as one would use a Qabbalistic Tree, and (b) and insight into the control of the Four Basic Elements.

It was considered in the past that man could help the Gods as the Gods helped man. In fact you will find that in many fairy stories they deal with this matter allegorically. It is from these and many similar stories, ie. Sir Gawain and the Hollen Bush, Tristam and Isolde, Launcelot and Geneveve, and others that a pattern of magical myth and legend may be woven, often with surprising with results and effects. To effect a magical ritual of this nature, one enacts it with various implements and tools that have the same symbolic meaning as the Gods involved.

It was these unions from the Gods and man, that the Art of Magic began. To those who have eyes, ears and heart that is pure. These deepest secrets are written upon the clouds, in the bark of trees, in the movement of water, and in the heart of fire. The genuine mysteries are open for all to see, and rediscover. There is no secrecy surrounding them. There is a great river flowing and twining round all Creation. Rushing out of Anwen. Binding the Seven Kingdoms together, and returning the Anwen in a great waterfall under which all must pass eventualy. The name of that river is Time and the place of Darkness to which it returns is not only Hel but Heaven also. It is Time and Time alone that binds us to blindness, and it is Love and Love alone that will let us see the Golden Heart of the Mysteries.

These are the subjects we will be dealing with over the next year, and examining the basic content:

The Five Rings of Power
The Four Castles and the Keepers
The Four Tides or Rivers
The Wisdom of the 72 Herbs and Trees
The Art of the Mirror

The Art of the Kippen

The Art of the Stang

The Art of the Bone

The Power of the Seven Planets

The Power of the Sun

The Power of the Moon

The Power of the Stars

The Art of the Three Knives

The Art of Cords and Binding

The Art of Symbols and their Interpretation

The Power of Desire

The Power of Will

The Twin Snakes

The Rings of Power

The Rings of Power Fall in this order:

1. The Wheel of Life.

2. The Moat

3. The Mill of Fate

4. The Necklace

5. The Ring of the Doorways.

The Wheel is the basic creation of witch magic. It is a vehicle of worship of the Goddess over Life, Love, Maternity/Maturity, Wisdom, Death. In the centre lies the heart within the coffin or as it is known within the Craft, The Rose from the Grave. Love and Death. Basically it is the most simple of all the Rings. But also the most complex. It corresponds with the Garter or Ladder of Devotion and the Ring, like the Garter should be fastened upon the Knot of Death. Its main use in Rituals of Death and Resurrection. In actions of Worship it is a religious device used to draw down the power of the Goddesses invoked, standing upon the horn of the aspect invoked. It is blessed in the Name of Love Water and Fire used to drive our Evil from the Five Points, Swept and Garnished and Censed. It should be enclosed once with Salt and Chalk. That is Life and the Moon. Upon certain operation, it is permissible to light a fire in the centre, thereby creating the Rose of Passion, or Unity. On no account should it be used for an operation of Cursing, neither should the witch work widdershins within it. It is the Vehicle of the Horn-ed Childe. By simple meditation it is possible to find more points than five, in fact there should be twenty-five with one more.

x..................................x

The following document is included in this retyped document but is very unlikely to have been on the original. As previously mentioned fragments only of this document survive having been typed and retyped many times, mainly by Norman Gills for his students and by others including Joe Wilson to whom he gave a copy. It is completely incongruous with the rest of the document.

The Tools of the Trade

Part One:

The Stang is the blasting rod, the rod of power. The iron rod of the bible. The origin of the Word has much in common with sting, mustang, etc [4 nid-stang] It country meaning is to beat one's wife. 'Giving her the stang'. Or a touch of whip o willy you can work out the connection from there. However, it is only part of the full number of rods that a witch can use. Basically these fall into this order.

The Keppen or Kippen

The Stang or the Stinger

The Bone or weaver's little man (distaff)

The word kippen means, divided or split. It is used in much the same way as the ceremonial magician's rod that is for pointing, directing, moving and commanding. It is normally devised of ash and correspond to the tree of Wisdom, but according to the ritual used these woods may be used also. Ash, Birch, Apple, Willow or Hazel. White thorn may be used instead of Birch, Rowan instead of Ash. It follows the same pattern as the Broom, and witches often carry the Keppen bound within the woods of the sacred tree. Hence wishing upon the Broom by withdrawing a twig of suitable wood. To complete the symbol there should be a binder of red roses and deadly nightshade upon the main staff. The use is dependent upon the operation viz. If it is to be an operation to find out something, an operation of wisdom, one should first of all prepare the Ring, and invoke the Power required. Then with considerable length of harvest twine, coloured to nature of the operation weave it upon the Bone in the Power's Name, then turning the Ring three times, weave it from the Bone to the Kippen, knotting once more at either end (note all the knots are treble tied)Proceed into the chant of the spell, holding the Kippen above the head and striking at the aspect invoked three times and turning the circle again. Work until the body is tired then unreal it off the Kippen, Knotting the spell into it with herbs and leaves, hairs, feathers etc at the point of the operation. The spell is ended by blessing, closing it in. Close circle, out.

X..................................X

(jj) 1965 August. 'Faith of The Wise.'
Pentagram August 1965

Notes: Enc: Bowers to Ronald White, comments about the recent edition of the *'Pentagram.'* This includes an amazing poem containing many folkloric elements pertaining to the mysticism of his 'Tradition' It refers to the inherent Luciferian current and to the Northern folkloric belief in the Universal Tree – Yggdrasil.

Transcript of Pentagram Letter to 'Ron' from 'Roy'

Dear Ron,

Here are the copies of the Pentagram as 'ordered.' There is one for you and one for George. According to the last series of experiments, things are going very well indeed. However thinking back upon my direction to your good self as to the nature of the keys. I realise that I must have sounded either obscure or heavily intellectual. The Three Mothers are: Air, Fire, and Water. Fire is ascendant, Water beneath, Air above as the magical principle. See the Qabbalistic Yetzirah and compare it with Graves' 'White Goddess' It will supply all answers. I cannot explain more than that since the explanation lies in poetic truth, not in logic. However my fingers itch, and this is what I now write:

> "Three Mothers the Witch has,
> One of Air, One of Fire, One of Water.
> Three Mothers older than Time,
> Each knowing the other,
> Turning aside the Male of Earth
> A triple stone upon a hill.
> Five Knights in a circle still.
> One for ether at the top.
> Black faced owl, Bitch on top.
> Two for air, the horse rider now.

Eight legged Ygdrassdill

Messenger Goddess of the Winds,

Speeding spiral of the Night,

Goddess of dark faced men and might.

Fire Goddess, Falling Star, Luciferous,

Wondrous Fire-Fly,

Glowing in the Night, the Verity

Of Deepest Sight.

Below those Turrets reign

Venus Rising from the Waves.

Water is Water, Air is Air.

Fire makes Ether, have some care.

For one is female, the others female male,

Plunder the Fern, look at the Lion's tail,

At the back of God is the Gate to the World.

And watching all is the earliest bird."

Speaking with tongues but it makes sense and will help you to see what I am pointing at.

In the exact centre of a ring there is a point that is neither male or female but perfect balance. It is that point in which one can stand still and turn without motion between three elements. A Castle builded in the Air, A Castle builded with Three Turrets upon, a silver sphere. The Castle has three towers and three doors, each door must open into a room that has eight doors and a tomb in one, a cauldron in another and a spear in the last. This world is but the beginning.

It's all right I haven't gone mad, this all makes sense if you can see what I am pointing to. Throw away all other ideas, and regard what I have written. There is no other way to explain what can be experienced. I have spoke with tongues the oldest poetry, It existed before syntax or logic. It is the sword in the stone, the philosopher's stone, the stone that makes lead into gold.... One is seven, seven seven. Roy

x...................................x

Transcript for 'The Faith Of The Wise' by Robert Cochrane *Pentagram* (4) August 1965

It is said by various "authorities" that the Faith of the Wise, when they do believe in its existence, is a simple matter: a pre-Christian religion based upon whatever Gods and Goddesses are the current vogue—full of simple, hearty peasants doing simple, hearty peasant-like things... things that in some cases complex, nervous sophisticates also enjoy doing in urban parlours. Consequently we have an interesting phenomenon: civilised sophisticates running round behaving like simple peasants—and simple peasants who have never heard of such things! It is also maintained by the same "authorities" that we follow a belief which, as one dear old fellow put it, is headed by a deity "Who is the sweetest woman, everyone loves her." To quote someone else who is just a student of the Craft, "Witchcraft is about rituals," which I suppose to be true, if one cares to accept the definition as witchcraft. All this worries me somewhat—since I am not a peasant and neither am I particularly interested in being led by a sweet woman, and ritual to me is merely a means to an end. So what is the Faith all about? Admittedly I can only speak for myself, and what I write here are my own opinions, but here goes.

Unfortunately for authorities, students and "mere seekers after truth," the Faith is not about anything that has been written above. The Faith is finally concerned with Truth, total Truth. It is one of the oldest of religions, and also one of the most potent, bringing as it does, Man into contact with Gods, and Man into contact with Self. As such the Faith is a way of life different and distinct from any theory promulgated by the authorities or historians. Within the disciplines of the Faith, man may offer devotion to the Gods, and receive certain knowledge of their existence by participation in something of the perfected Nature of Godhead, recalling that both within and without which is most true. The

Faith is a belief concerned with the inner nature of devotion, and finally with the nature of mysticism and mystical experience.

It has, in common with all great religions, an inner experience that is greater than the exterior world. It is a discipline that creates from the world an enriched inward vision. It can and does embrace the totality of human experience from birth to death, then beyond. It creates within the human spirit a light that brightens all darkness, and which can never again be extinguished. It is never fully forgotten and never fully remembered. The True Faith is the life of the follower, without it he is nothing, with it he has contained something of all creation.

Force requires form at this level of being, therefore ritual exists to contain that force. Godhead demands worship, therefore ritual exists to give and formulate that worship. Man needs help, therefore ritual is designed to give that help. It is possible to comprehend Godhead or Force without ritual, since the First Principle of Godhead is present at all levels and in all things at all times—but total perception is not present in humanity all the time. Therefore ritual basically becomes a matter of increasing perception until something of Godhead is finally revealed, and that which is within and without is partially understood: comprehended in the physical person of the participant until it becomes one with his total being. The forces comprehended are part of the living person, incorporated into everyday life as part of a spiritual, mental and physical discipline that returns the devotee again and again to the original Source.

Devotion requires proof. Therefore that proof exists within the disciplines of the Faith. The nature of proof cannot be explained, since force can only be shown by inference and by participation, not by intellectual reasoning. The nature of the proof falls into many forms, but amongst the most common are these:

a. POETIC VISION, in which the participant has inward access to dream images and symbols. This is the result of the unconscious being stimulated by various means. Images are taught as part of a tradition, and also exist.(as Jung speculated) upon their own levels. They are, when interpreted properly, means by which a lesser part of truth may be understood.

b. THE VISION OF MEMORY, in which the devotee not only remembers past existence but also, at times, a past perfection.

c. MAGICAL VISION, in which the participant undertakes by inference part of a Triad of service, and therefore contacts certain levels.*

d. RELIGIOUS VISION, in which the worshipper is allowed admission to the True Godhead for a short time. This is a part of true initiation, and the results of devotion towards a mystical aim.

e. MYSTICAL VISION, in which the servant enters into divine union with the Godhead. This state has no form, being a point where force alone is present.

These are proofs, since having enjoined with such forces, there cannot afterwards be any doubts as to the nature of the experience. Man suffers from doubt at all times, but to the participant in such experience, the doubt centres around the reality of the external world, not the inner. The reality of such experience illuminates the whole life.

Therefore it can be shown that the Faith is a complex philosophy, dealing finally with the nature of Truth, Experience and Devotion. It requires discipline and work; plus utter and complete devotion to the common aim. It can only be fulfilled by service, some labours taking many years to complete.

The Faith tolerates no nonsense, and those who would come to it, must come empty-handed saying "I know nothing, I seek everything," since within the structure of the Faith, all things may be contained and are contained. It has survived, in secrecy and silence, the attacks of persecution, indifference and misrepresentation. It is secret because those only who are best suited may enter the awful silences of the Places of the Gods. It is silent because in silence there is strength, protection and a future. It is also silent today, because as the Greeks said "Those whom the Gods would destroy, they first make mad." It is nearly impossible to enter unless the supplicant shows unmistakable signs of past memory and a genuine mystical drive, and is willing to undertake tests that will force him finally to disclose that matter which is most secret to himself.

The Faith has no secrets in the sense that there are formulas which can be readily understood and taught. It is finally and utterly the True Faith, standing immovable beyond space, time and all human matters.

———————————

*   Being requested by the Editor to clarify this statement I ask the interested reader to examine the Hebrew letters IHV as they would be in their original and matriarchal form, which will explain something of the basic nature of magical rite and ritual. It should be as clear as the Roebuck in the Thicket now.

X...............................X

Anchor points
Valiente leaves The Clan after the Pentagram débâcle in August
Bowers conducts Hand-fasting for J&V in Ross Nichols' Wood.
Autumn Rite of 65 citing V&J, A&C, R&J
Clan struggles to stay whole.

1966–Destiny calls

(kk) (s) Ritual For New Moon September 1965

Notes: As is proper within a Clan, a literal 'family,' Bowers addresses everyone as 'Brothers and Sisters.' This document supplements and supports the former document. It refers to a series of experiments Bowers intended to undertake in his explorations of the worlds described in that same, former document. After this, Bowers planned the culmination of all his aspirations within the '*Rite of the Star Crown*' - *a* highly mystical rite, engaging ancient keys and virtue. So long had he waited for a balanced coupling for his 'Eight Clan' to undertake this form of magick. Its disciplines are arduous and exacting. By all accounts it achieved everything and more than he'd ever hoped for. It was their most balanced and complete ritual held together, as Clan. Couples form each point of the Star Hexagram.*Instructions For Preparing Rite And Laying The Compass for Solomon's Star.* The diagram illustrates the Star; the Crown in truth.

Sadly, it was never to be repeated, Around this time, everything in his private life began to deteriorate. Witnessing the frailty of the human condition, he fears slowly escalated into eventual despair. But here, in this Rite of Four Parts/stages, the Tools of Arte meet with those of Will and Mind for the Oldest and Highest Magicks.

(1) Three & Four—A direct reference to the Three Mothers (Queens)as Fate and the Four Kings, the cumulative winds, planets, elements and days of the week.

(2) Kippen—forked staff, centralizes personal virtue, iconic tool of ancestry as the mace/sceptre. Symbol of the Warrior King. Weapon of Air – of Will and Intuition

(3) Sword—The Award of the Highest Craft. The channel of Mercy and Severity, the meter of Justice. Weapon of Fire - of Inspiration.

(4) Prayer—the supreme Invocation as an act of Theurgy (as the highest

level) to be transmuted via the Tools imbued with virtue as vehicle of manifestation, an act of Thaumaturgy. (lowest level)

Transcript for New Moon Ritual

Dear Brothers and Sisters,

Herewith the ritual for the New Moon September 25th. It follows in the beginning the usual pattern, that is the preparation of the site and the preparation of self. It is considered that eighteen days before any religious ritual, the witch of admission should prepare by a simple please of admission each night to the Godhead. This is usually created as a lesser ritual comprised of approaching the altar, and uttering a prayer for whatever is desired. The approach to the altar should be made by perambulating around it nine times, then followed by a prayer to Air Fire and Water (The Three Mothers). During prayer arms should be crossed upon the breast, and the witch should face North. The last seven days of the preparation should devoted to addressing three and four (1) separately for whatever is desired. The last day, both drinking and smoking should be eschewed, especially immediately before worship, since both alcohol and tobacco are depressants, and tend to stop the visionary aspects of the mind. It must also be remembered that the exercise of the Middle Pillar, must be practised at these times, combined with the ascending snake, a la Ygrasdaal. (Kundaline).

The time of gathering is as early as possible at this house. We must all be present by 5pm., and last minute queries answered.

Proceeding to the woods before nightfall, the site is to be prepared. The ritual which is composite of Air, Fire and Water is known in the Faith as 'Drawing the Sword from the Stone.' The ritual as such falls into three major parts.

Preparation of the site. Ring to be dug with central point. Northwards of the Ring is to be erected the Triad of the Cauldron.

North westerly is to be erected the Kippen (2) as a votive altar. The Cauldron three time bonded [bound] is to be the Altar of the Goddess, the Kippen the Altar of the Gods.

1. Admission and transference to Magister. This takes place by the Kippen.

2. Consecration of the Cauldron by Old Woman. Salutation to the Cauldron.

3. Drinking and eating the Sacred Food. Measured into the Horn Cup.

4. Entering the Ring (see diagram)

Considerable emphasis must placed upon correct positioning. The people will work according to this pattern and in absolute silence. Chalkie [sic] and Jane will Face inwards and work the principle of Air. George and Audrey will be partnered and will work the principle of Fire. John and Val will work the principle of Water. At first Jane will begin the Admission of Air from the Admission of the Star from myself, then it should be transferred around the Ring deosil until arriving at the principle of Water. John will then begin the Invocation of Water, working with Val as his emotional Charge. Ron will then take up the admission of Air, followed by Jane who returns the Virtue to myself. During the whole of this time the actual direction of the ritual is through the Sword (3), that is myself. Then upon completing the Round, the three are to be worked compositely through the Sword. At no time do the participants takes their eyes off the central figure who is the channel for energy. Uttermost, Will should be used, and the woman should supply the emotional reference.

This procedure, although it sounds complicated is quite easy. The inner invocations are prayers addressed to the aspect invoked, taking into consideration all the factors connected with that aspect. Briefly the downward spiral is merely a matter of passing on an imaginative concept of flowing velvet colour, the upward spiral is a more complicated procedure requiring an excellent knowledge of the element. For instance the aspect of water, is flowing, cool, slow fast, powerful subtle etc... Then to the next level Wisdom, Motherhood the Sea the first and Greatest Mother... The next aspect the Mother of Water. Worked into a prayer by the intellect by the man and "felt" by the woman it becomes a magical energy. Properly positioned upon the body and worked in collaboration with the sexual energies upon the spine, as an ascendant force directed to the Sword it gives power. The participants cross arms so that the right hand is locked with the partners right hand and left hand locked with partners left hand, so a chain that is unbroken forms around the Ring. In fact this is the "Blue Chain" written about by Taliesin. I will take the downward spiral to create the sea that basically supports the Ring, but each member in turn must build up from that point otherwise the working ritual will not work. It is essentially a matter of putting intellect and feeling (male) with emotional and intuition (female) and mixing them together. The final stage of the Ritual is pure Prayer (4) directed through the central point upwards. So the whole ritual then becomes a "Hand holding the Sword" this sword pierces through a Crown that is comprised of the Three Fates, thus 'Drawing Down the Moon'. There is to be absolutely no talking or sound, or passing round the Ring. The nine times nine about the Cauldron supplies the true approach to the Altar, and the sacred food will do the rest. This is a disciplined approach and considerable mental discipline is needed. It is also a basic matter, unless this can be done successfully, we as well work individually and forget all about the Clan, since we do not deserve one, or for that matter have the interest of the Gods.

X..................................X

(ll)

i - #6

ii - #7 Bowers to Norman Gills

Re: The Male and Female Mysteries

Notes: Initially the relationship between Bowers and Gills was all sparring and friction—a testing of the waters, indicating an absence of full trust. Bowers was neither close to, nor worked much with Gills, who certainly enjoyed a more convivial friendship and a frequent working relationship with Ronald White. Their later collaboration in the founding of The Regency, is testament to this. Other letters followed this one, all of which show a softening of that: see (nn). Here, Bowers thanks Gills for the unusual gift of a keppen rod. Offers him a vision of Caer Ochran, of the Starry Castle. Stresses that he hopes their two clans will <u>meet up</u> soon, suggesting that they had not yet done so. Bowers describes his vision of the High Queen in the Castle of Weeping and of the Noble Ones to be seen there. *'Bare on his bare back She rides, veiled in Her own Bright hair. How many shall enter the secret realms and survive.'* These final lines affirm the Clan Matriarch as the Pale Guiden, the absolute force of Destiny—the 'High' Goddess, Thrice-burned Gullveig-Heidr, Storm Mother of all Fates, Tides and Winds, Bountiful and Baleful Benefactress. Bowers feigns ignorance of plant-lore, deferring to a superior knowledge he trusted Gills to have.

Transcript for: Letter #6

Dear Norman,

Many thanks for your letter and enclosed keppen. I have seen a similar one made of two walrus teeth, and a narwhal tooth. However it is this time I have seen it in what appears to be elder wood. Still being a cockney bred and born (I was born in London and lived there all my childhood, Blitz, bombings the lot), I must confess I do not know one wood from another, or one plant, unless I use a book. Consequently, I am out of touch with the country traditions, and the symbolism of plants, herbs and woods. That is except when they directly affect my work as a witch.

I have not written to you before, because I was under the impression that you were busy with the R.A. exhibition. I was also worried because of the outburst of symbols. My own conclusion is that you were probably suffering from the after effects of deadly nightshade wine, but even so, I didn't want to push the issue at that point. You really should be careful, since all dream drugs can have a very dangerous side as well as a marvellous sensational side. There is a place in the other world (if place is the right way to describe it) which is literally chaos, and can destroy the human mind. In the past, they had very careful directions and sign-posts to help the congregation over the difficult way. Today much of those directions have been lost. It appears to be my own life's work to re-discover them. I have got as far as the Starry Castle…and entered it, and returned alive.

Here is a description of that place as written down by a member of my Clan:

"Before Caer Ochren
The winding of the ways of the ways is long
Before you come to the smooth white walls
Shining like pearls in the darkness

Before Glass Castle are the spirals of the maze
The lifting veils, the closing shadows
And the murk of night upon all

Before the Castle of Sorrow
Is drowning in the Sea of Darkness

The last light of the Moon, with Her sharp sickle.
The toothed portcullis, the quaking
drawbridge

Before Caer Arianrhod
Are the Gate and the Guardian
The armoured rider with a naked sword
Cold is the air as he passes by.

Red and flaming is the fire
Within that Hall of that High Queen
Filled with bright wine is the bowl in Her hand
Her eyes are blue and shining as the sea
How many shall go therein and return.

Her vesture half of blue, half of red
Life and death are in Her two hands
In the deeps of the bowl, the perilous vision
How many shall enter before Her and return
Through the empty Hall, a wind of laughter
Whirls us, frail straws, back across the drawbridge
Our boldness move the powers to mirth and mercy.
How many shall enter thc Castle and return?

Black and silver is the wood of bare trees
Wherein by moonlight treads Her unicorn's hoof
Bare on his bare back She rides, veiled in Her own Bright hair.
How many shall enter the secret realms and survive."[54]

I hope you like it. I will be delighted to meet you and the members of your Clan, on that trip or before. Perhaps we could come to some agreement and work together one time or another? But we will have to meet before and discuss things. Could you suggest a weekend? Either at your place or mine. Incidentally I recognise about two symbols out of that lot you sent me, I believe you are having me on. Motte a thee Roy.

X................................X

Bowers to Gills #7

Notes: Bowers refers to a talk he gave attended by bright young things from Kent, who hold future promise in forming another group within the Clan. He also mentions a book he is writing. Bowers seeks Gills help to aid a lady in grave distress. Refers to his need for a medium. Bowers suggests visiting Gills on the week-ending 26th March, bringing along John, Valerie, Ron and George to help prevent Audrey from thoughts of deep melancholy and suicidal trauma she is experiencing regarding her stormy relationship with her ex-husband. Bowers seeks to remove the hold her husband exerts over her. They makes provisional plans to meet up on Saturday the 26th March (now confirmed as 1966). Clan much diminished. In fact this particular letter describes events that take place at the beginning of 1966, just a few months after the following events have transpired in the latter part of 1965.

Transcript of Letter #7 from Bowers to Gills

Dear Norman,

Many thanks for your phone call. We will be very pleased to come and stay the week ending 26th march, and stay over-night in your cottage. Will it be alright to bring, John, V****** (his wife) Ron and George? With us and all muck in over the weekend? We propose to bring our own food, bedding and eating implements. We can have a weekend of working in a group – and see what results we get. I need your help as a medium here since I have tackled an extremely difficult job, and one that everything I have done seems to fail upon. The Tarot misbehaves and scrying won't work. No less than five attempts at ritual have failed – so I do need a fresh mind upon the subject. Do you remember little Audrey?, the Jewish girl and I think it is the Jewish background that is interfering – can you see whether or not she will re-marry soon, that is to her previous husband? I would be grateful if you would give me your opinion, and preferably attempt to date the matter. I cannot get anything at all – although I have worked no less than the Broom, the Sword and even the most complex of the lot – the Three Mothers. We even had a manifestation take place of the Noble Ones – but nothing seems to happen – and she is getting to the point where suicide seems to be a constant thought. This is my only genuine failure – and for the life of me I cannot discover what is wrong – since her grandmother was a Jewish Witch, so things should work for her. I would be exceedingly grateful for your help and opinion as soon as you can possibly manage it.

Things are pretty quiet down here – though I expect a group to form soon from some young people that come from Kent. I gave a talk last night, and some of these youngsters were very interested. They are phoning me this Sunday – so we may have a group comprised of people between the ages of twenty and thirty – which as you know as you know is the best time to catch them. They have a lot of natural power, and enthusiasm won't be far behind, so we have the basic beginings of a strong group – if Madam will allow such a thing.

Now why hav'nt I been writing – simple enough to answer, but I am hanging my head in shame – I have been writing a book, and consiquently my head is stuffed full of everything except consideration for my friends – my humble apologies to you, who has taught me some things.

Be seeing you on Saturday, 26th March – will let you know the expected time of arrival so that you can let us into the place.

Flags, flax and fodder - Roy

P.S. I am inclined to agree with you about the West-Country – a right miserable lot.

X.....................................X

(mm) Bowers to Joe Wilson: Letters #1, #2 & #3

Transcript of #1 ~20ᵗʰ December 1965, from Bowers to Wilson

Dear Mr. Wilson,

I read your advertisement in 'Pentagram' with considerable interest; being somewhat interested and involved with the Faith of the People.

I have recently been delving into the symbolism of the ley systems, and corresponding Herme posts that are scattered throughout Europe—and also America. I wonder if you have any knowledge of the Amerind system that was a marked part of the Sioux, and which appears to have extended from Mass: throughout the Great Plains, and into South America. I appear to have worded that somewhat badly—I meant the tradition of the ley-path, not the actual system itself. The South American maze leys are of particular interest, since they correspond very closely to part of a tradition that exists in Britain today; albeit the symbolism used is of a somewhat different origin.

I understand from your advertisement that you are also interested in Druidism, an interesting thing is that the original Druids still appear to exist—since I am in contact with an old man, born inside the pale of the Faith, who claims hereditary knowledge of the Druidical beliefs—and it appears that what he was taught as a child and young man, and what is claimed to be Druidism by modern sects and historians, are two very different things.

Are you a member of admission, and do you understand the order of 1734? A somewhat rude question, but since I cannot ask the traditional questions in writing, I have to ask somewhat impolite questions.

I understand from the family that there was at one time quite a considerable influx of the Faith into America—in settlements in the Midwest. The symbols used by the state of Texas point towards this being a fact. Some of the neo-pagan traditions of the hill folk also point towards a considerable belief in the religion of the Three Mothers, Kansas being one of the states in which this appears. The Horsemen, of which my father was a member, appear to have settled in force in the cattle and sheep areas, so it is very possible that the clan system is still present in the Midwest.

I appear to have asked many questions and given you no information about myself. I am male, married, a member of the People of two admissions, and aged 35. I know the right and left hand language, the story of the flood, and of the child that survived, I have seen One become Seven, and Seven One, "Whirled without motion between three Elements", as Gwion said and am still learning how many beans make five, and the number of steps in a ladder. I come from the country of the Oak, the Ash and the Thorn. I am against the present form of Gardnerism, and all kindred movements, although, like 'Taliesin', I believe they could become something far greater.

My religious beliefs are found in an ancient song, "Green Grow the Rushes O", and I am an admirer, and a critic of Robert Graves. Flags, Flax and Fodder Robert

x..............................x

Transcript of #2 from Bowers to Wilson
12th Night January 1966

Dear Mr. Wilson,

Many thanks for your letter, which I read with great interest. You obviously have a deep interest for the Faith, and I will attempt to explain something of it to you—this will be a difficult task, since talking about the People (We describe ourselves as such) is a matter that every hereditary group trains out of its members'. The religion is also more, mystical than most—

so words are very poor approximations of what we actually discover or feel about our beliefs.

A 'driving thirst for knowledge' is the for-runner of wisdom. Knowledge is a state that all organic life possesses, wisdom is the reward of the spirit, gained in the search for knowledge. Truth is variable—what is true now will not be true tomorrow, since the temporal truths are dependent upon ethics and social mores—therefore wisdom is possibly eternal truth, untouched by Man's condition. So we come to the heart of the People, a belief that is based upon eternity, and not upon social needs or pressures—the 'witch' belief then is concerned with wisdom, our true name then is the Wise People, and wisdom is our aim.

Some groups seek fulfillment in mystic experience—this is correct if one does not forget the duty of 'involvement'—the prime duty of the wise. It is not enough to see The Lady, it is better to serve Her and Her will by being involved in humanity, and the process of Fate (The single name of all God's is 'Fate'). In fate, and the overcoming of fate is the true Graal, for from this inspiration comes, and death is defeated. There is no fate so terrible that it cannot be overcome—whether by a literal victory gained by action and in time, or the deeper victory of spirit in the lonely battle of the self, Fate is the trial, the Castle Perilous in which we all meet to win or to die—Therefore, the People are concerned with Fate —for humanity is greater than the Gods', although not as great as the Goddess. When Man triumphs, fate stops and the Gods are defeated— so you understand the meaning of magic now. Magic and religion are aids to overcome Fate, and Fate is a cradle that rocks the infant spirit.

Now you know what 'witches' are.

You are confusing 'Lay', a story told to music, with 'Ley', which means in Keltic 'Flat'. The Ley paths were drover's roads, used by the Neolithic herdsmen to drive sheep and other cattle. They were designed

366

to go from one part of a country to another in an absolutely straight line. If you are in what was Indian country, and look along the horizon of hills or plains, you will sometimes see an artificial nick cut in the plains or hills, if you go to that point, you will notice that that mark corresponds to another within eyesight, and so on until you would have traveled either the whole length of Great Britain or Northern America. These ley paths are very strongly connected to the religion of the Wise, since the sheep-herders who carved out the hills also made the stone circles such as Stonehenge, Averbury, the Rollrights, and so on, and likely the great stone medicine wheels found throughout Northern America.

The Herme post is the solitary altar stone that one often finds upon these ancient roads, and if they are approached correctly may be used as places to gain whatever you desire by means of prayer and of magic. They are sites of ancient power now nearly forgotten, but still places where more than one world meets. I will see if I can send you some photographs later of such places, since they will help you to find the Amerind equivalent—and there you will find the answers to all your questions, although the form it will take at an Indian site will be somewhat different to how it comes to me. It is at such places that one may see the Goddess become Seven, and then return to One. The Seven are hinted at in the days of the week—but consider those days as feminine not masculine.

Likewise the order of 1734 is not a date of an event, but a grouping of numerals that mean something to a 'witch'. One that becomes Seven states of wisdom—the Goddess of the Cauldron. Three that are the Queens of the Elements—Fire belonging alone to Man, and the Blacksmith God. Four that are the queens of the Wind Gods. The Jewish orthodoxy believe that whosoever knows the holy and Unspeakable Name of God—has absolute power over the world of form. Very briefly, the

Name of God spoken as Tetragramaton ("I AM THAT I AM") breaks down in Hebrew to the letters IHVH, or the Adam Kadomon The Heavenly Man). Adam Kadomon is a composite of all Archangels—in other words a poetic statement of the names of the Elements. So what the Jew and the "witch" believe alike, is that the man who discovers the secret of the Elements controls the physical world. 1734 is the "witch" way of saying IHVH.

The language of the hands is complex and I will deal with it much later. The Oak, the Ash and the Thorn are the Names of the Three Elemental Mothers. All this is quite a complex philosophy—I will deal with it later.

Gardnerism is the title to the work of the late and unlamented Gerald Gardner—who, driven by a desire to be whipped, and to prance around naked devised his own religion which he called 'Witchcraft'. As you by now have gathered—we do nothing like this. Since the Gardnerians are very publicity conscious—they tend to give us a very bad name, and will one day possibly restart the persecution. Hence, they are thoroughly disliked. Graves' "White Goddess" contains the Predui Annwn—this will answer many questions if meditated upon—not only does it speak of the seven worlds, but it also tells you how to get there. "Where the evening star and the dark of night meet" is one way.

'Green Grows the Rushes O' is an archers' song from the Middle Ages. It is somewhat corrupt now from the Christian influence but parts of it are still original—"One is One and all alone, and ever more shall be so". The Stars on the American Flag are Pentagrams—The steer skull of Texas is another "witch" sign -as is the star within a circle. Diagonal bars and 'V' shaped bars are also "witch" in origin, like triangles, fleur de us, roses, etc. of heraldic tradition. Coats of Arms contain many pagan memories.

The man I work with is called John Armstrong, and he is an actual descendant of the Armstrongs of Cumberland and Durham. Armstrong was not only a bandit, but also a chieftain of no small merit.

My regards to yourself, wife and children.

Flags, Flax, Fodder

Robert Cochrane (I bless thee by Water, by Air and by Earth)

This breaks down into 7, work out what it means.

x...............................x

Transcript of #3 from Bowers to Wilson
1ˢᵗ February 1966

Dear Joseph,

Many thanks for your letter which I read with interest.

You appear to learn with speed. Your interpretation of 1734 is correct. the dialect name for this principle in Shropshire is the Broom, or the Seven Whistlers (so named because some of the Family summoned with a silver whistle). These first and feminine principles are Earth, Air and Water. Translated into the Broom they become Ash, Birch and Willow—the Besom broom that the Family "Turn without motion between three elements" upon. Which is the basic substance of magic, and mysticism. The fourth, and some postulate the fifth, metal, element is the one substance of power given freely to man—Fire. With fire, and its many spiritual and intellectual ramifications, man conquered the world of appearance. Therefore, the four elements conjoined come to mean Female and Male in One—represented by the figure of eternity, 8 or

Union. Fire, as such is the province of Alder, the God of Fire, of Craft, of lower magic and of fertility and death. All things that are of this world belong to him, the star crossed serpent. So you come to the true meaning of the Cauldron and the understanding of the Rite of the Cauldron. Bring forth the Star son, and you have Dionysus, the Horn Child and Jesus Christ in one—So the Cauldron is Generation and Re-generation. Taliesin asked 'what two words were not spoken from the Cauldron? A question I now ask you, giving these pointers. The Cauldron at this level means movement, a becoming of life—ever giving birth, ever creating new inspiration. There is within the Cauldron all things and all future— fate. Therefore, there is one state the Cauldron cannot be— What is it? In finding the answer you will come to understand the Cauldron.

As you have gathered, we teach by poetic inference, by thinking along lines that belong to the world of dreams and images—There is no hard and fast teaching technique, no laid down scripture or law, for wisdom comes only to those who deserve it, and your teacher is yourself seen through a mirror darkly. The answers to all things are in the Air— Inspiration, and the Winds will bring you news and knowledge if you ask them properly. The Trees of the Wood will give you power, and the Waters of the Sea will give you patience and omninesense, since the Sea is a womb that contains a memory of all things.

Obviously you wish to know how one asks correctly—This is known as 'Approaching or Greeting the Altar'. There are many altars, one is raised to every aspect you can think upon, but there is only one way to approach an altar or Godstone. There is a practice in the East known as "Kundalini", or shifting the sexual power from its basic source to the spine and then to the mind.

Cattle use this principle extensively, as you will note if you creep silently up to a deer or a cow—since there is always one beast that will turn its back to you, and then twist its neck until it regards you out of its left or right eye alone. It is interpreting you by what is laughingly known as 'psi' power and that is how an altar is used—with your back to it, and head turned right or left to regard the cross of the Elements and Tripod that are as sacred to the People as the Crucifix is to the Christians.

Before you do this however, it is necessary to offer your devotions and prayers by bowing three times to the Altar, with arms crossed upon your chest and then turn about the Altar (which for normal purposes should be round, hence King Arthur) the number of the Deity you are invoking or praying to. The Maid is usually three times three—the Mother six times three, the Hag (which is anything but the true title), nine times three. Upon the last turn stop with your back to the Altar, and there begin your great chant. With a group one works in absolute silence, but by yourself it is easier to utter your prayer and meditation aloud until you begin to speak as one possessed'.

Upon this point you will feel as if you are near a great bell that has begun to toll—this is the point of mysticism and magic—then you can achieve what you desire—do not be afraid, since it will feel as if you are in a boat on a stormy sea, and your body and spirit will part company, so that you will feel sensations of being in two different places at once. then you may journey to them and they will answer you when you are ready—but not before—so there is a long path of work, experience and failure ahead of you. They will also teach you what you need to know—but never confuse what you want with what you need, or else they are loathe to help. It is better to find an old sacred place and work there—rather than attempt it in the places of man. There is sure to be one place within six miles of you—usually in your case an Indian burial ground or stone ring.

I describe myself as a 'Pellar'. The People are formed in clans or families and they describe themselves by the local name of the Deity. I am a member of the People of Goda—of the Clan of Tubal Cain. We were known locally as 'witches', the 'Good People', 'Green Gowns' (females only), 'Horsemen' and finally as 'Wisards'.

Flags are a form of rush, a plant that grows in European waters—so the answer is Flags, water, Flax, being the weavers plant and blue—thus representing the Goddess of Birth and Death (Fate) being the principle of Air, and Fodder—which means grass, the Earth. The ancients swore an inviolable oath by grass roots—the answer will come to you if you think on it.

I will go into involvement more fully next letter—since I am somewhat tired.

Regards, 3, F's, /S/ Robert Cochrane

X....................................X

(nn) Candlemas

Notes: Bowers forwards (somewhat early according to the brief hand written message on the back of the typed document) *The Ritual Observance to Candlemas'* to 'Chalky' for the February next 1966. The message advises Chalky (and presumably George too in his own copy, noted as enclosed) that *they* should elect Anne S., as a 'scrying' maid in January for *their group, not his*. Observe again the instruction given to them, passing on advice for *their* group. Nothing in the syntax, tone, grammar or verbiage suggests that he refers to his own group here. Quite the opposite, this sentence only makes sense if deferred to another's group and working environment. The language used is very specific and without ambiguity. This Rite requires *'a woman for trance under the skull'* hence Bowers' suggestion to Chalky to give Anne some training as a 'maid' prior to this Rite for their event (the Greater Congregation Rite). Typically, the rites here reflect the strong northern traditions. This culture embraces the presence of spirit hearkened through a female guide, the Seeress, a position that requires much training to advance all psychic abilities. For all groups within the Clan. Anne S. did not stay with the group long enough to bring this to fruition.

J&V at D.V's for Candlemas Rite—February 1966

Through the Winter, the people of the Clan found working together very strained. Some of them began working in more discreet enclaves, split by frictions, tensions and personal traumas. Some come together to meet the knot with Doreen Valiente (John and V, and Justine Glass), others (Norman and Anne) begin to formulate new alliances that would form *The Regency*.

Transcript for the Ritual Observation to Candlemas

1. One. Confession   This should be willed to the Master, if felt necessary, "be thou bearer of my

sins" can be used to give reason to the procedure.

Two.   Expiation

Three.   Purification

2.   The Blessing. This is made before the altar Stang, no lights. The form of self Blessing should be used as per Mask. It is also the assumption of the magical personality. Major key is used by initiates.

3.   Drawing of New Moon into Cauldron. According to Major Sabbat Star. Sharpen Knife upon Stone. Candle bearers quarter Old Women, who takes mirror and Draws Moon into the Cauldron standing upon the ground before the Stang. Summoner takes Cauldron, swings over fire, after it has been crossed by the straps of Clan and worked round nine times. Cuveen join hands and dance round fire until pot is boiling.

Enter Old Woman and others.

4.   Elevate Platter to Moon place contents into pot. Enter Old Man.

5.   Plunges Sword into Cauldron. Summoner takes the Sword fashions Bridge.

6.   The Sacred Bread, Old Woman passes round the Cake, saying " You eat this bread in the Devil's Name with Great Terror (Girt) and Fearful Dread." The participants should groan when they eat it. The Old Man passes round the Wine, saying " You drink this wine in our Lady's name, and She'll gather ye home again."

7.   Old Woman to Cuveen, after centring 'Rejoice. A Child is Born.' Cuveen. " Who has borne the Child. What is it's name?"

Old Woman: "Thy Love in thine hearts has bore the Child. Her name is Compassion."

Cuveen" Then show us the Child of our Love."

8.   Maid is led forward by Magister, uncloaked and offered to the Cuveen. The Cuveen offer white candles and a kiss.

9.   Maid:

"Blessed Be the Plough, the lover of Earth,

Blessed Be the Tree, fruit and seed,

Blessed be the Ribbons and all that it binds,

Blessed is the Sweat of Creation.

Blessed are those who toil and use Craft,

Blessed forever be Adam's manufacture and Work.

Blessed Be all that wrests Life from the Earth,

Blessed are the Servants of Adam.

Fertile shall be the Cow and all Kine.

Fruitful shall be the Kine to Her young,

Powerful shall be the Bull,

Generation springs from his Loins.

Blessed unto all Life, Peace and Plenty,

To that which Lives.

Strength and Joy to that which is born.

And to that which still awaits.

To all creatures, Adam's help,

Naturals All.

Blessings, Food unto Thee.

May Old Tubal Shepered Ye All.

Blessed, Thrice Blessed Be..."

Cuveen: "Earth has awakened..Love is afoot."

Maid pours libation upon Earth, taking ladle from the Summoner, casts bread and salt to four quarters, taking them from Old Woman. Musician strikes up, join hands and dance around fire deosil. Devil leads off into Mill Dance round post with binders.

Feast, loving Cup.

[Hand-written note on the reverse:]

Dear Chalky,

See you on 19th—sending ahead Feb ritual—No Twelfth Night, except what you celebrate – Queen of Death. Meeting here 19th Party. Enclosed for George- comments required—January—suggest election of Anne to Maid for training.

    Roy

X..................................X

Anchor point:

Alleged Cursing Rite for M.M. by Roy Bowers, A. M and J.B.

Dated Letters to Wilson & Gills

X..................................X

(oo) Bowers to Norman Gills - #8 - #10

Notes: Bowers plans their meeting, raises the matter of food and sleeping arrangements. He expresses an interest in buying Gills' property. He derides Gills' interpretation of previous info shared on animal spirits and totems, especially with regard to Long Compton. Clearly, as he asserts himself, they have disparate views on these matters. He also corrects him on how to approach an altar, describing to him, how one swings on the chair, spinning without motion in the realms of the starry castle, hinting how this forms the basis for the ritual of the Broom and the Sword. He chides Gills for his confusion and affirms to him how his own knowledge comes from an Old man of the Craft, well versed in the wisdom of the Broom and Sword, a tradition centuries old. Humbly, he explains to Gills how he has glimpsed its power twice, only to lose it. Here again, it is plain to see that Bowers is teaching Gills, sharing with him also, the very special knowledge he receives from the 'Old Man.' Relates information on ritual, the dynamic of the Star of David, the masculine determinative of the alder rod, the Mother of Waters.

Transcript of Letter #8 Bowers to Gills

Dear Norman,

Many thanks for your letter—which I read with considerable interest. What time we will arrive is a matter of pure conjecture, since we will have to make it to Reading first, and then pick up the Oxford train—so I expect that we will arrive some time during the afternoon. We will be bringing our own gear and food, having for a long period lived with my total wealth upon my back a la gypsy, it is a matter of no consequence. Providing there is warmth and sanitation, we can manage the rest. If you are interested in selling the property—I may consider buying it although this is purely theoretical and dependent upon legal conditions, leases and the expectations of that lease and upon the actual structure of the building itself—and whether or not it can be restored to its original condition, and at the same time unobtrusively modernised. The better move for you to make would be to redecorate and modernise, and then open it up a boarding house to students. With eight rooms it would not be long before you made a considerable profit—since rooms are at least two pounds a week.

I read your remarks upon the practices you follow with interest, and perceive them in a conglomeration of various ideas that are not strictly of the faith I know. The animals you speak of I do possess a very considerable knowledge about, and I can assure you that a rat, as distinct from a mouse, is the last shape to be assumed by Long Compton any more than an alder rod would be used in a ritual devoted to the Mothers of the Waters. Trees like animals have a use and a meaning—and combined with a Maze pattern of the right sort and understanding, form a series of compound images that produce necessary effects. Taliesin was too fond of relying upon Toad, and the Taniast have lost because of this. Glorious dreams may be valid, but unless they have reason 'becoming,' they are of little use except in convincing the devotee of the beauty or horror locked away own unconsciousness.

The ritual you speak of is pretty basic although we begin with movement—for that is the correct way to greet the altar, and end with sitting still. To run about brings an emotional release that should for purity's sake be sexually released in its final stages—but for the big prizes one meets before the know the number of days devoted to the Goddess awakened, and then upon the knot invokes the Goddess through "the dark of the night and the evening star meeting together," which as you should know is brought about in the beginning by "in an uneasy chair above Caer Ochran."

"Spinning without motion between Three Elements," this was the way it was in Long Compton, Shropshire, Lancashire and the Isle of Man, and since one of my informant is now a very Old man who has been in it all his life—and understands both the Broom and the Sword I should think it has been traditional for centuries. I agree with you about movement—but as you know, movement of any spectacular sort is nearly impossible once "Bell Tone" has been reached, since by then you're verging on the Other World and preparing to enter beneath the Hall of the King. Forgive me for saying so, but you seem to be confused slightly as to the making of power—this of course is not suggesting that you have failed in discovering power but that you have discovered it instinctively—which will work for you, but for nobody else. The Star of David is, of course the basic explanation of the Sword and Broom—do you know how to apply this principle, or have you followed your instincts? As such it forms a cross pattern at the base of the throat and forehead—and is extremely difficult to operate since it is a point of perfect balance of two totally different yet complimentary forces—and the Noble Ones are loath to help since once it is mastered, it gives incredible power to the Master— but in search for it one can so easily be destroyed for it is the genuine philosophers work and stone, and twice in my life I have grasped it, only to lose it again.

Thank you for divining A for me. I see much the same thing and I cannot, or seem not to be able to alter her fate—or it is written that she will lose everything, and in the darkest hour, she will gain what she most desires. Otherwise, her distant fate is good, and marked with a considerable amount of wealth—which is more than mine is.

We will be seeing you on Saturday, there will be about five or six of us, until then, my best wishes. Incidentally, we will demonstrate our way of working, which you may find surprising. Regards, Roy Bowers

Addendum to letter 8

Dear Norman, Just a short time to ask whether you can bring the 'black mirror,' and a few suitable plants since I only possess a small reflector made of quartz and it would be of little value for work as a group because of its small size -

See you Saturday

fff

Roy Bowers

P.S. We will be there at three approx.

x....................................x

Letter #9

Notes: Bowers asserts the disparate views held between himself and Gills that are quite irreconcilable, regarding their beliefs and approaches to the 'True Faith.' *'Staffordshire and Warwick don't come* to *Long Compton,' maybe they went to another Well.'* Meaning, quite simply, they do not share the fundamentals of Tradition. He is underlining how their Clans are distinct. They do not share a common Ethos and Mythos. He refers much to the Faith, the memory of all things in the great Akashic record, and of Truth as Godhead. Bowers describes his feelings on what makes or breaks a ritual. He also discusses Sacraments, Ash Tree, sun symbols, and witch ointments. Particularly, he flags the imperative of Three Basic Rites—'The Three Rings' (see TGF) and The Law. He reveals the meaning of his name and how that becomes significant to him as Her standard bearer (Guiden) and mouth piece (Oss).

Transcript for: Letter #9

Dear Norman,

Many thanks for your letter, and my sincerest apologies for not answering it sooner. We seem to be at two very different angles in relation to our mutual attitudes towards the True Faith. In my way of thinking it is not what people know about ritual and symbolism that counts, but what they basically desire from the ritual, irrespective of what form the ritual takes. The important issue is not what form a ritual takes, but what force it invokes and shares among the participants. As far as I Know there are three basic rituals common to all members of the True Faith. One is the ritual that reaches the common pool of TOTAL knowledge, what the Qabbalists describe as the Akashics, this is a simple and straightforward matter. Two is the ritual of force, in which the various degrees of heavenly force is invoked and applied again going to a Godhead in the Akashics, and three, three is the most important one of all in which the participants invoke mystical energy, and this experience is shared by the whole group. Therefore these things are essential to the structure of any part of the Three Basic Rituals—Emotion—symbolism-direction and aspiration. Admittedly other aids are used, but the formative powers above and one other, unity are the basis of any ritual that will work properly. The other ingredients are the perfect couples and a suitable leader, the most important the Godhead present in physical and comprehended form.

Within the structures of the laws (and there are laws) above, the bits and pieces, the articles, the words etc, have value, but outside such a basic structure, whatever is used has no value at all except maybe to lead onto the level of Maya or delusion.

As such, dispensing with the various theatrical aids (which are also necessary) a ritual that covers all three traditionally is that which embraces the Three Mothers, Fire, Water and Air. As such it is very simple in format, the leader is male, and the structure of the rite is to do with eating and drinking. In fact the original form of the Sacrament of the Host, embracing unlike the Christian Sacrament, the principles of the Sun and the Moon. The male and females do not dance or pace round a ring (although that is done for other things) but stay still and a Maid is not used for such work. Incidentally, the concept of the Maid historically comes from either Spain or Italy and as such was to do with matters connected to a different religion that was relatively speaking, modern. Now the ritual I have spoken of can be traced by symbols and by grave goods many, many centuries back to the Neolithic or early Stone-Age. A sun symbol as such is still the form of a consecrated "Host" and means literally, resurrection. The concept behind the Horn Childe has much to do with this.

As a matter of fact I do know quite a lot about the Ash Tree and its meaning, since is the tradition of my own family. Even my name in its original form, BOWRAs, is Norse and means "Crookback" or to speak a la Truth Faith, The Herald. My own ashen staff, not the staff used for magic but the consecrated altar piece you have seen in symbolical form of the Ash Tree, and can be broken down into eight separate parts, and combined with a running noose and a single—edged knife (that has a spike on the spine), as being roughly representative of the Qabbalistic Tree of Life. The tree carried by a man wearing a red cap is a symbol of many things coalescing into two parts of the True and only Faith. You will find the same thing running in the Irish legends and in the Welsh. It appears in the Mysteries of Mithra. The Bulls tale is of three parts — The Trough-like shape was in the shoe she wore upon her left foot.

It was a traditional marking. Witch ointments presumably work of they are used upon an empty stomach and combined with one other thing, dandelion stems. The stems cause the nerves to swell, and become sensitive to other drugs. It is very dangerous to apply such ointments. They were usually incorporated into drinking or food. Roy

Bowers to Norman Gills #10

Notes: This letter refers to his use of the Broom for magical works. He also speaks of his growing personal issues, particularly of complications arising from his affair with a coven member. He discusses aspects of western Qabbalism. His despair over treachery, of a John's betrayal (not E.J.J., but possibly John Math for his Gardnerian defection and betrayal of principles) of how Admission to the Clan works and that he would like to meet Gills friend at Wayland's Smithy/Forge. A vital reference here to the emphasis Bowers places on 'the two deities who rule us,' which is another confirmation these are not carnate persons ruling the Clan!

Transcript of Letter #10 from Bowers to Gills

Dear Norman,

Many thanks for your kind letter, and the very good advice in it— however it is not what people said, but what they have done, which has hurt. John has also betrayed his trust—and spoken the name of a hereditary member to the Gardnerian's—who seeing that it is Taliesin, are now intent upon making trouble for him. As such when the Clans people get to hear about it, John will be put under the Ban—that I am sure of—and you know as well as I do, there is terror and death in that. The thing with Audrey and myself goes much deeper—but as you said— I should not get involved. Still enough of my troubles, and thank you for your attention and prayers.

The mystery you speak of is that of the Broom. It is the basic magical and mystical practice, and corresponds with the exercise of the Qabbalistic middle pillar. Unlike the principle and mystery of St. John though, the principle of Fire is removed, and that of Air put in its place. This practiced every day is the pathway to the Seven Gates of perception —Now what is it all about. Firstly then we must begin with the fundamental practice of the Faith—the correct way to approach an altar.

Have you ever watched cattle? The way one cow will always turn her back upon you and regard you over her shoulder? This then is the correct way to approach an altar. The cow is using 'kundalini' to analyse you, to sense out what you are, and whether you are dangerous, and she uses her spinal column as a sensory device—in much the same way as water diviners use a wand to sense water. Now the practice of kundalini, is as you know, the transmutation of sexual energy. So this is where the broom comes in—in the sense that this transmutes the energy of the sexual impulse into the higher grade energy of sensation, feeling and thought. Physically one perambulates a given number of times around the seven sided ring such as seven to call upon the seven stars. One stops in the exact center of the ring, and has the back to the altar, balancing upon the right foot, with the left foot pointing out, and looking over your shoulder at the altar—so that the spinal column forms a spiral— which incidentally you have already performed in your turning about the ring. At this point of balance—one begins the first principle of the broom—which equates to that of the Qabbalistic Malkuth.

Before the altar is greeted though, one prepares the ring by imagining a bright star very far away, and above your head. From this star should fall waves of light, and one should imagine that it is getting nearer—or rather you are getting nearer to it. The light should enter your body through the right shoulder, and work in a spiral downwards, and emit through the left foot upon stopping to greet the altar. As such the ring, which has been censed and purged by whatever method you use, is charged, and this in its turn becomes a well of wisdom—of the water of life. You like the trout spiral in this pool, and then by sheer poetry which should be spontaneous and inspired—take your body in an anti-clockwise spiral until it reaches the base of the spine—Malkuth—which is earth, and corresponds to the anus and the genital area surrounding it. This is the foundation, and the seat of all transmutation, since the area of skin between the anus and the sexual organs is that which holds the super-physical power. Hence broom stick riding, since in the past they rode a staff in order to activate that small area of sensation—and then transmuted it by mental power to the ascending snake.

The broomstick was anointed with the flying ointment. I will demonstrate the techniques of the broom when we meet—and if you can get Jill and her mother along since I have a distinct respect for Jill's psychism—I will show you how to approach the Holy Ones—that is the Deities who rule us. In this exercise, and once it is fully carried out and understood—the final stages is that when a sensation of being near a great bell is felt, and your mind and body appears to tremble with the vibrations.

It is at this point that you utter the prayer for whatever you are requiring—but always remember Norman—no man has power within himself, we are all but expressions of Godhead. This belief that tricks, or techniques bring power is a blasphemy since the magician is nothing but a channel for the forces he raises by prayer—and prayer and faith are the greatest secrets of them all. To be a channel of the force of Godhead is all we can ever hope to attain.

[Hand-written at the bottom of page squeezed in : *'Obviously you are well aware of this—but having told others—I always add this as a precaution, since some people think that power comes from within.'*]

Really it is impossible to teach this—just as it is to teach someone how to bring the 'Morning Star and the Dead of Night together' by writing. It has to be demonstrated so that faith is created, and so a standard is wrought to work by. As for other rituals—The Cad Goduie and the Predieu Anwm by Gwion, who was a poet in the twelfth century, will act as a gateway—since in poetic form (and that means in terms of images, a matter for which you have a gift) the answers are all ruled and laid out for the eye of the seer. You will find these in that very excellent book *'The White Goddess'* by Robert Graves. It costs 12/6 and is published as a paperback by Faber. In that book is indicated wisdom, and by unravelling some of the riddles—wisdom is to be found.

Thank you for your excellent reading—the power comes not from what I know, but from what I am—and this applies to you also. Human beings are alchemical metals—and we change from dross to gold slowly. Personal power is a little bit of gold in the dross—and it does not matter what the person knows, or how well educated, or how clever he or she is—it is the work of the Godhead upon that person, and the gold increases according to how it is cherished. Differences in personality make for nothing—or in religion or creed—what counts is the person. You have as much of that as I and no book will ever contain it—for it is the gold of the spirit—sometimes dulled by foolishness—other times shining bright. It is only bought by our personal search for the Grail, the Holy Cauldron, and the price is always blood and tears. The Gods give to man, but man always repays in the Gods coinage. Each of us pays in our little crucifixions, and all ritual must be prayer.

The news you gave me of a vision is of interest. You are saying in effect that I am to be awarded the sword. The Gate is that of Fire—the Serpent that of Earth, and the Rake the power that brings the two together. Water and Air is the First Admission—Fire and earth the Second—Air and Spirit the Last. I shall be pleased to meet any friend of yours— especially at Waylands Forge. Tell me, do they still have the Execution Stone in front of it?

Flags Flax and Fodder— I bless , Roy [sigil]

X..................................X

(pp) From Bowers to Joe Wilson #4

Transcript of letter #4 from Bowers to Joe Wilson 15 February 1966

Dear Joseph,

Many thanks for your letter which I read with interest.

"I am a Stag Who—survived the Flood,

I am a Flood—That destroyed the world, I am a Wind—Of God moving across the desolate world,

I am a Tear—The sorrow of Fate,

I am a Hawk—The Child who survived the Flood,

I am a Thorn—The beginning of Fate (Death), I am a Wonder—For I alone transform."

The Song of Amergin, combined with two other poems both of which are known, is like the Qabbala—a poetic commentary upon a religious work. The Song begins with a reference to the Golden Age of Man, in which men were Gods. This age of innocence was destroyed when movement began (Fate). The Child is Hope, borne out of the Flood by a stag of seven tines—and like the early Christian doctrine, the Horn Child travels the world seeking a place to rest. This is a common legend found in all mystery systems. Now to give a more detailed translation. The Stag is Welsh symbolism—it has seven tines on each antler, and represents 1 x 7 x 3 x 7, like 1734. It is the Roebuck, or the inner mystery of Godhead.

The Flood is again symbolic and represents Time. The Wind is the Shekinah, the feminine principle of Godhead—that which the Christians name the Holy Ghost.

The Tear is akin in principle to the passion of Christ. The Hawk is the young Sun King Baldar—Jesus—Buddah—Llew Llaw Gyffes.

The Thorn is Death or the process of Fate and as such the first principle, of the Broom.

The wonder is survival of Death -

The Wizard is Merridwen, the Sky re-creating Life out of Death—Now you explain something of the next five lines to me. What I have given is a basic translation only—it is far more involved, and to explain fully needs a considerable amount of time and space. However, it has a rough parallel with some of the Old Testament, and with the Babylonian epic of Gilgamesh—The five lines following are an explanation of the Pentagram, so that the pattern makes:

$$8 = 1 + 7 \quad 1$$
$$5 = * \quad\quad 2$$
$$8 = 1 + 7 \quad 3$$

---

21 or 3 x 7

Now this becomes also = 3

$24 = 2 + 4 = 6$

or the combined Cauldron ritual, in which both male and female meet—this is described as a Star of David.

I understand that you are corresponding with friend Taliesin—a nice fellow, albeit temperamental. He says that he belongs to a West Country group, and since he is ever so hush hush about it, I wouldn't be surprised. A friend of mine who has been in the People all his life made contact with them some time ago, but got on badly since they appeared to be very snobbish—not at all like the People in the Midlands, who will talk to anybody. Anyway, this old boy from the Midlands was put off by the cloak and dagger approach—he had to go through practically the whole history before they became interested—but got so fed up that he broke contact—it was a pity, since he was one of the last of the Long Compton People, and from my own experience of him he could have told them a lot. It was he that taught me the mechanics of the wand and stone—which is the secret behind the standing stones, if it is understood fully.

As you say, one is never through with learning about the Faith. It is a process that begins in childhood and continues throughout life. Some modern groups such as the Gardnerians have contained the active principle of belief and faith into dogma and ritual—this limits the process of wisdom severely, since wisdom cannot be contained but must be free to all that seek it. They appear to have confused the actual mystery, which is beyond words, with procedure—and evolved a secrecy about nothing except nudity and flagellation. The real mystery is only uncovered by the individual, and cannot be told, but only pointed to.

Any occultist who claims to have secrets is a fake—the only secret is that which man does not understand—otherwise, all wisdom is an open book to those who would read it. One is discreet about certain things because of blank incomprehension or misunderstanding, but wisdom comes only to those who are ready to receive it—therefore much of the nonsense believed by Gardnerians and some hereditary groups alike concerned with secrecy. There is no secret in the world that cannot be discovered, if the recipient is ready to listen to it—since the very Air itself carries memory and knowledge. Those then that speak of secrets and secrecy and not of discretion or wisdom are those who have not discovered truth. I personally distrust those who would make secrets—since I suspect their knowledge to be small. I was taught by an old woman who remembered the great meetings—and she took no terrible oath from me, but just an understanding that I would be discreet. She did not require silence, only a description of what I had seen and what I had heard and said when I was admitted. The Gods are truly wise—they know the future as well as the past and they admit not those who would abuse knowledge or wisdom.

Wisdom is cyclic—when one makes the discovery, one creates the alchemy that brings an answer—and in turn creates more questions from that answer. It is the pussy and hound. When the pussy is pursued by the hound it twists and turns, and turns until eventually it creates a great circle and crosses its own path. Therefore, Pussy pursues the hound at one point, and not the hound pussy. Symbolically the pussy then becomes the hound, and the hound the pussy—therefore they are but one thing— it is the same with knowledge and the pursuit of wisdom— one thing becomes the other, as also life becomes death, and death life. What is wise now is the desire for wisdom later.

The Cauldron is the same, constantly moving, creating, bringing forth, tearing down, building up, movement—therefore the simplest way of expressing what the Cauldron is not is by saying 'Be Still'. Even death is movement, one disintegrates and is recreated. The past moves in the future, since past shapes the future to come—this is Fate. All things that are of this world belong to the past, the flesh is heir to the sins and wisdom of the past— therefore the past lives on. There is no such time as 'Now' since that would require stillness to create it, and now is an impossible fragment of time—even to think of now is to think of the past. Therefore, and very simply to put your feet on the road—the words are 'Be Still'. Mayhap the true pursuit of man is in capturing stillness— since when the moment of silence is created magically man becomes as God.

The true cross is created out of four circles leaning slightly to the Northeast. It should be seen clearly—therefore it does not matter how it is fashioned. It should have the same quality as the dark mirror—that is it should reflect light softly so that the conscious world is lulled, and the world of dreams may come to the surface. It needs time and practice to use it but if a genuine desire to see is there, you will see. You will find that it assists in meditation if the gaze is fixed on it while a small light burns nearby.

I understand that in the past the Maid would wear a cloak sewn with little silver discs that the People would gaze upon—and she acted as a medium for the People whilst they reflected upon her cloak.

Flax is a common cultivated flower known as Linum. The variety known as Narbonense is very good—it is also a decorative in a garden. It is gathered and hung to semi-dry in darkness. When it is nearly dry beat it with a mallet made of wood until the fibres are separated from the stem. This produces a linen 'shoddy'. These are combed out with a teazle head until they are reasonably separate, then spun upon a distaff by a woman who 'sings' to the moon (sounds crazy?) This linen shoddy should be dyed before combing or spinning by Alder bark for red, blackberries (or equivalent) for blue, and bleached in lime or chalk for the white. Your whole length should be measured in this, then seven knots tied in the plait—and then you have the beginnings of a cord which is worn about the waist or neck and used as a meditational device, a la 1734. The remains should be kept in the separate colours and spun upon the distaff. This, used with Mother Broom, and symbolic herbs will assist the cure of most illnesses if a piece is tied and charmed around the afflicted part and three knots tied. I know it sounds crazy but— from personal experience I know it works. I have seen the common cold cured, cancer of the womb, warts, and bleeding stopped by this yarn—but it is dependent upon the moon's phases, and Mother Broom for the inner workings. The slow process of creating the yarn is a form of alchemy. If your wife uses it, she must not use the Alder, but instead turn to blackthorn for a black thread, but be careful of that yarn for it carries the power to blast.

What is known as 'witchcraft' is full of apparent superstitions that upon reflection have a sound scientific basis. Alchemical formula produces a resistance free copper—although analysis shows this copper to be of the normal purity rate, approx: 98%, yet normal copper has a resistance of 7% to electricity. The slow process of creation works its own magic— just in the same way that the innumerable firings of the copper produced a 'normal' article that has an unusual power. This applies to all materials used in working, since they are accumulated and collected carefully, and have power of their own.

It is intent and the love of God in creating the magical substance that transmutes it not any particular power in its own right. The best example of this is woman.

All females, irrespective of species is a lesser moon reflecting the Greater. She is made of three elements, the poor male possessing the fourth. Through these elements, she creates a chain unbroken that ranges from primitive childbearing and nest making to the Goddess woman flying in strange climates. Man is individualized and solitary—lead only by reason or passion. Woman by her physical structure is part of the cycle of evolution, and therefore part of the group soul. You notice in homemaking how they create a nest of security, a bond that is shared with all other females, and how the female passion embraces all creatures that have need—a bitch in whelp will mother kittens, etc. The woman, as a possessor of this common instinct, shares experience with the group soul—and what she and thousands of others do shapes that soul for time to come. Therefore, if one observes the way a woman instinctively works reflecting the tides of her body, and of the group soul—one learns about the creation of charms and remedies by 'magic' since the slow tide of growth and protection shapes the group entity, so can another principle, if undertaken as naturally shape it also. A plant grown with intent, a branch cut with intent and prepared according to the natural rhythms of life can affect any natural creature—the only creature it may not affect is man, and that man will be the product of a corrupt society in which nature has become a whore. The yarn spell has everything in common with the instinct that makes a mother knit for a forthcoming baby—each stitch is a spell for protection and comfort, wrought by love. Woman is a magickal creature, not because of the tides of her body as Graves suggests, but because she has this power to shape the group entity to her desire and following the tides of her soul she creates magic of no small order in making a home for her offspring. It is the Earth Mother working in her deep instinctive acts and she both creates and influences the group soul. It follows then, in charming, one should follow the tidal movements of the soul, and of the group soul, rather than the intellect and haste of the fire male. A rhythm worked upon like this strikes a resonance in the group—and power contacts are made. Alchemy and transmutation takes place not because of the material or what is done, but because of the resonance upon the group—and the power of the group. A tide is created, and another tide stilled—a balance wrought.

My regards and blessings to you and

yours, F,F,F Roy Bowers alias Robert Cochrane

P.S. This month's problem:

x...............................x

(qq) From Bowers to Gills: Letter #11

Notes: A brief hand-written letter urging Gills to offer further help and insight to assist the issue with a certain lady.

Transcript: #11 to Gills

Dear Norman,

I wonder if we can drop in and see you this Sunday. Just ourselves will be around that area... since we have transport, if we could get... a short chat. The friend, a lady, is not a member though she knows that we are. She herself is in trouble and is being helped by us. But she is absolutely distraught.

I have to cut a keppened broom for her daughter, a sweet little thing aged twelve. I wonder if you would be so kind as to show myself a useful spot where I might make one? If all is well, perhaps we could arrange this on the phone. My number is above and you can reverse the charge if you like. However, let me know via phone what your plans are this week since a letter will be no good as it will not get here in time.

Regards, Roy Bowers

X..................................X

(rr) From Bowers To Joe Wilson #5

Transcript of letter #5 from Bowers to Wilson April 5 1966

Dear Joseph,

Many thanks for your letter—which I enjoyed reading.I found your interpretation of the five Queen lines of Amergin of great interest, since it shows you are well on the road. Basically, they follow the Pentagram, that is Life, Love, Maternity, Wisdom, Death. Obviously, since the interpretation of the Faith is deeply personal, we differ somewhat in our approaches but basically we seem to be traveling in the same direction. The line "I am a Spear" refers to the Cauldron mystery—the original Holy Grail—in the sense that the Grail (Divine Inspiration) was activated originally by a priest bearing a spear, who like Sir Gawain performed the sacred marriage by thrusting the spear into the cauldron. Symbolically he was taking the principle of life made of ash and steel (Ash the Mother tree—earth—steel or iron the metal of Chronos—Wayland—the God of Time/physical life) and so continuing life by bringing down the principle of movement to earth—literally drawing down the Moon. In thrusting the spear the priest performed an act of love—thus bringing us to the next point of the ritual, "I am a Salmon". Ritually as you will find by reference to the Arthurian legends, he then withdrew the Spear, and cast drops of blood that fell from its tip upon the earth and surrounding congregation. This action was based upon observation of the actual mating habits of the salmon (a fish who anciently represented fertility and wisdom—there are records of trout or salmon being used for divination as late as the sixteenth century). The salmon comes in from the sea to spawn and die, but in dying the male salmon casts his sperm over the eggs—so a sequence of love and death is built up— which idea is confirmed by Gwion's further poem 'Preidui Annwn', when he writes—"Where the evening Star and the dark of night meet together". The ritual at this point is like the Catholic sacrament. The Host has been raised and transubstantiated—in other words spirit and matter have been brought together in the action of the ritual—as spirit and matter may be considered as the Female Spirit, and the Spear as phallic in the sense that the Goat God represents time or physical life, the ritual becomes that of Union or Love.

The contents of the Cauldron are now transformed into the Aqua Vitae—the Waters of Life. Anciently, as Taliesin pointed out, the Water of Life was impregnated with one of the plants that bring dreams such as Fly Agaric mushroom, or the Peyote cactus. However I am not suggesting that you do this, since they have extremely bad side effects and need care, caution and discipline to use efficiently. However, the sacred drink is now administered in the same fashion as the wine of the sacrament. Now how does this tie up with Motherhood? The Goddess feeds us, as a mother does—so in this aspect She is Bountiful Nature— Mother Earth, feeding Her children, in the same way as any mother feeds the child. The priests of Isis carried a dish that was shaped like a female breast, and from the nipple fell a constant stream of water and milk, with perhaps wine mixed in it. So then the congregation at the assembly are fed with the Water of Life—which as you already appreciate is inspiration or spirit brought to earth. This is, apart from the actual physical/differences, exactly the same concept as the sacrament to be found in Christianity.

Then we come to the extremely puzzling line 'I am a lure'. The lure was more than a snare, it was usually an imitation bird or animal used to attract the genuine article into the trap—Why is love a lure? Because it creates inspiration—and from inspiration comes the thirst for wisdom. The onset of physical love is also the onset of the two destructive/

creative forces in man. He can be fascinated by the object of his fancy, so that he will forget everything else. The stress of the love act produces poetry and in poetry is wisdom. Therefore, as we English say "A sprat to catch a mackerel"—something smaller to catch something bigger. The reason why the Goddess of Love in Britain was depicted as carrying a net, was that She ensnares the souls of Her men with a devotion that very few women are able to command. In Her love (this is a hard thing to say) there is death—and She rends Her poets/lovers apart before finally making them all wise. Graves follows this theme in the White Goddess—and there is always considerable truth in it. Be careful throughout your life of Her traps—They will make you wise, but you will sing sweetly and sadly afterwards. She is Fate, the Creatoress and the Destroyer. You will understand why She destroys, but the destruction will bring its own sorrow. As the Goddess of Love, She humbles us all at some time—and that sorrow is perhaps Her greatest gift to the moon-struck poet.

'I am a Hill' is a reference to Wisdom, since in vision you will see the Castle of the Seven Gates or Winds, standing upon a gloomy hill, turning four times to the Elements. The Hill is Life—the steady climb with its triumphs and disasters to Illumination or Wisdom. It is the Dark Tower that Roland fell in front of, it is the Castle Dolor of the legend of the Grail, the Caer Ochran of 'Predui Annwm'. The abode of the High Goddess—the One in Seven Wisdom, the destroyer and creator of men. You will die many times to be reborn in this religion, and each little death is the resurrection of new hope and spirit. Whatever Madame la Guiden has in store—the law is that you will overcome—and in the overcoming find spiritual strength. Never be like I was for a short while, arrogant in the knowledge of power, for She soon tripped me up, and brought me home across my black horse, and I like the knights of old lie wounded, and at this moment without hope.

Anciently the castle upon the hill is a very common motive in folk art. You will find many specimens of this in traditional Romany caravans—in that the inner walls are painted with roses (red and white), a roadway with nineteen trees lining it, and a castle at the end of the road upon a high hill. Armorial and coats of arms are also good examples, and about a 150 mile trot from here there is an old inn that has as a sign a castle founded upon three silver spheres. In qabbalism, the sphere becomes the moon—and is known in Hebrew as Yesod, or foundation. Now the three moons represent inspiration or spirit in these aspects: Life, the Virgin; Love, the Mother and Death/Wisdom, the Hag. As such then the hill is representative of the three major sources of inspiration and fate in physical life—the problems that we face are based upon these three foundations— Graves writes they are the poetic theme—but they are the structure of existence before that.

"I am a sow" or 'I am a boar'. This refers to Kerridwen—the greedy sow who in Keltic poetry eats her own farrow. The nightmare fertility and death in one creature—and so we come to the end of the Pentagram. The principle of Fate giving birth to life, then for reasons of her own destroying her own litter—a fact that any pig farmer will tell you about. As you have realized—the poetry of the ancients was based upon observed natural fact. From the lesser phenomena of nature, they drew conclusions about the greater and spiritual phenomena—reflecting as I do, that there is nothing created but it has a symbolic link with spiritual principles. I am not saying that physical creation has what the Theosophists like to call a purpose—that is something different—but in creation one uses a greater force to create the lesser—and there is an indivisible link between all things and their spiritual counterparts. As you say the Gods are in Man, and Man is in the Gods.

You will also find contained within my letters to you, a ritual which is the basic ritual of the Faith—that Of the Cauldron. You know now how to approach an altar, how to create an altar—how to create the sacrament houzle (bread and wine), and what to expect from it. You have in your possession the Broom—later we will speak of the Sword and Stone which is to do with Fire. But now you are girded, and can administer the Water of Life to your family—if you so desire. Remember though that male and female work together—and where the male intellect or fire gutters and burns out, the female water will wear at the problem gently, until it is reshaped and understood. In the final analysis rely upon what a woman feels rather than upon what you think is right. Of air and earth we have those between us.

Please do not thank me for helping you—you also help me. To describe the Faith is like teaching, but if you teach then eventually the pupil must turn on the teacher, since wisdom is only found in freedom, and teacher and pupil alike are not truly free, since the teacher is bound by dogma in order to explain—and therefore forgoes inspiration. The pupil has to follow the dogma in order to understand the teacher. Wisdom is not dogmatic—and when the pupil becomes wise he must necessarily break from the teacher, and interpret dogma and the promptings of his soul as he sees fit. Therefore I explain to you what I know—but I am not teaching you, you are taking from it what you require—and transmuting these ideas to your own needs.

The buckle in the photograph is a spouted pot used for pouring the Water of Life. You will find all the physical parenphanalia of ritual in it, and much of the symbolical stuff also.

If you wish I will do a complete reading upon your immediate future—or for that matter upon your complete future. It is easily done.

My best wishes to Daisy, yourself and the children—I sense that it will be a girl, and I got an impression that she will be fair headed. She (if

I am right) will live long and happily—and also be wealthy by marriage to a man that she will love.

FFF

Roy

X...................................X

(ss) From Bowers to Gills: Letter:s #12 & #13

Notes: Very short hand written letter from Bowers to Gills requesting Gills to print photos from negatives of his wife and son.

Transcript #12

Dear Norman,

Thanks for the weekend. Here are those negatives I spoke of. Will you do them as quickly as you can, I will pay for them, and other photograph you may have of Jane and Adrian brought up to a decent size. Make them as clear as you can please.

> Thanks a lot old friend, you're
>
> a true member of the faith
>
> Roy

The one of the Cauldron is the most important, also the one in the hut where we are all together.

> R.

X...................................X

Bowers to Gills: Letter #13

Notes: Bowers to Gills re his increasing personal issues, moving. Bowers contemplates moving to London, unable to cope alone with all the bad memories within the family home. He mentions how totally alone he is; Evan John Jones has moved to Brighton now that Valerie has a baby son, and Audrey has deserted him too. He appeals to Gills for help and refers to a photograph Gills had sent him as a warning about Audrey. He feigns optimism concerning his book and a television play he hopes to complete.

Transcript of Letter #13 Bowers to Gills

Dear Norman,

Many thanks for your letter, and the well-meant warning contained therein. The photographs you used as a warning, are only too well founded, and I am now, sans John- sans A, sans friends, and working by myself quite happily. It is surprising that the warning came the very week when the final and terrible painful blow fell. Old J. is no mean psychic since she warned me against A. many months ago—and I took little or no heed. So I have learned. I am, of course at the end of a phase—and being like yourself, a man without any true fate—except that which we shape ourselves—I would like to know where I go from here? Can you be a friend and have a look for me. For as you know, one cannot tell ones own future except by the merest glimpse, and I feel as if I am at the bottom of a well, with little or no hope for the future. If you do decide to help me, then I would be very grateful if you would tell me the truth, and not cover up any blows.

In spite of the fact that I am asking you about my future—I am trying to turn into a professional fortune-teller, see card enclosed—although I have little or no hope for it as a business, it will give me something to do. Perhaps you will be interested in seeing one of my cards—it is enclosed.

The books will not go right as yet—since I appear to have lost all desire to write about the Faith—although I am attempting to write about a television play—that if it is completed will be worth about £300 to me. But everything depends upon me completing it.

We are thinking of moving back into London—more or less to get away from this house which has many unhappy memories for us now. If we do not move, perhaps you would like to come and stay for the weekend with us occasionally—since it is easier for you to get to the smoke than it is to get here.

Thank you for saying that I have some personal power—I feel as flat as a pancake at the present time, and couldn't raise enough energy to swat or influence a fly. However unhappiness always causes me to go like that, especially when there is very little or no hope for the future.

I feel that the property deal that is verging at the moment will come through alright, and you will get what you desire—although not be quite as wealthy as you thought, and that the future is one of achievement for you, with passing of many of the old strains.

I will try to get to Oxford quite soon, and stay the weekend at .... perhaps we should all get together and have a talk. Regards. fff Roy

X................................X

(tt) Bowers to Joe Wilson #6

Transcript of letter #6 from Bowers to Wilson
8 April 1966

Dear Joseph,

I received your second letter, just as I was going to post the first. I am very glad you had your wife have come to an understanding—since domestic sorrow is a very big price to pay in order to belong to the Faith. There is no necessity that ones beloved should also belong—since one of the basic tenants of wisdom is that of tolerance. The people have had and experienced many centuries of intolerance, persecution and pain—therefore we make no attempt to convert—but instead we are just content to belong, that being enough in its own right. Your wife probably felt insecure in the face of a belief that inevitably obsesses its male followers—and to many people who have as yet to see the Goddess triumphant, the Faith is a strange and alien belief, intertwined with childhood memories of wicked witches, and later sensationalism from the gutter press. To a young girl looking in from the outside, it must seem frightening, since to her she must have seen the man she loves, subtly change and a side to his character appear that she does not understand—and although this character is not malignant in any way—it is alien to what normally passes as 'normal' in this world.

You no doubt have discovered that a whole new philosophy, a new morality, a new personality has begun to awaken in yourself and subtly alter your life—yet in spite of the excitement of the chase, and the desire to know that drives all 'witches', you must try to think of the effect this has upon someone who has not as yet kindled the flame.

This is a frightening experience, and one that brings a sensation of tremendous insecurity, especially to a girl with a child in her womb. A piece of advice if I may be allowed to give it; is that no philosophy, no creed, no God is worth more than the love that one human being may give and receive in their life time—this is what I meant by being 'involved'. It doesn't really matter how wise or knowledgeable one is—providing one can love and be loved in return—in this way the Christian ethos of 'loving ones neighbor' is very true all one needs after that is the witch 'Law':

Do not do what you desire—do what is necessary.

Take all you are given—give all of yourself. "What I have—I hold!" When all else is lost, and not until then, prepare to die with dignity. These may sound like peculiar laws, but they are wise and based upon experience—the first is perhaps one of the most difficult criterions to live by—since there is no room for illusion—the second allows you little time for yourself—the third is the keystone of wisdom and the fourth is the basic key to the "witch" personality.

Now how can I teach your wife—Shall I tell her that the Faith is the Mother of all Gods and Goddess's—that Christianity is only a part of the ancient faith, and not the whole, that the People are the direct descendants of the ancient shamans, priests, and priestesses of the Mysteries? Or shall I tell her that the Faith is basically feminine—and in it she will find her deepest self reflected?

It has been the repository for centuries of the deep feminine wisdom, the protector of the disposed female—in that it recognises her for what she is, man's total and absolute equal—and the Goddess's representative upon earth.

That the Gods created the world, and to man they gave Earth, Air and Fire—and to Woman they gave Earth, Air and Water—and that it was decreed that these elements would be worthless until they were brought together in male and female—therefore the Faith believes that both men and women play their separate and united roles in the comedy we call life—Still this is poetic and to a young mother sounds like a strange language—so I will put into the language of logic and rational thought, something of the Mysteries.

The Faith is made of three parts—of which I know two. The first part is the masculine mysteries—in which is enshrined the search for the Holy Graal—and is the basis of the Arthurian legends. This is the order of the Sun—the Clan of Tubal Cain. Under it come learning, teaching, skill, bravery, and truthfulness. In the distant past, the male clan was lead by a woman who was their priestess and chieftan. This is the origin of the legend of Robin Hood—and surprisingly enough began the Old Testament, and later, Christianity since both Jesus and Moses alike preached a version of the Masculine mysteries—Mithriasm was also a development of this—and the tradition was followed through into the middle Ages when the Plantaganet Kings were officers of the masculine aspect of the Faith (The name 'Plantaganet' means 'The Devil's Clan').

The effect of the masculine mysteries upon the world can hardly be under emphasized— since a very considerable portion of civilization owes its origin to them. To name but a few—Commerce, Lawmaking, Law- giving, Parliament, The early forms of universities and craftsmen's guilds—which lead to knowledge being contained and taught, surveying, all sciences such as metallurgy, astronomy and so on ad infinitum. The masculine mysteries were the direct creators of modern civilization as we know it now. It must also be remembered that originally the Mystery was conducted by a woman—and that she was the presiding genius behind many of the fundamental discoveries that created civilization. These mysteries are depicted as a javelin, a cockerel upon a pillar, a ladder, a flail, a twelve- rayed sun and a ladder of eight rungs and a sword or battle axe. Basically they have to do with control over three of four elements, especially that of Fire.

The feminine Mysteries are the deeper—connected with the slow tides of creation and destruction, of the cycle of life and death. they are best expressed in the pentagram—Life/Birth, Love, Maternity, Wisdom, Death/Resurrection. They are connected with all things that grow—all creatures of flesh—fertility and sterility—the mystery of the woman who is Virgin/Mother/Hag in one person. They are in essence the cycle of life, and the universality of life—and they express themselves in deep intuition and feelings—in other world terms they control the unconscious, as the male controls the conscious. That is they are what the Jews describe as the second emanation of the Sephiroth—emotion, sensation, imagery, empathy and intuition. They are expressed in symbols as a broom, a flask, a cup, a glove, a distaff and a shift—all of which have a symbolic meaning in the Faith. The clan of Women is lead by a man, who acts as a priest, and teaches the feminine mysteries. Each one of these symbols has a value in wisdom, and I will teach you both what I know about them in forthcoming letters. Today, since there are so very few, the old system has broken down and the families teach their children both mysteries, so that the tradition will not be forgotten entirely. In the past the male and female clans were separated except for the nine Rites or 'Knots' of the Year—when they came together and worshipped Godhead. Also, a great deal of traditional rite has been lost—but it will be recovered again one day, since things and thoughts alike do not die, they only change.

It was common for the People to meet once a week—like a service or a teaching session., or even to work some particularly difficult piece of magic. As the persecution grew harsher, the meetings became more secretive, and for security's sake the Clans divided and knew nothing of each other. The mysteries were also united so that nothing would be forgotten, yet I personally think it is better that they now divide since there is a mystery in sexual difference, and some things may only apply to men and some things only to women. No man may ever fully understand the mystery of menstruation or birth—and how it affects not only the female body but mind and emotion. No woman may fully understand the male passion for knowledge or craft etc., since it is a part of the male mind in which most women have difficulty in understanding. Yet the Faith teaches wisdom that has to do with both of these aspects of male and female and when it was taught properly as it was in the past it produced some really remarkable

One of the deepest and most appealing images in the Faith is that of the Virgin and Child—whom the Catholics stole from us as late as the twelfth century—yet the approach of a man and the approach of a woman are very different to this one Image.

I have enclosed a leaf out of a book which has the photograph of a French Menhir upon it—I helped the woman who wrote this book, and explained something of the menhir to her—but she is a fool, and her book is a shame to read since it is only interested in the sensational, and not in wisdom. However, the menhir contains all 'Witch' theology and belief—and if it is studied, it will answer many questions for you. The carvings date from the 17th century, the menhir is at least 2,000 years old. Archeologists believe it to be a depiction of the Passion of Christ, which shows how little they know. You will see upon it both male and female mysteries—with the bottom line reading as the third part— that of the Priest/Magician. Understand it, and you will have the basic groundwork of the Faith. Ask me questions about it, and I will explain them to the best of my ability.

You will be coming to Britain within one year, when you do, come to us when you have free time (or maybe it is me going to America).

FFF

X...............................X

(uu) Bowers to Gills: Letter #14

Notes: A short letter to Gills from Bowers that indicates a quite late date, possibly circa April 1966. This letter expresses his urgency and despair, his loss and he underlines again his confusion. Jane had finally left him, taking Adrian, leaving no trace of her whereabouts. Bowers asks Gills to bring along a lady named Jill Haddon, with whom Gills was working, and whom Bowers considers a marvellous and natural medium/ psychic.

Transcript of hand-written Letter #14

Dear Norman,

May I come and see you this weekend it is very urgent, Jane has left me, taking Adrian leaving no trace or letter, and I am worried out of my wits what to do next. I will be coming down with Jill – I hope and staying at 74, London rd for the weekend. Can you meet me there? I don't know whether you received my last letter or whether Jane destroyed it? Please let me know by telephone on Friday at about 8pm.

>   My Regards Roy

x..................................x

Anchor points:

End of March.

A.M has left R.B.

April. J.B. leaves R.B. Marriage over, she files for divorce -

Midsummer 1966 - Havamal

End Note: Midsummer 1966 Roy Bowers is found unconscious, in a coma.

>   **He died nine days later in hospital**

x..................................x

(vv) The Hinchliffe Folder

The Hinchliffe Folder contains re-typed copies of Bowers letters to Wilson in addition to various differing copies of those to Gills. There is also a Transcript in the Hinchcliffe Folder of an alleged Spirit Message from the deceased Bowers/Cochrane during a séance [using a Ouija Board] to Patricia Crowther in the Sheffield Coven. The querhent was Reginald Hinchcliffe. who recorded a spirit message in which Roy Bowers allegedly as apologised to Patricia Crowther for the former feud, before going on to state that *Gardner was right after all, and a good man.* Bowers then adds says *he did not commit suicide* and asks *who The Regency are.* The likely hood of this is left to the readers' individual discernment. This can either be dismissed as nonsense, or accepted at face value. It can even be considered a clever comment surrendered by someone who wished certain things to be known and to be considered which were being seriously overlooked.

Notes: The six official letters written between December 65 and April 66 to Joe Wilson in the USA from Roy Bowers exist only because copies were made via photograph and sent to a friend, Reginald Hinchcliffe. Happy foresight as it happens, for he was able to reconstruct them from the photo images after they were destroyed when Wilson and his wife separated company.

Both Gills and Wilson comment upon their usage and reformatting of much of the material in the letters Bowers sent to them. Freely cutting and pasting, the literature accrued several forms, dependent upon the recipients, Gills and Wilson were mentoring through them. Sifting through them to find a few genuine letters, intact and unadulterated, has been a painstaking task.

These were found in an old Manila folder containing with copies of various letters between Cochrane and Gills once in the possession of

411

Reginald Hinchcliffe, who was linked to several Gardnerian covens and High Priestesses, including Patricia Crowther's Sheffield Coven and to Lois Bourne's Brickett Wood. He was also, initially at least, a brief member of The Regency, but like many others soon became disillusioned by it and left, voting with their feet when Ruth Wynn Owen abandoned that project in 1969.

A commercial artist called Everley attracted Bowers and others into a traditional style coven he formed and acted as prime mover within through an advert in a newspaper about 'the White Goddess' [according to Hinchcliffe, who is certainly wrong about a good many things, especially that Roy Bowers was re-constructing 'west country craft', he was obviously either badly informed or his assumptions regarding the use of 'pellar' were wrong (both of which may not be mutually exclusive)

Due to the bad blood between the Crowthers and Cochrane/Bowers after their débâcle in the *Pentagram* Journal, Hinchcliffe appears to have been on a personal mission to collate information from any source available to him. Once in The Regency, Norman may have freely shared letters from his own correspondence with Bowers. Hinchcliffe made hand-written notes on the front of this folder and throughout his copies of the many letters within it, including invalid composites and valid originals. As polemics, they reflect well his perspective, and provide only retrospective conjecture. They do not offer facts, merely opinion & gossip. For example, he suggests that after Roy Bowers' suicide, Jane allegedly told Norman that he is the only group member Roy would wish to see if he were still alive.

However, all the facts of the matter reveal a very different dynamic altogether; so this is either an example of wishful thinking on Gills' part, or of Hinchcliffe's sheer malice. Certainly, Hinchcliffe litters his contempt for Bowers all over the re-typed copies of letters Bowers had written to Joe Wilson, with vitriolic marginalia.

NB: This material was ultimately sourced from the cache of letters donated to the Museum by Iain Steele/Plummer, who encloses a letter stating there is no provenance for any of the enclosures which came to him via his former wife Andrea F. who had been at one time, a student of Gills prior to 1985. For those interested in Gills' own works, the remainder of the archive contains considerable correspondence between Gills and Foreman. These stand as a record of his teachings to her and a fine example of the subjects he was interested in. These focussed largely upon astrology, plant-lore and fairies.

These documents are placed in Box 33 along with other correspondence material, mainly between Gills and members of The Regency during the early 1970s. Previously in the remit of Norman Gills, but shared with Joe Wilson during his stay in England 1971-72. Amongst these, a certain few stand out of place. These are Gills' correspondences with Bowers. One of these in particular appears to be made up of extracts from the 'BSotC' document as an Instruction to 'All Elders' (ii) that Roy Bowers had composed in 1965, posted to and discussed with members of his Clan.

Another much edited version of this document is included in the Capall Bann edition of the published letters of 'Robert Cochrane.' This confirms that sometime between 1972 and before 1985, copies were much edited and reassembled in numerous forms for Gills' students. Archived material within the Witchcraft Museum, includes a Manilla folder preserved by Hinchliffe, provides clear evidence of this; several differing examples are clear composites, with or without various handwritten sections. Once again, due to a pointed lack of provenance, flagged by Iain Steele, it remains unknown who edited and re-composed the document Wilson cites as letter three to Gills. Both Gills and Wilson shared a friendship, and extensive correspondence and a sometime working relationship with Chalky and George after Bowers' death, especially around 1970/2 when Wilson was in England.[57] But is also odd that Wilson, having been given so much by Gills, has only three complete letters written to Gills by Bowers and no more. These three, are now posted on the '1734' website.[58]

Wilson comments how his friend Reginald Hinchcliffe also once held copies of Bowers' letters Wilson had transcribed; an act of foresight that proved to be a mercy. They furnished Wilson with a duplicate set of those copies (but not, obviously of the originals), at a point in time when the originals became lost to him. Hinchcliffe was allegedly a member of the St. Albans' Coven, headed by Lois Bourne (née Pearson). She parted company however, from St Albans shortly after G. B. Gardner died in 1964. This cache of duplicate copies listed as 3263A, form an essential part of the Bowers papers within the archive. These may be found in a manila envelope containing not only the copies to Wilson, but also further copies of all Bowers' letters to Gills, some of these have not been previously published. Ironically, as Gills was also a Wican initiate, though he clearly discussed this material with Hinchcliffe and others, they have not been in general circulation.

In box 33, there is now a more recent letter dated March 30th 2004 from Andrew D. Chumbley that comments on the contents of these works, which were at that time of course, still in Mr Steele's possession. Chumbley advised Iain Steele to place them in the Witchcraft Museum's archives. Mr Steele (Plummer) reluctantly conceded to do so. Sadly, when we eventually did met up with Mr Steele in 2007, we discovered that it had been his wish to pass them onto ourselves, but had tried unsuccessfully for some years to make contact with us. He had even requested an introduction through the editor of *The Cauldron*, who had informed him we had no wish to be reached by anyone. This was an unfortunate misunderstanding of our wish for privacy. Yet several pairs of hands and eyes have witnessed their existence, ironically of select Wicans and also select personages of the Traditional Craft only, with ourselves excepted, despite Inductions into both streams. Our frequent requests to various people for copies of any such letters from Bowers, have to date, also been fruitless. None have been forth coming.

Mr Steele however, very kindly procured copies for us some of the material he'd donated to the Museum, including re-modelled drawings based on the original sketches that appear on Joe Wilson's '1734' web site. Mr Steele became a very close friend for the few years we were given together. Thankfully, by his deeds alone, we discovered these works eventually. It was to Iain's credit that even after that, and suffering failing health, he still sought us out and we became close friends. We shared Companie on many occasions before his death in the Spring of 2010. By invitation of his gentle Lady, we were privileged to attend his funeral, a green burial on a hill-top in Wales. We finally achieved full and proper access to these documents in their entirety, through the courtesy of Simon Costin, the current curator of *The Witchcraft Museum* in Boscastle.

Other papers included in the box, mostly concern Gills' own workings based on Bowers' material. They specifically regard how to approach the altar, Gills' (Celtic [sic]) names for the kings and queens of the castles, including the seven castles from the *Preiddeu Annwn* {3268/ 4}. This material becomes quite extensive with regard to his own tradition, on spells, poppets and the 'sight,' continuing into 3362CDG.

In box 3376, a diagram of a rather fanciful figure, assumes the posture of a Baphomet, albeit stood, rather than seated. The artist is Gills, (having the same face as his painting of Cernnunos, also exhibited at the museum) based on Bowers' 'Mask' and the 'Round of Life'.

One further bundle of notes {3386A-3386F}, include several diagrams and text entitled "*some extracts taken from the writings of Roy Bowers*" Most of these shift from the previous typed and handwritten pieces by Gills to composite photocopies in various states of edit, C&P on modern A4 paper. Importantly, we must note that the handwriting on these documents, text and drawings are consistent with those within handwritten letters from N.G. to A. F. {3302A} that discuss many of the peoples from Bowers' Clan and from The Regency.

Box 32 has Gills' letters from Bowers, and some of his notes in response to them. This contains copes of some of *the authentic letters* {3245, 3243 A+B} Documents {3249B, 3253, 3254B+A+C, 3256+7} covering the info in 'the BSoTC' as it appears in the (complete version as the) Letter (ii) 'To all Elders' of the Clan, sent by Bowers—all appear authentic, typed with the same characters (as those known and) authenticated of Bowers' works. However, the info in 3246A refers to the hand written material copied and part composed, with poetic edits by Gills; same for the poem 'The Ash Tree' in {3247} which sits incongruously on the page. The text is smaller and has different line spacing, certain 'lines of text' are different too, clearly edited.

All extant versions, in whatever form, are extrapolations taken from doc (ii) - the 'Structure of the Craft,' given by Bowers to the Clan; an almost complete version, where it is printed in the 'RCL.' Though it must also be noted, there are errors in this copy too, due to natural error or preferred edit. The original document (ii) that appears authentic from the typewriter's unique and quirky signature, lists 'Luci' not Lucet. And 'Node,' not Nodens. Tettens, not Toutes. And Carenos, not Cernunnos. Additional words, such as 'windyat,' typify example of its varient (re) constructions.

Much of the Gills material, including the so called 'Basic Structure of the Craft' is handwritten from originals and re-typed in several different forms as alleged 'teaching aids' in Gills hand and typewriter. {3344 ABCDEF} Overall, these composite documents remain a testament of the 'interest and adaptation incumbent' upon such material in the history of the Craft. They endure beside properly documented and authenticated originals.

i Diagrams & Illustrations 65/66

~b~

a. The Menhir Of St Uzec. Male & Female Mysteries

(Used in *Witchcraft, The Sixth Sense & us* by Justine Glass)

Copies of diagrams allegedly sent to Gills by Bowers as enclosures of a Letter of Introduction Wilson presents on his site, listed among those Gills shared with him. Allegedly, from Bowers - presumably to Gills, it is a composite of others, also found in various combinations amongst Gills' papers (see below)

X.................................X

b. Drawing and description of list of symbols and their meanings [Roys or Norman?]

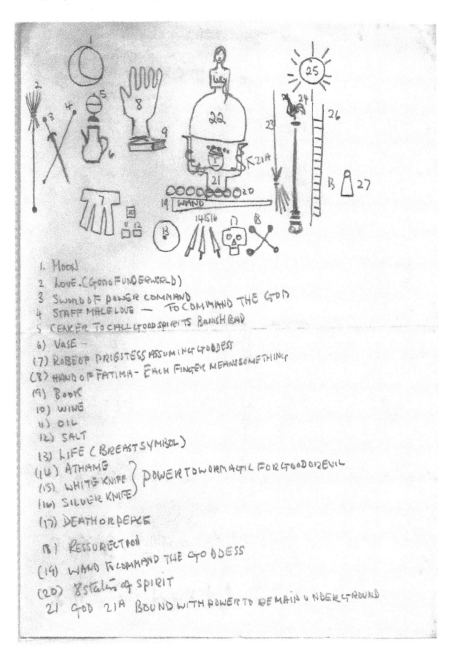

1. Moon
2. Love (God of Underworld)
3. Sword of power command
4. Staff male love — To command the God
5. Cenfer To call good spirits Banish Bad
6. Vase —
(7) Robe of Priestess Assuming Goddess
(8) Hand of Fatima — Each finger means something
(9) Book
10) Wine
11) Oil
12) Salt
13) Life (Breast Symbol)
(14) Athame
(15) White Knife } Power to work magic for Good or Evil
(16) Silver Knife
(17) Death or Peace

18) Ressurection
(19) Wand to command the Goddess
(20) 8 stalers of spirit
21 God 21A Bound with power to remain underground

22 GODDESS IN RITUAL POSITION

23 COPULATION

24 PHALLUS ERECTUS

25 FERTILITY — GOD OF PHYSICAL LIFE

26 THE CORDS LADDER TO to above from 23-25

27 - THE BELL TO CALL SPIRITS.

c. Oxford Stang with crossed arrows depicting the Supreme Altar –
    The Mask of God

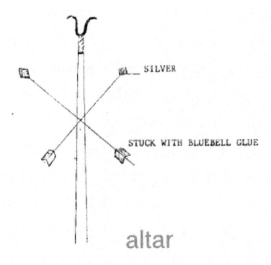

d. Transmutation of Mask as Triad, Hekate, Hermes & Saturn – Glyph
    as Monad

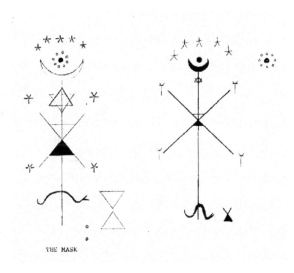

421

e.   Depicts folklore attached to the Two Brooms, a man's tool, not a woman's

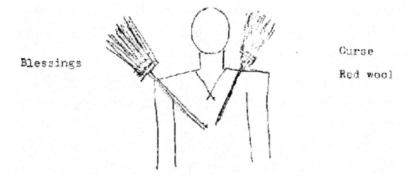

Blessings

Curse

Red wool

f.   How psi power works

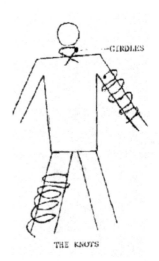

THE KNOTS

g. **Keppen within a Broom with belemnite fossil**

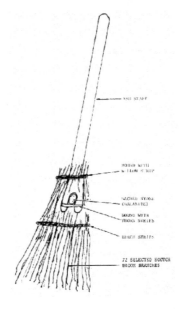

h. Necklace

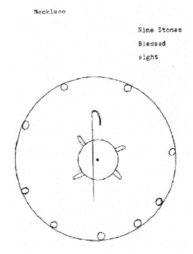

i.   Moat

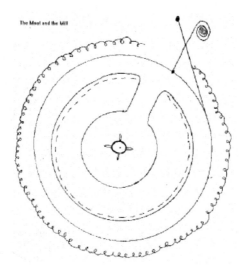

The Moat and the Mill

j.   Balanced Kundalene

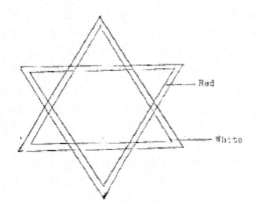

424

k. sigils used by Bowers to sign off

l. a Ring of crossed elements

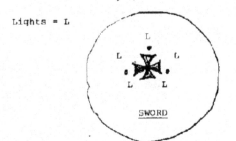

A silver or pewter disk for cross of Elements
- Tripod can be either broom or the three woods bound
with flax yarn thus ✳-bind. Upon Altar place thus:

Lights = L

L
L   L
. ✠ .
L   L

SWORD

put disk so that
it is seen easily

Surround ring perimeter with salt, sprinkle with   .
water thrown from broom -
    Ash from need fire makes outer perimeter surrounding
Altar.
    Incense is used to smoke area before beginning.

425

m.   further symbols enc. To Gills

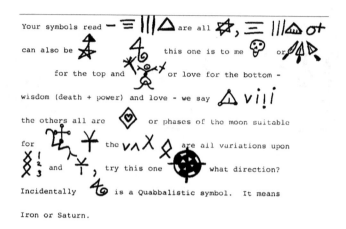

n.   Round of Life – Compass Rose

Original copies of pages with line drawings were developed by someone able to execute a slightly more diagrammatic perspective, very probably, Norman Gills who based his ideas on some preliminary sketches, allegedly provided by Roy Bowers during their correspondence and from Chalky and George during their time shared in The Regency.

The original sketches are mentioned by Valiente in her note-pads in some detail, as are her own diagrams that record them. She remarks upon them briefly in *Rebirth of Witchcraft*, as illustrations that may even have accompanied a possible article in *Psychic News* circa 62/63. Valiente penned her own sketches and notes from a nearby Witchcraft Exhibition in September 1961, held in Bourton-on-the-Water. Intrigued by these, she later must have discussed their purpose and origins with Bowers either by letter, during their long correspondence or in person once they'd met. And it is most telling of his character and his flair for intuitive cognition that Bowers was able to fully grasp their significance and place disparate oddments of folklore, gleaned from all manner of sources, to the fragmentary lore he had been gifted through various persons belonging to the old Craft; and all encountered along his journeying.

That Valiente was also able to contribute to the knowledge and folklore of the tools used by Bowers, is again a fine testament to their history and legacy which, we the Clan, hold dear. As these are all traditional tools included in the teachings and teaching aids as used by Roy Bowers in his directives to all members of his coven and Clan, including Chalky and George, it therefore registers some surprise as to why Monmouth is perplexed regarding the self-explanatory origin of the Sword & Broom Rites. He would prefer everyone to believe that it is drawn from knowledge of folklore that Chalky or George may have had, but clearly, this is not so. The paper trail simply does not lead back to them. We also know that Bowers shared these with Gills in at least three of their letters and possibly in person. Gills later shared them with Joe Wilson, by which time they had become re-drawn.

Both versions of these letters, written by Bowers, and Gills, courtesy of Iain Steele, remain in the museum for study). That they also became subject to popular knowledge and dispersal after his death is therefore no surprise.

Valiente lists the pertinent items amongst several others artefacts:

- wish mirrors, scrying bowls

- knives including a bronze knife,

- troy maze on black wax tablet,

- cauldron,

- 2 broomsticks, sometimes plain and sometimes with red and blue straps, bound with red thread, used in fertility rites male and female, one phallic, one forked, fossil belemnites used by witches as they are phallic shaped, one placed in the cleft for the male broom, another hidden in the brush, for the female broom.

- two written pieces on the witches cradle and the consumption of hallucinogenic Sabbat wine. Valiente sketches these in her note-pads, but they were not included on the museum transcript (they do remain in the archive).

X..................................X

(ww) Duplicates, Composites, and Alternative Published Documents between Bowers , Norman Gills and Joe Wilson

Alleged Appendage to Gills' Letter from Bowers concerning Joe Wilson 1966

Wilson's appendages as extra letters to Norman Gills [unverified, not validated, and not included amongst the earlier correspondences Gills shared with Wilson on his trip to England circa 1969]. During the many edits these letters underwent in the decades since Bowers' death, selected sentences and phrases have been changed and/or added to, in some cases using the typewriter George had kept which they had once shared. Certainly evident in the very early documents of The Regency, is how they are in fact typed upon the same typewriter Bowers used for his own correspondences. As for the letters written by Bowers to Wilson, he freely admits the originals were copied before they were tragically destroyed. And those copies were then subject to numerous different edits and reassembly, there is no longer a document that can be said to follow their original format. [59]

Wilson's suggestion for the 'Introductory letter' appears in the *Robert Cochrane Letters*, as Letter Eight to Gills.

The *end* of that document is *another letter to Norman Gills, and is also presented by Wilson on his website and in the RCL, as an enclosure. If these two separate document fragments (which appear to be distinct and authentic extracts of document (ii), were received as dated by Wilson, then, like so many others from the extant few letters made public, they too present considerable problems as (both) raise anomalies within some of the other letters where cross-references conflict markedly.

Nonetheless, they do sit well enough here in the chronology, so are included here for completion. Described amongst the 'Wilson' letters, is the way to approach an altar, which refers to how to prepare oneself for ritual; how to attain trance, even Lay a Compass. (the five motions of the round of life). In the last few months of his life, and pretty much left to his own devices, with no Clan to lead any more, Bowers so desperately needed to share his knowledge and experiences with someone, especially someone who was keen and showed interest in his work. He was not the first to do so, nor the last.

None of the following documents and letters reproduced by Gills or Wilson are edited or corrected for typos or spelling errors by ourselves as they appear here in the forms accepted as being the closest to the originals, or copies where the originals do not exist.

(xx) First example of an alternative (but composite and re-typed) Introduction letter from Roy Bowers to Norman Gills, cited by Joe Wilson as Letter 1.

I am a member of a cuveen, and come from a Crafter family, in which the Craft has been practiced for many generations. 'The local cuveen is small, consisting mainly of men, and of recent making since the last of the old Windsor cuveen died, when my mother was a girl back in Victoria's time. My mother helped her occasionally as a 'Maid' for scrying, but she did not tell her too much, and you may know her through reputation, her name was Mrs. Blomfield, and she was of high degree. As for my own Craft, it comes from the Midlands where my people originated. My family tell that my great-grand father was Grand Master for the whole of Warwickshire and Staffordshire, with some sixty "witches" under his care. How true this actually is though, I cannot say, although my aunt swears it is so, and she has a very impressive collection of "witch" things inclusive of a Maze that must be many centuries old. It seems to work out in the clan I belong to since we are interested in the old High Magic.

There are very few genuine cuveens left in Britain, most of the people who appear on television or in newspapers are fakes, and seem to originate from a man who lived on the Island of Man, and who made up the whole thing from his own head. I personally have very little time for them since they seem to be more interested in dancing naked than the real Craft, and as you know those sort of lies do nothing to help the real Craft.

I am married, Jane, my wife is a Crafter also, and my son Adrian, has all the markings of the pellar. Typical Craft, Jane and I met, fell in love and were married three weeks later. We have been together Fourteen years. We always work together, and I have found that from this we always get good results. Men and women are mirrors of each other, power cannot flow from man to man or woman to woman, it must flow together and mix. Not that we use power all that much, but when we have to, it works between Jane and I.

Nearly all the others have their hearts in the right place, but are inclined to use their brains too much, and not their wisdom. The small group I belong to falls into this trap, and I get very tired with trying to show them what is under their noses all along. A Crafter is born not made, or if one is to be made, then tears are spilt before the Moon can be Drawn.

What I can make of it, and I have been looking hard, the old Craft is nearly dead. Various groups of people call themselves witches, but this in many cases is an excuse for high jinx and tawdry orgies, rather than genuine Craft, although some of them are genuine enough in their beliefs. The real Pellar wisdom is almost lost, and the Gods are almost forgotten, yet today for the first time since the Christians came, more people are genuinely interested in the Craft from the religious and devotional viewpoint. I suppose the Industrial Revolution and the two wars are to blame really, but I think nearly all Pellars today work alone or nearly alone, with just one or two small clans still surviving, the real old ways are past, and it seems to break my heart when I think about it. Still enough of my miseries, you no doubt have enough of your own. I am trying to bring up what I know of the Craft, and apply it to the way of thought today. To do this I have had to read a tremendous amount about the old pagans and see what fitted and what didn't, and shape the religion as it was originally. To do this I have had to break away from the Knife and the Horn, but also keep them and make them into something slightly different. The Moon and the Mill—I have managed to bring that back to its original shape and symbolism, and ended up with the Castle, which seems to me to fit the old legends more correctly, and it works very

432

effectively, but to do this I have had to alter, and this by Craft standards is terrible, the old Ways quite a lot, but as I said High Magic, and it's attendant philosophy, is what we are interested in. Many of the old Craft ways were good and effective, but nobody knew why they worked. We do now.

The power comes not from what I know, but from what I am—and this applies to you also. Human beings are alchemical metals—and we change from dross to gold slowly. Personal power is a little bit of gold in the dross—and it does not matter what the person knows, or how well educated, or how clever he or she is—it is the work of Godhead on that person, and the gold increases according to how it is cherished. Differences in personality make for nothing—or in religion or creed—what counts is the person. You have as much of that as I and no book will ever contain it—for it is the gold of spirit—sometimes dulled by foolishness—other times shining bright. It is only bought by our personal search for the Graal, the Holy Cauldron, and the price is always blood and tears. The Gods give to man—but man always repays in the God coinage. Each of us pays in our little crucifixions, and all ritual must be a prayer.

In my way of thinking it is not what people know about ritual and symbolism that counts, but what they basically desire from the ritual, irrespective of what form the ritual takes. The important issue is not what form a ritual takes, but what force it invokes and shares amongst the participants. As far as I know there are three basic rituals common to all members of the True Faith. One is the ritual that reaches the common pool of TOTAL knowledge, what the Qabbalists describe as the Akashics, this is a simple and straight forward matter. TWO is the ritual of force, in which various degrees of heavenly force is invoked and applied, again going to a godhead in the Akashics, and three, three is the most important one of all in which the participants invoke mystical energy, and this experience is shared by the whole group. Therefore, these things are essential to the structure of any part of the three basic rituals—Emotion, Symbolism, Direction and Aspiration. Admittedly other aids are used, but the four motive powers above and one other, Unity are the basis of any ritual that will work properly. The other ingredients are the perfect couples and a suitable leader, and most important, the Godhead present in physical and comprehended form.

Within the structure of the laws (and they are laws) above, the bits and pieces, the articles, the words, etc. have value, but outside such a basic structure, whatever is used has no value at all except maybe to lead on into the level of Maya or delusion.

As such, dispensing with various theatrical aids, (which are also necessary) a ritual that covers all three traditionally is that which embraces the Three Mothers. Fire, Water, and Air. As such it is very simple in format, the leader is male, and the structure of the rite is to do with eating and drinking. In fact, the original form of the Sacrament of the Host, embracing unlike the Christian Sacrament, the principles of the Sun and the Moon. The male and females do not dance or pace round a ring (although that again is done for other things) but stay still, and a Maid is not used for such work. Incidentally the concept of a Maid historically comes from either Spain or Italy, and as such was to do with matters connected to a different religion that was relatively speaking, modern. Now the ritual I have spoken of can be traced by symbols and by grave goods many, many centuries back to the Neolithic period, or early Stone Age. A sun symbol as such is still the form of a consecrated 'host', and means literally resurrection. The concept behind the Horn Childe has much to do with this.

(xx) This is another example of a *(composite and re-typed)* letter. It is a pastiched version of letter. #11, and shows clear extraction from other letters.

Dear Norman,

Many thanks for your kind letter, and the very good advice in it—however it is not what people said, but what they have done, which has hurt. John has also betrayed his trust—and spoken the name of a hereditary member to the Gardnerian's—who seeing that it is Taliesin, are now intent upon making trouble for him. As such when the Clans people get to hear about it, John will be put under the Ban—that I am sure of—and you know as well as I do, there is terror and death in that. The thing with Audrey and myself goes much deeper—but as you said—I should not get involved. Still enough of my troubles, and thank you for your attentions and prayers. I am pleased to read that you know something of the old High Magic, not many do, although many claim to. Can you cast the Mound and the Skull? In fact thinking about it, I am more than pleased, since you are the first person I have met for many a long day who knows something about the Craft. I am in correspondence with a young man in the United States who seems to have a feel for it, but he has much to learn.

The mystery you speak of is that of the Broom. it is the basic magical and mystical practice, and corresponds with the exercise of the Qabalistic middle pillar. Unlike the principle and mystery of St. John though, the principle of Fire is removed, and that of Air put in its place. This practiced every day is the path way to the Seven Gates of perception—Now what is it all about.

The Faith is made of three parts—of which I know two. The first part is the masculine mysteries—in which is enshrined the search for the Holy Graal—and is the basis of the Arthurian legends. This is the order of the Sun—the Clan of Tubal Cain. Under it come learning, teaching, skill, bravery, and truthfulness. In the distant past, the male clan was lead by a woman who was their priestess and chieftan. This is the origin of the legend of Robin Hood—and surprisingly enough began the Old Testament, and later, Christianity since both Jesus and Moses alike preached a version of the Masculine mysteries—Mithriasm was also a development of this—and the tradition was followed through into the middle Ages when the Plantaganet Kings were officers of the masculine aspect of the Faith (The name 'Plantaganet' means 'The Devil's Clan'). The effect of the masculine mysteries upon the world can hardly be under emphasized— since a very considerable portion of civilization owes its origin to them. To name but a few—Commerce, Lawmaking, Law- giving, Parliament, The early forms of universities and craftsmen's guilds—which lead to knowledge being contained and taught, surveying, all sciences such as metallurgy, astronomy and so on ad infinitum. The masculine mysteries were the direct creators of modern civilization as we know it now. It must also be remembered that originally the Mystery was conducted by a woman—and that she was the presiding genius behind many of the fundamental discoveries that created civilization. These mysteries are depicted as a javelin, a cockerel upon a pillar, a ladder, a flail, a twelve- rayed sun and a ladder of eight rungs and a sword or battle ax. Basically they have to do with control over three of four elements, especially that of Fire.

Firstly then we must begin with the fundamental practice of the Faith—the correct way to approach an altar.

Have you ever watched cattle? The way one cow will always turn her back upon you and regard you over her shoulder? This then is the correct way to approach an altar. The cow is using 'kundalini' to analyse you, to sense out what you are, and whether you are dangerous, and she uses her spinal column as a sensory device—in much the same way as water diviners use a wand to sense water. Now the practice of kundalini, is as you know, the transmutation of sexual energy. So this is where the broom comes in—in the sense that this transmutes the energy of the sexual impulse into the higher grade energy of sensation, feeling and thought. Physically one perambulates a given number of times around the seven sided ring such as seven to call upon the seven stars. One stops in the exact center of the ring, and has the back to the altar, balancing upon the right foot, with the left foot pointing out, and looking over your shoulder at the altar—so that the spinal column forms a spiral—which incidentally you have already performed in your turning about the ring. At this point of balance—one begins the first principle of the broom—which equates to that of the Qabalistic Malkuth. Before the altar is greeted though, one prepares the ring by imagining a bright star very far away, and above your head. From this star should fall waves of light, and one should imagine that it is getting nearer—or rather you are getting nearer to it. The light should enter your body through the right shoulder, and work in a spiral downwards, and emit through the left foot upon stopping to greet the altar. As such the ring, which has been censed and purged by whatever method you use, is charged, and this in its turn becomes a well of wisdom—of the water of life. You like the trout spiral in this pool, and then by sheer poetry which should be spontaneous and inspired—take your body in an anti-clockwise spiral until it reaches the base of the spine— Malkuth—which is earth, and corresponds to the anus and the genital area surrounding it. This is the foundation, and the seat of all transmutation, since the area of skin between the anus and the sexual organs is that which holds the super-physical power. Hence broom stick riding, since in the past they rode a staff in order to activate that small area of sensation—and then transmuted it by mental power to the ascending snake. The broomstick was anointed with the flying ointment.

I will demonstrate the techniques of the broom when we meet— and if you can get Jill and her mother along since I have a distinct respect for Jill's psychism—I will show you how to approach the Holy Ones— that is the Deities who rule us. In this exercise, and once it is fully carried out and understood—the final stages is that when a sensation of being near a great bell is felt, and your mind and body appears to tremble with the vibrations. It is at this point that you utter the prayer for whatever you are requiring—but always remember Norman—no man has power within himself, we are all but expressions of Godhead. This belief that tricks, or techniques bring power is a blasphemy since the magician is nothing but a channel for the forces he raises by prayer—and prayer and faith are the greatest secrets of them all. To be a channel of the force of Godhead is all we can ever hope to attain. obviously you are well aware of this—but having told others—I always add this as a precaution, since some people think that power comes from within.

The ritual you speak of is pretty basic, although we begin with movement—for that is the correct way to greet an altar, and end with sitting still. To run about brings an emotional release that should for purity sake be sexually released in its final stages—but for the big prizes one meets before the Knot the number of days devoted to the Goddess awakened, and then upon the knot, invokes the Goddess through 'The dark of night and the evening star meeting together', which as you should know is brought about in the beginning by "in an uneasy chair above Caer Ochren".

"Spinning without motion between three Elements" this was the way it was in Long Compton, Shropshire, Lancashire and the Isle of Man, and since one of my informants is now a very old man, who has

been in it all his life—and understands both the Broom and the Sword—
I should think it has been traditional for many centuries. I agree though
about movement—but as you know movement of any spectacular sort
is nearly impossible once "Bell tone" has been reached, since by then you
are verging up on the other world and preparing to enter beneath the hall
of the King. Forgive me for saying so but you seem to be confused
slightly as to the actual making of power—this of course is not suggesting
that you have failed in discovering power, but that you have discovered it
instinctively—which will work for you, but for nobody else. The Star of
David is, of course, the basic explanation of the Sword and Broom—do
you know how to apply this principle, or have youfollowed your instincts?
As such it forms a cross pattern at the base of the throat and forehead—
and is extremely difficult to operate, since it is a point of perfect balance
of two totally different yet complimentary forces—and the Noble Ones
are loath to help, since once it is mastered, it gives incredible power to
the master—but in the search for it, one can so easily be destroyed, for it
is the genuine philosopher's work and Stone, and twice in my life I have
grasped it, only to lose it again.

Really it is impossible to teach this—just as it is to teach someone
how to bring the 'Morning Star and the Dead of Night together' by
writing. It has to be demonstrated so that faith is created, and so a standard
is wrought to work by. As for other rituals—The Cad Goduie and the
Predui Annwm by Gwion, who was a poet in the twelfth century, will act
as a gateway—since in poetic form (and that means in terms of images,
a matter for which you have a gift) the answers are all ruled and laid out
for the eye of the seer. You will find these in that very excellent book
'The White Goddess' by Robert Graves. It costs 12/6 and is published as
a paperback by Faber. In that book is indicated wisdom, and by unraveling
some of the riddles—wisdom is to be found.

Concerning your magic mirror .... with or without the horn? Or do you mean a scrying glass. I know of two mirrors, one the Lady holds by a very old piece of wood, and the other that is between my eyes. One mirror speaks of the trees (eight in all) of the forest, the other speaks of Tides that is still to come.

My question to you as to where the witch wears her garter—that needs an answer. However lets leave these things for the future. Perhaps we can meet some time in the new year. Perhaps your clan and mine could meet one day and discuss things. Staffordshire and Warwick don't come to Long Compton, maybe they went to another Well.

May the Hare, owl and pussy cat .. Robert

(yy) Example 3

Letter #6 in *The Robert Cochrane Letters* edited by Mike Howard (hereafter referred to as RCL), this letter forms the first section, followed by a second section in the RCL identical to the one Joe Wilson cites that similarly forms the second section of (qq4) after this example. Though none of them are validated and are clear composites, this one seems less so. But no document is yet forthcoming to prove its veracity.

Dear Norman,

A short letter to thank you for your hospitality during the weekend. We all enjoyed ourselves immensely. We have been experimenting with the balanite and the ash, and find that even without certain aids, it works remarkably well combined with the witches cradle. As far as we can see it has two effects. One is the activating of the power in a human body, and the other is moving a centre of power from one point to another. The thing that did strike us as interesting was that even without the cone of power being present from the ring it works as an activator. It evidently effects the nerve and mind power that has its centre just over the front of the head. The Indians call this a 'chakra' and it is supposed to spiral either left or right according to the sex. In sick people it looks like a closed flower, and in a psychic it looks like a vortex moving around. I have felt and seen this effect at time, so it is true I think. Now from what I can gather, when you move the cleft stick down, it also affects the other centres on the body, such as the one just under the heart and above the sexual organs. In other words, it is a far more advanced method than that used by the ceremonial magicians, who do all this by breathing.

Presumably, combined with the witches cradle, it helps the spirit to leave the body, anyway this is what we did with it. Also working in a ring, once the power has been raised it joins the directional power of the Maid or Master to the power of the group, and since the Maid has been instructed to go in a certain direction, the whole group will follow, and anything that happens must be shared by the group. It is very interesting. Now the idea of using it over water, bound to a wet tree, such as a willow, is interesting also, since it is forming a perfect link for the power to flow from heaven to earth, or earth to heaven according to which way the ring is being turned. As you already know, power must be a complete chain otherwise it will not work, since witch magic is like witch gods it is from the highest to the lowest and from the lowest to the highest. All is one and one is all.....

Thank you Norman for teaching us so much.

Obviously I cannot leave the matter like that, so here is a piece of knowledge that will help you, and which will explain the Castles and the Kingdoms. I have enclosed it, and I hope that you will understand it, since it really is a map of the other worlds, you are welcome to use our names, or use the ones you know personally. But I guarantee that this works, if it is combined with things that both you and I know, but will

441

not write down ... cords ... smoke ... tapers..etc, etc

I should think that if you were to summons and use your mirror it would be interesting also.

Will it be convenient if two members of my group come to see you? J. and I will be along also. And I wondered if we could come to some agreement to work together, since I feel that this will be right for both of us. Jane. is a very good sensitive [part of line missing]

Then I have the full permission of my group to invite you or your friends to work with us. We will not force you to work our way to see if it is possible for our two ways that are slightly different to be combined so that they will work together. If it is convenient we could drop in and see you on good Friday, which as you know is a very good day for the practice of the craft. I am making enquiries about your botanical paintings, and I think it may be possible to place them. Also Chalky, a member of my group says that he can get you an exhibition. He is..{rest of letter missing}

*Herewith is the basic structure of the Craft .....

(zz) Example #4 Letter #8 in RCL (composite and re-typed from several others), but cited by Joe Wilson as Letter #3

This letter is again another composite, formulated to emphasise 'The Basic Structure of the Craft.' These extracts are cited by Joe Wilson, as a collective missive (taken from the original full text document these passages are extrapolated). Of course, we now know this material has been extrapolated from the Document (**ii**) from within the Monmouth Cache. Wilson had posted up this composite document as an enclosure from Bowers to Gills for him entitled ...'*Herewith is the Basic Structure of the Craft* ' Within the Capall Bann publication *The Robert Cochrane Letters*, this extract is printed separately as a 'part or missing document.' Neither

442

version is complete; both are bereft of the first page of that document's title and vital 'Charge,' that is, the express instruction and intent with which Bowers addresses the Clan in 1965.

Dear Norman,

Thank you for your letter which I read with very great interest. I take it that you write in symbols, and your descriptions of Two Kings, and Two Queens are purely symbolic, since we have something very similar in my own branch of the Craft.

I was worried of the outburst of symbols. My own conclusion is that you were probably still suffering from the after affects of nightshade wine, but even so I didn't want to push the issue at that point. You should really be careful, since all dream drugs can have a very dangerous side as well as a marvellous sensational side. There is a place in the other world (if place is the right way to describe it) which is literally chaos, and can destroy the human mind. In the past they had very careful directions and sign posts to help the congregation over the difficult way. Today much of those directions have been lost.

I read your remarks upon the practices you follow with interest, and perceive in them a conglomeration of various ideas that are not strictly of the Faith I know. The animals you speak of I do possess a very considerable knowledge about, and I can assure you that a rat, as distinct from a mouse is the last shape to be assumed by Long Compton, any more than an alder rod would be used in a ritual devoted to the Mother of the Waters. Trees, like animals have a use and a meaning—and combined with a maze pattern of the right sort and understanding, form a series of compound images that produce necessary effects, and lead us into the place in the otherworld where we may gain wisdom. Taliesin was too fond of relying upon Toad, and the Taniast have lost because of this.

443

Glorious dreams may be valid, but unless they have a reason for 'becoming', they are of little use except in convincing the devotee of the beauty or horror locked away in his own unconscious.

We have been pretty busy recently, organizing a magical group along the Seven and One basis, as opposed to the old rural Twelve and One. The Clan seem to be responding, and our ancestors are appearing to give their approval, that is the only approval that counts for us. The Hallows of the Covenant went off all right, had to cover up somethings since strangers were present, but we got through a few results. Sorry about not bringing you along, but since it was already overbalanced with outsiders, there was not very much else we could do. We could not have helped you under those circumstances at all. The summoning of the Hound and the Raven had to be done symbolically as it was, and there were only four of us who knew what we were about. Still one of the outsiders said she had a vision of the Old Queen, and Old Tubal was definitely there. Not a bad night out all in all.

We have been experimenting with the balanite and ash, and find that even without certain aids, it works remarkably well combined with a witches cradle. As far as we can see, it has two effects. One is the activating of the power in a human body, and the other is moving a center of power from one point to another. The thing that did strike us as interesting was that even without the cone of power being present from the ring, it works as an activator. It evidently affects the nerve and mind power that has it's center just over the front of the head. The Indians call this a "Chakra", and it is supposed to spiral either left or right according to the sex. In sick people it looks like a closed flower, and in a psychic it looks like a vortex moving round. I have felt and seen this effect at times, so it is true I think. Now from what we gather, when you move the cleft stick down, it also affects the other centers on the body, such as the one just under the heart and above the sexual organs. In other words, it is a far more advanced method than that used by the ceremonial magicians who do all this by breathing.

Presumably combined with a witches cradle, it helps the spirit to leave the body, anyway this is what we did with it. Also working in a ring, once the power has been raised, it joins the directional power of the Maid or Master to the power of the group, and since the Maid has been instructed to go in a certain direction, the whole group will follow and anything that happens must be shared by the group. It is very interesting. Now the idea of using it over water, bound to a wet tree such as a willow is interesting also, since it is forming a perfect link for the power to flow from heaven to earth, or earth to heaven according to which way the ring is being turned. As you already know, power must form a complete chain otherwise it will not work, since "witch" magic is like "witch" Gods, it is from the highest to the lowest, from the lowest to the highest. All is One, and one is all.

Thank you Norman for teaching us so much.

Obviously, I cannot leave the matter like that, so here is a piece of knowledge that will help you, and which will explain about the Castles and Kingdoms. I have enclosed it, and I hope you will understand it, since it is really a map of the other worlds, you are welcome to use our names, or use the ones that you know personally. But I will guarantee that this works, if it is combined with things that both you and I know, but will not write down...cords...smoke...tapers...etc, etc.

*When the time comes pass this, and the other things which we have discussed, on to Mr. Wilson, whom I am afraid I will not see.

Flags, Flax and Fodder, Roy

*Herewith is the basic structure of the Craft .....

In the beginning there was only Night, and She was alone. Being was absolute, movement was there none. Being force without form, She desired form, and since She desired, that form was created .Woman. Being Woman, She desired union, and created Man from Her North side.

Having created Man, She discovered love, and so all things began. Here was the first of all sins, Desire. From desire sprang all movement, all Life, all Time, all Death, joy and sorrow alike.

From the Gods came seven children, who created seven worlds to rule over, and they formed a halo about the Great Gods as seven stars. They also created Earth, Air, Fire and Water, and gave these lands to four of the seven Gods. These Gods each live in a separate land bounded by the great Gulf of Annwn, which is the land of Chaos, and unredeemed souls.

The lands of the Gods are then:

A Castle surrounded by Fire that lies upon the East, ruled over by Lucet (The divine Child). The Supreme Goddess comes from here.

A Castle under the depths of the Sea, laying towards the West, ruled over by Node.

A Castle in the Clouds laying towards the North, ruled over by Tettens.

A Castle builded upon the Earth and surrounded by trees, laying towards the South, ruled over by Carenos.

To each of these rulers was given a wife,that sprang also from the love of the Gods. Each of these lands had power over human endeavour. Lucet is the King of Light, Fire, Love and Intellect, of Birth and Joy...The Child. He is visualized as a bright golden light moving quickly, with wings.

Thieving and mischievious.

Sometimes he comes as a tall golden man, moving rapidly, other times the wings of Fire surround him, but few can face that vision without aid from an even Higher Source. At times he is winged at the foot; at others upon the head, behind the glorious hair.)

For Thy Kingdom is past not away Nor Thy Power from the place hurled.

Out of Heaven they shall not cast the day They shall not cast out song from the world. By the song and the light they give

We know Thy works that they live

With the gift Thou hast given us of speech

We praise, we adore, we beseech We arise at Thy bidding and follow We cry to Thee, answer, appear Oh Father of us all Paian Appollo Destroyer and Healer hear!

In the North lies the Castle of Weeping, the ruler thereof is named Tettens, our Hermes or Woden. He is the second twin, the waning sun, Lord over mysticism, magic, power and death, the Baleful destroyer. The God of War, of Justice, King of Kings, since all pay their homage to Him. Ruler of the Winds, the Windyat.[60] Cain imprisoned in the Moon, ever desiring Earth. He is visualized as a tall dark man, shadowy, cold and deadly. Unpredictable, yet capable of great nobility, since he represents Truth. He is the God of magicians and witches, who knows all sorcery. Lord of the North, dark, unpredictable, the true God of all witches and magicians if they are working at any decent level at all. A cold wind surrounds Him, age and time so ancient that it is beyond belief flows from Him. Dark is His shadow, and he bears a branch of the sorrowing alder, and walks with the aid of a blackthorn stick. Sorrow is printed upon His face, yet also joy. He guards, as a rider upon an eight-legged horse, the approaches to the Castle of Night. He is also the Champion of the glass bridge after the Silver Forest. Cold is tho air as he passes by.

Some say tall and dark, I say small and dark, speaking in a faint voice which is as clear as ice.

(Lucet and Tettens are the Twins, the Children of Night and the Serpent, brothers and some say one and the same person. Fire and Air, growth and decay. One looks forward, the other backward. One creates, the other destroys, Castor and Pollox.)

In the South lies the Castle of Life. The ruler is named Carenos, He is the Lord of animals, of joy and of passion. Ruler of the woodlands, a wild hunter, yet the God of happiness, fruition, fertility, equivalent to the young Dionysus. Shown as a horned figure, with curling rams horns. He is the God of the fertility cultus, and everything about Him is connected with life, growth and strength.

In the West lies perhaps the most complex, and the greatest figure of them all. The God of Paradise, Node. He is the God of Rest, Sleep, Achievement, fruition of labour, spiritual growth. He is also noble, ever fighting against evil, and is equivalent to King Arthur. He is also the God of the Sea. He should be seen as a mature man, with golden light playing from Him, and a lion at His feet. Eyes that are wise and sad. He is the King of all true wisdom.

These four Kings are the reversed pentacle, thus [hexagram] and the fifth ray is turned into six points, or three and three, which in part represents Old Tubal Cain, or the All Father Himself. Hearne.

Above the head of the Moon, as shewn in the diagram lies five (seven) other stars, known as the Goddesses, that is they are to be seen in The Plough or Haywain. They fall into this sequence: Life, Love, Maternity, Wisdom, and Death. Since I maintain that knowledge is understood more fully if one has to work for it, I leave you to fit your own interpretation upon the five (seven) Stars, and how they fit as Queens within the Castles. By looking at the diagrams of both the Moat and the Mill, it is possible

448

to see how they become Queens, and also why in ancient mythology, why the Queen was always considered to play a harlot, or fallen woman. In other words, by the juxtaposition of King and Queens, it is possible to work out a magical formula concerned with (a) aspects within the Mask, as one would use a Qabbalistic tree, and (b) an insight into the control of the four basic elements.

It was considered in the past that Man could help the Gods, as the Gods helped Man. In fact, you will find that in many fairy stories, they deal with this matter allegorically. It is from these and many similar stories,

a. Sir Gawain and the Hollen Bush; Tristam and Isobel; Launcelot and Geneveve, and others that a pattern of magical myth and legend may be woven, often with surprising results and effects. To effect a magical ritual of this nature, one enacts it with various implements and tools that have the same symbolic meaning as the Gods involved.

It was from these unions between Gods and man, that the art of magic began. To those who have eyes, ears and a heart that is pure. These deepest secrets are written upon the clouds, in the bark of trees, in the movement of water, and in the heart of fire. The genuine mysteries are open to all to see and rediscover. There is no secrecy surrounding them. There is a great river flowing and twining round all creation. Rushing out of Annwn, binding the seven kingdoms together, and returning to Annwn in a great waterfall, under which all must pass eventually. The name of that river is Time and the place of Darkness to which it returns is not only Hell, but Heaven also. It is time and time alone that binds us to blindness, and it is love and love alone that will let us see the golden heart of the mysteries.

These are the subjects we will be dealing with over the next year, and examining the basic content.

The Five Rings of Power The Four Castles and the Keepers The Four Tides or Rivers

The wisdom of the Seventy-Two herbs and trees. The art of the Mirror

The art of the Kippen The art of the Stang The art of the Bone

The power of the Seven Planets The power of the Sun

The power of the Moon The power of the Stars

The art of the Three Knives The art of cords and binding

The art of symbols and their interpretation The power of desire

The power of will The twin Snakes

THE RINGS OF POWER

The Rings of power fall into this order:

i. The Wheel of Life

ii. The Moat

iii. The Mill of Fate

iv. The Necklace

v. The Ring of the Doorways

The Wheel is the basic creation of "witch" magic. It is a vehicle of worship of the Goddesses over Life, Love, Maternity/Maturity, Wisdom and Death. In the center lies the heart within the coffin, or as it is known in the Craft, the Rose from the Grave. Love and Death.

Basically, it is the most simple of all the Rings, but also the most complex. It corresponds with the Garter, or Ladder of Devotion, and the Ring, like the Garter should be fastened upon the knot of Death. It's main use is in rituals of Death and Ressurection. In actions of worship, it is a religious device used to draw down the power of the Goddesses invoked, standing upon the horn of the aspect invoked. It is blessed in the Name of Love, water and fire used to drive out evil from the five points, swept and garnissed and censed. It should be enclosed three times with Salt and Chalk. That is life and the power of the Moon. Upon certain operations, it is permissable to light a fire in the center, thereby creating the Rose of Passion, or unity. On no account should it be used for an operation of cursing, neither should the "witch" work widdershins within it. It is the vehicle of the Horn Child. By simple meditation, it is possible to find more points than five, in fact there should be twenty-five, with One more.

X..................................X

All Letter & Document Scans: Not yet released publicly, but may be viewed at the archived resources at the Witchcraft Museum in Boscastle. UK

X..................................X

Glossary of Terms:

An·a·go·ge also an·a·go·gy

A mystical interpretation of a word, passage, or text, especially scriptural exegesis that detects allusions to heaven or the afterlife.

Anagogic

Relating to literature as a total order of words. ie. fourfold model of exegesis (literal, allegorical, tropological, anagogic)

Achamoth

The Lower Sophia and daughter, in Valentinian Gnosticism, of the Upper Sophia (Wisdom).

Anthropos

Androgynous Angel /First Adam, spirit-endowed (created in the Upper Aeons), by the One in its own image. First, Perfect Man, as distinct from beasts/animals/demonic forms.

Ialdabaoth and his Archons then created the Second Adam, also androgynous, and who was soul-endowed (psychic Anthropos). But, in retrieving pneuma back from Adam, the third Adam (hylic Anthropos) was created – flesh endowed; then split from its androgynous state into male and female as Adam and Eve.

Aeons

Series of hypostases that emanate outward from a common 'Source,' as extensions of its being. *The Upper Aeons* are without spacial or temporal measure, they are boundless and eternal. They are silent, invisible and filled with light. Watery - the pleroma. A veil separates them from: *The*

Lower Aeons, that encircle the demiurge, Yaltabaoth, are multiple, and have temporal and spacial measures.

They are visible, mutable and filled with darkness. Fiery – the kenoma.

Androgyne

Possessing both male and female genders and virtues. Each of the seven Archons, being androgynous has a male and female name: (for) Adonaios, his feminine name is Kingship, and (for) Astaphaios, his feminine name is Sophia (Wisdom).

Angels

All angels are hypostasis existing as extensions/reflections of the One/Source within the Upper Aeons.

Apocalypse

c)   A 'revealed teaching.'

d)   The 'end of time,' the way of Chaos as instructional to Balance and the final resolution of forms.

Apocryphon

A 'hidden teaching'

Archons

Rulers of the Lower Aeons, known as: rulers, governors, gate-keepers, thieves, toll collectors, judges, corpse-eaters. Ruled by Yaltabaoth (created by Sophia). There are twelve Archons and their aeons that form the Lower Aeons: Seven heavenly Archons associated with the Seven planetary 'Heavens,' and Five Archons 'of the sub-lunary realms of the Abyss, each in turn possessing the qualities of earth, water, air and fire intermixed within the ether.

Atman

The higher self. The God Within.

Autogenes

The one who is 'self-begotten' - Christ.

Baptism

One of the five seals: A ritual that may be performed once, thrice of five (or more) times, all of which involve, being covered by water, either by full immersion, or by sprinkling/ pouring onto head, and/or body. Water is the vehicle for spirit/pneuma, and carries the reflection (image and gnosis of) the One, the Divine Source. To be 'covered' by water, one is born anew, filled with the essence, literally of the divine, now awakened to its light and virtue. Hence a new name is given, to represent that 'absorption.'

Call (the call)

To 'name,' to be named, to be summoned by The One, that is, to be sung home upon the name awarded within the Baptismal Rite – this the name the spirits will know us by, and allow us passage through the halls of oblivion and forgetfulness, where time is no more, and eternity lies ahead. It is the ancestral gift, the opposite to spiritual blindness, where ignorance of one's name , binds one to the limitations of the levels/realms known to them, in death, beyond death, and even before death.

Cosmogony

The origin and evolution of the universe as defined by religion, philosophy, mythology and science. These are not always mutually exclusive. Creation myths of the universe.

Cosmology

Historical record of a cultural consensus that considers how the world/

people will end – it concerns the action of fate upon man. This tends towards a religious and mythological perspective; it is an account of the shift toward the final things of eschatology. Man's endeavour to understand his fate and destiny within the greater schema.

Crown

Also a diadem, tiara, coronet

Father, Mother and Child each possess a Crown, composed of all beings, from all realms, pneumatic, psychic and hylic. The Crown shines with, and reflects back the stabilising and unifying 'light' created by all names of itself and of their virtue.

Dianoia

Meaning of a work of literature that may be either: the total pattern of its symbols (literal meaning); its correlation with an external body of propositions or facts (descriptive meaning); its theme, or relation as a form of imagery to a potential commentary (formal meaning); its significance as a literary convention or genre (archetypal meaning); or its relation to total literary experience: (anagogic meaning).

Disciples

Followers of a mentor – apprentices or labourers better known as 'apostles.'

Desire

A yearning akin to bitterness, a deep fire that is never sated, the wheel of repetition, a state of stupor, an emotive state of self –indulgence, passion, wrath and anger. Lack of clarity, clear sight.

Eschatology

The study of doctrinal issues that deal with the fate of mankind at the end of time, concepts of the life hereafter, judgment, paradise, Valhalla etc.

Esotericism

In modern times, the meaning of the word metaphysics has become confused by popular significations that are unrelated to metaphysics or ontology per se.

Eucharist

Ritual meal – a remembrance of life acquired through divine sacrifice, - gyfu. Primarily of Bread and Wine, it is another of the Five Seals, a sacramental meal, shared with and as, the presence of the divine. Continues the work of baptism, keeping body and soul in a 'state of readiness.' Salt for Sophia.

Fate

A gnostic premise states that Fate was created by The Archons to 'bind' humanity to the Lower Aeons. (In addition to time, oblivion and forgetfulness, these bonds, restrict elevation, ascent, evolution. They bind, preventing free movement through the gateways of all realms. It is the measure of one's life.

If an hallucination is experienced as the patient is falling asleep then it is described as hypnagogic.

Fundamentalism

Those who are concerned with separating their belief from those of others.

Hamingja

One who walks beside the self, as fate/providence – a guardian spirit akin to *flygia,* but in myth, is consigned to the head of a Clan specifically.

Hypnogogic Sleep inducing.

Hypnopompic and hypnogigic states

These dreams involve hallucinations either before (hypnogogic) or after a dream (hypnopompic). These may not just involve hallucinations - the dreamer may hear things, smell things, and even taste things. Such hallucinations usually last for just seconds but may continue for longer.

Kabbalah

A system of Jewish mysticism known as the Kabbalah displays many Neo-Platonic elements, and some have argued that the Kabbalah has an ultimately Greek origin. In the Kabbalah, God creates the universe through ten Sephirot, or vessels. These are, in order:

Kether, Crown Khokmah, Wisdom Binah, Understanding Khesed, Mercy Givurah, Strength Tifareth, Beauty Netzakh, Victory Hod, Glory Yesod, Foundation Malkuth, Kingdom

These ten Sephirot are linked by twenty-two paths, corresponding to the letters of the Hebrew alphabet. Many of the similarities are cosmetic: for example, in the Kabbalah there is a strong sense that the emanations are trinary in nature, each pair producing the next in a process of synthesis.

In Greek Neo-Platonism, this is not the case: usually, emanations are linear, each leading to the next. Also, in the Kabbalah, the letters of the Hebrew alphabet are, themselves, regarded as having some divine power. Although there is some evidence for similar attitudes in Greek theurgy, there they are not as developed.

Kairos

In the time of the gods, when fate decrees it is 'moot…beyond our rationale and kenning

Kenoma

The manifest cosmos. The divine within the mundane. The domain of the corporeal 'Sophia,' – Norea.

Logos

From the Greek word *logos* meaning: word, speech, discourse, definition, principle, ratio, or reason. The term is used in philosophy primarily to mean 'reason.'

Monism

Belief in an impersonal oneness.

Monotheism

Single, transcendental unity of One God.

Mysticism

[*mystikos*—secret] those who through arcane methods recognize the truth within all traditions as different paths to the same God.

Metaphor:

A relation between two symbols, which may be simple juxtaposition (literal metaphor), a rhetorical statement of likeness or similarity (descriptive metaphor), an analogy of proportion among four terms (formal metaphor), an identity of an individual with its class (concrete universal or archetypal metaphor), or statement of hypothetical identity (anagogic metaphor).

Mythos

The narrative of a work of literature, considered as the grammar or order of words (literal narrative), plot or 'argument' (descriptive narrative), secondary imitation of action (formal narrative), imitation of generic and recurrent action or ritual (archetypal narrative), or imitation of the total conceivable action of an omnipotent god or human society (anagogic narrative). One of the four archetypal narratives, classified as comic, romantic, tragic, and ironic.

mystagogue

A person who initiates others into mystical beliefs, an educator or person who has knowledge of the mystic arts

mys·ta·gogue (n.)

One who prepares candidates for initiation into a mystery cult. One who holds or spreads mystical doctrines.

Metaphysics

(Greek: meta = after/beyond and physics = nature) is a branch of philosophy concerned with the study of 'first principles' and 'being' (ontology).Problems that were not originally considered metaphysical have been added to metaphysics.

Other problems that were considered metaphysical problems for centuries are now typically relegated to their own separate subheadings in philosophy, such as philosophy of religion, philosophy of mind, philosophy of perception, philosophy of language, and philosophy of science. In rare cases subjects of metaphysical research have been found to be entirely physical and natural.

Neo-Platonism

The source of Western theurgy can be found in the philosophy of late Neo-Platonists, especially Iamblichus. In late Neo-Platonism, the universe is regarded as a series of emanations from the Godhead. Matter itself is merely the lowest of these emanations, and therefore not in essence different from the Divine. Although the number and qualities of these emanations differ, most Neo-Platonists insisted that God was both singular and good. Although Neo-Platonists were technically polytheists, they also embraced a form of monism: reality was varied, with varied gods, but they all represented aspects of the one reality.

Nephelae

Nephelim (plural of nephel) means 'rejects' and not giants. nominative female plural= nephelae

Consider too that plurals in Hebrew are designated by 'im' if masculine, and 'ot' if feminine. Think of Seraphim (masculine form yet of, hosted by Sephirot, feminine force). It is time, perhaps to delve into the more likely origin of this enigmatic and evocative term.

Neter / Netrit

Nature/laws, principles of God. Cognate with Yin/Yang.

Occultism.

Esotericism and occultism, in their many forms, are not so much concerned with inquiries into first principles or the nature of being, though they do tend to proceed on the metaphysical assumption that all being is 'One.'

Ontology

'The science of and study of being' What might be called the core metaphysical problems would be the ones which have always been considered metaphysical. (noun) The metaphysical study of the nature of being and existence. Other philosophical traditions have very different conceptions—such as 'what came first, the chicken or the egg?' The Metaphysics was divided into three parts, now regarded as the traditional branches of Western metaphysics, called (1) ontology, (2) theology, and (3) universal science. There were also some smaller, perhaps tangential matters: a philosophical lexicon, an attempt to define philosophy in general, and several extracts from the Physics repeated verbatim.

The science or art of perfecting the work, through devotion. And the practice of ceremonial, rituals, sometimes seen as magical in nature, performed with the intention of invoking the action of God (or other personified supernatural power), especially with the goal of uniting with the divine, or perfecting or improving oneself. The use of magic for religious and/or psychotherapeutic purposes, in order to attain 'salvation' or 'personal evolution,' as defined by P, E. I. Bonewits. This is often referred to as 'High Magic,' which is considered the best use of magic.

Palingenesis

Self-generation, evolving in perpetuity as a single organism.

Thaumaturgy

The use of magic for nonreligious purposes; the art or science of 'wonder working'; using magic to actually change things on the Earth Plane. Sometimes referred to as low magic.

The working of miracles or magic feats.

Thau'ma•tur'gic or thau'ma•tur'gi•cal adj.
Part of Speech: (noun) mass (no plural)

Miracle-working, wonder-working, the performance of a miracle, doing magic, legerdemain. However, one would soon notice that methods devised for theurgy can usually be used for thaumateurgy. While many believe that thaumaturgy (Magic performed with the help of beneficent spirits) is distinguished from theurgy, the branch which concerns itself with purely spiritual matters, this is not always the case.

Thaumaturgy deals with producing a desired effect within the material world, but it is not necessarily opposed to or distinct from theurgy in that the material effect produced may simply be a theurgical result caused to emanate downward from the more subtle, spiritual realm into the dense, material sphere. In this way, thaumaturgy may simply be considered as the visual manifestation of theurgy, just as the body is the visual manifestation of the spirit via the mind, as well as its vehicle. If one is intending to imply that the change produced has no higher effect other than a material effect for the purpose of physical gratification, then it would be more accurate to refer to it as low magic, in that it lacks any form of higher meaning or significance beyond self-gain. High magic would then be used to refer to both theurgy and also thaumaturgy, if this is just a material impression or actualization of spiritual forces or potentials.

Theology

Universal science is supposed to be the study of so-called first principles, which underlie all other inquiries; an example of such a principle is the law of non-contradiction: A thing cannot both be and not be at the same time, and in the same respect. A particular apple cannot both exist and not exist at the same time. It can't be all red and all green at the same time. This includes matters like causality, substance, species, and elements. Means the study of God or the gods and questions about the divine and how we come to understand them, rationalise them etc.

Theurgy

Divine –wonder working. Rites and rituals to evoke the presence of the divine as a conjunction of the self within it, in awareness. A method of creating the environment for that purpose.

Pleroma

The abode of the aeons. The plane of eternal ideas. The domain of the celestial Sophia – divine effulgence. Void of all sense of self.

462

Polytheism

Belief in the ineffable God, the ultimate of many attributes, each manifest through a series of hypostases, and in some cases, believed to be anthropomorphic entities, autonomous except unto fate.

Bibliography

The Robert Cochrane Letters by E. J. Jones ed M Howard. Capall Bann 2003

John of Monmouth, *Genuine Witchcraft is Explained,* Capall Bann 2012

The Roebuck in the Thicket' E.J.J. ed. MH. Capall Bann 2001

Doreen Valiente, *Rebirth of Witchcraft,* Hale 1989

E.J. Jones, 'The Cauldron Mythos' *Star Crossed Serpent II,* Mandrake of Oxford 2012

E. J. Jones 'Witchcraft a Tradition Renewed' ed Doreen Valiente Hale 1991

Shani Oates *Tubelo's Green Fire,* Mandrake of Oxford 2010

Shani Oates *Tubal's Mill* by Create Space 2016

Shani Oates *Crafting the Arte of Tradition,* Anathema Publishing. 2016

Museum of Witchcraft Archive

Doreen Valiente Trust at the Centre of Pagan Studies

Alan Grant, *Early Britain: Anglo-Saxon Britain,* 19th century

http://www.1734-witchcraft.org

http://clantubalcain.com/virtue-what-is-it/

Regency Resources: The Pagan's Handbook on line. Man, Myth and Magic 'The Messiah of Highgate *Hill' #1968* and numerous other interviews and articles in which their self-confessed views are profusely pagan.

John of Monmouth, *Genuine Witchcraft is Explained,* Capall Bann 2012

Notes & Refs:

1   1 Roy Bowers aka Robert Cochrane : 'The Craft Today' Pentagram#2 1964

2   *Tubal's Mill*, Midsummer 2016 Create Space

3   A separate critique on these papers is being self-published in the Spring 2016 see 2

4   First coined as such by Michael Howard in various publications, including his magazine, *The Cauldron*. Too numerous to list here, and not hard to find. Circa 94 -

5   Shani Oates - Clan Forum messages

6   Letter #I to Bill Gray

7   A deeper and more extensive explanation for this nomenclature is provided in 'Tubal's Mill. For an excellent understanding of operative and historical clanships,please consult:Alan Grant, *Early Britain: Anglo-Saxon Britain,* 19th century

8   Document from the 'old man' [cc]

9   Stuart Inman: "Wilson stated that 1734 had its own spirits and guardians, and much like Abra Melin, one should not approach it in too casual or disrespectful a way, for they would defend it." www.1734witchcraft.org

10   This was a 'method' Wilson adopted successfully, "teaching different things to different people. This didn't mean he was teaching "real" 1734 to one and "fake" 1734 to another, he was teaching them what they needed." Stuart Inman, Personal Correspondence. 10/6/2015

11   www.1734witchcraft.org

12   Described by Marian Green as a loose company of people who gathered 'ad hoc' to hold rituals. RCL p23

13   To be Clan, one is either an Inducted member or one is not. And if 'kindred, allegiance must be re-instated every seven years to remain within it's aegis (protection and inclusion) Membership to a Clan does not exist without Induction and inclusion as 'kindred' does not exist without renewed oaths of allegiance.

14   After Bowers' death, his widow, awarded singular authority to E.J. Jones only to continue Bowers' works, tradition and Clan. She dismissed utterly all association with Ronald White and George Winter. See 'Tubal's Mill,' Personal Correspondence, 13/10/98 [a] extract appears in *Tubal's Mill.*Create Space 2016 by Shani Oates.

15   30/9/67 Valiente Notepad entry. Monmouth mentions several letters from attendees throughout july and august confirming their expected attendance.

16   www.1734witchcraft.org

17   (see document 'i')

18   John of Monmouth, *Genuine Witchcraft is Explained,* Capall Bann 2012. Throughout the entire body of his book, Monmouth claims a very different origin for the works that sourced the Regency as quite distinct from Roy Bowers, asserting they are borne almost entirely from Chalky and George. Their works presented in the *Pagan Handbook* included in this book, clearly confirm that opinion. They are transparently distinct.

19   Oates, 2016 Tubal's Mill. op.cit.

20   Oates, 2016 Tubal's Mill. op.cit.

21   John of Monmouth, *Genuine Witchcraft is Explained,* Capall Bann 2012. p23 Letter is dated 1/9/63, which coincides with the first shift away from Bowers' former coven into 'The Clan' which included 'Dick' and John (E.J.J.).

22   John of Monmouth, *Genuine Witchcraft is Explained,* Capall Bann 2012 p78-82

23   Letters to Norman Gills, *The Robert Cochrane Letters* by E. J. Jones ed Howard. Capall Bann 2003

24 Doreen Valiente, *Rebirth of Witchcraft*, Hale 1989 p122

25 Valiente, Hale op.cit p126-129

26 Valiente, Hale op.cit p121-129

27 Letter #IV to Bill Gray

28 Round Robin see Doc (z) to Bill Gray #XIV

29 Letters to Norman Gills, *The Robert Cochrane Letters* by E. J. Jones ed M Howard. Capall Bann 2003As editor to this book, Mr Howard suggests in his notes regarding a letter to Norman Gills that Bowers posted a document referring to the Castles & Kingdoms of the BsoTC. That letter is a composite, and did not contain those addenda . For a better illustration of that artificial construction, please see the section on SCSIII that examples this document (qq). What is very odd however, is that Michael Howard sent to us a copy of the following document (jj) in 2006 minus the first and last page, questioning us as to our familiarity with it. Even without it's first and last page, it is clear it is not an addendum to any letter to Gills or anyone else for that matter. The wording and the links to the Gills letter that Michael Howard asigns in TRCL do not appear on this document – anywhere!

30 Confirmed by personal conversation and correspondence with E. J. Jones, V, Iain Steele and Doreen Valiente. The document here (ii) 'To all Elders' is the full and complete document composed by Bowers and sent to members of the Clan informing them of his summary not only of the Mythos he'd been relaying to them over the previous year, but what he intended to study with them over the course of time – until they all 'got it.' see pp 337-345

31 Greater detail of the entire book is given in the forthcoming— *Tubal's Mill* 2016

32 Ibid.

33 Russell Erwin – FaceBook 'Traditional Witchcraft in America ' 2015 {site now removed]

34 "The Craft Today" - *Pentagram* #64

35 Letter# 3 to Joe Wilson

36 Letter IX to Bill Gray

37 Bowers explains to Joe Wilson the wonder of Woman as the Lesser Moon to the Goddess

38 30/9/67 Doreen Valiente, Notepad entry.?

39 A more in-depth exploration of what virtue signifies may be found on http://clantubalcain.com/virtue-what-is-it/

40 E.J. Jones (dated 24th May 2001)Bowers creation myth explained via personal correspondence, 1998 but John wrote it up as an article which appeared in 'The Cauldron' in 2002

41 Robin-the-dart

42 Reginald Hinchcliffe's notes on a manilla folder in the Witchcraft museum at Boscstle UK Box 333/Norman Gills

43 John of Monmouth, *Genuine Witchcraft is Explained,* Capall Bann 2012. p23 Letter is dated 1/9/63,

44 Ibid.

45 Oates, Shani 2016 *'Tubal's Mill'* Create Space, Amazon UK

46 Monmouth. op.cit. p97

47 This document is cited as the 'Final Version' by Monmouth and appears in two parts - 282-87 & 302- 315. In fact the pages 302-315 are also covered in addenda and scribbles.

48 Marian Green *'The Roebuck in the Thicket'* E.J.J. ed. MH. Capall Bann 2001 p. 38

49 Editor of the *Pentagram* magazine and co-founder of The Regency. The magazine does not begin to appear until 1964, an event by which we may rationally date the period this letter refers to is after Bill Gray had first introduced Bowers to Gerard Noel late in 1964.

50 Thames Valley Coven, the group Bowers may have started when he left the London mob to settle in Slough, hence recent local coven. His coven was soon abandoned for the Clan.

51   As Roy and Jane were married in London in December 1951, this would date this letter (if authentic) to 1965.

52   Quite a substantial portion of this letter is extracted from Doc (ii) To All Elders.

53   Ibid.

54   Reginald Hinchcliffe, a Gardnerian Priest via Lois Bourne, and a member of The Regency for a short time, left a manilla folder in the archives of the Witchcraft Museum. Enclosed are several documents, mostly composites of Gills letters from Bowers and a copy of Bowers' letters to Joe Wilson

55   Personal Correspondence Confirmed to Mike Howard in 2006 when he sent a 'snipped' and poorly photocopied section with missing pages, which was a similar document to the one that appeared in *The Robert Cochrane Letters* by E. J. Jones ed M Howard. Capall Bann 2003. The last page (7) missing also, and he'd asked me if I had seen the original and if so what did I know of its contents.

56   Ibid

57   Note here that Chalky is listed as being a member of Bowers' group, and as someone unknown to Gills. Again, this begs the question, how then, did he become listed as present in a letter allegedly written at least three years prior to these recent meetings between Gills and Bowers.

58   www.1734witchcraft.org

59   In fact, like so many others, I have seen only snippets and edits of various documents in circulation, alleging to be 'part of something else.' These are all together for study in box 334F in the Museum of Witchcraft's archive. Boscastle, Cornwall. UK.

60   3257 A+B Museum of Witchcraft archive. Boscastle Original document does not include this addendum, 'the Windyat' - this is an edited comment, inserted by Gills or Chalky, after Bowers' death. See document [ii] 'To All Elders'

Index

472

Printed in the USA
CPSIA information can be obtained
at www.ICGtesting.com
LVHW021246130124
768548LV00141B/1363/J